PASSAGES

A Writer's Guide

PASSAGES

A Writer's Guide

Third Edition

RICHARD NORDQUIST

St. Martin's Press
New York

Senior editor: Karen Allanson
Revisions editor: Edward Hutchinson
Associate development editor: Steven Kutz
Managing editor: Patricia Mansfield Phelan
Project editor: Diana Puglisi
Production supervisor: Joe Ford
Art director: Sheree Goodman
Text design: Angela Foote
Cover design: Sheree Goodman
Cover photo: FPG International

For information, write:
St. Martin's Press, Inc.
175 Fifth Avenue
New York, NY 10010

ISBN: 0-312-10117-1

Acknowledgments

The American Heritage Dictionary of the English Language, Third Edition. The entry "pacify." Copyright © 1992 by Hougton Mifflin Company. Reprinted by permission of The American Heritage Dictionary of the English Language, Third Edition.

Toni Cade Bambara. "The Lesson" from *Gorilla, My Love* by Toni Cade Bambara. Copyright © 1972 by Toni Cade Bambara. Reprinted by permission of Random House, Inc.

Roy Blount, Jr. "Gather Round, Collegians," from *Now, Where Were We* by Roy Blount, Jr. Copyright © 1988 by Roy Blount, Jr. Reprinted by permission of Villard Books, a division of Random House, Inc.

Mike Brake. "Needed: A License to Drink" from *Newsweek*, March 14, 1994. All rights reserved. Reprinted by permission.

Tertius Chandler. "Education—Less of It" from *The College Board Review.* Copyright © 1987 by College Entrance Examination Board. Reprinted by permission of The College Board Review and the author.

K. C. Cole. "Hers; Women and Science" from *The New York Times*, December 3, 1981. Copyright © 1981 by The New York Times Company. Reprinted by permission.

Nora Ephron. "Living with My VCR" first appeared in *The New York Times*, December 23, 1984. Copyright© 1984 by The New York Times Company. Reprinted by permission.

Bob Greene. "Cut" from *Cheeseburgers* by Bob Greene. Copyright © 1985 by John Deadline Enterprises, Inc. Reprinted by permission of Scribner, an imprint of Simon & Schuster.

Maxine Hong Kingston. Excerpt from "Shaman" from *The Woman Warrier*, by Maxine Hong Kingston. Copyright © 1976 by Alfred A. Knopf, Inc.

Acknowledgments and copyrights are continued at the back of the book on page 421, which constitutes an extension of the copyright page.

Preface

The third edition of *Passages* contains many new readings and whole-discourse exercises; a quicker transition from paragraph-length assignments to short essays; and more occasions for journal writing, critical thinking, and collaborative work. Yet the fundamental premise of the text remains the same: to become a better writer, a student needs to write—and rewrite and keep on writing—on a wide range of topics, for various audiences, and with different aims in mind. Based on this assumption, *Passages* guides students through the writing process, teaching strategies and skills in the context of particular assignments. In conventional terms, Part One is a rhetoric, Part Two a grammar, but neither part of the book is wholly conventional.

In terms of both structure and subject, the assignments in Part One progress from the fairly simple to the more complex. For example, the list of observations called for in the first chapter reappears as a discovery (or prewriting) strategy in later assignments. Likewise, the methods of paragraph development discussed in the opening chapters are recalled in the essay-length assignments in Chapters Seven through Fourteen. Thematically, the assignments proceed from the personal world of the student in the early chapters to more public concerns later on. Nonetheless, all of the assignments are broad enough to accommodate the particular interests of each writer. And, while the sequence of assignments is incremental, it is not inflexible: instructors can alter and reorder assignments to suit their own teaching needs.

Each chapter in Part One offers numerous examples and exercises to guide students through all stages of the assignment: discovering and exploring a topic, writing a rough draft, and revising (perhaps several times). This approach does not ignore the recursive nature of the writing process, nor is it an attempt to prescribe a single method of writing. On the contrary, by gradually introducing a wide variety of composing strategies, the assignments help students gain greater control over the way they write. What this book cannot provide, of course, is a sympathetic, sharp-eyed reader—someone to encourage, question, and commend students as they work their way through each assignment. What *Passages* does offer are abundant opportunities for the instructor—and for the students themselves—to perform these important tasks. The Instructor's Guide suggests how the text can be used effectively in conferences and writing workshops as well as in more formal classroom settings.

Part Two of *Passages*, titled *A Guide to Writing Sentences*, is unique in its integration of sentence-combining exercises, writing suggestions, and more traditional methods of grammar instruction. Chapters Fifteen and Sixteen give students practice in manipulating sentence structures to help them achieve clarity, variety, and coherence in their writing. Succeeding chapters reinforce these skills while also demonstrating how to eliminate the most common types of errors. The various combining, editing, and proofreading exercises are more extensive than those found in standard handbooks and workbooks. The Instructor's Guide, in addition to supplying sample answers, explains how the exercises and writing suggestions can be used to supplement the assignments in Part One. Additional exercises appear in the software package that accompanies the text.

Following Part Two are five brief appendices. The diagnostic tests in Appendix A will help students determine which chapters in Part Two they need to concentrate on. Appendix B explains how the skills needed to write effective examination essays are closely related to the skills discussed in Part One. Appendix C, which provides practical advice on writing a résumé and letter of application, may be used with the assignment on *Work* in Chapter Six. Appendix D provides advice on composing with the help of a word processor. And finally, Appendix E contains the paragraphs and short essays that served as models for the paragraph-building exercises in Chapters Fifteen and Sixteen.

This short survey has pointed out the chief aims and approaches of *Passages*, but it has not yet identified the most distinctive quality of the book. The instructions are clear, the advice is sound, the exercises work, but none of these things would matter if the illustrative writings were not lively, thoughtful, and carefully crafted. This third edition of *Passages* contains numerous short selections from the works of various contemporary authors. Just as significant, however, are the many paragraphs and essays written by students who have since completed their passage through freshman composition. These writings should serve as encouraging guides to those students who must still take the journey.

Acknowledgments

To the many people who assisted and encouraged me in the writing of the third edition of *Passages*, I owe much more than just the customary expressions of thanks. The following reviewers provided countless suggestions that helped to shape this revision: Kathy Albertson, Georgia Southern University; Margaret Borden, Willmar Community College; Santi Buscemi, Middlesex College; Sylvia Gillett, Dundalk Community College; Maureen Hogan O'Brien, Springfield Technical Community College; Luke Robins, Laramie County Community College; Carol Wilson, Mission College.

I am also grateful to Karen Allanson, Edward Hutchinson, Alda Trabucchi, Diana Puglisi, Steven Kutz, and the rest of the staff at St. Martin's Press for their patience, guidance, and help.

I owe special thanks to my colleagues at Armstrong State College, in particular my assistant, Katharine Clarke, who has always attended to the details with enthusiasm and good humor; Anne Muller, a superb editor and teacher who provided encouragement and sound advice; and the staff of the Office of Nontraditional Learning, including Jason Richardson, Grace Robbins, Deanne Skinner, Heather Wainright, Douglas Walker, and Michael Walker.

Finally, I am most grateful to the many hundreds of students I have had the pleasure of working with over the past twenty years. In particular, I want to thank the student authors and editors of the writings that enliven and distinguish these pages. As ever, *Passages* is dedicated to them:

Kathy Albertson	Maria B. Dunn	Quan Nguyen
Jesse Albright	Alison Earley	Jane Nineham
Lori Alexander	Diane Esposito	Ruth Norris
Linda Arnold	Roz Evans	Trusan Ponder
Mike Ayala	Rita Faircloth	Paige Porter
Mary Baltes	Casandra Ferguson	Flo Powell
Nancy Barbee	Jill S. Gerard	Pamela Remler
Heidi Becker	Ashley LaJane German	Darcy Rosario
Paula Betlem	Eric V. Gilbert	Frederick Roth
Lynn Bigbie	Kim Grier	April Scott
Rita Black	Devi Griner	Louis Sobrero
Jobie Bowen	Sandra Harris	Vanessa Sutlive
Margaret Brockland-Nease	Diane Jervis	Stacy Swofford
Jeremy Burden	Mary Alsten Johnson	Katie Sydney
Adam Butcher	Angela Jones	Betty Talley
Curtis Carter	Linda King	Alvaro Veale
Debra Cavenah	Brenda Lain	Jason Walker
Pae Choi	Melanie Leopold	Michael Wetzstein
Ann Clarke	Mark Lisicia	Paul Widner
Anthony F. Clarke	Linn McCoy	Mary Ann Wilharm
Ann M. Cullina	Kevin Matthews	Shelby Wilson
Linda Cummings	Anne Miller	Dee Wu
Elisha Cuyler	Julia Moody	Mary Zeigler
Alfreda Darden	Joe Morgan	Diane Zelinski
Ivy Davis	Kiedra Mullet	

Richard Nordquist

Contents

CHAPTER FOURTEEN
Additional Essay Assignments 175

Strategies and Skills

Discovering

Organizing

The Writer and the Writing Process

Preview

Each chapter in *Passages* begins with a "Preview" like this one to let you see at a glance what writing assignment you will be working on and what skills you will be practicing. In this chapter, you will consider how your attitudes toward writing can help or hinder your development as a writer. After examining your writing background, your methods of writing, and the kinds of writing you do, you will take a look ahead at the design and purpose of the rest of the book.

Your Attitudes toward Writing

Be honest: how do you feel about having to write? Do you tend to view a writing assignment as a challenge or as a nerve-wracking chore? Or is it merely a dull duty, one you have no strong feelings about at all? Whatever your attitude may be, one thing is certain: how you feel about writing both affects and reflects how well you can write.

Let's compare the attitudes expressed by two students:

❏ I *love* to write and I always have, even in elementary school—when there wasn't any paper I would write on the walls. I keep a journal and write a lot of letters. And I always get pretty good grades from teachers who let me write.

❏ I get so nervous when I have to write that my eyes sweat. I put off taking this course for as long as I could. Maybe if I had lots of time and didn't get so anxious I could be a good writer. But I'm not very good.

Although your own feelings may fall somewhere between these two extremes, you should be able to recognize what these students have in common: their attitudes toward writing are directly related to their abilities. The one who enjoys writing does well because she practices often—and she practices because she does well. On the other hand, the one who hates writing avoids opportunities to improve. Therefore, as you begin working to become a better writer, you must first examine—and perhaps reconsider—your attitudes toward writing.

The questionnaire that follows will give you a chance to examine your attitudes carefully. Respond to each statement by circling one of the numbers at the right:

1. I agree.

2. I am unsure or indifferent.

3. I disagree.

Respond to the statements thoughtfully and honestly. Your aim is not to impress an instructor but to understand yourself.

Your Writing: Public and Private

	Agree	Unsure	Disagree
1. I enjoy writing.	1	2	3
2. The only time I write is when I'm required to.	1	2	3
3. Writing something well gives me a sense of satisfaction.	1	2	3
4. I don't think I write as well as most other people do.	1	2	3
5. I sometimes write just for myself—to express my feelings or think out my problems on paper.	1	2	3
6. Having to write makes me nervous or afraid.	1	2	3

Your Background in Writing

Answer questions 7 through 10 if you graduated from high school within the past four years.

	Agree	Unsure	Disagree
7. I wish I had been made to do more writing in high school.	1	2	3
8. My teachers in high school put a lot of emphasis on good writing skills.	1	2	3
9. In my senior year, I was required to write at least one essay every two weeks.	1	2	3
10. Recent high school graduates should not be required to take a writing course in college.	1	2	3

Answer questions 11 through 14 if it has been more than four years since you graduated from high school.

	Agree	Unsure	Disagree
11. My writing skills have gotten rusty over the years.	1	2	3
12. One reason I have stayed out of college has been my fear of having to write.	1	2	3
13. Although I have not studied writing recently, I have kept up my skills by writing on the job and at home.	1	2	3
14. Older students should not be required to take writing courses in college.	1	2	3

The Value of Writing

15. I don't see the value of taking a writing course in college.   1 2 3

16. The ability to write well will help me to succeed in many
     college courses.   1 2 3

17. In college, only English instructors care about good writing.   1 2 3

18. I would rather take an objective test (multiple choice and
     fill-in-the-blanks) than an essay examination.   1 2 3

19. I avoid taking classes with instructors who give writing
     assignments (essays, reports, term papers).   1 2 3

20. Writing a paper helps me to understand a subject better than
     memorizing facts for an objective test.   1 2 3

21. Once I get out of college, I don't think it will matter very
     much how well I can write.   1 2 3

"Good" Writing

22. The ability to write well is a gift a person must be born
     with—either you've got it or you don't.   1 2 3

23. Being a good writer primarily involves knowing the rules
     of grammar, spelling, and punctuation.   1 2 3

24. A good piece of writing should contain lots of difficult words
     and long sentences.   1 2 3

25. Even the very best writers often have to work hard to make
     the words come out just right.   1 2 3

26. A piece of writing can often be improved by reading it over,
     thinking about it, making changes, and writing it over again.   1 2 3

The Writing Process

27. I usually don't like to reread something I've written.   1 2 3

28. When I'm given a writing assignment, my mind often goes
     blank and I have trouble getting started.   1 2 3

29. I write very slowly because I spend a lot of time worrying
     about correct grammar and spelling.   1 2 3

30. When I sit down to write, I usually have plenty of good ideas,
     but I often have trouble putting those ideas into words.   1 2 3

31. If I have enough time, I usually rewrite a paper (sometimes
     several times) until I'm satisfied with it.   1 2 3

32. I like to show my writing to others for suggestions on how to
     improve it.   1 2 3

Agree Unsure Disagree

33. I usually try to write a perfect paper the first time so I won't have to go back and rewrite it.   1 2 3

34. If I take the time and make the effort, I can usually improve something I've written.   1 2 3

In the next section of this chapter, we will consider some of the implications of your responses to this questionnaire.

Shaping a Positive Attitude toward Writing

Now, in looking over your responses to this questionnaire, how would you define your attitude toward writing? What matters is not whether you think you are a good writer or a bad one, but the extent to which you are willing to work to become a better one. If you are convinced that good writing skills are unimportant or beyond your reach, then you lack the motivation to become a better writer. On the other hand, if you recognize the value of good writing skills and want to improve your own, then you're ready to learn.

Your Writing: Public and Private

Public writing is the work you do for others, usually because you are required to. If this is the only sort of writing you do, then it's understandable why you might feel uncomfortable—even nervous or frightened—when you sit down to write. You're just following orders, doing a chore, writing to please someone else. One way to become more relaxed and confident is to do some writing for yourself—*private writing*—as these two students explain:

❑ Whenever I'm bothered about something, I pick up a pen and go to work writing down my problems. In this way I am able to see solutions to my troubles appear on the page right before my eyes.

❑ For many years I have kept a journal, a place where I express my thoughts and feelings about different experiences in my life. I enjoy this type of writing. My journal is a private book that no one else ever reads.

Without the pressures of deadlines or grades, such private writing can be relaxing, therapeutic, even fun. In a journal, you can write whatever you please—your thoughts, dreams, observations—and nobody can ever criticize you for bungling a sentence, misspelling a word, or leaving out a central idea.

Keeping a journal should not take much of your time—perhaps ten or fifteen minutes each day. With regular practice, you will improve your writing skills and create a file of ideas and observations, some of which may later be developed into formal paragraphs and essays. In time, as you practice making discoveries in your private writing, you should also gain confidence in your ability to write for others.

A kind of writing that might be described as *semi-private* (or perhaps *semi-public*) is the personal letter: a note to a friend or family member about your everyday experiences, great and small. Although letter writing means keeping a reader other than yourself in mind, it resembles journal writing in a number of ways: generally, you can express opinions freely, switch easily from one subject to another, and write without fear of being marked down for making mistakes. Likewise, the practice gained by writing personal letters should in time help you gain confidence as a writer.

Writing Suggestion: Journal Writing

On a sheet of paper or in a notebook, try your hand at private writing by explaining to *yourself* what your attitudes toward writing are. You may want to recount some past experiences (the term paper that drove you crazy or the essay that turned out just right). Or you may instead look to the future, explaining in what ways you hope to improve your writing by the end of this course. Write for ten or fifteen minutes. Then write again tomorrow, this time on a different subject—any subject.

If you have trouble getting started, consider the following suggestions:

1. Make a list of your goals, problems, chores, favorite foods, or whatever else comes to mind.

2. Write a letter that you will never send. Write to someone you haven't seen in a long time, someone who is making life difficult for you, or someone you have never met but would like to know.

3. Describe something that recently amused, interested, or troubled you.

4. Describe the person you would like to be five years from now.

William Safire's essay "On Keeping a Diary" (at the end of this chapter) and the *Writing Suggestions* in Part Two provide additional journal-writing advice and topic ideas.

Your Writing Background

If you recently graduated from high school, you might find it strange (if not a little annoying) to be taking a writing course in college. Isn't this a step backward? The answer is no—not at all. Certainly you will be reviewing some of the principles of writing that you learned in school, but you will also be making the transition to college-level writing. Your work in this book will prepare you for the various types of writing commonly assigned by college professors.

If you have been out of school for a number of years—perhaps even decades—you may have different concerns. How can I be expected to remember things I forgot so long ago? Will I be able to keep up with the younger students? You shouldn't be concerned—for several reasons. One reason is that this book proceeds in step-by-step fashion, reminding you along the way of things you may have forgotten.

Another reason is that you may not be as rusty as you think you are: consider the various kinds of writing you have done at home and at work since you left school. And finally, remember that you have experience on your side: the more you have lived, the more you have to write about.

Writing Suggestion

Write a note to your instructor, telling him or her something about your writing background. Be as specific as you can. If your memories of high school are still fresh, mention what English courses you took and what sort of assignments you were given. If you have been out of school for some time, explain what sort of writing you have done at home and on the job.

The Value of Writing

You probably don't need to hear a lecture on how important good writing skills are to success in college. Nor do you need to hear stories from people in business and industry detailing all the types of writing they have to do every day on the job. What you do need to consider is the importance of writing in your *own* career, college work, and personal life. If you see writing as nothing more than a punishment inflicted by English instructors, you won't be motivated to become a better writer. However, if you recognize that writing is a skill you will need throughout your life, you will have good reason to improve this skill.

Writing Suggestion

Make a list of all the different kinds of writing you do in your life—everything from shopping lists to job applications to term papers. Be as specific as you can. Then add to this list any additional kinds of writing that you think you might be called on to do in the future.

Characteristics of Good Writing

Experiences in school leave some people with the impression that "good" writing is that which contains no "bad" mistakes—that is, no errors of grammar, punctuation, or spelling. But, in fact, good writing is much more than just correct writing. It is writing that responds to the interests and needs of the reader. Briefly, here are the basic characteristics of good, effective writing:

1. It makes a clear point.
2. It supports that point with specific information.
3. The information is clearly connected and arranged.
4. The words are well chosen, and the sentences are clear, concise, emphatic, and correct.

The assignments in Part One of *Passages* focus on the first three of these characteristics. Sentence structures are treated in Part Two, and word choice is considered in both parts. However, this arrangement does not mean that you must complete Part One before going to Part Two. The exercises in Part Two are intended to *supplement* the assignments in Part One. Indeed, if you need practice in building clear, correct sentences, you should turn to the Part Two exercises early in the course. Just remember that correctness is only one aspect of good, effective writing.

Good writing is the result of much practice and hard work. This fact should encourage you: it means that the ability to write well is not a gift some people are born with, not a privilege extended to a few. If you are willing to work, you can improve your writing.

Professional writers, the ones who make writing *look* easy, will be the first ones to tell you that often it's not easy at all:

> There is no rule on how to write. Sometimes it comes easily and perfectly; sometimes it's like drilling rock and then blasting it out with charges.
>
> *(Ernest Hemingway)*

> Writing is just work—there's no secret. If you dictate or use a pen or type or write with your toes—it is still just work.
>
> *(Sinclair Lewis)*

Don't be depressed by the thought that writing rarely comes easily to anyone. Instead, keep in mind that regular practice will make you a better writer. As you sharpen your skills, you will gain confidence and *enjoy* writing more than you did before. In short, your attitude toward writing will improve as you grow more satisfied with your work.

Writing Suggestion

Help out your instructor by preparing a list of the "Rules of Good Writing"—those rules that you remember from school and still try to follow. For instance, were you ever forbidden to use certain words in your writing or told when to use a comma? Were you told how many sentences should be in a paragraph, or how many paragraphs should be in an essay? If so, write down these "rules" and others like them. Your list will make your instructor aware of some of the things you already know about writing as well as some of the things you may yet need to know. And, if you discuss these rules in class, you may discover that some of them are not really rules at all.

The Writing Process

Once you have decided that you're ready to work to improve your writing, you need to understand just what you will be working on. In other words, you need to think about how you handle the various steps involved in the whole process of writing: from discovering ideas for a topic, through successive drafts, to a final revision and proofreading. Let's look at how two students have described the steps they typically follow when writing a paper:

- I usually prepare myself by getting my notebook and pen and a clean sheet of paper. Then I'll just stare at my bird until he gets paranoid enough to turn his back on me. That's when I head for the refrigerator. Eating never seems to give me inspiration, but it does let me postpone having to write for awhile. When I return to my seat, my mind is as blank as the paper in front of me. I start to wonder why I ever decided to go to college in the first place. But eventually something hits—not great, but something. I start to scribble down everything I can think of. And I mean *scribble*—write fast, make a mess. When I finally figure out what I have scrawled, I fix it into an orderly, halfway decent essay. Then I turn it over (after making another trip to the refrigerator), so I can't see it. Then I take my great idea and start over. When I'm done, I compare both papers and combine them by taking out things that don't suit and by adding more details. Then I read my paper out loud. If it sounds better and it is better, I've revised it. If not, I start all over and work till I'm satisfied.

- In trying to put together a paper, I go through four phases. First, there's the *idea phase*, where I get this bright idea. Then there is the *productive phase*, where I'm really smoking and start thinking Pulitzer Prize. After that is the *block phase*, and all those prize-winning dreams turn into nightmares of this big, six-foot guy jammed into a first-grader's desk and being made to print the alphabet over and over again. During this phase I'll go through two or three pencils, chewing them into sawdust. I slam my head against the wall, pull out my hair, scream at the cat, and just generally go nuts. Eventually I hit the *deadline phase*: I realize this sucker has *got* to be written, and so I start burning it out again. This phase often doesn't start until ten minutes before a paper is due, which doesn't leave a heck of a lot of time to *proofread*—a phase I never seem to get around to.

As you can see, there is no single method of writing followed by all writers in all circumstances. Each of us must discover the approach that works best on any particular occasion. We can, however, identify four basic steps that most successful writers follow in one way or another:

1. *Discovering:* finding a topic and something to say. Because for many people getting started is the hardest part of writing, the early assignments in Part One introduce you to some specific discovery strategies: listing, probing, mapping, freewriting, and brainstorming.

2. *Drafting:* putting down your ideas in rough form. A first draft is generally messy and full of mistakes: your aim is to capture the shape of your ideas on paper, not to compose a perfect paragraph or essay on the first attempt.

3. *Revising:* studying, changing, and rewriting a draft to make it better. In this step you respond to the needs of your readers by rearranging your ideas and reshaping your sentences to make clearer connections.

4. *Proofreading:* examining your paper to see that it contains no errors in grammar, spelling, or punctuation. The exercises in Part Two will help you become more adept at proofreading.

The four stages overlap, but that doesn't mean you must be concerned about all four stages at the same time. In fact, trying to do too much at one time will only frustrate you, not make the writing go faster.

To give you practice in all stages of the writing process, the assignments in Part One are broken down into four steps. To get the most out of each assignment and to discover the process that works best for you, be sure to perform all four steps. But don't let this plan mislead you into thinking that composing is a straightforward sequence of activities, like following a recipe. In fact, the process of writing is exploratory—two steps forward, one step back. As you work on successive drafts, for instance, you will often find it necessary to rediscover your subject through new details and examples. And as you edit and proofread your work, you may find yourself revising as well. So be prepared to move back and forth as you practice the four basic stages of the writing process.

Accompanying the various steps are exercises, which you may be directed to do on your own or in collaboration with others in the class. These exercises will give you additional practice in developing, organizing, and revising paragraphs and essays.

At the end of each chapter in Part One, you will find two passages: the first usually by a student writer and the second by a professional. In addition to illustrating different writing strategies, these passages provide you with opportunities to exercise critical reading skills.

The overall purpose of the assignments in Part One is to make you an effective, independent writer. Therefore, as you move from writing paragraphs in the early chapters to writing essays in the later ones, you will find that the instructions offer you more and more freedom to choose your own strategies and approaches. By the time you reach these later assignments, you should have enough confidence in your writing ability to exercise this freedom thoughtfully and productively.

Writing Suggestion

Describe your own writing process—the steps you ordinarily follow when writing a paper. How do you get started? Do you write several drafts or just one? If you revise, what sort of things do you look for and what sort of changes do you tend to make? How do you proofread, and what types of errors do you most frequently find? Hold on to this description of your writing process, and then look at it again in a few weeks to see if you have made any changes in the way you write.

Passage

In the following essay, *New York Times* columnist William Safire considers the value of keeping a diary or journal and offers a few "rules" for those who would like to adopt the habit. Before reading the essay, jot down some of the reasons that *you* think people keep diaries.

On Keeping a Diary

Diaries are no longer dear; as the invention of the telephone began the decline of letter-writing, the invention of the tape recorder has led to the atrophy of the personal diary. Many of us record our words but few of us record our thoughts.

Why is a diary stereotyped today as the gushing of a school-girl or the muttering of a discontented politician, unworthy of the efforts of a busy person? Perhaps because we are out of the habit of writing, or have fallen into the habit of considering our lives humdrum, or have become fearful of committing our thoughts to paper. . . .

Diaries remind us of details that would otherwise fade from memory and make less vivid our recollection. Navy Secretary Gideon Welles, whose private journal is an invaluable source for Civil War historians, watched Abraham Lincoln die in a room across the street from Ford's Theater and later jotted down a detail that puts the reader in the room: "The giant sufferer lay extended diagonally across the bed, which was not long enough for him. . . ."

Diaries can be written in psychic desperation, intended to be burned, as a hold on sanity: "I won't give up the diary again," wrote novelist Franz Kafka; "I must hold on here, it is the only place I can." Or written in physical desperation, intended to be read, as in the last entry in Arctic explorer Robert Scott's diary: "For God's sake look after our people."

But what of people who are neither on trial nor freezing to death, neither witnesses to great events nor participants in momentous undertakings? To most of us, a diary presents a terrible challenge: "Write down in me something worth remembering," the neatly dated page says; "prove that this day was not a waste of time."

For people intimidated by their own diaries, here are a handful of rules:

1. *You own the diary, the diary doesn't own you*. There are many days in all our lives about which the less written the better. If you are the sort of person who can only keep a diary on a regular schedule, filling up two pages just before you go to bed, become another sort of person.

2. *Write for yourself*. The central idea of a diary is that you are not writing for critics or for posterity but are writing a private letter to your future self. If you are petty, or wrongheaded, or hopelessly emotional, relax—if there is anybody who will understand and forgive, it is your future self.

3. *Put down what cannot be reconstructed*. You are not a newspaper of record, obligated to record every first time that man walks on the moon. Instead, remind yourself of the poignant personal moment, the remark you wish you had made, your predictions about the outcome of your own tribulations.

4. *Write legibly*. This sounds obvious, but I have pages of scribblings by a younger me who was infuriatingly illiterate. Worse, to protect the innocent, I had encoded certain names and then misplaced my Rosetta Stone; now I will never know who "JW" was in my freshman year at college, and she is a memory it might be nice to have.

Four rules are enough rules. Above all, *write about what got to you that day*, the way a parched John Barrymore did during a trip to Mexico in 1926 when he discovered a bar that to him was an oasis:

"The beer arrived—*draft* beer—in a tall, thin, clean crystal of Grecian proportions, with a creamy head on it. I tasted it. . . . The planets seemed to pause a moment in their circling to breathe a benediction on that Mexican brewer's head. . . . Then the universe went on its wonted way again. Hot Dog! But that *was* a glass of beer!"

That is the art of the diarist in its pure form, unafraid, intimate, important in its insignificance, ringingly free. Who can compare Barrymore's frothy recall with the insecure jottings-down of most of us on little expense ledgers?

Wish I still kept a diary. But you see, I get very tired at the end of the day, and besides, nothing interesting happens any more. And so to bed. . . .

(William Safire)

Questions

1. Define the following words as they appear in Safire's essay: *atrophy, gushing, invaluable, psychic, momentous, posterity, tribulations, Rosetta Stone.*

2. According to Safire, what are some of the reasons that people keep diaries? Can you think of any additional reasons?

3. What does Safire mean when he writes that "a diary presents a terrible challenge"?

4. What are the distinctive features of the sample diary entries from Welles, Kafka, and Barrymore? What do you think is the point of each of these examples?

5. The final phrase in Safire's essay ("And so to bed") echoes a recurrent line in the famous diaries of the seventeenth-century English writer Samuel Pepys. Why do you think Safire concludes by admitting that he no longer keeps a diary?

Postscript

By examining your attitude toward writing, you have already begun working toward becoming a better writer. If you recognize the value of writing in your own life and accept the fact that writing can be improved through practice, then you will understand the purpose of your work in the rest of this book. In other words, you are ready to write.

PART ONE

A Guide to Writing Paragraphs and Essays

CHAPTER ONE

Observations
(DETAILS)

Preview

This assignment will give you practice in the discovery technique of listing and will show you the importance of using specific details in your writing. You will begin by taking notes on what you see in a particular place at a particular time. Then you will expand your notes into complete sentences, focusing on a different detail in each sentence. Finally, you will revise your list of sentences, making them as clear and descriptive as you can.

Step 1 ## *Observe and Take Notes*

Look! Put simply, that's the watchword of this assignment, the motto of all good writers: pay attention to the details and *show* the reader what you mean. Specific details create word pictures that make writing easier to understand and more interesting to read.

Before you can report interesting details, you need to discover them. So, with notebook in hand, begin by selecting a particular location. If you like to observe people, visit some crowded place, such as a cafeteria, a church, or a shopping mall. If you prefer to observe nature, take a walk through a field or park, find a quiet spot beside a stream or river, or spend some time in your backyard. Whatever the location, you may either walk around to find interesting details or just sit still and observe what is in front of you.

Now, look carefully, particularly if the place is familiar to you. Because we often take for granted the things we see every day, we need to concentrate to observe the details right in front of our eyes.

Only after you have spent some time observing your surroundings should you begin to take notes. At this point, you don't need to write complete sentences, just key words and phrases that describe what you see—and also hear and smell, if appropriate. However, do try to make your notes specific. "A crushed red carton from Kentucky Fried Chicken," for example, is a more vivid description than simply "trash." Try to fill a page (or more) with notes.

The following exercise illustrates how one student took notes for this assignment. After completing the exercise, check that your own notes are clear and specific.

EXERCISE NOTING SPECIFIC DETAILS

The following notes record a student's observations while caught in a traffic jam. Some of the notes are vague and general ("loud noise") while others are more specific ("jackhammers blasting" and "Red Hot Chili Peppers screeching"). Put a checkmark in front of those notes that you think are particularly descriptive—that *show* as well as tell the reader something.

small hyper black poodle

wet nose prints on window

teenager driving

lots of cars

sound of music

dog at window

bright orange warning cones

boy in car

on floor: hairbrush, sticky ice-cream spoon, Lloyd Cole and the Commotions cassette

silver Volvo with tinted windows

big hair

man reading

road construction

Red Hot Chili Peppers screeching

stuff on floor

loud noise

jackhammers blasting

wood-paneled station wagon

huge black hairdo with pink ribbon

baby

woman applying mascara

man eating lunch

jackhammer shooting up clouds of dirt

old man reading folded newspaper

nearly bald man combing hair in mirror

crusty peanut butter and jelly sandwich

yellow pollen on windshield

| Step 2 | *Put Details into Complete Sentences* |

After reviewing your own page of notes, choose the details that you find most interesting. Then, on a fresh sheet of paper, put those details into complete sentences, as shown below:

Notes old woman—gray bun, print dress, reading *Seventeen*
Sentence Her gray hair pinned back into a neat bun, the old woman in the flowered print dress sat slumped in her chair reading the latest issue of *Seventeen* magazine.

Notice how the details in this sentence help us to see the woman. She is wearing not just any dress, but a *flowered print dress*. The woman isn't just *sitting* in the chair; she is *slumped* in it. And she is reading not any old magazine, but *the latest issue of Seventeen*. Use specific details in your own sentences to show your readers what you have observed.

In a sentence or two each, describe at least six particular items in detail. For this assignment, you do not have to compose a paragraph: simply list your observations in complete sentences. Skip a line after each one.

Don't be concerned at this point if your sentences sound a bit awkward: you will have a chance to improve them in the next two steps. For now, just put your notes into sentences (no matter how rough) that capture the details you have observed.

The following exercise will give you additional practice in arranging specific details in complete sentences. After you have done the exercise, check that your own sentences are both detailed and complete.

EXERCISE USING SPECIFIC DETAILS IN SENTENCES

Here is the opening sentence from a student's report on his first impressions of a new apartment:

> Last Saturday morning, I toured my "exclusive" new apartment in the Cambridge Arms, an apartment that I had foolishly rented sight unseen.

Below you will find six sets of notes and short sentences describing some of the things that the student observed as he walked through the apartment. On your own paper, organize these details into six complete sentences. (The first set has been completed for you, though other combinations are possible.) Try to include all of the specific details, but leave out anything that sounds vague or repetitious.*

1. Footprints marched across the ceiling.
    living room ceiling
    stiff wedges of pizza
    pizza ground into the carpet

    > Footprints marched across the ceiling in the living room, and stiff wedges of pizza were ground into the carpet.

2. Lightbulbs were smashed in their sockets.
    Several sets of initials were carved into the coffee table.
    torn sofa cushions
    sofa cushions dusted with crushed saltines

3. stale odor
    dozens of Miller cans lined up on the windowsills
    Miller cans stacked up in a pyramid in one corner

4. puddles of milk and orange juice in the kitchen
    half-empty cat food cans on the counter
    mound of eggshells in the sink

*For additional guidelines on ways of effectively combining sentences, see Chapters Fifteen and Sixteen in Part Two.

5. The refrigerator door was wide open.
   old tennis shoe inside the refrigerator

6. The bathroom was just as bad.
   shaving cream on the walls
   sock jammed into the drain of the bathtub
   name "Fred" written in toothpaste on the mirror ■

Step 3 *Create an Opening Sentence and Revise Your Descriptions*

Now you will *revise* (or "look again") at your sentences to see if you can make them clearer and more specific. Begin a new draft with an opening sentence that identifies just where you were when you made your observations, as the student did in the previous exercise:

> Last Saturday morning, I toured my "exclusive" new apartment in the Cambridge Arms, an apartment that I had foolishly rented sight unseen.

Notice that the writer specifies the time that the observations were made ("Saturday morning") as well as the place. Be as specific as you can in your opening sentence.

Now go on to rewrite each of your descriptions, making any changes you like. After looking over your first draft, you may want to omit certain items and add some different ones. Go right ahead. Experiment with different words to make your descriptions more interesting, and try rearranging words to make your sentences clearer. You might also try reading your sentences aloud, *listening* to different versions of the same description until you find the one that sounds best to you. Don't hesitate to cross out and rewrite. Remember that revising is an opportunity to experiment with your writing—and, at this stage, neatness *doesn't* count.

The following exercise provides additional practice in revising descriptive sentences.

EXERCISE REVISING DESCRIPTIVE SENTENCES

Here is the opening sentence from a student's report on what he saw one afternoon on a city street:

> One brisk afternoon in late September, I took a walk down Liberty Street.

What follows are six sentences from the student's first draft. Revise each of these sentences according to the instructions in parentheses. Of course, there is no single set of "right answers" to this exercise. Rely on your imagination to create details that are precise and vivid, and then compare your responses with those of your classmates.

1. Music squealed out of the Record Ranch and mingled with some of the other noises of the city.

(Identify the kind of music that "squealed out of the Record Ranch," and give some specific examples of "the other noises of the city.")

2. Garbage danced along the sidewalk and lay crushed against the curb.
   (For the word "garbage," substitute specific examples of litter.)

3. A woman reading a book was sitting on the curb.
   (Describe the woman, and identify the book she was reading.)

4. Steam blew out of the air vents of a restaurant, carrying with it various smells.
   (Name the restaurant, and identify some of the smells coming from it.)

5. An old man was talking to "George," even though he was walking by himself.
   (Describe the old man in more detail.)

6. A red-faced man was pleading with a traffic cop as the cop was doing something.
   (*What* was "the cop" doing?) ■

Step 4 *Revise and Proofread*

Now let someone else read your sentences and suggest ways you might further improve them. This reader may be your instructor, a classmate, or a friend. Then, taking your reader's comments into consideration, revise your sentences once again. Use the following checklist as a guide.

REVISION CHECKLIST

❏ In the opening sentence, have you identified where you were when you made your observations?

❏ Are all of your descriptions clear?

❏ Are your descriptions specific?

❏ Have you put each of your descriptions into a complete sentence? (If you need help in determining what makes a sentence complete, turn to the exercises in Chapter Fifteen.)

❏ Have you proofread your paper carefully?

The final stage in the writing process is *proofreading*—carefully rereading a paper to make sure that it contains no distracting errors. The following suggestions should help you to proofread effectively.

1. Read your work aloud when you proofread: you may *hear* errors that you haven't been able to *see*.

2. Hold a ruler or a sheet of paper just below each line as you read. Doing this may keep you from being distracted by other words on the page.

3. Look for particular problems, one by one. Look for the kinds of errors you know you have a tendency to make—missing or misspelled words, for in-

stance, or faulty punctuation or incorrect verb endings. Read your paper several times, each time looking for a different type of error.

The exercises throughout Part Two of this text will give you a great deal of practice in finding and correcting sentence errors. Still, the best way to practice is to edit your own writing.

Passages

A. What follows is the final version of the student's report on the observations she made while caught in a traffic jam. Compare the student's original notes (in the first exercise) with the sentences below to see which details she selected and how she chose to organize them into sentences.

Traffic Jam

Driving to class this morning in the conjested traffic, I had plenty of time to observe the cars around me.

In the silver Volvo in front, a woman with huge black hair topped by a pink ribbon was vigorously applying mascara, while in the van to my right a shirtless young man pounded on his air guitar and screeched along with the Red Hot Chili Peppers.

Another driver, a gray-haired man in a business suit, gnawed on an apple while he skimmed the morning newspaper.

Flipping impatiently through the radio stations, I glanced at the wood-paneled station wagon to my left and noticed a plump infant strapped tightly into a baby-seat on the passenger side.

The young man driving the car was munching happily on what appeared to be a crusty peanut butter and jelly sandwich.

Out of nowhere, a tiny black poodle popped up between the two and sniffed the pollen-dusted windshield, its head darting from side to side as if it were thinking very serious thoughts.

The station wagon jerked forward, nudged a bright orange warning cone, and then stopped again suddenly, propelling the poodle back onto the seat and sending the baby into fits of laughter.

(Katie Sydney)

B. In the following selection, journalist Jane O'Reilly observes an evening's activities in the ladies' room of a Las Vegas casino. As you read, consider what thoughts might be occurring to the attendant who works (and observes) silently while the various patrons arrive, chat, and depart.

In Las Vegas: Working Hard for the Money

Eight o'clock in the evening is a slow, sullen hour in Sin City, a.k.a. Lost Wages. "I'm tired," whines a member of the United States Twirling Association. "C'mon, we're supposed to be having fun," snaps her companion, a clone. In razor-crease jeans and stiletto heels they stamp into the ladies' room, flounce around the corner past the polished washbasins and disappear into the two long rows of toilet stalls.

They are the kind of girls who obey their mother's warnings never to sit on strange toilet seats. Attendants have to nip in after that type, making sure the next woman will have no unpleasant surprises. That is the sort of job specification that made Donna Summer's song about a ladies' room attendant, *She Works Hard for the Money*, a big hit, especially in the neon city.

A circle of flattering pink mirrors catches multiple reflections of the plaster statue of Diana. On the dusty-rose settee, two elderly ladies in Orlon lace sweaters tell each other racist jokes and giggle. The attendant, who is black, has just unwrapped twelve rolls of toilet paper and is now dragging two huge bags of trash out the door. She passes an aghast English-speaking European tourist, who apparently expected Las Vegas to be more in the style of James Bond at Monte Carlo.

Two women on the far side of 45 stand next to each other before the washbasins, excavating makeup from the inside corners of their eyes. Vision restored, they notice they are wearing the same velour jogging suit. The turquoise version is from Pasadena, Calif., the deep pink from Evanston, Ill. Imagine that! Instant sisterhood. Evanston, who is in real estate and relaxes by playing the slots, says, "Have you got one of those rooms with the round bed and the mirror on the ceiling? Just out of curiosity, I asked the bellboy what it would cost me to get some company. He said, 'It's hard to get any kind of a sharp looker in here for less than $100. But you shouldn't have any trouble on your own.' So I checked out the craps tables. This adorable guy, my type, with the Southern drawl, the boots and the $500 chips, told me to step right up and be his good luck. Well, after ten minutes, I realized I'd have to stand there all night to shift his attention away from the table."

"Yeah," says Pasadena, "I'm married to one of those kind of guys." Pause. "Did you say $100? That seems sort of high." Both women scrub hands blackened from pushing hundreds of coins into slot machines and then each takes one thin quarter from the paper cup holding her slot-machine supplies and deposits it on the tip plate. An attendant, sweeping together the wreckage of paper products they have left behind, says, "Women don't tip like men. Sometimes I don't take home more than $6 in tips."

At 11 o'clock everyone is friendly, wide awake and ready for action. A response of "Nice dress" to "You like that mascara?" leads, within minutes, to "So I told him, if he wants to see those children, he has to stop tearing them up emotionally." A circle of strangers, all intricately wielding lip pencils, choruses sympathetically, "Baby, I know just what you mean." A dealer from another casino drops in to visit a friend, who looks at the dealer's name tag and says, "Bernadette? Since when?" The real name is Pamela, but, she says, "I'm sick of it. I tried Edith one time and all I got was 'Oh ho, Edith, have your cake and Edith too, eh?' Mona is best. It sounds sort of untouchable." The false Bernadette says she had dinner with "someone influential, very prominent in town." This is code for someone with reputed underworld ties. "It was boring. I'm not going out again until I find someone as smart as my ten-year-old son."

A classic bimbo comes in, a sincere (as opposed to commercial) bimbo, a woman who has chosen her life-style and works hard at it. She is accompanied by a bimbo-in-training, a young woman who has not yet imagined all the places blusher can be applied. Both wear draped and beaded jersey jumpsuits. It is hard to go to the bathroom in such garments, and the subsequent readjustment involves lots of friendly bantering with the attendant.

"We came with some degenerates who went straight to the tables. They haven't even been up to our rooms." ("Degenerate" is an acknowledged category of gambler in Las Vegas, one step ahead of "compulsive" on the road to ruin.) In perfect synchronization, the two women lean over with brushes in both hands, and each beats her hair into a froth. Upright again, both declare, "Ugh! Straw!" The little bimbo says, "I'd never put color on my hair. People would think I was phony." Her mentor, wiser and blonder, lets the remark pass. She takes out a small bottle and sprays her face. "Baby oil. Gives you that fresh, dewy look." But doesn't it smudge? "Oh, you never let them play kissy face—it ruins your makeup." They depart from the premises, the big bimbo's cleavage prompting admiring stares from a mother and daughter in windbreakers. Says Mom to newlywed daughter: "How'd you like to have a pair like that?"

At 2 o'clock in the morning the tourists are as blurred and fading as children allowed up past bedtime. The women who work the graveyard shift sneak in for a cigarette. Says a cocktail waitress: "We're supposed to go to designated areas for our breaks, and otherwise the bosses want us out on the floor all the time." "The bosses" is the Las Vegas equivalent of "the Man," covering every rank of power from a floor supervisor to a casino manager to the Mob to God. The bosses are, almost without exception, men. "Dorks, all of them," says a cashier. "A boss asked me out last week. We'd go to the mountains, he said. You guessed it. No mountains. Halfway through dinner he says, 'Are we going to get between the sheets or not?' Cute, huh? Lucky thing I brought my own car." She takes out a tube of Super Glue and, in a surrealistic gesture worthy of Buñuel, reattaches a thumbnail that is one and a half inches long.

Fingernail maintenance seems to fill the hours women once devoted to straightening stocking seams and rolling pin curls. The ladies' room crowd admires a tourist, the owner of a nail shop in California, who reveals a gold nail set with diamonds on her left ring finger. But the home champ is Leta Powers, whose nails are polished, striped with silver and pierced with little gold circles and charms. Leta works as a Goddess, which means she is a cocktail waitress at Caesars Palace, a hotel and casino organized around a spurious Greco-Roman theme. Locally, the Goddesses are dubbed coneheads, after the shape of the false hairpiece that is part of the costume. Unchanged since the hotel opened in 1966, the uniform, with its uncomfortable corset top and cutie-pie short pleated skirt, is as archaic as the clothes in a Currier & Ives print. The Goddesses, carrying a tray of drinks in one hand, give a thin gloss of glamour to a job that is a grueling eight-hour hike in high heels. But, says Goddess Bonnie Arrage, "I'm one of nine sisters, born in Kentucky. I was working as a secretary in Michigan, and I got laid off. I decided I wanted to go where there was money left in the world. For someone like me, with only a high school education, this is opportunity city."

All night the conversation threads along: aching feet, daughters' weddings, chemotherapy, whether or not it will rain that weekend—and men. A coffee-shop hostess says, "You know Howard? My old boyfriend? He's seeing a new girl. She's 30, with two kids. They've already got an apartment together. Well, last night he comes into my place. I gave him one of my superduper dirty looks. He says I've got to talk to him because the two of them need money. He wants to borrow some. Can you imagine?"

Jean Brown is the attendant from 2 a.m. to 10 a.m., and she knows what to say: "You keep a positive outlook. Don't give up. Keep faith in yourself. You never know when Mr. Right will show up."

The hostess sighs, "I never thought I'd be carrying menus at 35." And then, "What do you think I ought to wear when he comes back to get the money?"

(Jane O'Reilly)

Questions

1. Define the following words as they are used in O'Reilly's essay: *sullen, clone, aghast, excavating, bantering, synchronization, mentor, surrealistic.*

2. Discuss how specific details are used in any one paragraph of O'Reilly's essay to *show* the reader some aspect of the ladies' room.

3. Identify the overall mood of the ladies' room as it is described by O'Reilly. Point out some of the specific details that contribute to this mood.

4. Discuss how O'Reilly uses dialogue to help characterize the visitors to the waiting room and contribute to the mood of the essay.

5. What do you think is the main idea or central purpose of O'Reilly's essay? Identify particular descriptive details and lines of dialogue that support your interpretation.

Postscript

Whether making observations in a journal, collecting your thoughts, or drawing up plans, you will find that listing details is a quick and useful way of starting many writing projects. Later assignments will demonstrate other ways to apply this technique, and will also give you additional opportunities to use specific details in various kinds of paragraphs and essays.

CHAPTER TWO

Belongings
(*DESCRIPTION*)

Preview

In this assignment you will continue to make observations and record specific descriptive details. After selecting one of your belongings to describe, you will create a list of details by *probing* your topic—that is, responding to a series of questions about it. You will then put these details into sentences and arrange the sentences in a paragraph. Finally, you will revise the paragraph to make sure that it is unified and clearly organized.

Step 1 | ## *Probe Your Topic*

Our possessions are reflections of who we are, what we have done, and what we value. In this assignment you will take one of your belongings and describe it in detail, showing why it is important to you.

Probably the best way to get started is to walk through your house and take inventory of those things that carry a special personal meaning. Rummage through closets, drawers, wallets or purses; check shelves, mantels, and desk tops. The items may be intrinsically valuable (or at least costly)—a stereo system or a diamond ring, for instance. Or they may have sentimental value—an old baseball glove or a knick-knack won at a fair. Make a list of these items.

Now, choose one of the items from your list, an item that you can study carefully and describe in detail. *Probe* your topic by answering (on paper) as many of the following questions as you can:

❑ What does this item look, sound, feel, taste, and smell like?

❑ What size is it?

❑ What shape is it?

❑ How heavy is it?

❑ What color is it?

❑ What are its outstanding characteristics?

❑ What other thing(s) does it resemble?

By carefully observing the item and responding to these questions, you should be able to create a long list of precise descriptive details.

EXERCISE PROBING FOR SPECIFIC DETAILS

Probing is a discovery strategy that can help you to get started on many different kinds of writing assignments. In a small group or with the rest of the class, practice this strategy using any item in your classroom. This item may be something unusual that your instructor has brought along, or it may be as common as a wastebasket or an eraser. Study the object carefully, and then answer as many questions as you can regarding its size, shape, weight, color, and outstanding characteristics. ■

Step 2 | *Draft a Descriptive Paragraph*

Now that you have carefully probed the item you selected in Step 1, you are ready to draft a descriptive paragraph. Begin the paragraph with a *topic sentence* that identifies your prized belonging and briefly explains its significance to you. Next, describe the item in four or five sentences, using the details that you listed in Step 1. Finally, conclude the paragraph with a sentence that emphasizes the personal value of the item.

The paragraph below follows this pattern of topic sentence, supporting sentences, and conclusion:

Title
Topic
sentence

Supporting
sentences

Concluding
sentence

My Tiny Diamond Ring

On the third finger of my left hand is the pre-engagement ring given to me last year by my sister Doris. The fourteen carat gold band, a bit tarnished by time and neglect, circles my finger and twists together at the top to encase a small white diamond. The four prongs that anchor the diamond are separated by pockets of dust. The diamond itself is tiny and dull, like a sliver of glass found on the kitchen floor after a dishwashing accident. Just below the diamond are small air holes, intended to let the diamond breathe, but now clogged with grime. The ring is neither very attractive nor valuable, but I treasure it as a gift from my older sister, a gift I will pass along to my younger sister when I receive my own engagement ring this Christmas.

Notice that the topic sentence in this paragraph not only identifies the belonging (a "pre-engagement ring") but also implies why the writer treasures it (". . . given to me last year by my sister Doris"). Such a topic sentence is more interesting and revealing than a bare announcement: "The belonging I am about to describe is my pre-engagement ring." Avoid merely announcing your topic in this way, and instead focus your paragraph and interest your reader with a complete topic sentence—one that expresses an attitude or reason as well as identifies the object you are going to describe.

Once you have introduced a topic clearly, you should stick to it, developing it with details in the rest of the paragraph. The writer of "My Tiny Diamond Ring" has done just that, providing specific details that describe the ring: its parts, size, color, and condition. Thus, the paragraph is *unified*—that is, all of the supporting sentences relate directly to one another and to the topic introduced in the first sentence.

Don't be concerned if your first draft does not seem as clear or as well constructed as "My Tiny Diamond Ring" (the result of several revisions). Your aim now is to introduce your belonging in a topic sentence and then draft four or five supporting sentences that describe the item in detail. You will have opportunities to improve and rearrange these sentences as you revise in later steps. (For an example of an essay-length version of this assignment, see the section "Mementos" in Chapter Fourteen.)

EXERCISE SUPPORTING A TOPIC SENTENCE

What follows is an effective topic sentence for this assignment:

My most valuable possession is an old, slightly warped, blond guitar—the first instrument I taught myself how to play.

This sentence not only identifies the belonging ("an old, slightly warped, blond guitar") but also suggests why the writer values it ("the first instrument I taught myself how to play"). Some of the sentences below support this topic sentence with specific descriptive details. Others, however, offer information that would be inappropriate in a unified descriptive paragraph. Put an **X** in front of those sentences that do *not* support the topic sentence with precise descriptive details.

_____ 1. It is a Madeira folk guitar, all scuffed and scratched and fingerprinted.

_____ 2. My grandparents gave it to me on my thirteenth birthday.

_____ 3. I think they bought it at the Music Lovers' Shop in Portland where they used to live.

_____ 4. At the top is a bramble of copper-wound strings, each one hooked through the eye of a silver tuning key.

_____ 5. Although copper strings are much harder on the fingers than nylon strings, they sound much better than the nylon ones.

_____ 6. The strings are stretched down a long slim neck.

_____ 7. The frets on the neck are tarnished, and the wood has been worn down by years of fingers pressing chords.

_____ 8. It was three months before I could even tune the guitar properly, and another few months before I could manage the basic chords.

_____ 9. You have to be very patient when first learning how to play the guitar.

_____ 10. You should set aside a certain time each day just for practice.

_____ 11. The body of the Madeira is shaped like an enormous yellow pear, one slightly damaged in shipping.

_____ 12. A guitar can be awkward to hold, particularly if it seems bigger than you are, but you need to learn how to hold it properly if you're ever going to play it right.

_____ 13. I usually play sitting down because it's more comfortable that way.

_____ 14. The blond wood has been chipped and gouged to gray, particularly where the pick guard fell off years ago.

_____ 15. I have a Gibson now and hardly ever play the Madeira anymore.

■

Step 3 | # *Revise for Effective Organization*

Now you will revise your descriptive paragraph, concentrating on its *organization*. That is, you will check to see that your sentences follow a clear and logical order, each detail related to the one that came before and leading to the one that follows.

There are various ways to organize the details in a descriptive paragraph. You may move from the top of the item to the bottom, or from bottom to top. You may start at the left side of the item and move right, or go from right to left. You may start with the outside of the item and move in, or go from inside to out. Choose the one pattern that seems best suited to your topic, and then stick to that pattern throughout the paragraph.

The following paragraph is an example of a well-organized description:

A Friendly Clown

On one corner of my dresser sits a smiling toy clown on a tiny unicycle—a gift I received last Christmas from a close friend. The clown's short yellow hair, made of yarn, covers its ears but is parted above the eyes. The blue eyes are outlined in black with thin, dark lashes flowing from the brows. It has cherry-red cheeks, nose, and lips, and its broad grin disappears into the wide, white ruffle around its neck. The clown wears a fluffy, two-tone nylon costume. The left side of the outfit is light blue, and the right side is red. The two colors merge in a dark line that runs down the center of the small outfit. Surrounding its ankles and disguising its long black shoes are big pink bows. The white spokes on the wheel of the unicycle gather in the center and expand to the black tire so that the wheel somewhat resembles the inner half of a grapefruit. The clown and unicycle together stand about a foot high. As a cherished gift from my good friend Tran, this colorful figure greets me with a smile every time I enter my room.

Observe how the writer moves clearly from a description of the head of the clown (in sentences two, three, and four), to the body (sentences five, six, seven, and eight) to the unicycle underneath (sentence nine). Notice, also, how the concluding sentence helps to tie the paragraph together by emphasizing the personal value of this gift.

As you revise your paragraph, check to see that it is both unified and clearly organized. In other words, make sure that you stick to the topic and arrange your descriptions clearly and logically.

EXERCISE ORGANIZING THE DESCRIPTIVE PARAGRAPH

What follows is the topic sentence of a paragraph titled "The Candle":

I treasure my candle not for its beauty, its sentimental value, or even its usefulness, but for its simple, stark ugliness.

The rest of the paragraph appears below; however, the sentences have been rearranged so that the descriptions appear in no logical order. Number the sentences from 1 to 8 to show how they should be arranged to make a clear, well-organized paragraph.

_____ **A.** Rising crookedly out of the cup and collar is the candle, a pitifully short, stubby object.

_____ **B.** Abandoned by a previous occupant of my room, the candle squats on the window sill, anchored by cobwebs and surrounded by dead flies.

_____ **C.** This ugly little memorial consists of three parts: the base, the reflector, and the candle itself.

_____ **D.** This aluminum flower is actually a wrinkled old Christmas-light collar.

_____ **E.** The base is a white, coffee-stained Styrofoam cup, its wide mouth pressed to the sill.

_____ **F.** And by lighting the wick, any time I choose, I can melt this ugly candle away.

_____ **G.** From the bottom of the cup (which is the top of the base) sprouts a space-age daisy: red, green, and silver petals intended to collect wax and reflect candle light.

_____ **H.** The candle is about the same size and color as a man's thumb, beaded with little warts of wax down the sides and topped by a tiny bent wick. ■

Step 4 ## Revise and Proofread

Invite someone to read your paragraph and suggest ways you might further improve it. Then, taking your reader's comments into consideration, revise the paragraph once again. Use the following checklist as a guide. ·

REVISION CHECKLIST

❑ Does your paragraph begin with a topic sentence—one that identifies the item you are going to describe and suggests its significance to you?

❑ Are your descriptions clear and specific?

❑ Have you put your descriptions into complete sentences?

❑ Is your paragraph unified—that is, do all of the supporting sentences relate directly to the topic introduced in the first sentence?

❑ Have you followed a logical pattern in organizing the sentences in your paragraph?

❑ Have you concluded the paragraph with a sentence reminding the reader of the item's personal value?

❑ Have you proofread your paper carefully?

Passages

_A._ What follows is the final version of "The Blond Guitar," a paragraph that you first saw in the exercise on supporting a topic sentence. Compare this version with the earlier one to see which descriptions have been retained, what information has been omitted, and how sentences have been reworded and rearranged.

The Blond Guitar

My most valuable possession is an old, slightly warped, blond guitar—the first instrument I taught myself how to play. It's nothing fancy, just a Madeira folk guitar, all scuffed and scratched and finger-printed. At the top is a bramble of copper-wound strings, each one hooked through the eye of a silver tuning key. The strings are stretched down a long, slim neck, its frets tarnished, the wood worn by years of fingers pressing chords and picking notes. The body of the Madeira is shaped like an enormous yellow pear, one that was slightly damaged in shipping. The blond wood has been chipped and gouged to gray, particularly where the pick guard fell off years ago. No, it's not a beautiful instrument, but it still lets me make music, and for that I will always treasure it.

(Jeremy Burden)

B. The following paragraph opens the third chapter of Maxine Hong Kingston's lyrical account of growing up female and Chinese-American in California, *The Woman Warrior: Memoirs of a Girlhood Among Ghosts*. Notice how Kingston integrates informative and descriptive details in this account of "the metal tube" that holds her mother's diploma from medical school.

from "Shaman"

Once in a long while, four times so far for me, my mother brings out the metal tube that holds her medical diploma. On the tube are gold circles crossed with seven red lines each—"joy" ideographs in abstract. There are also little flowers that look like gears for a gold machine. According to the scraps of labels with Chinese and American addresses, stamps, and postmarks, the family airmailed the can from Hong Kong in 1950. It got crushed in the middle, and whoever tried to peel the labels off stopped because the red and gold paint came off too, leaving silver scratches that rust. Somebody tried to pry the end off before discovering that the tube pulls apart. When I open it, the smell of China flies out, a thousand-year-old bat flying heavy-headed out of the Chinese caverns where bats are as white as dust, a smell that comes from long ago, far back in the brain.

(Maxine Hong Kingston)

Questions

1. What appears to be the special significance of the metal tube described by Kingston?

2. What are *ideographs?*

3. Identify two of the colorful comparisons used by Kingston to convey an image and suggest the significance of the tube.

Postscript

The strategy of probing or questioning a topic, which you practiced at the beginning of this assignment, is one that is useful in all stages of the writing process. Probing helps us first to discover ideas and later to improve our drafts by drawing out more specific details. Like the strategy of listing, probing can help us with many different kinds of writing assignments.

This assignment also gave you practice in composing a unified, well-organized paragraph. Although later chapters will present some variations on the strategies introduced here, you should keep in mind these basic principles:

1. focus your paragraph in a topic sentence;
2. stick to the topic throughout the paragraph;
3. arrange your sentences clearly and logically.

The next assignment will give you additional practice in composing an effective descriptive paragraph.

CHAPTER THREE

Places
(Place Description)

Preview

In Chapter One (*Observations*), you listed sentences that described a particular place, and in Chapter Two (*Belongings*), you organized a descriptive paragraph. This assignment calls on you to combine these approaches by composing a one-paragraph description of a place. After discovering and focusing a topic through clustering, you will draft a paragraph that describes a place and conveys your attitude toward it. Then you will revise your paragraph to ensure that the descriptions are precise and clearly connected.

Step 1   *Discover and Develop a Topic through Clustering*

We all know places that evoke strong feelings, whether of nostalgia or regret, pleasure or disgust, peacefulness or fear. Such a place might be a vacation spot or a place of worship, an exotic locale or just a corner of the kitchen. In this assignment you will describe one of these places.

Consider several possible topics before you settle on one. Think of particular places that you associate with good times in your life—or with bad times. Recall the spot where you first met your boyfriend or girlfriend, husband or wife. Did you have a "secret hiding place" when you were a child, or do you have one now where you go to get away from it all? Think of particular places that have ever frightened, inspired, depressed, or excited you.

A discovery strategy called *clustering* may help you to identify a topic for this assignment. Clustering is a simple way of mapping out ideas as they come to you. Begin with a blank sheet of paper, and in the center write a key word or phrase—the name of your hometown, for instance, or of your college. Then, draw a short line from the middle of the phrase outward and write down something associated with the place: perhaps the name of a street in your hometown or the name of one of the buildings on campus. Continue making associations in this fashion, jotting down related words and drawing lines to indicate connections. Let one thought lead you to another, and don't stop to make corrections or to criticize yourself.

In this assignment, clustering can help you to focus a topic so that you can describe a particular place adequately in a single paragraph. In the sample below

(Figure 3.1), notice how the student moved from a large place ("campus") to a particular building ("Old Student Union") to a room in that building ("Records Office"). Another way to focus your topic is to describe the place at a particular time of the day or year. For instance, a description of the library on the first day of classes will probably differ from a description of the same place a few days before final exams. Your aim is to find an approach that allows you to describe your topic in detail.

Of course, if the place you have chosen is nearby, you may simply want to visit it and take notes on what you see there (as you did for your *Observations* report). But if you can't visit the place in person, you will have to rely on your memory of it. Clustering can also help you to recall and organize specific descriptive details. Once you have settled on a particular location (the Records Office in the Old Student Union, for example), repeat the process described above: write the name of the place in the center of a fresh sheet of paper, and then jot down all of the things that you associate with it: sights, sounds, and smells; the people who go there and the things it contains; details that help evoke the mood or atmosphere. Notice in the sample below (Figure 3.2) how the student has begun to group related details together. The notes that you take while clustering will be useful when you draft your paragraph in the next step.

EXERCISE OBSERVING A PLACE AND CLUSTERING

With the other members of your class, spend several minutes carefully observing your own classroom or some other location on campus. Then, working on your own or in a small group, jot down as many details as you can using the clustering strategies just described. When you are done, compare your notes with those of your classmates. Consider some of the various possible ways of focusing a description of

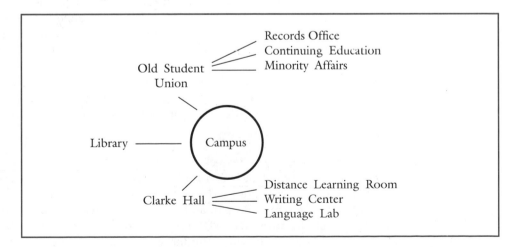

Figure 3.1

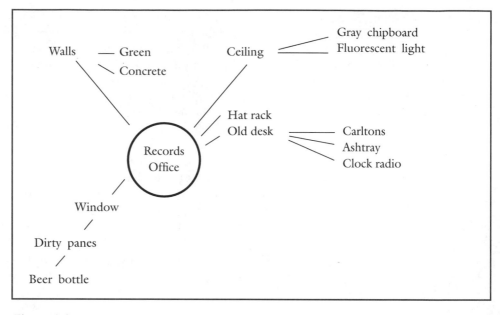

Figure 3.2

your classroom, and discuss how certain specific details might help to evoke a particular mood. ■

Step 2 | *Draft a Place Description*

From the list of details that you came up with in the first step, select the ones you
think are most significant and revealing. Then draft a paragraph in which you organize these descriptions. Begin with a topic sentence that clearly identifies the place
and suggests your attitude toward it. Then go on in the rest of the paragraph to describe the place in detail.

In addition to creating a vivid picture, carefully chosen details can also convey the
single dominant mood of a place. The following paragraph, which grew out of the
clustering exercises illustrated in Step 1, demonstrates this quality:

The Cubicle

Topic
sentence

<u>I spend fifteen hours every week in a bleak, six-by-six foot cubicle on the sec-
ond floor of the old Student Union Building.</u> The walls are bare concrete blocks,
painted a dull industrial green. The ceiling is gray perforated chipboard, interrupted only by a fluorescent light, and the floor is cracked brown linoleum. The
single wooden door, always closed, wears last year's calendar on its back. By the
door is an empty hat rack, and along the wall beside it is the old oak desk, still
sturdy despite the initials, emblems, and obscenities gouged into it. On the desk

are a pack of Carltons, a cheap green aluminum ashtray, two blue Spirit pens (both run dry), a broken clock radio, and a stack of the IW-24 forms that I collect and correct, return or reject every day. The room is otherwise empty and undistinguished, except for the small, dusty window to the left of the desk. There, barely visible beyond the grime on the panes, is the shadow of a Black Label beer bottle on the outside sill. The bottle is empty.

Notice that only in the topic sentence does the writer *tell* us that this room is "bleak"; in the rest of the paragraph he *shows* how bleak it is. Identify particular details in the paragraph that convey this mood.

Don't be concerned if your rough draft is not nearly as polished or well organized as the paragraph above (the product of several revisions). For now, simply put down as many details as you can in whatever order seems clear and logical. Later, when you revise, you can change and rearrange your descriptions.

EXERCISE FOCUSING PLACE DESCRIPTIONS

Each of the following paragraphs could be improved through careful focusing and the addition of more specific details. On your own paper, suggest ways to make these improvements by answering the questions that follow each paragraph.

Boulevard of Broken Dreams

Los Angeles was not at all what I had expected. I found myself driving down a dark section of that famous street, Hollywood Boulevard. I had never been there before. Glittering in the dull lights were broken wine bottles, and crumpled up fast-food containers blew across the street. There was a disturbing smell in the air. An endless trail of cigarette butts and hard black wads of gum littered the Walk of the Stars. I was frightened by all the strange, loud noises. Standing against a cold, dark concrete wall was a girl of about fourteen or fifteen. She was wearing very little clothing. She was fidgeting nervously from coming down off of her heroin high. Walking back and forth, twisting and tangling her fingers together, she could hardly stand still. I was wearing a new pair of shoes, and my feet began to ache from all the walking we were doing. Just down from the girl lay a gentleman on the walkway. He was drinking from a bottle half hidden in a paper bag. His dark brown coat was torn, and his pants were raggedy. His white tennis shoes were blackened from the grime on Hollywood Boulevard. Thank goodness my cousin was with me. Lying there drinking, the man began to talk to himself, turning his head from one side to the other. I don't know exactly what he was saying, but I understood that he was telling me that it was time to go home.

1. Remember that your description should begin with a topic sentence that identifies the particular place and suggests the mood that you want to evoke. With this guideline in mind, which of the opening sentences should be eliminated from the preceding paragraph?

2. What particular place is the writer attempting to describe?

3. What is the dominant mood that the writer is trying to evoke?

4. Using your answers to questions 1, 2, and 3, create an effective topic sentence for this paragraph.

5. Certain parts of this paragraph *tell* something without *showing* very much. Identify those things that need to be described in greater detail.

6. Which sentences should be eliminated (or at least modified) because they are not directly related to the main purpose of the paragraph?

Augusta, Kentucky

I grew up in a poor family in a poor town. We did not have much money or many of the good things in life, but we did have one another. One year the flood wiped out our home. In fact, it wiped out all of River Street. I'll never forget the morning I saw River Street for the last time. The river was on one side of the street and the houses were on the other. We lived in one of these houses before the flood hit. There was mud on the walls of the houses, and many windows were broken. The roofs were in terrible shape. There were many gigantic trees. Children were still playing here, and I remember hearing music. There was a bar at the end of the street and after that a lot of weeds. The whole scene was pretty desolate.

1. This paragraph does not begin with a clearly focused topic sentence. Which of the opening sentences should be eliminated?

2. What place is the writer attempting to describe?

3. What is the dominant mood that the writer is trying to evoke?

4. Use your answers to questions 2 and 3 to create an effective topic sentence for this paragraph.

5. What are some of the items *mentioned* in the paragraph that need to be *described* in more detail? ■

Step 3 ## *Revise Your Place Description*

Be prepared to add, change, or leave out particular words and sentences as you revise your place description. Make sure it begins with a clear and accurate topic sentence, one that prepares the reader for what follows. Also, check that the sentences in the rest of the paragraph are clearly related both to the topic sentence and to one another.

Organizing a place description is not that different from the way you organized your paragraph in the last assignment (*Belongings*). You can arrange the details down, around, or across, letting the natural order of the place determine the arrangement of the descriptions in your paragraph.

To help guide your reader from one sentence to the next, you may want to use some of the following *place signals*:

above	in front
across	in the center
alongside	nearby
at one end	next to
at the near (or far) side	on top of
beneath	opposite
beyond	to the left (right)
farther along	under
in back	upon

These words and phrases show direction and help to connect place descriptions. Observe how the writer of the following paragraph has relied on a number of these signals to steer us around the room he is describing:

The Cabin at Jackson Lake

I know of no place more reassuring and secure than my grandparents' sturdy one-room cabin at Jackson Lake. The floor is made of thick slabs of oak, always waxed and highly polished. The walls are made of pine, and they are criss-crossed by rough black beams. One of the walls lets in light through two large windows that were salvaged from an old gas station. Above each window is a row of German beer steins, and just in front of them is a double bed covered with a warm quilt comforter. Across the room, occupying half the opposite wall, is a great stone fireplace, with an old musket hanging to the left and a Civil War sword on the right. In front of the fireplace is a knotty gray rug, about an inch thick. And a few inches away, in the center of the room, stands a rectangular oak dining table, large enough to sit eight hungry adults. Surrounding the table are various wooden chairs, no two of which are the same. This roughly constructed cabin will exude charm and provide comfort for many years to come.

As you revise your paragraph, rearranging sentences and adding place signals, again check that your descriptions are as specific as you can make them. Try to evoke a mood by creating a vivid picture.

EXERCISE USING PLACE SIGNALS

Identify the place signals used in each of the following paragraphs.

Mabel's Lunchroom*

Mabel's Lunch stood along one wall of a wide room, once a pool hall, with the empty cue racks along the back side. Beneath the racks were wire-back chairs, one

---

*Adapted from *The World in the Attic*, by Wright Morris (New York: Scribner's, 1949).

of them piled with magazines, and between every third or fourth chair a brass spittoon. Near the center of the room, revolving slowly as if the idle air was water, a large propeller fan suspended from the pressed tin ceiling. It made a humming sound, like a telephone pole, or an idle, throbbing locomotive, and although the switch cord vibrated it was cluttered with flies. At the back of the room, on the Lunch side, an oblong square was cut in the wall and a large woman with a soft, round face peered through at us. After wiping her hands she placed her heavy arms, as if they tired her, on the shelf.

The Laundry Room

The windows at either end of the laundry room were open, but no breeze washed through to carry off the stale odors of fabric softener, detergent, and bleach. In the small ponds of soapy water that stained the concrete floor were stray balls of multicolored lint and fuzz. Along the left wall of the room stood ten rasping dryers, their round windows providing glimpses of jumping socks, underpants, T-shirts, and fatigues. Down the center of the room were a dozen washing machines, set back to back in two rows. Some were chugging like steamboats; others were whining and whistling and dribbling suds. Two stood forlorn and empty, their lids flung open, with crudely scrawled notes that said "Broke!" A long orange shelf ran the length of the wall, interrupted only by a shut door. Alone, at the far end of the shelf, sat one empty laundry basket and an open box of Tide. Hanging above the shelf at the other end was a small bulletin board decorated with yellowed business cards and slips of paper: lost dogs, cats for sale, requests for rides, and phone numbers without names or explanations. The machines hummed and wheezed, gurgled and gushed, washed, rinsed, and spun on and on and on. ■

Step 4   *Revise and Proofread*

Let someone else read your place description and offer suggestions on how you might further improve it. Then, using the following checklist as a guide, revise your paragraph once again.

REVISION CHECKLIST
❑ Does your paragraph begin with a topic sentence that clearly identifies the place and suggests the dominant mood?
❑ Are your descriptions clear?
❑ Are your descriptions specific?
❑ Do the descriptive details evoke a particular mood as well as provide a picture?

❑ Is your paragraph unified—that is, do all of the supporting sentences relate directly to the topic sentence?

❑ Have you used place signals to guide your reader from one detail to the next?

❑ Have you followed a logical pattern in organizing your paragraph, using the natural order of the place to determine the arrangement of the descriptive details?

❑ Have you proofread your paragraph carefully?

Passages

A. What follows is a thoroughly revised version of "Augusta, Kentucky," the second paragraph in the exercise on "Focusing Place Descriptions." Notice that this revised paragraph is not only more descriptive than the original but also better organized.

River Street

I will never forget that desolate spring morning when I saw River Street for the very last time. On the east side of the street, the Ohio River waited menacingly. The west side was lined with a single row of flood-damaged houses, sitting dark and abandoned, so completely decayed that even the poor could no longer live in them. Walls that once were pastel blue, green, or yellow were now layered with mud six or seven feet high. Paneless window jambs were opened like dark mouths to gulp down the muddy flood tides. Once-sturdy beams that supported porch roofs stood shakily, missing chunks of molded wood from their damp middles. These rotting houses were still shaded by the enormous limbs of the old oaks. Fed by the rich river soil, the trees loomed over the street like strange, dark mourners. Their massive gnarled roots had broken through the sidewalk, pushing up great chunks of jagged concrete. Tattered, dirty children played on these slabs while twangy country music drifted down from the saloon at the end of the street. And that is where my memory ends, at the end of the street, lost in mud, weeds, and rubble. This was the last view I had of the street where I had grown up.

(Flo Powell)

B. Educator Joseph H. Suina grew up on the Cochiti Pueblo Reservation in New Mexico, where he still lives today. As you read the following paragraph, in which Suina describes the one-room house that he shared with his grandmother, notice how he reveals certain feelings—indirectly—through the descriptive details he provides.

A Goody Bag in a One-Room House

During those years, Grandmother and I lived beside the plaza in a one-room house. It consisted of a traditional fireplace, a makeshift cabinet for our few tin cups and dishes, and a wooden crate that held our two buckets of all-purpose water. At the far end of the room were two rolls of bedding we used as comfortable sitting "couches." Consisting of thick quilts, sheepskin, and assorted blankets, these bedrolls were undone each night. A wooden pole the length of one side of the room was suspended about ten inches from the ceiling beams. A modest collection of colorful shawls, blankets, and sashes draped over the pole making this part of the room most interesting. In one corner was a bulky metal trunk for our ceremonial wear and few valuables. A dresser, which was traded for some of my mother's well-known pottery, held the few articles of clothing we owned and the "goody bag." Grandmother always had a flour sack filled with candy, store-bought cookies, and Fig Newtons. These were saturated with a sharp odor of moth balls. Nevertheless, they made a fine snack with coffee before we turned in for the night. Tucked securely in my blankets, I listened to one of her stories or accounts of how it was when she was a little girl. These accounts seemed so old fashioned compared to the way we lived. Sometimes she softly sang a song from a ceremony. In this way I fell asleep each night.

(Joseph H. Suina)

Questions

1. Define the following words as they are used in Suina's paragraph: *makeshift, modest, sashes, saturated*.

2. What is the dominant mood or impression evoked by the author's description of the one-room house?

3. Point out specific descriptive details in Suina's paragraph that not only show what the one-room house looked like but also suggest the mood of the place.

4. Identify the place signals used in this paragraph.

5. Discuss how Suina's description of the one-room house also suggests something about the character of his grandmother.

6. Toward the end of the paragraph, Suina refers to the "stories or accounts" told by his grandmother. What is the difference between a *story* and an *account*?

Postscript

In this chapter, you practiced the discovery strategy of *clustering*—a simple method of mapping out information and ideas. Like listing and probing, clustering is a strategy that may be applied to any writing assignment.

In addition, this chapter, like the earlier *Observations* and *Belongings*, has given you practice in using and arranging specific descriptive details in your writing. Although the assignments that follow will introduce you to types of writing other than description, you will still be called on to develop, organize, and connect specific details. In other words, you will continue to build on the strategies that you have learned so far.

CHAPTER FOUR

Virtues and Vices
(EXAMPLES)

Preview

In the assignments so far, you have collected and organized details that have *described* something. In this assignment, you will collect and organize details that *explain* something—something about yourself. After identifying one of your character traits (a virtue or a vice), you will use the discovery strategies of listing, probing, and clustering to develop a number of examples of this trait. Next, you will draft a paragraph containing a clear topic sentence supported by three or four brief, specific examples. You will then revise the paragraph to make sure that your examples are clearly and logically connected.

Step 1 · Develop Examples through Listing, Probing, and Clustering

What are your virtues and vices, your good points and bad? Do you consider yourself to be patient or impatient? Generous or selfish? Hard-working or lazy? Begin this assignment by making a list of what you see as your outstanding character traits. Write down at least ten adjectives that you think accurately describe your temperament or personality.

Look over your list of character traits, and choose one that you feel you will have no trouble explaining. How do you *explain* a virtue or a vice? One way is to give examples that *show* how you are generous or selfish, hardworking or lazy, patient or impatient. Jot down several examples.

To be convincing and interesting, your examples should be specific. For instance, if you claim to be a generous person, you might give as an example the time you drove twenty miles out of your way to take a stranger to the airport. This example would be much more convincing than merely saying, "I am nice to strangers."

Try using the discovery strategies of probing (discussed in Chapter Two) and clustering (Chapter Three) to develop examples of a virtue or vice. You might begin by asking the questions used by reporters to probe their subjects: *who? what? where? when? how?* and *why?* When you demonstrated generosity, for example, who was involved, what happened, where and when did it occur, how did you behave, and why did you behave in that fashion? Clustering may help you to recall additional examples. In the center of a clean sheet of paper, identify your virtue or vice, and then (in no particular order) jot down any examples that come to mind. Try to find several brief examples so that you will have plenty to choose from when it comes time to draft a paragraph. If you have trouble recalling more than two or three specific examples, clustering should help you to find an alternative topic—another virtue or vice but one that is easier to illustrate.

EXERCISE IDENTIFYING SPECIFIC EXAMPLES

Although we use general statements ("I am nice to strangers") to introduce specific examples, such statements should not be confused with the examples themselves. For each set of notes below, put an X in front of general statements and a checkmark in front of specific examples.

VICE: I am too talkative.

Support:

_____ I used to talk a lot in school when I should have been paying attention.

_____ I used to talk so much in class that one day Mrs. Barnard, my history teacher, tied her scarf around my mouth.

_____ One day in church the priest stopped his sermon and invited me up to the altar to finish what I had been "whispering" to my brother.

_____ My father used to yell at me for talking so much in church.

_____ My girlfriend says that I talk too much.

_____ Once when I was talking on the phone to my girlfriend, I was interrupted by the doorbell: there she was on the front step! My girlfriend had hung up the phone and driven to my house, and I was so busy talking I never noticed that for ten minutes I was talking to myself.

VIRTUE: I am an honest person.

Support:

_____ Last week at Kroger's, I was given a dollar too much in change, and I returned it to the cashier.

_____ I always count my change to make sure it is correct.

_____ I have never cheated on a test at school.

_____ My boyfriend once offered to show me a copy of the math test I was scheduled to take that afternoon. I didn't look.

_____ When people ask me for my opinion, I give it to them, whether they like it or not.

_____ When my boyfriend asked me what I thought of his new "skinhead" hair style, I told him his head looked like a moldy old cantaloupe.

VICE: I am a very forgetful person.

Support:

_____ I usually pay my bills on time, but I often forget to mail them.

_____ A few weeks ago I came home to find that the water in my house had been shut off. Sure, I had paid the bill on time, but it was still sitting on the dashboard of my car.

_____ Although I have never yet forgotten that Christmas was approaching, I have managed in the past year to forget to buy gifts in time for Mother's Day, my sister's graduation, and my father's birthday.

_____ My absent-mindedness causes me to forget a lot of things.

_____ Because of my absent-mindedness, I have managed, just recently, to lose my gloves, two umbrellas, a gas cap, a notebook, my French textbook, and my gym shorts. ■

Step 2 | ## *Draft a Paragraph with Examples*

Study your list of examples and choose the three or four that you think are most interesting and best illustrate your virtue or vice. Then use these examples in a rough draft of a paragraph. Begin the paragraph with a topic sentence that clearly identifies the trait you are about to illustrate. This topic sentence may be quite simple:

I am an extremely forgetful person.

Or you may start with something a little more imaginative:

I am not ashamed to confess my outstanding vice, but I just can't seem to remember what it is.

Just make certain that the topic sentence is clear.

Your paragraph should contain at least three or four examples, explained in a sentence or two each. Don't be too concerned just yet about the arrangement of the examples in your draft: you will have a chance to revise them later on.

To get an idea of what this step calls for, read the following draft of a student's paper on the "vice" of excessive worrying.

Worried to Death

I worry entirely too much. My worries range from the tiniest things to extremes. ~~I usually~~ My biggest worry is how I will accomplish everything I have to do within the day. ~~A good example would be today~~ For example, today I woke up fifteen minutes late, so I worried the whole time I was getting ready. Then I drove to school, and during the long drive I worried about ~~making it~~ arriving to Spanish class on time. When I finally made it to my first destination, I then proceeded to worry ~~if I was really listening to the lecture, and what would happen if~~ about the test that I was sure I was about to fail. I really wanted an *A*, and I stressed over the consequences if I didn't make it. ~~Then I~~ My professor returned my test, and amazingly I did make an *A*. But I couldn't relax. Then I worried about the next five tests I would take and what could possibly go wrong. After that I went to lunch, and while I ate I worried that I would mess up my speech ~~that I was supposed to give in my speech class~~. I worried that I would spill the marinara sauce on my white blouse and that I was eating too much butter on my muffin and whether the Sweet'n Low contained cancer-making agents. I worried that it would make my fingernails brittle and my hair fall out. ~~After lunch I realized that~~ I was so busy worrying through lunch that I realized I was already twenty minutes late for work and still had to stop to get gas. I worried that I wouldn't have enough gas to reach the gas station. ~~Did I go over the limit on my credit card? What if I had to hitch a ride with a crazy serial~~ But most of all I was most worried about how much I was worrying about everything.

The many crossings-out in the paper show that the student was already revising as she was making her rough draft. Later in this chapter you will see the final version of the paragraph: the examples are the same, but the sentences have been reworded and rearranged.

EXERCISE FORMING TOPIC SENTENCES

This exercise will give you practice in expressing a main point in a topic sentence that catches the interest of your readers. Each paragraph below illustrates a single character trait. After reading each paragraph, try to create an imaginative topic sentence that clearly identifies the particular trait being described.

A. Topic Sentence: _____

_____

_____

For example, recently I began taking my two-year-old dog to obedience school. After four weeks of lessons and practice, she has learned to follow only three commands—sit, stand, and lie down—and even then she often gets confused. Frustrating (and costly) as this is, I continue to work with her every day. After dog school, my grandmother and I sometimes go grocery shopping. Inching along those aisles, elbowed by hundreds of fellow customers, backtracking to pick up forgotten items, and standing in the endless line at the checkout, I could easily grow frustrated and cranky. But through years of patience I have learned to keep my temper in check. Finally, after putting away the groceries, I might go out to a movie with my fiance, to whom I have been engaged for three years. Layoffs, extra jobs, and home problems have forced us to reschedule our wedding date several times. Still, my patience has enabled me to cancel and reschedule our wedding plans again and again without fuss, fights, or tears.

B. Topic Sentence: _____

_____

_____

For instance, when I was in kindergarten, I dreamed that my sister killed people with a television antenna and disposed of their bodies in the woods across the street from our house. For three weeks after that dream I lived with my grandparents until they convinced me that my sister was harmless. Not long afterwards, my grandfather died, and that sparked new fears. I was so terrified that his spirit would visit me that I put two brooms across the doorway of my bedroom at night. Fortunately, my little trick worked. He never came back. More recently, I was terribly frightened after staying up late one night to watch *A Nightmare on Elm Street*. I lay awake until dawn with my hand on the telephone, ready to dial 911 the moment Freddy Kreuger appeared. Just thinking about it now gives me goosebumps.

C. Topic Sentence: _____

_____

_____

When I was a young girl, I would make a tent out of my blankets and read Nancy Drew mysteries late into the night. I still read cereal boxes at the breakfast table, newspapers while I am stopped at red lights, and gossip magazines while waiting in line at the supermarket. In fact, I'm a very talented reader. For example, I've mastered the art of talking on the telephone while simultaneously reading Erma Bombeck or James Herriot. But what I read doesn't really matter all that much. In a pinch, I'll read junk mail, an old warranty, a furniture tag ("DO NOT REMOVE UNDER PENALTY OF LAW"), or even, if I'm extremely desperate, a chapter or two in a textbook. ■

Step 3   *Revise for Clear Organization*

Now, read over your draft and consider how you might improve it. Is the topic sentence clear? Are you satisfied that all the examples are specific and relevant to the topic? Are they organized clearly and smoothly? Does your paragraph have a clear conclusion?

As you prepare to make your revision, consider some of the ways writers introduce and connect examples. One common technique is to begin a sentence with an *example signal*—a word or phrase that tells the reader that an example lies ahead. Here are some of the common example signals:

another example	for instance
another instance	specifically
as an illustration	to illustrate
for example	

In some cases, you may want to present your examples in chronological order—that is, the order in which they occurred in time. Following are some of the common *time signals:*

after	next
afterward	now
as long as	once
at the same time	previously
before	simultaneously
currently	since
earlier	subsequently
finally	then
immediately	when
in the meantime	until
in the past	until now
later	whenever
meanwhile	while

Examples may also be organized according to where they took place, and if so, *place signals* (listed in Chapter Three) may be used to introduce the examples and make clear connections. And there are still other ways to arrange examples: from least important to most important, or from most important to least. As you revise your paragraph, consider various ways of organizing the examples until you find the order that is clearest and most logical.

Another important part of organizing a paragraph is concluding it effectively. You might conclude a paragraph on a vice by explaining how you plan to change your behavior—or why you probably never will. You might conclude a paragraph on a virtue by defining the limits of your strength or explaining the benefits that come with such a virtue. Whatever approach you take, your concluding sentence should give readers a clear sense that you have completed the paragraph, not just run out of examples.

Now revise your paragraph, paying particular attention to the way that you introduce and arrange your examples and the way that you bring the paragraph to a satisfactory close.

EXERCISE IDENTIFYING CONNECTIONS AND ADDING CONCLUSIONS

Both of the following paragraphs are well organized, but each lacks a satisfactory concluding sentence. On your own paper, respond to the questions after each paragraph.

Junk Food Junkie

I am the worst junk food junkie in the world. You can keep your lentils, granola, and prunes. I want calories and carbohydrates, burgers and fries. Within minutes after waking up grouchy and puffy-eyed in the morning, I stumble to the kitchen and pour myself a tall glass of ice cold Pepsi. Ahh, my tongue tingles and my eyes pop open. I then have the energy to eat. I rummage through the refrigerator, push aside the eggs and apples, and there it is: a fat slice of cold pepperoni pizza. That's enough to get me off to school and through my first class. Of course, I head to the store on my first break for a Snickers bar and a Tab. The diet drink, you see, compensates for the calories in the candy. An hour or two later, for lunch, I gobble down a row of Oreos and a peanut butter sandwich, all sloshed down with a pint of chocolate milk. Later in the afternoon I stop at Burger King to devour a double cheeseburger and a large order of fries. Finally, before going to bed, I knock off a bag of potato chips dripping with onion dip.

1. The writer uses time order to organize her examples. List the time signals that you find in the paragraph.

2. What short sentence does the writer use to guide us from the Pepsi example to the pizza example?

3. What sentence does the writer use to guide us from the pizza example to the Snickers-and-Tab example?

4. Add a sentence that would conclude this paragraph effectively.

Confessions of a Slob

A quick tour through my house will convince you that I am an extremely messy person. In fact, some would say I'm a slob. Starting in my bedroom, you will see clothes thrown around as if thieves had just looted the place. T-shirts dangle from door knobs, socks sit balled up on top of the dresser, and blue jeans cover the floor like a dropcloth. A trail of shoes and sneakers leads you out of the bedroom and into the bathroom. There you will stand on a sopping towel and see a blowdryer and a copy of *Newsweek* lying on the sink alongside an uncapped tube of Crest. Just behind you is the towel rack: no towel, of course, but a dripping shirt and a crusty old bathrobe belt. Next to the bathroom is the kitchen: slob headquarters. To the left are erupting bags of garbage, a bald tire, and a tall stack of yellow newspapers. To the right are a greasy oven stacked high with pots and—beside it—a sink full of gray water and dirty dishes.

1. The writer uses place order to organize his examples. List the place signals you find in the paragraph.

2. What sentence does the writer use to guide us from the bedroom to the bathroom?

3. Add a sentence that would conclude this paragraph effectively. ■

Step 4 | *Revise and Proofread*

Let someone read your paragraph and suggest ways that you might further improve it. Then, taking your reader's comments into consideration, revise the paragraph once again. Use the following checklist as a guide.

REVISION CHECKLIST

❏ Have you clearly identified the vice or virtue in your first sentence?

❏ Have you given at least three or four specific examples?

❏ Do all the examples clearly relate to the trait you identified in your topic sentence?

❏ Have you organized the paragraph clearly and logically?

❏ Have you guided the reader from one example to the next using appropriate place, time, or example signals?

❏ Have you concluded with a sentence that gives the paragraph a sense of completeness?

❏ Have you proofread carefully?

Passages

A. Here is the revised version of the paragraph on worrying that you read earlier. Notice that the writer has added more specific details, used clear transitions from one example to the next, and developed an effective concluding sentence.

Worrying Myself to Death

I worry entirely too much. Waking up fifteen minutes late this morning, I was instantly worried that I would be running late the rest of the day, beginning with Spanish class at eight o'clock. When I made it to Spanish (fifteen minutes early), I then proceeded to worry about the upcoming test, which I was sure to fail. I dwelled on the awful consequences: being thrown out of college, losing my friends, being disowned by my family, and left pushing a shopping cart down some lonesome highway. Then, instead of relaxing after I completed the test (with an *A*, by the way), I redirected my worries to the next five tests and how they could go wrong. After that I went to lunch at Mary's Spaghetti House, and while eating I worried about spilling marinara sauce on my white blouse. Nervously, I wondered whether I was putting too much butter on my roll and whether the Sweet'n Low contained cancerous agents that would make my fingernails brittle, my hair fall out, or my firstborn emerge with radioactive orange eyes. I was so busy worrying through lunch that I was twenty-two minutes late for work and still had to stop for gas. I grew increasingly anxious. Would I be able to reach the service station on fumes? Had I exceeded the limit on my BP card? Would I then have to drive (walk? hitch a ride with a serial killer?) to the bank to get cash? That thought made me worry about the prospect of getting mugged at the automatic teller machine while trying to decide how much money to withdraw. I pondered whether ten dollars would be enough or twenty dollars too much. What agony! But underlying all of these concerns, day in and day out, is the biggest worry of all—that I'm worrying myself to death.

(Linda Cummings)

B. In his essay "The Sentimentalist," educator and freelance writer Frank Cappella considers the ways in which sentimentality may serve to disguise certain emotional inadequacies. In the following excerpt from the opening of that essay, Cappella offers numerous examples of sentimental experiences in his own life. As you read the passage, consider whether you agree or disagree with Cappella's central conviction that sentimentality is a vice.

The Sentimentalist

By nature, I'm a sentimental fool—a sucker for orphaned lion cubs and abandoned aliens, widowers in Seattle with precocious sons and twitchy club owners in Casablanca whose problems "don't amount to a hill of beans." Watching these tear-jerkers for the umpteenth time, I don't just sniffle mawkishly. I sob. I blubber. Rivulets of salty tears course down my puffy cheeks. Likewise, a corny greeting card (signed by the right person), a cruelly manipulative AT&T commercial, a child's crayoned rendition of a happy sun, even the often irritating tinkle of an ice cream van on a summer afternoon—all, without warning, can break my cheap, cheating heart. Certain songs—even those that have been homogenized by A Thousand Strings in a supermarket or an elevator—can induce gut-lurching fits of nostalgia for places never visited and people scarcely known. Oh, I'm a sentimental fool, all right.

But I've learned the hard way not to confuse sentimentality (a squishy kind of emotion that won't hold up under any kind of pressure) with genuine sensitivity. "Sentimentality," according to hard-boiled novelist Norman Mailer, "is the emotional promiscuity of those who have no sentiment." It's a soft, seemingly innocent vice, like munching cashews for breakfast or whistling in the office. But for one who still finds it hard to hug without discomfort and almost impossible to utter "I love you " convincingly, sentimentality is a sad little substitute for the real thing.

(Frank Cappella)

Questions

1. Define the following words as they are used in Cappella's essay: *precocious, mawkishly, manipulative.*

2. See if you can identify the four films that Cappella alludes to in his opening sentence. What, if anything, do these movies have in common?

3. What evidence, if any, can you find in the first paragraph to support Cappella's later assertion that sentimentality is "a sad little substitute for the real thing"?

4. Explain why you agree or disagree with Norman Mailer's view of sentimentality, as quoted by Cappella in the second paragraph.

Postscript

Explaining an idea with examples is a very common writing strategy. Specific examples not only clarify general principles but also make writing more interesting and easier to follow. In a number of later assignments you will have additional opportunities to develop paragraphs and whole essays with examples.

CHAPTER FIVE

Growing
(NARRATION)

Preview

In this assignment you will write about a particular incident in your life—one that taught you a lesson or deepened your understanding of others. In telling your story, you will use specific details that both describe and explain. You will begin by exploring your topic through *freewriting*—that is, nonstop writing without rules. Then you will draft a paragraph and revise it to make sure that your story is clearly focused and logically organized. Finally, you will proofread the paragraph carefully.

Step 1 ## *Freewrite*

The theme of this assignment is *growing*—the process of coming to a deeper awareness of ourselves and the world around us. This process is subtle (an inkling here, a suspicion there) and continuous. However, in looking back at our lives, we can usually point to several particular experiences that have had a profound effect on our attitudes, our values, and our behavior. In this assignment, you will relate one such experience.

Begin by reflecting on some important occasions and incidents in your life. Consider, for instance, some of the following experiences:

a serious illness or accident

the death of a family member or close friend

the beginning or the breaking up of a relationship

a personal victory or defeat

graduation from school

the loss of a job or the start of a new one

Make a list of such experiences, whether they occurred years ago or just this morning. And don't restrict yourself to dramatic incidents only: sometimes a casual remark or a trivial action can affect us deeply.

After jotting down several ideas, study your list of experiences and select one that is significant and yet not so painful to recall that you may have difficulty writing about it. Make sure that you identify a *particular* incident: not "My three years with Bobo," but perhaps "The first time I met Bobo."

You are now ready to explore your topic through *freewriting*. Freewriting is a kind of nonstop writing without rules. Your purpose is to capture on paper some of the thoughts that are flying about in your head. After writing down the topic you are considering, don't pause to ponder or correct: just write, write, write. If you get stuck for something to say, simply repeat the last word you have written, or write "I'm stuck, I'm stuck" until a new idea emerges. Your wrist will ache and your paper will probably be a mess, but you will have begun to explore your topic. Freewrite for ten minutes.

Following is one student's first attempt at freewriting. Spelling errors have been corrected, but otherwise this is an accurate transcript of the student's work. Notice that the student did not have a specific topic in mind when he started freewriting. In fact, he was using freewriting to help discover a topic for this assignment. Judge for yourself how successful he was.

First Freewriting

Freewriting is something that can really help you help you. You write about whatever you like. Of course you don't stop stop stop to fix errors or go back you just write. You can write you can write about what I just said you can write about dogs, gorillas cats horses birds etc. Dogs are very very special animals I believe they provide the best kind of pet. They wag their tails meet you at the door they stay by your side, sometimes they protect you. I'm stuck stuck I'm dogs they sometimes get run over by cars Fred hit by car an accident they didn't even stop stop stop Writing like this can sure put a cramp in your hand and it really hurts but I guess the pay off is really worth it. Glad this is not being graded for grammar spelling neatness it would surely be a double F F F F. I would hate to get an F in any subject. Math test last week got an F. Did it teach me a lesson a lesson? Don't get another F. I'm stuck I'm stuck dogs and math tests and accidents accidents wrecked the Camaro brand-new used 69 Camaro boy did I learn a lesson insurance and safety and time's up!

If we were to judge this piece of writing as a paragraph, we would find many problems. But as a first exercise in freewriting, this is quite successful. In just ten minutes of nonstop scribbling, the student discovered three possible topics: Fred's accident, a failed math test, and the wreck of the Camaro. Which topic did the student settle on? The answer is found in the student's second try at freewriting, below.

Wrecking My Camaro (Second Freewriting)

It happened so fast I can hardly remember what really happened now but I'll try anyhow. Traveling down Ferguson Ave. in my new car a Camaro I was faced with a situation unlike any situation that I did had ever been in before. There in the oncoming lane was a Caddie that was about to kiss the front of my car or the other way around. Anyway before I could even react we hit. All I remember then was asking my girlfriend if she was all right and then getting out of the car and walking in all the glass that was on the road. A witness who saw the accident walked walked up to my car and looked in and saw what happened and that I had nothing to worry about because it wasn't my fault she thought. I was still worried sick. The police came and the ambulance and then and then all the confusion started. The cop's first question was have you been drinking and I said no. He then wanted me to put me in his car but understood the situation and was very understanding. The crowd broke up and the ambulance left and the confusion seemed to be over this night even though it had just started what would soon prove to be one of the worst Christmas eves in my entire life. This would not be the last time that I would have to discuss this terrible incident because court was right down the road and so was a huge lawsuit where I learned a lesson about the importance of safe driving and also the importance of excess liability coverage because you never know how much someone, and I mean anyone, might sue you for. The amount is limitless and it all comes down to what a jury says.

This second freewriting has produced a rough draft. Key details of the accident are here for the student to clarify and rearrange in successive revisions. Freewriting, then, has not only helped the student discover a topic, but has also allowed him to explore that topic.

Examine the results of your first freewriting. Although you may find much there that is nonsense, you might also find some important items of information and description that can be used later in your draft. If so, underline or highlight these items. This freewriting may give you a clearer idea of exactly what you want to write about. After giving your hand a rest, do another ten minutes of freewriting to see what else you can discover about your topic.

EXERCISE ANALYZING FREEWRITING

Following is a slightly edited transcript of a student's second effort at freewriting—an unusually productive effort. Read this tale of a family crisis, and then answer the questions that follow it.

Terror on Sunday Morning (Second Freewriting)

I've never been so scared in my life. It all started on a Sunday beautiful Sunday morning when we were getting dressed for church. I remember that the video of *Beauty and the Beast* was on the VCR and nobody was watching as usual but I was singing along. It was one of those perfect mornings. I was dressing David and myself and Amy was out on the deck in her playpen playing by herself. I checked on her every fifteen minutes to check and see if she was okay doing okay. I always dressed Amy last if I didn't she would get herself all messed up before before we even got to church. Sometimes she acted up so bad we had to turn around and go back go back. Everything was fine the usual rushing around to get everybody ready. Then I went out to check on Amy and this time I knew right away that something was wrong terribly. David came running out after me when he heard me yelling. Amy was on the floor of the playpen not moving, choking. I picked her up and screamed for her father to come help me help me he went and called the EMS. I stuck my finger in her mouth and found a leaf stuck there and she kept on choking and started turning blue. I didn't even think of CPR at the time though I signed up for a course a week later. I just kept pounding Amy on the back and she kept crying and choking and then suddenly the rest of the bits of the leaf popped out. She was okay thank God. The EMS arrived and they checked to make sure Amy was okay but she was fine. I couldn't stop crying. We never even made it to church that morning but I did a lot of praying.

1. The student has good material here for a paragraph. Begin to focus this information by writing down what you think is the main point of the student's story.

2. Go back through this sample freewriting, and underline or highlight what you think are the key details in it—details that the writer would probably include in a carefully focused paragraph on the same subject.

3. What part(s) of the story do you think the writer should reduce, move, or cut out when she comes to draft a more carefully focused paragraph?

4. What items of description or information do you think the writer needs to add when she drafts her paragraph? ■

Step 2   *Draft a Paragraph That Tells a Story*

Drawing on the information contained in your freewritings, draft a paragraph in which you relate your experience and explain its effect on you. Identify your topic in the first sentence, and then in chronological order report the details of what happened. Because you are writing for someone who has not heard of this experience before, make certain that you provide those details that will let your reader understand what happened and appreciate the lesson you learned. Be sure to identify who was involved and where and when the incident occurred. Conclude your paragraph with "the moral of the story"—the lesson you learned, the understanding you achieved.

EXERCISE ELIMINATING UNNECESSARY INFORMATION

As you proceed from freewriting to drafting and then again from drafting to revising your paragraph, knowing what to cut out of your writing is as important as knowing what to put in. This exercise will give you practice in eliminating information that is irrelevant or repetitious.

Following are the first two sentences of a paragraph titled "Close to Dying":

During a brief stay at Hunter Leggett as a member of an army medical support unit, I watched a young man come close to dying. On this particular afternoon, P.F.C. Johnson and I were playing euchre in the truck when we received a bee sting patient.

The rest of the paragraph appears below. Although most of the sentences are in chronological order, some of them should be eliminated because they are repetitious or irrelevant to the story. Put an **X** in front of each sentence that should be eliminated.

_____ **A.** Weakly, the patient told us that he had been stung four hours earlier and that he was allergic to bees.

_____ **B.** Knowing then that the sting could be fatal, we started treatment immediately.

_____ **C.** Right now I can't recall the patient's name or even his rank.

_____ **D.** The young man fainted while I was holding his hand, and when I checked the vital signs, I found no sign of breathing and no trace of a pulse.

_____ **E.** We had received several other bee sting victims earlier that day.

_____ **F.** While I performed CPR on the patient, Johnson put ice bags around his neck.

_____ **G.** After several frightening seconds had passed, the patient resumed breathing on his own.

_____ **H.** The patient was now breathing in and breathing out.

_____ **I.** When he opened his eyes and saw the tears in mine, he asked me what the problem was.

_____ **J.** I had been at Hunter Leggett just a few days when all this happened.

_____ **K.** When I assured the young man that everything was going to be fine, he clasped my hand and asked me not to leave him.

_____ **L.** Then he slipped back into unconsciousness, and I revived him again, even as we were loading him into the ambulance.

_____ **M.** Three times the patient "died" during that ride to Small Troop Clinic, and three times he came back to life.

_____ **N.** P.F.C. Johnson was as new to Hunter Leggett as I was, and she took care of the driving.

_____ **O.** Johnson and I were partners.

_____ **P.** When we reached the clinic, the doctor was waiting to take over.

_____ **Q.** Then about twenty minutes later, once the patient was stable, we helped the doctor load him onto the helicopter that would carry him to the main hospital.

—————————— **R.** I had never even visited the main hospital at that time.

—————————— **S.** As the helicopter lifted off, I stood there in the field, crying.

—————————— **T.** Before this day, I had known of death and I had known people who had died, but never before had I seen a person actually dying. ■

| Step 3 | # Revise for Vivid Details and Clear Organization |

Now, as you revise your paragraph, see if you can make the story more vivid with sharp descriptions and dialogue. You should also be careful to guide your readers clearly from one sentence to the next, from moment to moment.

Your readers will find the story more interesting and convincing if you let them see and hear what you experienced. Just a few carefully chosen details can bring a scene to life. For example, compare these two accounts of the same incident.

> The little girl fell off the plank and dropped into the water.
> Suddenly the plank tipped, throwing the little girl head first into the dark green water of the creek.

The first sentence merely *tells* what happened; the second sentence, with its more vivid descriptions, *shows* what happened. Therefore, in your revision of this assignment, keep in mind the principles of good descriptive writing that you practiced earlier.

In addition to providing precise descriptions, you can make your story more dramatic through the careful use of dialogue—that is, by quoting the actual words spoken by the people in your story. Compare these two accounts of a young soldier's arrival at Fort Benning:

> A drill instructor boarded the bus and told us to get off. As we did, he shouted abuse at us.
> A drill instructor boarded the bus and shouted, "You have thirty seconds to disembark from this vehicle. Twenty-six are gone." As we scrambled out, he glared at each of us and barked an order or a threat. "Don't look at me, boy," he hollered at one. "You're going to regret this day," he warned another.

Through direct quotations as well as vivid active verbs (*scrambled, glared, barked*), the second version dramatically conveys the character of the drill instructor and the tension of the scene. As you revise, try quoting—instead of just summarizing—an important conversation or even just a key remark.*

---

*The standard practice in reporting dialogue is to write what each person says as a separate paragraph:
  "How did *you* get an application?" the manager asked me. "We don't usually give one to anybody wearing jeans."
  I stared at my shoes. "The secretary gave me one," I whispered.
See section 21.A of Chapter Twenty-one for advice on punctuating direct quotations.

As useful as descriptive details and direct quotations can be, don't bore your readers by overworking either strategy. Describe only those things you want to emphasize. Quote only those remarks that convey the flavor of the incident. Keep in mind that your purpose in this assignment is to provide details that will let your readers understand what happened and appreciate the lesson you learned.

As you have already seen, the most effective way to relate a story is usually through chronological order—step by step in time. In Chapter Four you saw how *time signals* can be used to introduce examples in a paragraph. Time signals can also help you to relate an experience clearly. Use the list of time signals on page 46 as a guide when you revise your narrative paragraph.

Finally, as you revise, check that you have clearly identified your topic in the first sentence and stated the lesson learned from the experience in your final sentence.

EXERCISE EVALUATING NARRATIVE PARAGRAPHS

Read each paragraph below, and respond to the questions that follow.

A.   **Making the Grade**

My parents were always telling me to raise my grades, but they would never tell how. After getting one bad report card after another, I knew I had to do something drastic. When my December card arrived with three Cs, two Ds, and an F, I was afraid to show it to my mother. That's when I came up with the brilliant idea of changing the F to an A. It was really quite simple just to give the F another leg. I was in the third grade at the time. When I showed the card to my mother, she was very excited to see the one good grade. She gave me a hug and a kiss and, most important of all, a bigger allowance. Everyone was happy in my house until two nights later when the phone rang. My mother answered it, listened, and then looked at me with blood in her eyes. She told me that there were some things much worse than failing, and that cheating was one of them. I tried to argue. I said that she was the one who had told me to change my grades. That made her really angry, and she said that I knew that's not what she had meant. Then she gave me a whipping and took away my allowance for a month. Since then I have learned to *make* the grade, not change it on the card.

1. One sentence in this paragraph seems to interrupt the story. Identify that sentence and suggest a more appropriate place for it.

2. Make up a topic sentence for this paragraph—one that clearly prepares the reader for what follows.

3. (a) Where in this paragraph do you think dialogue would be particularly effective?
   (b) Rewrite part of the paragraph using dialogue to dramatize an important conversation.

B.
My Summer Dream

I was twelve years old the summer my parents sent me to Rock Eagle Camp, the summer I learned about arts and crafts—and mindless hatred. The first few days of camp were fun, plenty of hiking, boating, and swimming, but I had trouble making friends with any of the five other girls who shared my cabin. They ignored me when I would try to join a conversation, and they never sat with me in the dining hall or around the campfire at night. I was both surprised and pleased, therefore, when one afternoon the girls invited me to sneak out and go swimming with them while the other campers had their rest period. We had this rest period for two hours every afternoon, but it was really just a chance for the counselors to get a rest away from us. We took a rowboat out to the middle of the lake and then swam around the boat for half an hour or so. The girls were strangely quiet, but, happy to be one of the gang, I just figured they were as shy as I was. Then, one by one, the girls climbed back into the boat, until I was the last one left in the water. They were all watching me as I swam to the boat and started to hoist myself in. I knew we were breaking the rules by going out there, but I went along because I so badly wanted to be accepted. Just then, one of the girls picked up a shoe and began hammering at my fingers. Too terrified to let go of the boat, I hung on until my hand started to bleed. The other girls just watched. I cried and called for help, but I was sure I was going to drown without anyone there to help me. Finally, one of the other girls grabbed me by the strap of my bathing suit and yanked me into the boat. During the trip back to shore and the walk to our cabin, I just stared at my bruised hand and nobody said a word. Later, without offering any reason, I asked to be transferred to another cabin, and that night I was allowed to move. Until now, I have never told anyone of my experience that summer, and I still don't know what there was in me, in my personality, to make the other girls hate me so. It was my first experience with madness, stupidity, and savagery. I dream of it still.

1. One sentence in this paragraph contains some fairly irrelevant, unimportant information and should probably be eliminated. Which sentence is that?

2. One sentence in the paragraph appears to be misplaced because it upsets the chronological order of the story. Identify that sentence and suggest where it should be placed.

3. The writer has not used any dialogue in her story. Can you identify any place where it might have been used effectively? Or, can you think of a reason why the writer might have felt that dialogue wasn't necessary?

4. Identify at least four different time signals used in this paragraph. ■

Step 4

Revise and Proofread

Now invite someone to read your paragraph and suggest ways you might further improve it. Then, taking your reader's comments into consideration, revise the paragraph once again. Use the following checklist as a guide.

REVISION CHECKLIST

❑ In your first sentence, have you clearly identified the experience you are about to relate?

❑ Have you clearly explained who was involved and when and where the incident occurred?

❑ Have you organized the sequence of events in chronological order?

❑ Have you focused the paragraph by eliminating unnecessary or repetitious information?

❑ Have you used precise descriptive details to make your story interesting and convincing?

❑ Have you used dialogue to report important conversations?

❑ Have you used time signals to give the paragraph unity?

❑ In your concluding sentence, have you clearly explained the lesson you learned from the incident or the understanding you achieved?

❑ Have you proofread carefully?

Passages

A. The following paragraph, "A Sweet Magnolia Leaf," grew out of the freewriting you saw in the first exercise in this chapter. Notice how the writer has eliminated details that she felt distracted from her narrative and added others. As you read the student's paragraph, compare her revisions with the suggestions you made on how to focus the original material effectively.

A Sweet Magnolia Leaf

It was a beautiful Sunday morning, and I had just placed Amy inside her playpen on the deck while I hurried to dress her four-year-old brother. Experience had taught me to dress the baby last if I had any expectation of her reaching the church with her dress still clean and unrumpled. As I had been doing every fifteen minutes or so all morning, I stepped out to check on Amy and make sure that everything was okay. But what I found on this check was not the smiling, kicking, happy baby I had visited a few minutes earlier. Instead, to my horror, Amy lay in her playpen lifeless and choking, unable to get her breath or utter a cry. Immediately, I snatched her up from the bottom of the pen, screaming for her father to come help me. Then, sticking my finger into her mouth, I found a slice of a magnolia leaf that had dropped into her pen from the tree overhead. Turning Amy upside down, I began to pound on her back, desperately hoping somehow to dislodge the bits of leaf still trapped in her windpipe. Now Amy was gasping for air, still unable to make a cry, and I noticed that her lips were starting to turn blue. As I dropped to my knees, her father, who had just called the EMS, came running to help me. Yet we both felt so helpless, crying, pounding this baby on the back, and praying that somehow the leaf would dislodge itself from her throat. After a few minutes that seemed like hours, Amy began to squall at the top of her lungs, and we were relieved to see the tiny piece of magnolia leaf that had caused Amy's choking now lying on the floor of the deck. It was amazing to think that so slight a thing had almost killed my baby. I clutched her and for a long time cried with her. There were practical lessons learned from that experience, beginning with the need to take a course in CPR. But at the moment all that I understood, and I understood it deeply, was how sweet and precious life is and how quickly and simply it can be taken away.

(Diane Jervis)

B. In the following essay, columnist Bob Greene recalls a moment of acute disappointment and explains the effect that this experience has had on his life. As you read the essay, consider how Greene maintains our interest in his boyhood experience even though very little action is reported.

Cut

I remember vividly the last time I cried. I was twelve years old, in the seventh grade, and I had tried out for the junior high school basketball team. I walked into the gymnasium; there was a piece of paper tacked to the bulletin board.

It was a cut list. The seventh-grade coach had put it up on the board. The boys whose names were on the list were still on the team; they were welcome to keep coming to practices. The boys whose names were not on the list had been cut; their presence was no longer desired. My name was not on the list.

I had not known the cut was coming that day. I stood and I stared at the list. The coach had not composed it with a great deal of subtlety; the names of the very best athletes were at the top of the sheet of paper, and the other members of the squad were listed in what appeared to be a descending order of talent. I kept looking at the bottom of the list, hoping against hope that my name would miraculously appear there if I looked hard enough.

I held myself together as I walked out of the gym and out of the school, but when I got home I began to sob. I couldn't stop. For the first time in my life, I had been told officially that I wasn't good enough. Athletics meant everything to boys that age; if you were on the team, even as a substitute, it put you in the desirable group. If you weren't on the team, you might as well not be alive.

I had tried desperately in practice, but the coach never seemed to notice. It didn't matter how hard I was willing to work; he didn't want me there. I knew that when I went to school the next morning I would have to face the boys who had not been cut—the boys whose names were on the list, who were still on the team, who had been judged worthy while I had been judged unworthy.

All these years later, I remember it as if I were still standing right there in the gym. And a curious thing has happened: in traveling around the country, I have found that an inordinately large proportion of successful men share that same memory—the memory of being cut from a sports team as a boy.

I don't know how the mind works in matters like this; I don't know what went on in my head following that day when I was cut. But I know that my ambition has been enormous ever since then; I know that for all of my life since that day, I have done more work than I had to be doing, taken more assignments than I had to be taking, put in more hours than I had to be spending. I don't know if all of that came from a determination never to allow myself to be cut again—but I know it's there. And apparently it's there in a lot of other men, too.

(Bob Greene)

Questions

1. How is the third paragraph of Greene's essay different from the second paragraph? If the third paragraph were omitted, would Greene's narrative still be clear? Would it be as effective?

2. Toward the end of the fourth paragraph, Greene switches from the first person (*I*) to the second person (*you*). Why?

3. What is the main point of Greene's narrative? Where does he express that point most clearly?

Postscript

This assignment has given you valuable practice in freewriting—a quick way of overcoming writer's block and discovering ideas for any writing project. Because freewriting violates all the customary rules of writing, you may have to practice the technique several times before it becomes a comfortable and productive way of starting an assignment. In addition, you have learned some valuable strategies for developing and organizing narrative paragraphs. Because narratives are useful ways of illustrating problems and explaining concepts, you will probably have many opportunities to apply these strategies in longer essays and reports.

CHAPTER SIX

Work
(OBJECTIVE REPORT)

Preview

As this assignment will demonstrate, the "voice" you assume when you write is directly related to your reason for writing and the type of audience you are addressing. Here you will compose two paragraphs on the same subject. You will begin by drafting a personal, informal report describing a particular job, one you now hold or once held. You will then adapt some of the material in this report to suit a more formal, objective description of the same job. Finally, you will revise this job description and proofread it.

Step 1 | ### *Draft a Personal, Informal Job Description*

In this chapter, you will begin to pay even greater attention to the interests and needs of your readers as you move from personal kinds of writing to more public or objective writing. The assignment calls on you to describe a particular job that you now hold or once held. In fact, you will describe it twice: first in a personal, informal way in this step, and later in a more formal, objective manner.

Begin by taking inventory of the jobs you have held and the chores you have performed in your life. Make a list of places where you have worked, positions you have held, and duties you have performed on each job. Even if you have never held a formal job with pay, you should be able to identify some sort of work or chore you have done at home, at school, or in your community.

Next, select one of the jobs from your list and freewrite on this topic for ten minutes. Jot down whatever comes to mind regarding your regular duties, the equipment you had to operate, the skills required to perform the job, and the pay and benefits it provided. Because this is freewriting, you don't need to be concerned with sentence sense, organization, or neatness; just fill a page or two with your thoughts about the job.

You should now be ready to draft a personal, informal description of this particular work experience. *Personal* means you will write in the first person (*I*) and reveal your feelings about the job as you describe it. *Informal* refers to the English we use in everyday speech—the sort used in conversations with friends or in personal letters. Informal writing is usually characterized by contractions (*can't* and *don't*, for instance, instead of the more formal *cannot* and *do not*) and the vocabulary used in ordinary conversations.

Read aloud the following example of a personal, informal job description, and *listen* to the conversational tone of the writing.

Booth Operator at the Fairgrounds

I don't ever want to see a clown, hear a carousel, or smell a hamburger again. I've just barely survived a week working as a booth operator at the fairgrounds. I've made $180, and I've lost a lot of sleep. You wouldn't believe what I had to do. From nine in the morning until midnight—fifteen hours!—I had to stand in this crummy little booth and sell lousy food to obnoxious people. Sure, I could eat for free, but how long can a body survive on a diet of hot dogs, hamburgers, cotton candy, popcorn, and candied apples? By the end of the first day, the smell of the stuff was enough to make me sick. And then, if I wasn't burning my fingers on the grill or getting grease from the popcorn in my hair, I was slapping a mop around the floor or wiping the counter with a filthy rag. The customers were as bad as the food. Bratty kids would accuse me of giving them poisoned hot dogs, and their bossy parents would accuse me of short-changing them. Of course, I probably was. You see, there was no cash register, so I had to figure out all the prices in my head—you know, 79¢ for a candied apple, $1.12 for a burger, plus four percent tax. Well, you know what a math wizard I am. If I wasn't ripping off the customers, I was ripping off the guy who owned the booth. I figure it all evened out in the end. All I can say is that I'm very glad the fair moved out of town last night. I just feel sorry for the next person hired to operate that booth in the next town.

This is a good, lively job description, written informally, as if addressed to a friend. The writer has used contractions and colloquial language (that is, the language of everyday speech). See if you can find several examples of each. The references to the reader (*you*, as in "Well, you know what a math wizard I am") also contribute to the informal tone of the paragraph.

Keep in mind that *informal* does not mean "vague" or "general." The writer of "Booth Operator at the Fairgrounds" has provided specific information about her duties, hours, pay, and benefits. Also, the way she presents this information clearly reveals her feelings about the job: "I had to stand in this *crummy little* booth and sell *lousy* food to *obnoxious* people."

The personal, informal style is appropriate when we are writing to an audience of friends or acquaintances—or to people we would like to treat as acquaintances. And thus, this style is best suited to writing that aims to reveal the personality of the writer as well as convey information about a subject. Journals, autobiographies, personal letters, and familiar essays fall into this category.

Cast your own informal job description as a letter to a friend. In the language you would ordinarily use when addressing this person, relate your experience on the job. Through your descriptions, explanations, and examples, let your friend know how you feel about this experience.

EXERCISE EVALUATING AN INFORMAL JOB DESCRIPTION

This exercise will help you to identify the characteristics of personal, informal writing, and it will also prepare you for the next step in revising your own job description. Read the informal job description below, and then answer the questions that follow it.

Teacher's Aide

You know, sometimes I wonder if it's worth it. For just five measly bucks an hour (and that's *before* deductions), I do some of the toughest jobs of a teacher without any of the public recognition. I spend the day wiping noses, grading papers, drying tears, running equipment, and keeping the children lined up straight, and still most of their parents—and even some of the teachers—seem to think I'm one of the cafeteria or maintenance workers. Sure, I passed the Board of Education test with flying colors, but without a degree I can't go anywhere. *I* know I'm intelligent and helpful, and the kids know it, too, but I get frustrated sometimes being treated as a hired hand or a second-class citizen. Then, just when I start thinking about chucking it all, something really nice happens: a shy girl gives me her drawing of the sun, a troublemaker calms down long enough to give me a hug, or the whole class catches on to a reading passage they'd been stuck on all week. The hours are pretty good (Scooter and I leave the house together at seven and get back around three), and I *love* summer vacations. Still, every August I get impatient to return to work. Of course, I miss the children, even the hyperactive ones that try to drive me crazy. Heck, I even miss the film projector that's always breaking down. So here's what I've decided to do: I'm going back to college to get a degree in education, and then I'm going to become a "real" teacher. I don't know if it will make me any happier or even any smarter. But I'll be able to keep doing what I love best, and I'll have a chance to show *myself* that I can do it.

1. "Teacher's Aide" is an informally written paragraph. Give several examples of words and expressions that have been drawn from the vocabulary of everyday speech.

2. The writer of this paragraph takes a personal look at her topic, revealing her feelings about the job. In your own words, summarize what she likes and what she doesn't like about being a teacher's aide.

3. According to the writer, a teacher's aide has various duties and responsibilities. List those duties in simple outline form.

4. What skills and personal qualities are needed to perform this job, and what rewards and benefits does the job offer? ■

Step 2

Draft a Formal, Objective Job Description

You will now transform your informal job description into a more formal, objective description, one your employer might use to recruit someone else to take over your job. Write this description in the third person, describing the worker as *he* or *she* rather than *I*. This step in the assignment is not meant to imply that more formal writing is superior to informal writing, but to show how the two approaches differ.

Begin by reading over your informal job description, locating key information concerning job duties, requirements, and benefits. Then list these points in a simple outline. If you see that you left out any important information in your original paragraph, add that information to the outline.

Here is a simple outline of the main points brought out in the paragraph seen earlier, "Booth Operator at the Fairgrounds":

JOB TITLE: Booth Operator at the Fairgrounds

DUTIES OF THE JOB:
1. Prepare and serve hot dogs, hamburgers, cotton candy, popcorn, and candied apples.
2. Keep floor and counter clean.
3. Make change and collect money.

SKILLS AND QUALITIES REQUIRED:
1. Must be able to operate grill and other equipment.
2. Must have a pleasant disposition.
3. Must be willing to work hard and keep long hours.
4. Must be able to make change quickly and accurately.

PAY AND BENEFITS:
$30 per day for six days. No charge for food.

Notice that all the information in the outline is contained in (or can be deduced from) the original paragraph. What is missing from the outline is any reference to the worker's attitude toward the job. As you carry out this step of the assignment, your purpose for writing changes. No longer are you primarily concerned with relating your personal job experience; instead, you are interested in informing your reader about the job itself and the skills needed to perform it. In other words, your aim now is to write a more formal and objective job description.

The following paragraph is an example of just such a description. Read this paragraph aloud, as you did the original in Step 1, so that you may *hear* the differences between them.

Booth Operator at the Fairgrounds

A booth operator at the fairgrounds manages one of the several fast-food booths, and therefore he or she must be able to operate a grill and the equipment for making popcorn, cotton candy, and candied apples. This temporary position should be filled by someone who has a pleasant disposition, a willingness to work hard, and the ability to make change quickly and accurately. The operator must serve the public efficiently and courteously from nine in the morning until midnight for as long as the fair is in town. This person must grill and serve hot dogs and hamburgers, make sure the condiment containers are always filled, and keep grease and popcorn in the popper at all times. The operator also needs to keep the candied apples warm and the cotton candy machine unclogged. In addition, he or she must mop the floor of the booth several times throughout the day and keep the windows and counter clean. Finally, the operator must compute prices, add tax, and give correct change—all without the aid of a cash register. The booth operator receives $30 a day and is entitled to eat at the booth at no charge.

This second version of the job description is clearly more *objective* than the original: the writer provides facts, not feelings or opinions, leaving it up to the reader to decide how attractive or unattractive the job is. Also, this version is more *formal* than the original. This does not mean that a more difficult vocabulary or longer, more complicated sentence structures have been used. In fact, the writing in the second version is quite clear and direct. The writer has, however, eliminated the colloquial expressions and contractions found in the original version. Likewise, the writer has avoided the casual use of *you* in this more formal version.*

In short, the overall effect of the more formal and objective paragraph is to focus attention on the requirements of the job itself, not on the experiences or the voice of the writer. This formal, objective approach to writing is commonly called for in technical articles, scientific reports, and college term papers.

After preparing and studying your simple outline, write a more formal and objective description of your job. You will now explain what *the worker* does, not what you have done. After identifying the job clearly in the first sentence, respond to the following questions as you develop the body of the paragraph:

1. What specific duties does the job call for?

2. What particular knowledge, skills, or personal qualities should the worker possess?

3. What benefits does the job have to offer?

Don't be too concerned at this point with the order in which you present the information. You will have opportunities to reorganize and revise your formal description in the next two steps.

---

*Note that the writer uses the phrase *he* or *she* in her formal description to avoid discriminating against either sex. To be effective, this phrase should not be overworked. When repeated too frequently, *he* or *she* can sound awkward and monotonous. To avoid such a problem in this assignment, you may use a feminine pronoun (*she, her, hers*) to refer to the worker if you are a woman, and a masculine pronoun (*he, him, his*) if you are a man. This problem of the "common gender" is discussed in more detail in Chapter Twenty, section 20.B.

EXERCISE TRANSFORMING A PERSONAL, INFORMAL JOB DESCRIPTION INTO A FORMAL, OBJECTIVE REPORT

The paragraph below is a personal, informal description of the job of parcel post clerk. After reading the paragraph, complete the simple outline that follows it; then, on your own paper, use the information in your outline to draft a more formal and objective description of the same job. When you are done, compare your work with that of your classmates.

Parcel Post Clerk

For one year, seven months, and one day, I was a parcel post clerk for the United States Postal Service. You know, the guy who takes your package stamped "Fragile" and jams it into a sack filled with bricks, axes, and heavy farm equipment. At least that's what most people think parcel post clerks do. I hardly ever intentionally smashed anything. In fact, after the supervisors got on my case for breaking that shipment of Wedgwood china, I was practically gentle with the mail. Every day, Monday through Saturday, I would punch the clock at four in the afternoon and then for eight hours stand around a tall chute full of parcels and toss them into the mail sacks. I had to be able to read an address label, match the address with the right sack, and then, whenever a sack filled up, lug it over to the loading cart. Some of those sacks weighed as much as sixty or seventy pounds, so I had to learn how to carry them without breaking my back. Most guys who work the parcel post for a few years have screwed-up backs. Don't get me wrong, though; this is no job for dummies. Because I sometimes had to move from the national sack racks to the local state rack, I had to "learn the code." That means I had to memorize the zip codes for all 1,600 post offices in the state—every town from Kinderhook to Watervliet, Clifton Springs to Hicksville. It drove me crazy memorizing those stupid codes. If I had failed the test, I would have been demoted from clerk to mail handler. As it turned out, I passed with a score of ninety-eight percent. The pay was excellent, about $24,000 a year to start, but I quit because the job got boring and I wanted to go back to school.

JOB TITLE: _____

DUTIES: _____

_____

_____

_____

_____

SKILLS AND QUALITIES REQUIRED: _____

_____

_____

_____

PAY AND BENEFITS: _____

Now use the information in this outline to draft a more formal and objective description of the same job. ■

Revise Your Formal Job Description for Clear Organization

You will now revise your formal job description, paying particular attention to how you have organized your information. Although you should start the paragraph by clearly identifying the job, and you will probably conclude it by stating the pay and benefits that come with the job, there are various ways to organize the information in between.

If the duties of the job tend to follow a set pattern each day, you may want to organize them chronologically, using time signals to guide the reader from one duty to the next. However, if the work varies from day to day, you may want to present the duties in the order of importance or frequency. Such a pattern is used in the following paragraph, in which the chief duty is described before all other chores:

Coke and Ore Operator

A coke and ore operator has a number of daily job requirements, as well as other occasional duties. His chief responsibility is to run the ore drying system. The operator uses a front-end loader to fill a hopper with ore, which is then run through the drying system by means of a conveyor belt. The operator then places the dried ore in a storage bin. Another daily requirement is the operation of the cooling tower. The operator must periodically check the water flow to maintain a constant temperature. He must also mix chemicals into the tower water to keep it clean and free of bacteria. On occasion, the coke and ore operator is expected to help unload coke cars. After opening the slide gates on the bottom of the car, he must set hoses down by the coke that falls from the bins into the car; he then switches on the "coke unloading blower" to transport the coke by vacuum to a storage bin. All of the procedures described above can be learned by the coke and ore operator during the first few weeks on the job. Strong physical endurance and mental alertness are the prime characteristics of the competent operator. Starting operators receive full company benefits and an hourly wage of $8.75.

Notice that the writer of "Coke and Ore Operator" waited until the end of the paragraph to identify the skills and personal qualities demanded of a worker on this job. You may follow his example, or you may wish to provide this information before or even while you describe the duties of the job. Let the nature of the job itself help you determine the best way to organize the information in the paragraph.

EXERCISE ORGANIZING A FORMAL, OBJECTIVE JOB DESCRIPTION

Here is the introductory sentence of a student's formal, objective job description:

An opening exists immediately at Haven Pool for the position of lifeguard assistant.

The rest of the paragraph appears below; however, the sentences have been rearranged so that the information appears in no clear order. Number the sentences from 1 to 9 to show how they should be arranged to make a clear, well-organized description of the lifeguard assistant's job. Different arrangements are possible, some more effective than others. When you are done, compare your responses with those of your classmates.

_____ **A.** When the lifeguard assistant is not distributing or collecting the baskets, he or she must clean the showers and mop the floor in each rest room.

_____ **B.** Benefits include free use of the pool after the final swim session of the day.

_____ **C.** The job begins at ten in the morning by the dressing rooms, where the lifeguard assistant checks the children's identification cards and hands each child a clothes basket.

_____ **D.** Because the job involves working closely with young children, the lifeguard assistant must be particularly patient and conscientious.

_____ **E.** These check-in and check-out procedures are repeated each hour throughout the day.

_____ **F.** The pay is $4.25 an hour, forty hours per week.

_____ **G.** He or she must also be a competent swimmer.

_____ **H.** The assistant then collects these baskets at the end of the fifty-minute swim session.

_____ **I.** After the final swim session ends at four in the afternoon, the assistant must hose down the pool area and measure the chlorine content of the water. ■

Step 4 · *Revise and Proofread*

Now let someone else read and evaluate both of your job descriptions, the informal version and the more formal, objective report. Then, taking into consideration your reader's comments, revise the formal job description once again. Use the following checklist as a guide.

REVISION CHECKLIST
❏ Have you clearly identified the job in your opening sentence?
❏ Have you clearly described the duties of the job?
❏ Have you written your descriptions in the third person (*he* or *she*)?
❏ Have you described the job objectively, providing facts rather than feelings or opinions?
❏ Have you organized the duties clearly—either in chronological order or in order of importance or frequency?
❏ Have you identified the particular skills or personal qualities required of someone who must perform this job?
❏ Have you concluded the paper by stating what pay and benefits the job offers?
❏ Have you proofread the paragraph carefully?

Passages

A. The following paragraph is the more formal and objective version of the job description that appears in the first exercise in this chapter. Compare the two versions, noting which details have been added in this version and which have been omitted.

Teacher's Aide

The main concern of an elementary school teacher's aide is for the welfare of the children in her class. Though an aide's duties vary from day to day, her primary responsibility is to follow the teacher's directions on the best ways to assist children with their lessons. The aide must possess a basic knowledge of mathematics, reading, and language skills. Without two years of college credit, an applicant for the position must demonstrate proficiency in these areas by passing a test given by the Board of Education. The aide must also see to the general needs of the children in her class. For example, she must take temperatures, make certain that children abide by class and school regulations, pass out papers and tissues, and change torn or wet clothing. The aide is also expected to run various pieces of equipment, including filmstrip projectors, video players, and photocopiers. Above all else, a tremendous amount of patience is a most desirable quality in an aide. She will draw on this resource many times during an eight-hour day in a room full of thirty-two children. The position offers an attractive work schedule for a parent whose children are also in school. In addition to two weeks off at Christmas and one week in the spring, the aide enjoys two-and-one-half months off in the summer. Other benefits are unlimited hugs, generous gifts of artwork, a chance to join in the thrill of learning, and genuine demonstrations of appreciation from the children. Although there is no opportunity for advancement without further education, it is a good position for a mother of school-age children — assuming that the mother is not the sole provider. The pay is about five dollars per hour for a forty-hour week.

(Rita Faircloth)

B. Essayist and journalist Irene Oppenheim has also worked as an editor, a receptionist, and an interviewer for a mental health survey. In the following excerpts from her essay "On Waitressing," Oppenheim describes her experience working as a waitress at Canter's, "a sprawling twenty-four-hour-a-day Jewish (though non-kosher) bakery, delicatessen, and restaurant" in the Fairfax district of Los Angeles. As you read, consider the ways in which Oppenheim combines objective reporting about the restaurant with her own judgments and feelings.

On Waitressing

While I don't wish to discredit my powers of persuasion, getting hired at Canter's was hardly a difficult affair. The "Help Wanted" sign in Canter's front window was a faded, permanent fixture. And in the two months I ultimately worked at the restaurant, the volume of employee comings and goings was never less than impressive. There were, however, exceptions to this transitoriness, and some among the large Canter crew had been with the restaurant for ten, twenty, or even thirty years. These were mostly older women who remained through a combination of loyalty, age, narrow skills, and inertia. The younger people tended to find the work too demanding and the income increasingly unreliable. Canter's heyday had been in the pre-McDonalds, pre-cholesterol days of the 1950s and 60s. And while the erosion was gradual, it was clear that the combination of fast food and *nouvelle cuisine* was steadily reducing Canter's corned beef/pastrami/chopped liver clientele. Despite trendy additions to the menu, such as an avocado melt sandwich (not bad) and the steamed vegetable plate (not good), there were now many quiet afternoons when the older waitresses, wiping off ketchup bottles and filling napkin holders to pass the time, would tell you about the days when the lines for Canter's stretched right down from the door to the corner of Beverly Boulevard.

Canter's could still get enormously busy — on holidays, for instance, or weekend nights. Sometimes for no reason at all the place would suddenly be mobbed. But it all had become unpredictable. And while this unpredictability made the owners niggardly and anxious, its more immediate toll was on the waiters and waitresses, who were almost totally dependent on customer tips. Canter's is a "union house," which means that for sixteen dollars a month the workers are covered by a not-too-respected grievance procedure and a well-loved medical/dental plan. The pay for waiting on tables, however, remains $3.37 per hour (two cents above minimum wage), so at Canter's, as with most restaurants, any real money has to come from tips. . . .

I've never worked anywhere that had more rules than Canter's. The staff bulletin board was so crammed with admonitions that the overflow had to be taped to the adjacent wall. The topics of these missives varied. One sign, for example, warned that bags and purses might be checked on the way out for purloined food; another that those who didn't turn up for their shifts on holidays such as Christmas (Canter's is open every day of the year except Rosh Hashanah and Yom Kippur) would be automatically dismissed; a third firmly stated that no food substitutions were permitted, which meant that it was against regulations to give a customer who requested it a slice of tomato instead of a pickle. When working on the floor, one encountered even more elaborate rules. All ice cream, juice, or bakery items, for instance, had to be initialed on your check by that shift's hostess, lest you serve something without writing it down. To further complicate matters, orders for deli sandwiches had to be written on a slip of paper along with your waitress number (mine was #35), and these slips were then matched against your checks to make sure, for example, that if you ordered two pastrami sandwiches the customer had paid for two. I was castigated by Jackie one day for—along with the more major infraction of not charging fifty cents extra for a slice of cheese—charging ten cents too little for a cup of potato salad. It seems like a small thing, said Jackie (I concurred), but then she added grimly that little mistakes like mine with the potato salad cost the restaurant many thousands of dollars each year. I was tempted to point out that undoubtedly an equal number of errors were made in the restaurant's favor. But I held my tongue, knowing by then that, in the face of a documented Canter's money loss, anything that could be construed as less than acute remorse would only serve to bring my checks under even closer scrutiny. . . .

One of the more graphic symbols of Canter's changing times was the uniform closet. The male waiters—a relative novelty at Canter's—were allowed to work in a black-pants/white-shirt combo, with some of them opting to appear in the "I Love Canter's" T-shirt available for eight dollars (*their* eight dollars) at the front cash register.

The women could get "I Love Canter's" stenciled free on the off-work shirt of their choice, but their on-the-job dress code was more severe. No one's memory reached back to a time when Canter's waitresses had worn anything other than cream-colored outfits with a single brown stripe running down from each shoulder. There were many of these lined up in the uniform closet. In most cases the uniforms were well-worn, with underarms stained an irreparable gray and hems which had been let up or down more than once. But their dominant characteristic was size. Most of the available uniforms could have doubled as small tents. And no matter how many pins or tucks you employed, material would billow out over your tightly pulled apron strings, an irrepressible tribute to the amplitude of your predecessors.

Although there was a locker room at Canter's it was deemed dangerous for reasons I never explored, and I always arrived with my uniform already on. At first I'd worked various shifts—twelve P.M. to eight P.M., eight P.M. to four A.M.—but finally was assigned to days, primarily because I was considered easy-going and the day shift had a contentious reputation. My first task was to relieve Pauline at the counter. She went on duty at six A.M., and technically I was to relieve her at nine A.M. when my shift began. Though the management preferred you didn't clock it in, the rules at Canter's required you to be on the floor fifteen minutes before your shift time, and I'd generally show up around 8:40, which would give Pauline a chance to finish off her checks and put together her own breakfast—usually a mixture of Frosted Flakes and Wheaties from the little boxes kept on display right near the coffee machine. . . .

My Canter's career was to come to an unfortunately abrupt end. A restaurant as large as Canter's was bound to have "walk-outs" who'd leave without paying their checks, and I'd had a few. There was one obese woman who asked me a couple of times if she could pay with a credit card (Canter's didn't accept them) and then left me a tip before managing to get away without paying for her hamburger and coke. Another man had me take his bacon and eggs back to the kitchen twice for repairs; he left me a tip too, but the eggs and bacon went unpaid for. Though there was an element of disgrace in having a walk-out, these small incidents were too common for much of a fuss to be made. But one busy Saturday I had a party of seven who each ordered around ten dollars worth of food and then made a calculated escape while I was in the back adding up their check. Jackie sat me down at the staff table and grimly said that while she didn't blame me for what happened, she did want me to know that it was the largest walk-out loss in the history of Canter's. Nothing was mentioned about my leaving, though Jackie did say that from this point on she wanted me immediately to report to her or the hostess any of my customers who seemed suspicious. I worked the rest of my shift, but everyone I served began to look vaguely suspicious. And with my reputation securely if infamously etched into Canter's history, it seemed time to move on.

(Irene Oppenheim)

Questions

1. Define the following words as they appear in Oppenheim's essay: *transitoriness, inertia, grievance, admonitions, missives, purloined, castigated, construed, graphic, irrepressible, contentious, calculated, infamously.*

2. Locate particular instances in Oppenheim's essay where she combines straightforward reporting about Canter's with her own judgments and feelings.

3. Identify the various signal words and phrases used in paragraph three ("I've never worked anywhere . . . ") to achieve coherence.

4. What is Oppenheim's overall impression of her job at Canter's? Point out specific details that contribute to this impression.

5. Based on the information in Oppenheim's essay, compose a formal and objective description of the job of waitress at Canter's restaurant.

Postscript

Good writers are flexible, able to alter their voice and style to suit their particular subject, audience, and purpose for writing. The intention of this assignment has been to make you a more flexible writer, one sensitive to the differences between informal and formal prose, between a personal approach to a subject and a more objective one. The assignments that follow will allow you to adopt various voices and experiment with different approaches as you continue working to become a more confident and versatile writer.

CHAPTER SEVEN

Complaints
(FORMAL LETTER)

Preview

In this assignment you will make the transition from writing paragraphs to composing essays. You will begin by selecting and focusing a topic—a complaint about a particular product or service. Next, you will draft a paragraph explaining the exact nature of your complaint. You will then turn this paragraph into a formal letter (a short essay, in fact) consisting of an introduction, a body, and a conclusion. Finally, you will revise and proofread the letter.

Step 1

Identify and Focus Your Complaint through Brainstorming

Why don't we complain? That question is both the title and the subject of an essay by William F. Buckley, Jr. In it, after giving examples of his own failure to complain about an overheated train and an out-of-focus movie, Buckley offers this answer to the question:

> We are increasingly anxious in America to be unobtrusive, we are reluctant to make our voices heard, hesitant about claiming our rights; we are afraid that our cause is unjust, or that if it is not unjust, that it is ambiguous; or if not even that, that it is too trivial to justify the horrors of a confrontation with Authority; we will sit in an oven or endure a racking headache before undertaking a head-on, I'm-here-to-tell-you complaint.*

In this assignment, you will be neither passive nor complacent; you will, instead, write a "head-on, I'm-here-to-tell-you complaint."

But what do you have to complain about? You don't want to gripe about something that can't be changed ("all that rainy weather we've been having") or whine about some slight discourtesy ("Laverne passed me in the bookstore without saying hello"). No, you want to find a legitimate subject for complaint—a particular case of fraud, incompetence, damage, injustice, or inconvenience. Now, that doesn't

---

*William F. Buckley, Jr., "Why Don't We Complain?" *Esquire*, 1960.

75

mean you will attempt to right all the wrongs in the world through this one short assignment, but you will have a chance to express your disapproval of certain behavior or your disappointment with a certain product or service. In other words, narrow your topic: complain not about noise pollution in American cities, but perhaps about your neighbor's blaring stereo.

Responding to the following questions should help you find several possible topics for your complaint:

Have you recently purchased a product that you think was advertised or packaged misleadingly?

Have you purchased something that turned out to be defective?

Have you bought a product or used a service that you think was highly overpriced?

Have you used a service that did not do what you expected it to do?

Have you been dissatisfied with the quality of the service you received at a particular restaurant, store, service station, or other business?

Have you been needlessly inconvenienced or bothered by someone or something?

If, after considering these questions, you still have difficulty settling on a topic, turn to your family or friends for ideas. You may write your letter on someone else's behalf.

For additional topic ideas, or for suggestions on ways to develop a topic that you have already selected, join with three or four other students in a *brainstorming* session. In this session, each of you will, in turn, introduce a particular complaint and then encourage the others to suggest ways of generating specific information in support of the topic. Ask and invite questions about the circumstances and purpose of each complaint:

What particular product, service, or experience are you complaining about?

When did you purchase this product, use this service, or have this experience?

What *specific* complaint do you want to make?

Have you already made an effort to register your complaint, and, if so, what happened?

To whom are you addressing this complaint?

What do you hope to achieve by making this complaint?

What information will the reader need to know if he or she is to respond effectively to your complaint?

By asking questions and offering suggestions, your classmates may either help you to focus your complaint or lead you eventually to discard it in favor of another.

The most important quality of an effective brainstorming session is its openness: the members of the group should feel free to share any ideas that come to mind. Don't stop to criticize or reject a suggestion; instead, let one idea lead to another. In this way, brainstorming is like freewriting: it helps us to discover information and a sense of direction without inducing the fear of making mistakes or appearing foolish. Take notes either during the session or right afterwards. The information that you gather while brainstorming should prove useful later when you prepare your draft.

EXERCISE EVALUATING TOPICS THROUGH BRAINSTORMING

The following sentences identify various complaints, some better suited to this assignment than others. Working with three or four of your classmates in a brainstorming session, decide whether each topic is effective (one that focuses clearly on what appears to be a specific, legitimate complaint) or ineffective (one that appears to be too vague or broad to be dealt with competently in a short letter). Discuss your reasons for making these judgments, and consider ways that the weaker topics might be effectively reshaped or narrowed.

1. The crime rate in this city is outrageous, and something must be done immediately to make our town safe for good, law-abiding citizens.

2. I am registering a complaint against the local school system for hiring an individual with only an Associates Degree in Home Economics to teach radiation physics to twelfth graders at Millhouse High School.

3. The clerks and cashiers at Gallery Mart, the largest department store in Westerly, are the rudest human beings on the face of the earth.

4. When I was growing up, your neighbors were your friends, always looking out for one another and ready to lend a helping hand, but the people who live in my neighborhood now are selfish, unfriendly, and inconsiderate.

5. Last Friday evening at Mary's Spaghetti House on Fleetwood Street, I had to wait over an hour to be seated (though I had made reservations earlier in the day); then I was overcharged $4.36 for scallopini that was served cold and dangerously undercooked.

6. My complaint concerns arrogant college professors who ridicule students in front of their classmates.

7. Because they must be so dissatisfied with their own unhappy lives, gossips like Christina enjoy hurting others with their malicious lies.

8. As every student on this campus knows, the prices charged by the college bookstore are simply outrageous.

9. While assembling my new Blodgett 211X Seed Spreader, I discovered that the following parts were missing from the package: one "D" bolt, three "C" screws, and the restraining bolt for one wheel.

10. Children are exposed to far too much violence on American television. ■

| Step 2 | *Draft a Complaint Paragraph* |

Using the information that you gathered in the last step, draft a paragraph in which you explain the exact nature of your complaint. *Be specific.* Identify and describe the product you are complaining about, state where and when you purchased it, and explain exactly what is wrong with it. Or, if you are complaining about a particular experience, clearly explain when, where, and how the problem occurred.

Deliver your complaint with facts, not emotions. Although anger may spur us into making a complaint, we should control our temper when presenting the complaint in a letter. Be forceful and direct, not enraged or threatening. Highly emotional letters often serve only to garble the main point and put the reader on the defensive. Consider, for instance, how *you* would respond to the following complaint:

> I wasted $3.21 of my hard-earned money to buy two pairs of your lousy pantyhose, and they don't even fit! I don't even weigh 120 pounds, and they don't fit me. Imagine if some big old horse tried to squeeze into them! The store wouldn't give me a refund, even after I drove all the way back there and complained to the manager. I've got better things to do, buddy, than drive all over town trying to replace a couple pairs of pantyhose. I tell you I'd like to wrap them around your neck and strangle you with them!

You might pause to question the sanity of the letter writer, but you probably wouldn't take the time to write back. The writer was so busy venting her anger that she failed to include some important information (the name of the store, the date of purchase, the size of the pantyhose, and the particular type)—information that you, as head of the company's complaint department, would need if you were to send the writer a replacement or a refund.

In contrast, consider how you might respond to this calmer, more objective version of the same complaint:

> The two pairs of Vari-close pantyhose that I purchased on February 7 from Big Buck department store were not the size printed on either the package or the Vari-close measurement chart. According to this chart, supersheer Vari-close pantyhose, #63 taupe, should fit a person from five-feet-four-inches to five-feet-eleven, weighing between 120 and 165 pounds. In fact, I am slightly smaller than this, standing five-feet-three-and-three-quarter inches and weighing just 117 pounds. Nonetheless, the pantyhose were too small for me. I do not know whether the problem is with the measurement chart, the package, or the pantyhose themselves, but I am asking you to honor your guarantee of "100% satisfaction or your money back." I am returning the two pairs of pantyhose and look forward to receiving a full refund of $3.21.

Factual rather than emotional, this version of the complaint is much more effective because it explains the problem fully without antagonizing the reader.

Writing *can* serve as an opportunity to let off steam. In fact, discharging our anger and frustrations on a sheet of paper can be healthy and refreshing. However, don't *mail* that sheet of paper if you want someone to respond positively to your complaint. Instead, set it aside and rewrite your complaint with facts, not emotions. The more factual your paragraph is in this step, the easier it will be for you to fashion a formal letter of complaint in the next step.

EXERCISE ANALYZING THE AUDIENCE AND WRITING WITH FACTS

In the previous chapter (*Work*), you practiced altering your voice in a piece of writing by transforming a personal, informal job description into a more formal and objective report. Here you will do something similar as you rewrite a complaint paragraph. The writer of this paragraph appears to have a valid complaint, but it is couched in emotion-charged language that may distract the reader from the facts of the case. Rewrite this complaint addressed to the President of Springdale College: adopt a calmer, more objective voice, using the facts provided in the paragraph, and leave out the unsubstantiated rumors and highly charged emotions.

I'm perfectly aware, President Bosco, that college professors are expected to be a little bit eccentric, absent-minded, and even wacky, but let's face it, man: Dr. Legree, my history professor, is out of his freaking mind. He's a certifiable bull-goose looney, and everybody on campus knows it. We're supposed to be learning about American history in this class, right, and yet all Dr. L. seems to want to talk about is the Middle Ages and some lady, an old friend of his, I think. Frankly, I think he's got some personal problems that are getting in the way. He hardly ever talks about anything that's in our textbook, and when somebody tries to say something or ask a question he either ignores him or says something rude, like "Now who really cares?" He gave only two quizzes all term and never returned either one, and we never even had a midterm because he says that he "lost it." You know, some students say the guy drinks, keeps a bottle of Wild Turkey in his filing cabinet. Dr. L. can be very insulting, even to students like me who work hard. "How can you children ever hope to understand history," he said the very first day of class, "when you hardly have a past yourselves and your heads are full of mush." Well, for one thing, we're not "children" around here. Some students are even in their thirties and forties. And another thing is that some of us do know something about history (I was an *A* student in history in high school, you might be interested to know), but we sure haven't learned much of it from Dr. Legree. He's always walking around campus at night, like some sort of pervert nightcrawler, talking to himself. And he's hardly ever in his office when he says he's going to be. I'm very sorry if he's going through a rough time, you know, but I didn't pay my tuition for this kind of nonsense. Last week, when I went to visit him for some help getting ready for the final exam, I found him sitting in his office with the lights out, whistling "Bye, Bye, Blackbird" or something and drawing something with a pencil in his gradebook. I don't think he even knew I was there. At our last class meeting, when we asked him why he wasn't letting us do evaluations of his course, the crazy guy just said, "I've got tenure. Nobody cares what I do or what you think of me." So that's why I'm writing you. I'm a good student, and, because I read the history textbook, I expect to pass the course okay. So don't get all stiff and huffy on me thinking that I'm just some kind of whiner who screwed up all term and then decided to blame it on the professor. I just think you ought to know that there's a nutcase running loose in your college, and I think it's high time that you did something about it. ■

Step 3 *Draft a Letter of Complaint*

Now that you have carefully focused your topic and explained the details of your complaint in a paragraph, you are ready to draft a formal letter of complaint. Follow the standard business-letter format shown below:

Your name
Your Address
Date

Name and/or Title of Person to Whom You Are Complaining
Address

Dear Mr. or Ms. X (or To Whom It May Concern):

Introductory Paragraph

   [Clearly identify what you are complaining about.]

Body Paragraph

   [Clearly and specifically, explain the nature of your complaint.]

Concluding Paragraph

   [State clearly what you expect to be done as a result of your complaint.]

Sincerely,

Your Name

This standard business-letter format is similar to the basic essay plan of *introduction, body,* and *conclusion*. Let's consider what approaches you should take and what material you should include in each of these three paragraphs.

An *introductory paragraph* in an essay is like the topic sentence of a paragraph: it identifies the subject to be discussed in the rest of the paper. In a formal letter, your introduction should go straight to the point: tell what you are complaining about. In addition to identifying your complaint, you may also want to provide some background information (such as date and place of purchase, if you are complaining about a product). Notice how the writer of the following introduction has managed to pack several specific details into just two sentences:

Last Thursday, February 7, I purchased two pairs of Vari-close pantyhose from the local Big Buck department store. Because the pantyhose were not the size printed on either the package or the Vari-close measurement chart, I am asking you to honor your guarantee of "100% satisfaction or your money back."

This concise introduction lets the reader see at a glance what the writer is complaining about and what she wants done.

The *body* of an essay provides specific support for the subject announced in the introduction. Here, your single body paragraph will be a revised version of the paragraph you wrote in Step 2. Make sure that you provide all the information your reader will need to know if he or she is to respond effectively to your complaint. And again, make sure that your complaint is delivered with facts, not insults, sarcasms, or threats. Here is the body paragraph to the "Vari-close" letter.

> According to the measurement chart, super-sheer Vari-close pantyhose, #63 taupe, should fit a person ranging from five-feet-four inches to five-feet-eleven and weighing between 120 and 165 pounds. In fact, I am slightly smaller than this, standing five-feet-three-and-three-quarters and weighing just 117 pounds. Nonetheless, the pantyhose are too small for me. I do not know whether the problem is with the measurement chart, the package, or the pantyhose themselves, but clearly your company is at fault.

Notice how closely this body paragraph follows the objective version of the complaint paragraph shown in Step 2.

The *concluding paragraph* of an essay is similar to the concluding sentence of a paragraph: it gives the writer an opportunity to emphasize or restate the main point of the paper. In your letter, the conclusion should state clearly what you expect to be done as a result of your complaint. If you want a refund, state how much. If you would like to see a change in policy, explain what that change should be. If you want an apology, say so. State your request firmly and directly. Here is the concluding paragraph to the Vari-close letter:

> Because Big Buck department store does not give refunds on pantyhose, I am returning the two pairs to you with the request for a full refund of $3.21. I also recommend that you provide your customers with a more accurate measurement chart.

As this paragraph demonstrates, you can be forceful in your conclusion without being impolite.

To emphasize to the reader that you are approaching the end of the letter, you may wish to use one of the *concluding signals* in your final paragraph. Following are some of the common concluding signals:

and so	in conclusion
after all	in short
at last	on the whole
finally	to conclude
in brief	to summarize
in closing	

Such words and phrases send the signal that we are drawing our ideas to a close.

The kind of information you provide in your letter and the way that information is arranged will depend to some extent on the nature of your particular complaint. Nevertheless, be guided by the three-paragraph format described in this step: identify your complaint in the introduction, explain your complaint in the body, and request specific action in the conclusion.

EXERCISE ORGANIZING THE COMPLAINT LETTER

The sentences in the following complaint letter have been rearranged so that the information appears in no clear order. On your own paper, rewrite the letter, arranging the sentences in logical order and organizing them into a separate introduction, body paragraph, and conclusion. Different arrangements are possible, some more effective than others. When you are done, compare your responses with those of your classmates.

Kenny L. Thompson
121 Jacquelyn Drive
Westerly, R.I. 05909
December 13, 1994

Mr. Fitz Kurtz, Manager
Gallery Mart
Westerly, R.I. 05908

Dear Mr. Kurtz:

1. After I had worn the Neki Air Tennis Shoes only three times, the leather began to crack and the color turned from white to yellow.
2. Clearly, I had purchased a defective pair, and I imagined that a simple exchange would not be a problem.
3. On October 31, 1994, I purchased a pair of size ten Neki Air Tennis Shoes for $94.99 from the Westerly Gallery Mart.
4. I am requesting an immediate replacement of the shoes or a full refund of $94.99.
5. When I returned to Gallery Mart on November 7, the sales assistant—Pat Howard—assured me that she would notify me as soon as a replacement shipment of Neki's arrived (she had no size tens in stock).
6. Since then, I have visited your store twice and called several times requesting information, but no one has given me any help.
7. More troublesome is the fact that your salespeople have not lived up to Gallery Mart's promise of "complete customer satisfaction."
8. The problem, I think, lies not with Neki's shipping but with your inability to communicate effectively with your customers.

9. Although in the past I have been satisfied with the quality of Neki footwear, I was distressed to find that the particular pair of shoes I received this time were in fact substandard.

Sincerely,

Kenny L. Thompson   ■

Revise and Proofread

Now ask someone else in the class to read your letter of complaint and respond to it as if he or she had received it in the mail. See if your reader is clearly convinced that your complaint sounds valid. Then revise the letter, using your reader's comments and the following checklist as a guide.

REVISION CHECKLIST

❑ Does your letter follow the standard business-letter format shown in Step 3?

❑ Does your letter consist of an introduction, a body paragraph, and a conclusion?

❑ Does your introductory paragraph clearly identify what you are complaining about?

❑ Does your body paragraph clearly and specifically explain the nature of your complaint?

❑ In the body paragraph, have you provided the reader with all the information needed if he or she is to respond effectively to your complaint?

❑ Have you delivered your complaint with facts rather than emotions?

❑ Have you clearly organized the information in your body paragraph so that one sentence leads logically to the next?

❑ In your conclusion, have you clearly stated what action(s) you want your reader to take?

❑ Have you proofread the letter carefully?

Passages

A. The letter that follows is a revision of the complaint against Dr. Legree that you saw earlier in this chapter. Observe how the writer has modified the tone of his complaint and focused on the facts of the case.

Frederick Roth
3667 Robling Avenue
Yardley, Pennsylvania 19327
December 20, 1994

Dr. Elizabeth Scott, Chair
Department of History
Springdale College
640 Booker Drive
Yardley, Pennsylvania 19350

Dear Dr. Scott:

I have just completed American History 301, taught by Dr. Thomas Legree, and would like to make you aware of some problems that occurred during the term. Dr. Legree's lack of organization, apparent indifference to student concerns, and inadequate grading procedures made this class a particularly frustrating experience for me and my classmates.

Despite his impressive academic credentials, Dr. Legree demonstrated some serious shortcomings in the classroom. His failure to provide a syllabus or even to project the goals of the course left the class frequently confused about deadlines, assignments, and grades. During the term we were given only two tests, which were never returned. Although he had scheduled a midterm examination, Dr. Legree cancelled it at the last minute, claiming to have "lost it." Equally disturbing was his rude treatment of students: "children," he called us, "with heads full of mush." He often ignored questions asked in class and rarely kept office hours.

Though I expect to receive a satisfactory grade in the course, I am writing because the class was not given the opportunity to evaluate Dr. Legree. "I've got tenure," he told us at our final class session. "Nobody cares what I do or what you think of me." I prefer to think that you do care about what happens in your history classes and that you will make an effort to consult with other students enrolled in American History 301 as you carefully review Dr. Legree's professional performance.

Sincerely,

Frederick Roth

B. In the following letter, essayist E. B. White responds humorously to a complaint from the A.S.P.C.A. As you read White's letter, look for the serious points that underlie his cheerful descriptions and seemingly irrelevant digressions.

Open Letter to the A.S.P.C.A.

New York, N.Y.
12 April 1951

The American Society for the Prevention of Cruelty to Animals
York Avenue and East 92nd Street
New York, N.Y.

Dear Sirs:

I have your letter, undated, saying that I am harboring an unlicensed dog in violation of the law. If by "harboring" you mean getting up two or three times every night to pull Minnie's blanket up over her, I am harboring a dog all right. The blanket keeps slipping off. I suppose you are wondering by now why I don't get her a sweater instead. That's a joke on you. She has a knitted sweater, but she doesn't like to wear it for sleeping: her legs are so short they work out of a sweater and her toenails get caught in the mesh, and this disturbs her rest. If Minnie doesn't get her rest, she feels it right away. I do myself, and of course, with this night duty of mine, the way the blanket slips and all, I haven't had any real rest in years. Minnie is twelve.

In spite of what your inspector reported, she has a license. She is licensed in the State of Maine as an unspayed bitch, or what is more commonly called an "un-spaded" bitch. She wears her metal license tag but I must say I don't particularly care for it, as it is in the shape of a hydrant, which seems to me a feeble gag, besides being pointless in the case of a female. It is hard to believe that any state in the Union would circulate a gag like that and make people pay money for it, but Maine is always thinking of something. Maine puts up roadside crosses along the highways to mark the spots where people have lost their lives in motor accidents, so the highways are beginning to take on the appearance of a cemetery, and motoring in Maine has become a solemn experience, when one thinks mostly about death. I was driving along a road near Kittery the other day thinking about death and all of a sudden I heard the spring peepers. That changed me right away and I suddenly thought about life. It was the nicest feeling.

You asked about Minnie's name, sex, breed, and phone number. She doesn't answer the phone. She is a dachshund and can't reach it, but she wouldn't answer it even if she could, as she has no interest in outside calls. I did have a dachshund once, a male, who was interested in the telephone, and who got a great many calls, but Fred was an exceptional dog (his name was Fred) and I can't think of anything offhand that he *wasn't* interested in. The telephone was only one of a thousand things. He loved life—that is, he loved life if by "life" you mean "trouble," and of course the phone is almost synonymous with trouble. Minnie loves life, too, but her idea of life is a warm bed, preferably with an electric pad, and a friend in bed with her, and plenty of shut-eye, night and day. She's almost twelve. I guess I've already mentioned that. I got her from Dr. Clarence Little in 1939. He was using dachshunds in his cancer-research experiments (that was before Winchell was running the thing) and he had a couple of extra puppies, so I wheedled Minnie out of him. She later had puppies by her own father, at Dr. Little's request. What do you think about *that* for a scandal? I know what Fred thought about it. He was some put out.

Sincerely yours,

E. B. White

Questions

1. Define the following words as they are used in White's letter: *harboring, feeble, circulate, solemn, synonymous, wheedled*.

2. E. B. White is perhaps best known as an author of children's books, in particular *Charlotte's Web* (which he was in the process of revising when he wrote this letter). What do you find in White's descriptions of Minnie and Fred that reminds you of a children's story?

3. White's letter contains a good deal of information that does not appear relevant to the complaint made by the A.S.P.C.A. Give an example of such irrelevant information, and explain what its purpose might be.

4. Playful as this letter is, White does deliver some complaints. What are they?

Postscript

By introducing you to the basic essay format of introduction, body, and conclusion, this assignment has prepared you for the longer essay assignments that will follow. It has also reminded you again of the importance of considering the needs and interests of your readers when you come to revise your work. Finally, this assignment has shown that writing is much more than just a method of packaging information: it can be a means of protesting wrongs and claiming our rights. Thus, you may wish to repeat this assignment, perhaps many times, after your writing course is over.

CHAPTER EIGHT

Skills
(PROCESS ANALYSIS)

Preview

This assignment should make you particularly sensitive to the needs of your readers, for you must teach them how to perform a particular task. Beginning with a variety of discovery strategies (probing, listing, and freewriting), you will first identify one of your skills and then prepare a simple instructional outline. Next, you will turn the outline into a short essay containing step-by-step instructions on how to perform the task. Finally, you will revise and proofread the essay.

Step 1 | ## Discover and Narrow a Topic

In this assignment, you will play the role of an instructor as you explain how to perform a particular task. Your aim will be to share your knowledge and skills with someone who has never performed the task before.

Begin by taking an inventory of your skills—that is, things you know how to do. What do you know how to make, break, fix, or improve? What do you know how to play or cook or arrange? *What do you know how to do?* Jot down your responses to these questions. The combination of probing and listing should help you to develop quite an inventory of skills.

Now, select one of the skills from your list—one that you have performed often enough and know well enough that you can teach it to someone who lacks your experience and knowledge. In ten minutes of listing or freewriting, jot down all you can think of concerning this particular skill: how long it takes to perform, what equipment or materials are needed, what steps are involved, what precautions should be taken. Your aim in this discovery activity is to see if you know your subject well enough to write about it. If you have trouble recalling how to perform the skill, you should consider another topic. On the other hand, you may discover that you have more than enough to say. The following notes show how listing ideas can help us to narrow a topic.

How to Go Fishing

Start before dawn—the earlier the better

Find a good fishing spot—not crowded

You need a sturdy fishing rod

Decide what kind of fishing you want to do

Wear shorts or a bathing suit

Wear a shirt with plenty of pockets for lures, hooks, bait

Get all your equipment ready the night before

Make sure you hve the right equipment

You need different lures and lines and bait for different fish

Some cases you need a boat

Fishing for bass or catfish or going crabbing—all different things

Going Crabbing

boat, crab lines, scoop nets, crate

Use chicken necks for bait

Best time is low tide

Drop the lines slowly

Keep bait close to surface

Snatch crabs with scoop

Store crabs in crate

Discovering that her original topic was too big for a one-paragraph assignment, the student narrowed her topic by focusing on one particular item from her original list. Likewise, you should settle on a topic that can be explained in detail in a short essay. "How to Repair an Engine," for example, is too ambitious for this assignment; "How to Clean a Carburetor," however, should work just fine.

EXERCISE NARROWING THE TOPIC FOR A SKILLS PARAGRAPH

The following subjects are too broad to be dealt with adequately in a short essay. Working either on your own or with others in a brainstorming session, derive from each general subject at least three or four subtopics that are more focused and specific.

1. How to Repair an Automobile
2. How to Succeed in College
3. How to Get a Job
4. How to Save Money
5. How to Look Your Best
6. How to Lose Weight and Keep in Shape
7. How to Be a Good Ball Player
8. How to Prepare Dinner for Twelve People and a Dog
9. How to Get Along with Others
10. How to Play a Musical Instrument ■

Step 2 *Prepare an Instructional Outline*

In Chapter Six, you prepared a simple outline to check the organization of your draft. Here you will complete an *instructional outline* as a way of organizing your steps before you draft a short essay. You will need to provide the following information in the outline:

1. *Skill to be taught:* Clearly identify the skill.
2. *Materials or equipment needed:* List all the materials (with proper sizes and measurements, if appropriate) needed to complete the task.
3. *Warnings:* Explain under what conditions the task should be carried out if it is to be done safely and successfully.
4. *Steps:* List the steps according to the order in which they are to be carried out. In your outline, jot down a key phrase to represent each step. Later, when you draft a paragraph, you can expand and explain each of these steps.
5. *Tests:* Tell your readers how they will be able to know if they have carried out the task successfully.

After examining the sample outline on "Breaking in a New Baseball Glove," complete an instructional outline of your own topic.

Instructional Outline

Skill to be taught: Breaking in a New Baseball Glove

Materials or equipment needed: a glove, linseed oil, a baseball or softball, heavy string

Warnings: Be sure to work outside or in the bathroom: this process can be messy. Also, don't count on using the glove for at least a week.

Steps:
1. Smear oil over the glove.
2. Pound the ball into the pocket of the glove.
3. Wedge the ball into the pocket.
4. Tie the string around the glove.
5. Let the glove sit for one week.
6. Clean the glove.
7. Repeat the process.

Tests to see that steps have been carried out successfully: The pocket
should be snug, and the glove should be flexible (though not
floppy).

◼

Instructional Outline

Skill to be taught: _____

_____

Materials or equipment needed: _____

_____

_____

_____

Warnings: _____

_____

_____

Steps: _____

_____

_____

_____

_____

_____

_____

_____

Tests to see that steps have been carried out successfully: _____

_____

_____

_____

EXERCISE EXAMINING THE OUTLINE FOR LOGICAL ORDER

Clear instructions need to be given in a logical, step-by-step order. The following instructions on "How to Bathe a Cat" are confusing because they are arranged out of sequence. After reading all the steps, renumber them to show the order in which they should appear.

How to Bathe a Cat

_____ 1. When the cat is completely wet, rub the soap or shampoo into the fur.

_____ 2. Grasp the cat firmly by the back of his neck (he will wriggle out of a collar), and place him in the tub.

_____ 3. Once you have washed the cat thoroughly, you are ready to rinse and dry him.

_____ 4. Without loosening your grip on the cat, douse his fur thoroughly with warm water from a hose connected to the faucet.

_____ 5. Continue to hold him by the back of his neck so that he will not be able to get his claws close enough to wound you.

_____ 6. When the fur is completely free of soap, empty the tub and use a towel to dry the excess water from the fur.

_____ 7. A final word of warning: do not let the cat outside until he is completely dry.

_____ 8. Next, set the hair dryer on "warm," and rub the cat under the warm air until his fur becomes fluffy. ■

Step 3 *Draft the Skills Paragraph*

Once you are satisfied that the steps in your instructional outline are clearly and logically arranged, you are ready to turn the outline into a short essay. As you write your draft, keep in mind that you are writing for readers who do not share your knowledge of this particular task. Thus, you must be careful not to omit any steps (what may appear obvious to you may not be so obvious to your readers) or to confuse your readers with technical language. If you must use one or two technical terms, be sure to explain them or illustrate them in a diagram.

In many cases, the three-paragraph format that you followed in developing your letter of complaint in the previous chapter should also work well for you here. In the introductory paragraph, be sure to identify your topic clearly and explain briefly the value of learning this skill. If not included in your introduction, the list of required materials and any warnings that you need to provide should appear in the opening sentences of your body paragraph. The rest of that paragraph will consist of clear, step-by-step instructions. Finally, in a brief concluding paragraph, give your readers some way of knowing whether or not they have completed the task successfully.

Following is an example of a clearly organized skills essay. Notice that the writer has provided a list of necessary materials, explained why, when, and where this task may be done, given warnings, and arranged the steps in logical order:

How to Break in a New Baseball Glove

Breaking in a new baseball glove is a time-honored spring ritual for pros and amateurs alike. A few weeks before the start of the season, the stiff leather of the glove needs to be treated and shaped so that the fingers are flexible and the pocket is snug.

To prepare your glove, you will need a pint of linseed oil, a baseball or softball (depending on your game), and a heavy string. Because this process can be messy, you should work outdoors, in the basement, or in the bathroom—certainly not over a shag carpet in the living room. Begin by smearing the linseed oil all over the glove, especially in the palm. Then take the ball and pound it into the glove for at least twenty minutes to form a pocket. Now, wedge the ball in the pocket, tie heavy string around the glove, and let it sit for a week. Then, after a few games of catch, you should clean the glove with a mild detergent and repeat the entire process.

The end result should be a glove that is flexible, though not floppy, with a pocket snug enough to hold a ball caught on the run in deep centerfield. During the season, be sure to clean the glove regularly to keep the leather from cracking.

Observe how smoothly the writer has guided us from one step to the next:

Begin by . . .
Then take . . .
Now, wedge . . .
Then, after . . .
The end result should be . . .

The writer has used *process signals* to take us clearly from one step to the next. You may want to use some of the common process signals as you write and revise your skills essay:

after	following
before	once
begin	next
first, second, third . . .	now
the first step, the next step . . .	then
	when

Use these signals rather than numbers (1, 2, 3, . . .) when you turn your instructional outline into an essay.

EXERCISE EVALUATING A SKILLS ESSAY

The following skills essay has both strengths and weaknesses in terms of content, organization, and coherence. Evaluate this essay by responding to the questions that follow it.

Fortress

For young and old alike, a trip to the beach means relaxation, adventure, and a temporary escape from the worries and responsibilities of ordinary life. Whether swimming or surfing, tossing a volleyball or just snoozing in the sand, a visit to the beach means fun. The only equipment you need is a twelve-inch deep pail, a small plastic shovel, and plenty of moist sand.

Making a sandcastle is a favorite project of beach-goers of all ages. Begin by digging up a large amount of sand (enough to fill up at least a half-dozen pails) and arranging it in a pile. Then, scoop the sand into your pail, patting it down and leveling it off at the rim as you do. You can now construct the towers of your castle by placing one pailful of sand after another face down on the area of the beach that you have staked out for yourself. Make four towers, placing each mound twelve inches apart in a square. This done, you are ready to build the walls that connect the towers. Scoop up the sand along the perimeter of the fortress and arrange a wall six inches high and twelve inches long between each pair of towers in the square. By scooping up the sand in this fashion, you will not only create the walls of the castle, but you will also be digging out the moat that surrounds it. Now, with a steady hand, cut a one-inch square block out of every other inch along the circumference of each tower. Your spatula will come in handy here. Of course, before doing this, you should use the spatula to smooth off the tops and sides of the walls and towers.

You have now completed your very own sixteenth-century sandcastle. Though it may not last for centuries or even until the end of the afternoon, you may still take pride in your handicraft. Do make sure, however, that you have chosen a fairly isolated spot in which to work; otherwise, your masterpiece may be trampled by beach bums and children. Also, make a note on the high tides so that you have time enough to build your fortress before the ocean arrives to wash it all away.

1. What important information is missing from the introductory paragraph? Which sentence from the body paragraph might be placed more effectively in the introduction?

2. Identify the *process signals* used to guide the reader clearly from step to step in the body paragraph.

3. Which piece of equipment mentioned in the body paragraph does not appear in the list at the end of the introduction?

4. Notice where two warnings appear in this essay. Where should these warnings have been placed, and why?

5. Apparently, two of the steps have been given in reverse order. Rewrite these steps, putting them in a logical sequence. ■

Step 4 *Revise and Proofread*

The best way to measure the success of your skills essay is to invite someone to follow the instructions you have provided. If this person understands each step and can complete the task without error, then your paragraph works. If such an experiment isn't possible, at least let someone else read and evaluate your paragraph. Then, guided by your reader's comments and the following checklist, revise the paragraph.

REVISION CHECKLIST

❑ In the opening paragraph, have you clearly identified the skill to be taught?

❑ Have you provided enough background information for your readers to know when, where, and why this skill may be practiced?

❑ Have you provided necessary warnings in appropriate places?

❑ Have you arranged the steps in the exact order in which they are to be carried out?

❑ Have you explained each step clearly?

❑ Have you used process signals to guide your readers smoothly from one step to the next?

❑ Will all your language be clear to your readers? If you have used any technical terms, have you defined them?

❑ Have you concluded the essay by explaining how your readers will know if they have carried out the procedures correctly?

❑ Have you proofread carefully?

Passages

A. In Step 1, you saw how a student derived the topic "How to Catch Crabs" from her original subject, "How to Go Fishing." Here is the final version of that student's skills essay. Notice how many details appear here that were not on the original list. Observe, also, how carefully she has organized her instructions.

How to Catch Crabs

As a lifelong crabber (that is, one who catches crabs, not a chronic complainer), I can tell you that anyone who has patience and a great love for the river is qualified to join the ranks of crabbers. However, if you want your first crabbing experience to be a successful one, you must come prepared.

First, you need a boat, but not just any boat. I recommend a fifteen-foot long fiberglass boat complete with a twenty-five horsepower motor, extra gas in a steel can, two thirteen-foot long wooden oars, two steel anchors, and enough cushions for the entire party. You will also need scoops, crab lines, a sturdy crate, and bait. Each crab line, made from heavy-duty string, is attached to a weight, and around each weight is tied the bait—a slimy, smelly, and utterly grotesque chicken neck.

Now, once the tide is low, you are ready to begin crabbing. Drop your lines overboard, but not before you have tied them securely to the boat rail. Because crabs are sensitive to sudden movements, the lines must be slowly lifted until the chicken necks are visible just below the surface of the water. If you spy a crab nibbling the bait, snatch him up with a quick sweep of your scoop. The crab will be furious, snapping its claws and bubbling at the mouth. Drop the crab into the wooden crate before it has a chance to get revenge. You should leave the crabs brooding in the crate as you make your way home.

Back in your kitchen, you will boil the crabs in a large pot until they turn a healthy shade of orange. Just remember to keep the crab pot covered. Finally, spread newspapers over the kitchen table, deposit the boiled crabs on the newspaper, and enjoy the most delicious meal of your life.

(Mary Zeigler)

B. In the following essay, free-lance writer Jill Young Miller offers some practical advice on effective ways to study and prepare for examinations.

Making the Grades: How to Cram

Frances Avila learned the hard way not to expect miracles overnight. A chronic crammer, the New York University senior did the usual for her midterm in "Major British Writers" last fall: she pulled an all-nighter. Fighting off fatigue and anxiety, Avila forced herself to concentrate on the novels and her notes through dawn, breaking only to splash cold water on her face. Near noon, she closed her books to head for the test.

The first question—"Expand on the gap between her front teeth"—was a lulu. Avila didn't recognize the allusion to Chaucer's Wife of Bath, even though she'd read the section only hours before. "Not only did I blank out, but I was also frightened," she recalls. "I didn't expect the test to be that elaborate." The bad situation only got worse. She fumbled through 14 more stray lines before plunging into part two, which wasn't any easier. Avila had studied innumerable facts for hours, but she knew only one thing for sure: she was in trouble.

"I failed the exam," she explains, "because I had to compare and contrast two poets from different time periods. In order to do that, I had to elaborate on all the details within the poetry. But I'd absorbed just enough information the night before to understand what I was reading and not enough to catch all the details."

Sound familiar? Almost all of us have stood (and sleepwalked) in Avila's shoes at one time or another. Sometimes push comes to shove, crunch comes to cram, and before you know it, you have to read 450 pages in six hours. Pour on the caffeine, you mumble.

About 90 percent of all students cram, estimates Don Dansereau, a psychology professor at Texas Christian University, who defines cramming as "intense studying the night before or the day of a test." Quips Ric Schank, a University of Florida senior, "Down here, it's the rule rather than the exception."

Despite its popularity, cramming gets low marks from educators and memory experts, who claim that the last-minute nature of the act kills your chances for payoff at test time.

A quick stroll down memory lane explains why. Most experts identify three types of memory: immediate, short-term, and long-term. You use your immediate memory as you read this, remembering each word just long enough to make the transition to the next.

Short-term memory is limited, too. For example, you use it when you look up a phone number, close the book, and dial. Short-term memory can supposedly hold a maximum of seven items for only a few seconds.

Long-term memory is the big daddy, the one that holds everything you know about the world. It's the memory that last-minute learners need to respect.

How well you organize information on its way into your long-term memory determines how quickly you can retrieve it later, or whether you retrieve it at all. Think of a backpack you'd take on a hike, says Laird Cermak, a research psychologist at the Boston Veterans Administration Hospital and the author of *Improving Your Memory* (McGraw-Hill, 1975). "If your backpack is organized and you get bit by a snake, you can go right for the snakebite kit," he explains.

The magic lies in spacing your study over days, weeks, or even months. That gives you time to mull over the new stuff, relate it to what you already know, and organize it for exam-time recall. "The reason you forget the information is not because it was learned the night before," Cermak explains. "It's because when you crammed you didn't give yourself good ways to remember it in the future." In other words, last-minute studying limits the number of mental retrieval routes you can create.

But it doesn't take a psychologist to explain why cramming often fails. "You throw things into your mind, knowing that you're going to spit them out in a couple of hours and forget them. It's not a good way to learn at all," says NYU journalism senior David Reilly.

No quick-and-dirty detours to long-term retention and instant recall exist. But if you're forced into a late-night, last-minute study session, the results don't have to be disastrous. Here's some advice to help make the morning after less anxious than the night before:

Find out what kind of test you're in for. If you cram, you're likely to fare better on multiple-choice and fill-in-the-blank tests because they jog your memory with cues, Cermak says.

Find a quiet place to study. When Avila crams, she seeks out a small room at the library that's devoid of distractions. "I'm cornered," she says. "I have no choice but to look at the print."

If you like to study with music in the background, go for something without lyrics and keep the volume down low. Classical music such as Bach can have a soothing effect if your nerves are impeding your studies, says Danielle Lapp, a memory researcher at Stanford University and the author of *Don't Forget! Easy Exercises for a Better Memory at Any Age* (McGraw-Hill, 1987).

Compose a scene that you can recreate during the exam. If you can, study at the desk or in the room where you'll take the test, or do something while you study that you can do again when you take the test. For example, Dansereau suggests that you chew grape gum. "The flavor acts as a cueing device," he explains.

Build your concentration. Spend 10 minutes warming up with a novel or magazine before you tackle a tough chapter. Says Cermak, "It helps you block out whatever else is going on."

Watch what you eat and drink. Avoid heavy meals and alcohol. Both could make you drowsy, cautions Lapp. If you need a cup of coffee to perk up, fine. But putting too much caffeine in your system can make you jittery and break your concentration.

Mark your book. Even if you only have time to read the chapter once, it helps to highlight important terms and sections. Identifying the key words and passages requires you to be mentally alert and forces you to be an active rather than a passive reader.

Spend time repeating or discussing facts out loud. Recitation promotes faster learning because it's more active than reading or listening. (Try it out when you study for your next foreign-language vocabulary quiz.) Discussion groups are helpful for this reason.

Take short breaks at least every few hours. They'll help you beat fatigue, which takes a heavy toll on learning. Two hourlong sittings separated by a 15-minute break are more productive than one two-hour session in which your mind wanders throughout the second half. It doesn't matter what you do during those breaks; just take them.

Experiment with memory techniques. They impose structure on new information, making it easier to remember at test time. The "house" method is one of the oldest. Let's say you want to remember a list of sequential events for a history exam. Try to imagine the events taking place in separate but connected rooms of your house. When the test asks you to recall the events, take a mental amble through the rooms.

Another simple technique involves acronyms. You may have learned the names of the Great Lakes (Huron, Ontario, Michigan, Erie, and Superior) with this one: *HOMES.*

Try some proven learning strategies. Richard Yates, a counselor and time-management expert at Cleveland State University, recommends the SQ3R method: survey, question, read, recite, review. Survey the material to formulate a general impression; rephrase titles and headings into questions; read through the material quickly to find the main points and the answers to your questions; recite those main ideas, taking brief notes; and review. Even when you're pressed for time, the strategy can help. "It may take a little longer," says Yates, "but it's worth the effort."

Get some sleep. UF's Schank quit all-nighters after his freshman year. "I'd go into a final and be so wired from staying up all night that I'd lose my concentration," he says. "I'd miss questions that I knew I wouldn't miss if I were in a good frame of mind." Now he crams until about 3 A.M., sleeps for about four hours, and hits the books again at 8 A.M.

Psychologists and memory researchers can't specify how much sleep you need—everyone has his or her own threshold—but they do stress its importance. Says Lapp, "You're better off getting some sleep so that your mind is rested for the exam than you are cramming the whole night." Just don't forget to set that alarm clock before you go to bed.

For an early-morning exam, it's best to do heavy-duty studying right before you go to sleep. In other words, unless you've got back-to-back exams, don't cram and then do something else for a few hours before a test. Freshly learned material is remembered much better after a period of sleep than after an equal period of daytime activity.

Relax. It may sound simplistic, but it's key to good test performance. "Anxiety is enemy number one of memory," Lapp explains. She compares a student taking a test to a singer performing onstage. "There's no way a completely anxious singer can utter a sound," she says.

Cramming is like going to the dentist; if you have to do it, you want it to be as painless and as productive as it can be. After all, no one goes to college to take a semester-long class and promptly forget all the new information that's been taught. At least Frances Avila didn't. After her disastrous midterm, she didn't dare risk cramming for her "Major British Writers" final exam. This time, she spaced her studying over a period of weeks, earned an A, and salvaged her grade for the semester.

That doesn't mean she's quit cramming for good—in fact, she hasn't even tried to. Instead she's perfected her technique. Ditto for Reilly, who's tried unsuccessfully to break the habit. "Every semester I kick myself a million times and scream that I'm not going to cram next semester," he laments. "But it never seems to work."

(Jill Young Miller)

Questions

1. Define each of the following words as they are used in Miller's essay: *chronic, allusion, innumerable, devoid, sequential, salvaged, laments.*

2. Summarize Miller's central point regarding the value of cramming for examinations.

3. Almost half of Miller's essay is taken up with the introduction and the conclusion. Identify the body paragraphs that focus on step-by-step instruction.

4. Throughout this essay, Miller provides brief guidelines and instructions for applying various study skills and strategies. Choose any one of these skills, and offer some additional advice based on your own experience.

Postscript

For this assignment, you prepared a simple instructional outline before drafting a short essay. Such an outline can be particularly helpful when you have to organize a sequence of steps or events. Of course, the outline is just a guide, and you may choose to rearrange information when you draft or revise your essay. The most important lesson to be learned from this assignment is concern for the needs of your readers: provide them with all necessary information and present that information as clearly as you can. This lesson holds true for all writing that you do for others.

CHAPTER NINE

Changes
(COMPARISON)

Preview

In this assignment, you will show how some person, place, or thing has changed over a period of time. After exploring your topic and listing some details from the past and from the present, you will draft two paragraphs: a "then" paragraph (showing what your subject used to be like) and a "now" paragraph (revealing the changes that have taken place). Next, you will incorporate these paragraphs in an essay made up of an introduction, two body paragraphs, and a conclusion. Finally, you will revise and proofread your work.

Step 1 ## Explore Your Topic and List Details

No matter what your age, you have experienced and witnessed many changes—some in your own life (changing interests, relationships, residences) and others in the world around you (changes in fashion, commerce, and technology). The first step in this assignment is to settle on one person, place, or thing that has undergone a change, for the better or the worse, and then to explore that subject to see exactly how it has changed.

You already have some experience in writing about people (Chapter Four), places (Chapter Three), and things (Chapter Two), and you may want to turn back to these earlier assignments for tips on selecting a topic and generating details. Just keep in mind that you need to consider what your subject used to be as well as what your subject is now. Perhaps you know of an athlete, a politician, or an entertainer who has changed in recent years: a baseball pitcher who has traded his fastball for a slider, a liberal who has turned conservative, or a heavy-metal rock singer who has begun crooning ballads. Or maybe a recent visit home revealed some dramatic changes in a place you have known since childhood—your old house, school, or playground, for instance. Think also of changes that have occurred in what people eat, wear, and use—in frozen foods, wristwatches, and children's toys, for example. Jot down several potential topics, and then select the one you find most interesting.

Make sure you know your subject well, its past as well as its present state. If you have not observed the changes firsthand, you may need to gather additional information before you begin writing. This doesn't mean you must visit the library to research your subject; instead, interview an older acquaintance or family member who is familiar with your subject and the changes it has undergone. Look for someone who seems to enjoy talking about "the way things used to be." Prepare for the interview by drawing up a list of questions that will help you get the facts you need. Then, during the interview, take notes—or (if the person you are interviewing doesn't mind) record the conversation and take notes afterwards. Right after the interview, while the information is still fresh in your head, you can expand and clarify your notes.

Once you have decided on a topic, given it some thought, and perhaps discussed it with someone else, you should be ready to list specific details about your subject. On a sheet of paper, make two columns, one marked "Then" (the way your subject was at some particular time in the past) and the other "Now" (the way your subject is today). Here is how one student explored her subject, the transformation of a small, family-owned grocery into a modern supermarket:

Mullett's (15 years ago)	*IGA (today)*
Essex: population 400	Essex: population 500
squeaky wooden door	automatic doors
single small room	huge supermarket
restaurant: grill, bar, booths	processed & packaged food
miniature juke box	Muzak
small grocery: figured by hand	eight computerized cash registers
house in back (4 bedrooms)	big parking lot
Mom ran store herself	cashiers, baggers, etc.
friendly, small talk	impersonal

Notice that the writer has carefully arranged past and present details in parallel fashion, contrasting the old wooden door with the automatic door, the juke box with the Muzak, and so on. Although you may not be able to match all the details in the two columns, you should look for corresponding qualities and try to make your columns roughly equal in length. If one column or the other is short on specific details, you may want to consider another topic, one you are more familiar with. The more specific information you can come up with in this step, the easier it will be to draft two paragraphs in the next.

EXERCISE LISTING CORRESPONDING DETAILS

The essay that follows was written by Eudora Welty, a professional novelist and storyteller from Jackson, Mississippi. In the essay, she gives us a child's view of a small neighborhood store in the early years of this century. Read the essay, first, just for pleasure: the precise descriptive details invite us to share the child's experience as well as see the store. Then respond to the instructions that follow the essay.

The Little Store

Our Little Store rose right up from the sidewalk: standing in a street of family houses, it alone hadn't any yard in front, any tree or flowerbed. It was a plain frame building covered over with brick. Above the door, a little railed porch ran across on an upstairs level and four windows with shades were looking out. But I didn't catch on to those.

Running in out of the sun, you met what seemed total obscurity inside. There were almost tangible smells—licorice recently sucked in a child's cheek, dill-pickle brine that had leaked through a paper sack in a fresh trail across the wooden floor, ammonia-loaded ice that had been hoisted from wet croaker sacks and slammed into the icebox with its sweet butter at the door, and perhaps the smell of still-untrapped mice.

Then through the motes of cracker dust, cornmeal dust, the Gold Dust of the Gold Dust Twins that the floor had been swept out with, the realities emerged. Shelves climbed to high reach all the way around, set out with not too much of any one thing but a lot of things—lard, molasses, vinegar, starch, matches, kerosene, Octagon soap (about a year's worth of octagonal-shaped coupons cut out and saved brought a signet ring addressed to you in the mail. Furthermore, when the postman arrived at your door, he blew a whistle). It was up to you to remember what you came for, while your eye traveled from cans of sardines to ice cream salt to harmonicas to flypaper (over your head, batting around on a thread beneath the blades of the ceiling fan, stuck with its testimonial catch).

Its confusion may have been in the eye of its beholder. Enchantment is cast upon you by all those things you weren't supposed to have need for; it lures you close to wooden tops you'd outgrown, boys' marbles and agates in little net pouches, small rubber balls that wouldn't bounce straight, frazzly kite string, clay bubble-pipes that would snap off in your teeth, the stiffest scissors. You could contemplate those long yellow boxes of sparklers gathering dust while you waited for it to be the Fourth of July or Christmas, and noisemakers in the shape of tin frogs for somebody's birthday party you hadn't been invited to yet, and see that they were all marvelous.

You might not have even looked for Mr. Sessions when he came around his store cheese (as big as a doll's house) and in front of the counter looking for you. When you'd finally asked him for, and received from him in its paper bag, whatever single thing it was that you had been sent for, the nickel that was left over was yours to spend.

Down at a child's eye level, inside those glass jars with mouths in their sides through which the grocer could run his scoop or a child's hand might be invited to reach for a choice, were wineballs, all-day suckers, gumdrops, peppermints. Making a row under the glass of a counter were the Tootsie Rolls, Hershey Bars, Goo-Goo Clusters, Baby Ruths. And whatever was the name of those pastilles that came stacked in a cardboard cylinder with a cardboard lid? They were thin and dry, about the size of tiddlywinks, and in the shape of twisted rosettes. A kind of chocolate dust came out with them when you shook them out in your hand. Were they chocolate? I'd say rather they were brown. They didn't taste of anything at all, unless it was wood. Their attraction was the number you got for a nickel.

Making up your mind, you circled the store around and around, around the pickle barrel, around the tower of Cracker Jack boxes; Mr. Sessions had built it for us himself on top of a packing case, like a house of cards.

If it seemed too hot for Cracker Jacks, I might get a cold drink. Mr. Sessions might have already stationed himself by the cold-drinks barrel, like a mind reader. Deep in ice water that looked black as ink, murky shapes that would come up as Coca-Colas, Orange Crushes, and various flavors of pop, were all swimming around together. When you gave the word, Mr. Sessions plunged his bare arm in to the elbow and fished out your choice, first try. I favored a locally bottled concoction called Lake's Celery. (What else could it be called? It was made by a Mr. Lake out of celery. It was a popular drink here for years but was not known universally, as I found out when I arrived in New York and ordered one in the Astor bar.) You drank on the premises, with feet set wide apart to miss the drip, and gave him back the bottle.

But he didn't hurry you off. A standing scale was by the door, with a stack of iron weights and a brass slide on the balance arm, that would weigh you up to three hundred pounds. Mr. Sessions, whose hands were gentle and smelled of carbolic, would lift you up and set your feet on the platform, hold your loaf of bread for you, and taking his time while you stood still for him, he would make certain of what you weighed today. He could even remember what you weighed the last time, so you could subtract and announce how much you'd gained. That was goodbye.

(Eudora Welty)

So that's the way a neighborhood store *used* to be. Now think of what a child might notice in one of today's "convenience stores," such as a Seven-Eleven or a Golden Pantry. In fact, think of a particular store in your own neighborhood, and consider in what specific ways it differs from the store described by Eudora Welty. Then fill in the two columns below with corresponding details: on the left, jot down some of the items mentioned in Welty's essay (the ceiling fan, for instance, or the Goo-Goo Clusters); on the right, put down items more likely to be found in the modern store (an air conditioner, probably, and Gummi Bears).

Then

_____

_____

_____

_____

_____

_____

_____

Now

_____

_____

_____

_____

_____

_____

_____

_____   _____
_____   _____
_____   _____
_____   _____
_____   _____

■

Step 2　*Draft Two Paragraphs: "Then" and "Now"*

Now that you have listed several details about your subject, past and present, you are ready to draft two paragraphs: a "then" paragraph, showing what your subject used to be like, and a "now" paragraph, revealing the changes that have taken place.

In your "then" paragraph, clearly identify at what time in the past you are considering your subject. Don't rely on such vague phrases as "long ago" or "in the olden days"; instead, name the particular year or at least the decade ("late 1970s," for example, or "early 1980s") in which your observations held true. Then arrange your facts and descriptions in clear, logical order. Again, you may want to review previous assignments for advice on how to organize a paragraph about a person, place, or thing. The "then" paragraph below begins by identifying the time in the past ("fifteen years ago") and goes on to provide specific descriptions of the young magnolia tree:

The Magnolia Tree (Then)

Fifteen years ago, when my family first moved to a house on East 37th Street, we decided to plant a tree in the middle of the front lawn. We chose a small magnolia tree, just a few feet tall. Its eight tiny branches, no larger than my fingers, were dotted with small lime-colored leaves. To keep this frail tree from being uprooted, we placed a foot-high white picket fence around it. But the fence was no protection against the heavy storms that struck that winter and left the magnolia stunted, wilted, and bare. I was sure the tree was dead, but my Dad said to wait for spring: time has a way of healing.

Use your "then" paragraph to guide you in developing your "now" paragraph: reconsider particular parts or characteristics of your subject to show how they have changed or stayed the same. Notice how the present-day descriptions of the magnolia tree, below, correspond to the past descriptions in the earlier paragraph:

The Magnolia Tree (Now)

Although many winters have come and gone since then, the tree still stands in the front lawn. The little sapling is now a beautiful budding magnolia, taller than the house and spreading its shade across the entire lawn. Its boughs, enormous and sturdy, are home to several varieties of birds—cardinals and bluejays as well as sparrows and hummingbirds. The leaves are no longer pale, but green and glossy. And its thick roots have upset the little picket fence, now rotten and splintery. The tree is so huge that when I go to hug it my arms reach only halfway around.

The small tree, "just a few feet tall" in the first paragraph, is now "taller than the house." The "tiny branches" have become "enormous and sturdy" boughs. The "small lime-colored leaves" are now "green and glossy." And the "foot-high white picket fence" has become "rotten and splintery." These corresponding descriptive details combine to create a vivid impression of how the tree has developed over the past fifteen years.

Describing how a person or a place has changed over the years may be more challenging than recounting the growth of a tree. Nonetheless, the basic approach is the same: identify and illustrate particular aspects of your subject in the "then" paragraph; consider corresponding qualities in your "now" paragraph. For example, if you give examples of how selfish and spoiled your brother was in the past, you might show his change in behavior by offering examples of his thoughtfulness and generosity in the present. Likewise, if you describe how clean and new a classroom appeared fifteen years ago, you might go on in your "now" paragraph to show how run-down that same room has become.

Be as specific as you can in both paragraphs, and arrange the details in clear, logical order. However, don't be too concerned if the paragraphs are not yet as well organized as you would like them to be: you will have an opportunity to revise them in the next step.

EXERCISE EVALUATING "THEN" AND "NOW" PARAGRAPHS

Read the "then" and "now" paragraphs below, and answer the questions that follow each pair.

A.   **Creating Rest**

Then   A typical Saturday for Rick used to begin at four A.M. with a two-page letter to his mother in Seattle, Washington. Then he would turn on CNN to catch up on the news that he had missed during the week. As the sun rose, he began working out on the Stairmaster or roughhousing with his Maltese dogs, Luke and Stinky. Rick had bought the dogs in Newport a few years before. Throughout the morning, he answered countless phone calls from employees, family, and friends. If there was no sign of rain, he would take his usual ten-mile run down to Bakker's Deli, ignoring the brilliant sunshine and colors of the world to focus on his shopping list: Mighty Dog dog food, Healthy Choice sliced ham, Sunbeam whole wheat bread, and a six-pack of Bud. By the time Rick had completed his chores, it was usually dark—party time. With a few friends he would head down to Wet Willy's for a night of drinking or to Victory Cinema to catch the latest film. Often he would stay out until the next morning.

Now   Now that Rick has chosen to follow traditional beliefs for celebrating the Sabbath, he has made Saturday a day of rest. From Friday just before sundown until Saturday night, he doesn't write, shop, turn on the television or radio, ride in a car or even use the telephone. He has learned how to plan ahead so that material concerns (such as running out of beer or dog food) won't intrude on his day of rest. He sleeps in Saturday mornings until nine or ten o'clock, and his day is shaped by leisurely meals, walks to the park, reading, and an afternoon nap. He tries not to think about deadlines, family problems, or the tensions of earning a living. In fact, he doesn't even wear a watch. During the rest of the week, he keeps up with the news. Saturday is now a day for *not* doing things: not spending money, not being interrupted by the telephone, not being tyrannized by an extensive to-do list.

1. Using the information in these two paragraphs, create two columns ("Then" and "Now") filled with specific facts and descriptions. Wherever possible, arrange the details in parallel fashion (that is, match a detail from a Saturday of the past with a corresponding detail from a present-day Saturday).

2. What single overall impression of Rick's typical Saturday are we given in the "then" paragraph? List any details that *don't* contribute to this impression.

3. What single overall impression of Rick's typical Saturday are we given in the "now" paragraph? List any details that *don't* contribute to this impression.

4. Which of the two body paragraphs appears to be more effective? Suggest some ways in which the less effective paragraph might be improved.

B.   **Children**

Then

In the early days of America, children found ways to entertain themselves. The girls were usually inside helping mom with dinner and housekeeping chores or else attending the baby. The girls helped mom because they usually were married by sixteen, and helping in the house gave them good experience. The boys, on the other hand, spent most of their time helping dad in the barn or out in the fields. About the only time you found a young lad sitting around was when he and pa went fishing. After doing his homework, a boy would hurry through his chores so maybe he could go fishing. The kids of that day were definitely not lazy.

Now

The children of the modern times are exactly the opposite. The girls sit around talking on the phone and watching soap operas. The common conversation between two girls is the soap operas. When the mother comes home from work, the house is just the way she left it. It's not the kids' fault that they are lazy; it's the fault of the parents. They don't make them do anything. The boys still go outside sometimes. They usually go out to play, never to work. Some sit inside and watch the cartoons and stuff their faces. If they are the only boys, their parents really pamper them. They might get yelled at once in a lifetime. This laziness will just get passed down from generation to generation.

1. Using the information in these two paragraphs, create two columns ("Then" and "Now") filled with specific facts and descriptions. Wherever possible, arrange the details in parallel fashion (that is, match a detail from the past with a corresponding detail from the present).

2. What single overall impression of children are we given in the "then" paragraph? List any details that *don't* contribute to this impression.

3. What single overall impression of children are we given in the "now" paragraph? List any details that *don't* contribute to this impression.

4. In his "then" paragraph, how has the writer identified at what time in the past he is considering his subject?

5. Suggest some ways that the writer of these two paragraphs might have further narrowed his topic and made the examples more specific.

6. Which two paragraphs do you think are more effective, the ones on "Creating Rest" or the ones on "Children"? Explain your answer. ■

Step 3 ## Draft a "Then" and "Now" Essay

Now you will revise your two paragraphs as you turn them into the body paragraphs of an essay. This essay will begin with an introductory paragraph containing a clear *thesis*—a sentence that identifies your topic and the main point you are about to demonstrate. You will then support this thesis with specific facts and descriptions in your two body paragraphs ("then" and "now"). Finally, in a one-paragraph conclusion, you will remind your readers of your main point.

There are various strategies you might follow in developing your introduction. Perhaps the simplest is to move from a general statement about your subject to a specific thesis, as shown below:

> We have all known someone who seems to fit the observation, "Oh, she'll *never* change." Regardless of what cataclysmic events might occur, what bombs may fall on their lives, or what dreams may come true, some people, we are convinced, will never change. My own mother, I once felt, was just such a person, but a family tragedy miraculously transformed her from a gruff and miserly house-tyrant to a warm and generous friend and mother.

Notice how the writer moves from observations about a *type* of person in her first two sentences to a thesis concerning a *particular* person in her last sentence. This thesis is complete, for it identifies not only the subject of the essay (the writer's mother) but also the main point the writer intends to make about her subject (the transformation from "tyrant" to "friend"). As you can see from this example, the thesis sentence in an introduction works like the topic sentence of a body paragraph: it reveals the subject and suggests the purpose of what follows.

Another introductory strategy is to provide information that anticipates the pattern (in this case, "then" and "now") of your essay. In other words, begin with one or two sentences describing your subject in the present. Here is an example:

> Once there was a street, Bay Street, where teenagers could go at night to get together with old friends and meet new ones. The air was filled with friendly chatter, good-hearted laughter, and rousing music from boom boxes and car radios. But now the teenagers are gone, driven away by city officials who are more concerned with making money off of tourists than with offering their own young citizens a place in which to have a good time.

This introduction foreshadows the structure as well as the substance of the essay. And, like the previous example, it ends with a strong thesis sentence that clearly identifies the writer's attitude toward the change his subject has experienced.

A variation on this introductory approach is to move from specific examples drawn from the present (the way your subject is now) to a thesis that identifies and comments on the change that has taken place. This strategy, as the following introduction demonstrates, can be effective in catching your reader's attention:

> Welcome to the modern American playroom. A rocking horse gallops on house current. A plastic lady with permanently waved hair and a sexy swimsuit poses for her plastic boyfriend on her plastic yacht. And at the push of a button, a robot stalks across the floor, its aluminum eyes rolling as its motor hums. Bored and restless, the children in the playroom *watch* their toys. In fact, there is little else for them to do. Unlike the simple gadgets and cuddly playthings of yesterday, the sophisticated toys of today are robbing our children of the true imaginative pleasure of play.

As you draft your introduction, try out different strategies to find the one that best suits your subject and your purpose for writing.

Follow your introduction with a revised version of the "then" paragraph you wrote in the last step. If in your introduction you have not already identified the particular time in the past you are writing about, be sure to do so at the beginning of this first body paragraph. Also, check that the information in this paragraph does, indeed, support your thesis. Let's return to the essay on toys to see how the writer has developed her "then" paragraph:

> When I was a little girl, just fourteen or fifteen years ago, I played every day with a small blackboard and a classroom of cuddly, overstuffed rag dolls. They would line up on my bed for their lessons in spelling, arithmetic, and history. I, the teacher, was a strict disciplinarian: no funny stuff in my classroom. My students knew that whispering, giggling, and gum chewing would be punished by a long spell under the bed. Of course, now and then I would have a student miss class through no fault of her own. Once, for instance, panda was in bed with the measles—a case made real by the addition of Mercurochrome dots (which, unfortunately, never healed). All of this was so much fun because I was exercising my imagination; in a word, I was *playing*.

Here the writer has used an extended illustration from her own experience to support her thesis. Notice that she has chosen to place the topic sentence at the end of the paragraph rather than in its more customary spot at the beginning. Such an arrangement can be an effective way of preparing your readers for the shift to the present in the next paragraph. However, just be sure the implicit point of the paragraph is clear from the start.

Your second body paragraph, a revised version of the "now" paragraph you wrote in the last step, should also clearly support your thesis. Read this second body paragraph from the essay on toys, and judge for yourself how successful the writer has been in justifying her thesis that "the sophisticated toys of today are robbing our children of the true imaginative pleasure of play":

I wish I could say that little Alicia, who lives next door to me, could play with such enthusiasm. Certainly she has no shortage of toys. Her collection of Madame Alexander dolls sits proudly on her closet shelf. "You may look," she is cautioned, "but you mustn't touch." And so these exquisitely crafted ceramic aristocrats, being museum pieces rather than playthings, just gather dust. However, Alicia does have a baby doll: with the aid of a string it says (over and over) what the manufacturer has dictated, not what Alicia would have it say. She also has a record player that sings to her, an electronic organ that plays for her, and even a Play-Doh Factory that makes little clay houses for her. No wonder she complains that she's bored: it's her toys who are having all the fun.

Although we may not be altogether convinced by the writer's argument, we can see that she has provided several examples in support of her thesis.

Your concluding paragraph offers an opportunity to reemphasize the main point of your essay. Make it clear here whether you think the change you have observed has been for the better or the worse. Or you may want to qualify your observations, noting that both gains and losses, good and bad, have resulted from this change. Finally, you might want to end the paragraph with a look to the future to see what changes may lie ahead. Let's now consider the paragraph that concludes the essay on toys:

Playtime should offer children a chance to exercise their imaginations, to make worlds of their own, not just passively occupy the worlds created by toy manufacturers. In recent years, at least for some children, the delight of play has been lost. As a result, will the children of today grow up to be the robots of tomorrow, dully punching buttons and staring vacantly at a world that passes them by? I hope not. In fact, I trust that our children will outwit the toymakers. Why, just this morning I saw Alicia sitting in a cardboard box on her front lawn, riding her "rocket ship" to the stars.

In the first two sentences of this conclusion, the writer echoes her thesis, repeating the key words *children, toys, play,* and *imagination.* In her third sentence, she looks to the future and considers some depressing consequences. But she qualifies her observations at the very end of the paragraph, where she frees Alicia from her boring playroom (and the tyranny of toy manufacturers) as she describes the child's imaginative escape.

Just how you support and arrange the information in your essay will depend to a large extent on what you are writing about and the point you are making. Be guided, however, by the general plan discussed here: an introduction, two body paragraphs ("then" and "now"), and a conclusion.

EXERCISE DEVELOPING INTRODUCTIONS AND CONCLUSIONS

Below are two pairs of "then" and "now" paragraphs. Read them carefully, and decide what you think is the main point of each pair. Then, on your own paper, turn each pair into an essay by adding an introduction and a conclusion. Make sure that your introduction includes a clear thesis. Your conclusion should emphasize the main point implied by the writer of the original paragraphs. When you are done, compare your work with that of your classmates.

A.   **Watching the Wristwatch**

Then
As recently as ten years ago, the wristwatch served just two basic purposes: to tell time and to look nice. It had a single button on the side with which to set the time and wind up the spring (a daily chore). The watch had two hands to count off the hours and minutes, and sometimes a third to count the seconds. The only additional function available on the old-fashioned watch was a little window that displayed the day of the month (a figure which was almost always wrong). In those days to say that you owned a fancy watch meant that the timepiece was made of gold and the strap was made of an expensive leather.

Now
In today's watches, electronic circuits have replaced gears and springs. As a result, they no longer have to be wound up: a tiny battery will keep them running for years. The two or three hands of the clock have been replaced by digital numbers, and they do much more than just tell the time. They will also announce the date (day, month, and year), count laps, and tell you if it is A.M. or P.M. Some modern watches even contain built-in calculators and video games. The watch of today will ring an alarm to wake you in the morning and play musical scores to keep you awake during class. Nowadays, how fancy a watch is is determined more by what it does than by what it looks like.

B.   **Basic Training**

Then
Thirty years ago, my Uncle Bob joined the United States Air Force. His first duty assignment was Lackland Air Force Base in San Antonio, Texas—an eight-hour plane flight from Chicago. When he arrived at the airport, he had to make his way to the base alone on a Greyhound Bus. There, Security Police directed him to the base library, where he met Sergeant Jones, his training instructor. Uncle Bob was then taken to the barracks—an old brick building that had been used as a supply depot during the Korean War. Fifty men were in his unit, with four people assigned to each room. The poorly lit room was furnished only with lockers and bunk beds. The day after Uncle Bob's arrival, he was marched to the military clothing store, where he was issued boots that were too tight and an oversized uniform (one size fits all). That same day he received from the base quarter-master twenty dollars (called the "flying twenty" because it took only a minute to spend). The next six weeks consisted of military indoctrination and intense physical exercise, with no opportunities to leave the base or even use the telephone. Uncle Bob still considers those six weeks to be the grimmest time of his life.

Now
Now, thirty years later, the young men and women of the nineties see basic training as an investment in their future. When my brother Eric joined the Air Force last year, he also took a flight from Chicago to San Antonio—in just two hours. When he arrived at the airport, he was met by Sergeant Jones, Training Instructor, who drove him to Lackland Air Force Base. There he was escorted to a private room in a brand new dormitory. The room was large, with freshly painted

walls, a newly carpeted floor, and a large, comfortable bed. The next day, when he visited the military clothing store, an attendant took Eric's measurements and later custom-made his uniform. Next, he was given a $210 check to spend on personal items. In addition to military indoctrination and physical exercise, basic training itself included a great deal of free time. At the end of four weeks, Eric called to tell me that he never wanted to leave Lackland because he was having the time of his life. ■

Step 4 — *Revise and Proofread*

Let someone else read and critique your essay. Then, guided by your reader's comments and the checklist below, revise the essay.

REVISION CHECKLIST

❑ Have you chosen a *particular* person, place, or thing for your topic?

❑ Is your essay made up of four paragraphs: an introduction, two body paragraphs, and a conclusion?

❑ Does your introduction clearly identify your subject and attract the interest of the reader?

❑ Does your introduction contain a thesis that clearly states the main point you are about to demonstrate?

❑ Does your "then" paragraph identify a particular time in the past?

❑ Have you developed the "then" paragraph with specific facts and descriptions?

❑ Have you organized the information in the "then" paragraph clearly and logically?

❑ Is your "now" paragraph approximately the same length as your "then" paragraph?

❑ Does the information in the "now" paragraph correspond with the information in the "then" paragraph?

❑ Have you developed the "now" paragraph with specific facts and descriptions?

❑ Have you organized the information in the "now" paragraph clearly and logically?

❑ Does your conclusion reemphasize the main point of your essay?

❑ Have you proofread the essay carefully?

Passages

A. Back in Step 1, we saw how one writer explored the transformation of her family's small grocery and restaurant into a modern supermarket. Here is the essay that finally evolved from her initial investigation. Notice that many of the details that appeared in the student's original list reappear here.

From Mullett's to IGA

On Main Street in Essex, Illinois, there once stood a small wooden structure called Mullett's—a grocery and restaurant that was owned and operated by my mother. When visiting this past summer, I had hopes of finding the same, old-fashioned building crowded with familiar faces and buzzing with friendly conversation. Nonetheless, I knew that the store had changed owners many times since we had left and that even in Essex, Illinois, time does not stand still.

Fifteen years ago, when the population of Essex was about 400, our store was always filled with the same friendly characters. The squeaky wooden door led into a single room containing both the restaurant and the grocery store. The grill that lined one wall was enclosed by a bar and a few scattered stools. A half-dozen booths, each equipped with a mini-juke box (three songs for a quarter), crouched in the back. Along the other two walls were shelves stocked with groceries. A short hallway led to our home, which contained four bedrooms, a living room, and a bathroom. This arrangement was ideal because my mom ran the store by herself: flipping pancakes on the grill, serving customers in the booths, and bagging, stocking, and pricing all the groceries. We had no cash registers: Mom just figured each bill on her pad. Our store was home, not just to my family, but to everyone in Essex.

On my recent visit, I was shocked to find a huge IGA supermarket covering the land where both our store and our home had once sat. More than ten times the size of Mullett's, the new store could probably hold the entire town of Essex (population 500 now). Two sets of automatic doors stand on each side of the building, leading into a room filled with carts and a Coke machine. Just beyond this room is the store itself. In place of the few shelves of groceries are eight well-stocked aisles and eight cash registers. Fifteen years ago, Mom would have been amazed to hear the computerized voices on these registers announcing how much change is needed. She would have been even more amazed to see the number of cashiers, baggers, and stock people doing the jobs that she used to do alone. There are always lines at the checkouts now; it seems as if the whole town goes shopping at the same time.

Of course, the people aren't as friendly and the conversation isn't as personal in the IGA as in the old Mullett's. And it's hard not to feel some sense of loss when you find that the house you grew up in is no longer there. But I'm really not surprised. Throughout the country, small, family-owned groceries and restaurants have become increasingly rare reminders of the past. Nowadays, like everyone else, I eat lunch at the Burger King and shop at the IGA.

(Kiedra Mullett)

B. The following essay by journalist Andrew Ward provides a humorous account of how gas stations have changed in recent years. As you read, consider how Ward's use of specific, descriptive details contributes to your enjoyment and understanding of the essay.

They Also Wait Who Stand and Serve Themselves

Anyone interested in the future of American commerce should take a drive sometime to my neighborhood gas station. Not that it is or ever was much of a place to visit. Even when I first moved here, five years ago, it was shabby and forlorn: not at all like the garden spots they used to feature in the commercials, where trim, manicured men with cultivated voices tipped their visors at your window and asked what they could do for you.

Sal, the owner, was a stocky man who wore undersized popped-button shirts, sagging trousers, and oil-splattered work shoes with broken laces. "Gas stinks" was his motto, and every gallon he pumped into his customers' cars seemed to take something out of him. "Pumping gas is for morons," he liked to say, leaning indelibly against my rear window and watching the digits fly on the pump register. "One of these days I'm gonna dump this place on a Puerto Rican, move to Florida, and get into something nice, like hero sandwiches."

He had a nameless, walleyed assistant who wore a studded denim jacket and, with his rag and squeegee, left a milky film on my windshield as my tank was filling. There was a fume-crazed, patchy German shepherd, which Sal kept chained to the air pump, and if you followed Sal into his cluttered, overheated office next to the service bays, you ran a gauntlet of hangers-on, many of them Sal's brothers and nephews, who spent their time debating the merits of the driving directions he gave the bewildered travelers who turned into his station for help.

"I don't know," one of them would say, pulling a bag of potato chips off the snack rack. "I think I would have put 'em onto 91, gotten 'em off at Willow, and then—Bango!—straight through to Hamden."

Sal guarded the rest room key jealously and handed it out with reluctance, as if something in your request had betrayed some dismal aberration. The rest room was accessible only through a little closet littered with tires, fan belts, and cases of oil cans. Inside, the bulb was busted and there were never any towels, so you had to dry your hands on toilet paper—if Sal wasn't out of toilet paper, too.

The soda machine never worked for anyone except Sal, who, when complaints were lodged, would give it a contemptuous kick as he trudged by, dislodging warm cans of grape soda which, when their pop tops were flipped, gave off a fine purple spray. There was, besides the snack rack, a machine that dispensed peanuts on behalf of the Sons of Garibaldi. The metal shelves along the cinderblock wall were sparsely stocked with cans of cooling system cleaner, windshield de-icer, antifreeze, and boxed head lamps and oil filters. Over the battered yellow wiper case, below the Coca Cola clock, and half hidden by a calendar from a janitorial supply concern, hung a little brass plaque from the oil company, awarded in recognition of Salvatore A. Castallano's ten-year business association.

I wish for the sake of nostalgia that I could say Sal was a craftsman, but I can't. I'm not even sure he was an honest man. I suspect that when business was slow he may have cheated me, but I never knew for sure because I don't know anything about cars. If I brought my Volvo in because it was behaving strangely, I knew that as far as Sal was concerned it could never be a simple matter of tightening a bolt or re-attaching a hose. "Jesus," he'd wearily exclaim after a look under the hood. "Mr. Ward, we got problems." I usually let it go at that and simply asked him when he thought he could have it repaired, because if I pressed him for details he would get all worked up. "Look, if you don't want to take my word for it, you can go someplace else. I mean, it's a free country, you know? You got spalding on your caps, which means your dexadrometer isn't charging, and pretty soon you're gonna have hairlines in your flushing drums. You get hairlines in your flushing drums and you might as well forget it. You're driving junk."

I don't know what Sal's relationship was with the oil company. I suppose it was pretty distant. He was never what they call a "participating dealer." He never gave away steak knives or NFL tumblers or stuffed animals with his fill-ups, and never got around to taping company posters on his windows. The map rack was always empty, and the company emblem, which was supposed to rotate thirty feet above the station, had broken down long before I first laid eyes on it, and had frozen at an angle that made it hard to read from the highway.

If, outside of television, there was ever such a thing as an oil company service station inspector, he must have been appalled by the grudging service, the mad dog, the sepulchral john. When there was supposed to have been an oil shortage a few years ago, Sal's was one of the first stations to run out of gas. And several months ago, during the holiday season, the company squeezed him out for good.

I don't know whether Sal is now happily sprinkling olive oil over salami subs somewhere along the Sun Belt. I only know that one bleak January afternoon I turned into his station to find him gone. At first, as I idled by the no-lead pump, I thought the station had been shut down completely. Plywood had been nailed over the service bays. Sal's name had been painted out above the office door, and all that was left of his dog was a length of chain dangling from the air pump's vacant mast.

But when I got out of the car I spotted someone sitting in the office with his boots up on the counter, and at last caught sight of the "Self-Service Only" signs posted by the pumps. Now, I've always striven for a degree of self-sufficiency. I fix my own leaky faucets and I never let the bellboy carry my bags. But I discovered as I squinted at the instructional sticker by the nozzle that there are limits to my desire for independence. Perhaps it was the bewilderment with which I approach anything having to do with the internal combustion engine; perhaps it was my conviction that fossil fuels are hazardous; perhaps it was the expectation of service, the sense of helplessness, that twenty years of oil company advertising had engendered, but I didn't want to pump my own gas.

A mongrel rain began to fall upon the oil-slicked tarmac as I followed the directions spelled out next to the nozzle. But somehow I got them wrong. When I pulled the trigger on the nozzle, no gas gushed into my fuel tank, no digits flew on the gauge.

"Hey, buddy," a voice sounded out a bell-shaped speaker overhead. "Flick the switch."

I turned toward the office and saw someone with Wild Bill Hickok hair leaning over a microphone.

"Right. Thanks," I answered, and turned to find the switch. There wasn't one. There was a bolt that looked a little like a switch, but it wouldn't flick.

"The switch," the voice crackled in the rain. "Flick the switch."

I waved back as if I'd finally understood, but I still couldn't figure out what he was talking about. In desperation, I stuck the nozzle back into my fuel tank and pulled the trigger. Nothing.

In the office I could see that the man was now angrily pulling on a slicker. "What the hell's the matter with you?" he asked, storming by me. "All you gotta do is flick the switch."

"I couldn't find the switch," I told him.

"Well, what do you call this?" he wanted to know, pointing to a little lever near the pump register.

"A lever," I told him.

"Christ," he muttered, flicking the little lever. The digits on the register suddenly formed neat rows of zeros. "All right, it's set. Now you can serve yourself," the long-haired man said, ducking back to the office.

As the gas gushed into my fuel tank and the fumes rose to my nostrils, I thought for a moment about my last visit to Sal's. It hadn't been any picnic; Sal claimed to have found something wrong with my punting brackets, the German shepherd snapped at my heels as I walked by, and nobody had change for my ten. But the transaction had dimension to it; I picked up some tips about antennas, entered into the geographical debate in the office, and bought a can of windshield wiper solvent (to fill the gap in my change). Sal's station had been a dime a dozen, but it occurred to me, as the nozzle began to balk and shudder in my hand, that gas stations of its kind were going the way of the village smithy and the corner grocery.

I got a glob of grease on my glove as I hung the nozzle back on the pump, and it took me more than a minute to satisfy myself that I had replaced the gas cap properly. I tried to whip up a feeling of accomplishment as I headed for the office, but I could not forget Sal's dictum: Pumping gas is for morons.

The door to the office was locked, but a sign directed me to a stainless steel teller's window which had been installed in the plate glass of the front window. I stood waiting for a while with my money in hand, but the long-haired man sat inside with his back to me, so at last I reached up and hesitantly knocked on the glass with my glove.

The man didn't hear me or had decided, in retaliation for our semantic disagreement, to ignore me for a while. I reached up to knock again, but noticed that my glove had left a greasy smear on the window. Ever my mother's son, I reflexively reached into my pocket for my handkerchief and was about to wipe the grease away when it hit me: at last the oil industry had me where it wanted me— standing in the rain and washing its windshield.

(Andrew Ward)

Questions

1. Define the following words as they are used by Andrew Ward in his essay: *walleyed, aberration, accessible, contemptuous, sepulchral, retaliation, semantic.*

2. In your own words, explain what Ward misses about the gas station of the past.

3. Select one paragraph from this essay, and discuss how the author uses precise descriptive details to convey an idea or impression.

4. Compare Ward's essay with the previous selection, "From Mullett's to IGA." In what ways are they alike or different in terms of structure and detail? Consider how each writer uses personal experience to make a point. Do the two writers reach similar conclusions about changing times?

Postscript

In showing how a particular subject has changed over a period of time, you have followed the common writing strategy of *comparison.* That is, you have identified similarities and differences between "then" and "now." Comparison can also help us to understand the relation between two separate subjects (two presidents, two plants, two methods of treating snakebites, for instance). A short comparison essay is often organized according to the "block" method you have followed here—examining first one subject and then the other in separate paragraphs. Longer comparison essays may be organized according to a "point by point" approach, which you will find discussed in the assignment *Choices* in Chapter Fourteen.

CHAPTER TEN

Modern Times
(EVALUATING EFFECTS)

Preview

In this assignment, you will examine both the good and bad effects of some recent invention or innovation. You will begin by selecting a topic and listing its advantages and disadvantages. Then you will expand each of your points into a short paragraph containing specific supporting evidence. Next, you will arrange these paragraphs into a coherent essay. Finally, you will revise and proofread your essay.

Step 1

List and Illustrate Advantages and Disadvantages

Many of the inventions and innovations of modern times have turned out to carry mixed blessings. Certainly such items as the telephone, the television, the computer, and the credit card all have proven benefits, but they bring disadvantages as well—discomforts, disruptions, inconveniences. As one writer has commented, "What we call *progress* is often just the exchange of a nuisance for an annoyance." You will begin this assignment by considering how some of these recent inventions and innovations have affected our lives—both for the better and for the worse.

Before passing any judgments, make a list of some of the products and services that you associate with modern times. Here are a few items to start you thinking:

cable television	rock videos
artificial organs for the body	compact discs
cellular telephones	videocassette recorders
personal computers	microwave ovens
artificial sweeteners	fast-food restaurants

Of course these items are not equally important, but even the smallest, most trivial things can have an effect on the way we live. Add at least ten more items to this list.

As you look over your list, see if any of the items can be broken down into more specific inventions or innovations. For example, if you put "television" on your list, you might break it down into a number of different topics: commercials on television, news on television, cable television—even a particular cable service such as MTV.

The next step is to take a few of these items and list some of the advantages and disadvantages of each. Here is an example:

Credit Cards

ADVANTAGES	DISADVANTAGES
convenient	time-consuming credit checks
easy credit	embarrassing if rejected at checkout
easy access to your money	high finance charges
clear record of purchases	misuse can lead to bad credit rating
good for bargains, sales	impulse buying
protected if lost	hassle if stolen

After you have explored a few topics in this way, select the one you are most familiar with and interested in.

Once you have chosen a topic, jot down some specific facts and examples that support the points you have listed:

Credit Cards

good for bargains, sales: bought gloves 50% off at Belks—no cash one-day sale

high finance charges: stereo cost an extra $80 in interest because I paid for it by Visa card and took eight months to pay it off—18% annual interest

You may not use all of these facts and examples when you go to write your essay, but you will use some. And locating this information now lets you see whether you know your topic well enough to support your ideas in an essay. If you have trouble coming up with supporting details, you should either research your topic (locate additional information in magazines or reference works) or find another topic that you are more familiar with.

EXERCISE DISTINGUISHING BETWEEN MAIN POINTS AND SUPPORTING DETAILS

Each topic below is followed by four statements. Put an **M** in front of each main point (an advantage or disadvantage). Put an **S** in front of each supporting point (a fact or example demonstrating an advantage or disadvantage).

TELEPHONE ANSWERING MACHINES

_____ 1. Answering machines help us to avoid dealing with pesky callers.

_____ 2. By checking with my answering machine when I was visiting friends in Atlanta, I found out that I had been invited to a job interview the following Monday.

_____ 3. Our answering machine allows us to avoid disruptions at mealtimes and late at night.

_____ 4. Answering machines allow us to stay in touch with family and friends even when we are out of town.

POWER WINDOWS IN CARS

_____ 1. They can be quite an inconvenience at times.

_____ 2. The power system failed in the middle of January, and for three weeks I had to drive around with the windows open.

_____ 3. With my finger on the control, I feel secure knowing the kids in the back seat can't go bouncing out the window into a lane of traffic.

_____ 4. They increase fuel consumption in a midsized automobile by almost eight percent.

THE DESIGNATED HITTER IN AMERICAN LEAGUE BASEBALL

_____ 1. Dave Winfield added years to his career (as well as hundreds of thousands of dollars to his income) by becoming a designated hitter.

_____ 2. The role of designated hitter gives many aging ball players an opportunity to prolong their careers.

_____ 3. With a designated hitter available, managers no longer have to make some important tactical decisions.

_____ 4. Weak-hitting pitchers in the American League are generally happy to sacrifice their spot in the lineup to a designated hitter.

X-RAYS

_____ 1. X-rays help doctors to diagnose different diseases.

_____ 2. An X-ray can detect the extent of tooth decay or damage to the gums.

_____ 3. X-rays can cause damaging physical and chemical changes.

_____ 4. Overexposure to radiation can cause skin burns, a reduction of the blood supply, or even cancer. ■

Step 2 *Draft Several Short Paragraphs*

Guided by the notes you took in the first step, develop at least three or four short paragraphs. Begin each paragraph with a topic sentence that identifies a particular good or bad effect. Then go on to support this topic sentence with specific examples, facts, and explanations.

You may support a point with two or three brief examples, as in this paragraph:

Television commercials can be extremely irritating. How could that whining, finger-tapping Mr. Whipple convince anybody to buy his toilet paper? Most viewers would like to squeeze this charmer's *head*—in a vise, preferably. And I know that I would love to batter and fry that clucking geek in a chicken costume who peddles aluminum siding during the breaks in the midnight movie.

Likewise, you can use one extended example—or short narrative—to demonstrate an advantage or disadvantage:

Losing a credit card can be a traumatic experience. I will never forget the time a pickpocket made off with my wallet, which contained a shiny new MasterCard. As soon as I discovered the loss, I called the police, who didn't seem to care, and a representative of the credit card company, who interrogated me for half an hour as if I were the thief. Two weeks later I received a new card, along with a $2,176 bill for charges I never made. The problem was settled six months later, and my only loss was $50 and my peace of mind.

You may want to refer to earlier assignments for advice on developing a paragraph with examples (Chapter Four) or a narrative (Chapter Five).

You can also support a point with *facts*—information based on your own studies or on the reports of others:

Nicotine patches have helped many people quit smoking in recent years. According to a study reported in the *American Medical Journal* of August 1994, thirty-one percent of those who used the patches for five weeks or longer still were not smoking at the end of one year. This figure compares with just twenty-one percent of those who chewed nicotine gum and nineteen percent of those who used a placebo (Beard and Burden 237).

If you rely on information from an outside source, be sure to identify that source in your paper.

To demonstrate that something is easy or difficult to operate, you can offer a step-by-step explanation:

Oven-cleaning pads are easy to use. After putting on a pair of rubber gloves, you simply poke a pin through the pad to release the cleaner, squeeze the pad a few times, and then rub it over the grunge in your oven. After letting the cleaner sit for half an hour, you just wipe the oven with a damp sponge.

Chapter Eight (*Skills*) offers tips on writing step-by-step explanations.

You may use any combination of these methods to develop your short paragraphs. Just make sure that your examples, facts, or explanations clearly support the advantage or disadvantage expressed in the topic sentence of each paragraph.

EXERCISE SUPPORTING TOPIC SENTENCES

On your own paper, support each topic sentence below with at least two or three sentences. Provide the kind of support indicated in parentheses.

1. Most fast-food restaurants live up to the name, serving their customers within minutes, if not seconds.
   (Provide a step-by-step explanation.)

2. Digital alarm clocks operate according to the whims of the electric company.
   (Provide two or three brief examples or one extended example.)

3. Vending machines sometimes break down, leading to some very frustrating encounters.
   (Provide an extended example.)

4. The automobile is a dangerous form of transportation.
   (Provide facts or an extended example.)

5. Some television commercials offer better entertainment than the programs they sponsor.
   (Provide two or three brief examples.)

6. A lost contact lens can be far more upsetting than a misplaced pair of glasses.
   (Provide an extended example.) ■

Step 3

Draft an Essay

You will now organize your short paragraphs into an essay. There are various ways to do this.

Perhaps the simplest way is to use just two body paragraphs—one treating the advantages (or good effects) of your topic, the other dealing with the disadvantages (or bad effects) of your topic. The basic format of your essay would be something like this:

Introduction: *Identify your topic, comment on its significance in modern life, and then—in your thesis sentence—note that your topic has both good points and bad.*

Body paragraph 1: *Identify the advantages one by one, and briefly support each observation.*

Body paragraph 2: *Identify the disadvantages one by one, and support these observations.*

Conclusion: *State whether or not you think the advantages outweigh the disadvantages, and explain your response. Or suggest how your readers may enjoy the good effects and avoid the bad.*

This approach (similar to the one you followed in Chapter Nine, *Changes*) will work if your main points are simple to explain and your supporting materials are brief.

However, you may find that some or perhaps all of the paragraphs you wrote for Step 2 are strong enough to stand on their own—that your readers might, in fact, be confused if you were to combine paragraphs. If so, then it's quite all right to draft an essay containing several body paragraphs—two or three considering the advantages, and another two or three considering disadvantages.

A third approach is to pair each advantage with a disadvantage in a separate body paragraph. This method of organization is effective only when particularly good and bad points are closely related—when, for instance, you consider both the convenience of using an automatic teller and the inconvenience of having to reclaim a bank card that the machine has "eaten."

Finally, you may combine these last two approaches, as demonstrated in the following essay.

Frozen Spaghetti

Introduction   Frozen foods are convenient, but are they anything else? Are they nutritious? Are they economical? Are they even food at all? One thing is for certain: the frozen meals of today—such as Stouffer's, Budget Gourmet, and Lean Cuisine—are better and more popular than the papier mâché concoctions that used to be called "TV dinners." A close examination of one of these new frozen meals, the Lean Cuisine spaghetti dinner, reveals that with the good points come some bad.

Advantage   Any busy person will appreciate the convenience of this product. You simply open the box, punch a few holes in the two plastic pouches (sauce in one, pasta in the other), and pop the pouches into a microwave oven. While your meal cooks, you can return to your English homework or the six o'clock news: no stirring, seasoning, or tossing pasta against the wall to see if it sticks. Your dinner is ready in five minutes. To serve, remove each pouch from the microwave and slit one corner with a knife. Then pour the contents of both packets onto a dinner plate, grab a fork, and dig in. The tedious chore of cooking, particularly if you are eating alone, has been virtually eliminated.

Advantage   But how are your taste buds affected by a product that has been cooked, frozen, shipped, nuked, and served? Remarkably enough, there's very little flavor at all. To those who prefer a bland diet, this is an advantage. However, if you like to taste **Disadvantage** what you are chewing, you will be disappointed. One danger of the increasing dependence on frozen meals is that our sense of taste is being steadily dulled. It may be getting to the point where a "spicy dish" will soon be Lean Cuisine spaghetti with an extra dusting of synthetic Parmesan.

Advantage   Perhaps it isn't fair to expect good taste (or any taste at all) from a product that calls itself "lean." Diet-conscious pasta lovers will be glad to hear that a single serving of Lean Cuisine spaghetti contains a mere three hundred calories. So, can we then conclude that such "lite" fare will help us to stay thin and trim? Not re- **Disadvantage** ally, for a "single serving" is mighty small—just a few ounces of wet spaghetti. I suspect that many Lean Cuisiners, after congratulating themselves for counting their calorie intake so carefully, will an hour or two later answer their growling stomachs with a bag of Doritos and a can of pop. Thus, disguised as a diet food, this frozen package of starch may actually be making us fat.

Advantage   These thoughts may bring up another question: how are the pocketbooks of the Lean Cuisiners affected? A single serving of spaghetti costs just $1.69—darn cheap for a meal these days. But what meal? With a can of tomato paste and a few strands of spaghetti you can make the same thing for half the price. And your **Disadvantage** homemade version would probably be better for you. Lean Cuisine promises you a few percentage points worth of niacin and riboflavin, but certainly not enough vitamins to get you through the day—or even the rest of your homework assignment. And Lean Cuisine spaghetti is about the cheapest frozen meal available. You can pay up to four or five dollars for midget portions of equally unnutritious chicken and beef—in fancier containers, of course. So the final effect is that the frozen-food manufacturers are making a bundle off us while our bodies are being starved of basic nutrients.

Conclusion   Nevertheless, as I said at the start, today's frozen dinners are superior to those of the past. Bland food is better than foul-tasting food substitutes. And a little riboflavin beats a lot of monosodium glutamate. But only if convenience is the most significant value in your life will you be satisfied by Lean Cuisine and its cool cousins in the frozen food section. These foods are tasteless, unnutritious, expensive—and fattening.

Be guided by the structures shown here, but don't force your paragraphs to fit a pattern. Experiment with different arrangements until you find the one that allows you to develop your ideas clearly and effectively.

EXERCISE EVALUATING ESSAYS

Read the following draft carefully, and then respond to the questions that follow it.

Distance Learning

Distance learning is a high-tech method of taking college classes on live TV. Through two-way interactive video, students sitting in a classroom at one college are able to participate in a class that is being taught at another college miles away.

Distance learning gives more people an opportunity to take a wider variety of college courses without having to travel far away from their homes. Because I work forty hours a week while trying to raise a family, I can't spare the time to commute two hours to Savannah to take education courses. Distance learning classes at the nearby community college will help me to complete my degree much more quickly. Of course, a distance learning class isn't quite the same as a "live" class. Although you can see and hear the professor (and she can see and hear you), there's not much opportunity for personal contact. I called my education professor on the phone two or three times to get help with assignments. Although some of my friends refuse to sign up for distance learning classes, I know of others who wouldn't be in college otherwise.

Distance learning works well until it stops working. I discovered that when we lost the sound in my education class and had to rely on a tape of the class that was mailed the next day. At least we didn't miss any important information. I thought at first that there might be other problems: students ducking out of camera range to sneak out of class early or to cheat on examinations. But these things were all worked out. After a few classes, I almost forgot that I was staring at a TV screen and not at a live person. Handouts were faxed to us in the classroom, and Dr. Cosgrove knew all of us by name and kept classes interesting with photographs and slides and videos. Of course, all this technology is very expensive ($2,000 a month just for telephone line charges), but it might save money in other ways.

So is distance learning a good thing or a bad thing? Easy answers can be found on both sides of the issue: the technocrats say that these new technologies will lead to better teaching and smarter citizens; their opponents are afraid that distance learning means the defeat of higher education by morons clutching remote controls.

1. Complete the following simple outlines for the two body paragraphs in this draft:

   First Body Paragraph

   Topic Sentence: _____

   Advantage: _____

   Disadvantage: _____

   Advantage: _____

   Second Body Paragraph

   Topic Sentence: _____

   Disadvantage: _____

   Disadvantage: _____

   Advantage: _____

   Advantage: _____

   Disadvantage: _____

2. Which points in the first body paragraph might be presented more effectively in a separate paragraph?

3. Which of the advantages and disadvantages in the first body paragraph are supported with specific facts or examples?

4. Which statement in the second body paragraph needs to be clarified with additional information or examples?

5. The introductory paragraph lacks a clear thesis sentence. Based on your reading of this draft, create an appropriate thesis sentence.

6. Suggest how the conclusion to this draft could be improved. ■

Step 4 | ## *Revise and Proofread*

Let someone else read your essay and recommend some ways you might improve it. Then revise the essay, using the following checklist as a guide.

REVISION CHECKLIST

❑ In your introduction, have you clearly identified your topic and suggested why it is worth considering in an essay?

❑ Does your introduction contain a clear thesis—one that lets the reader know you will be considering both good effects and bad?

❑ In the body of the essay, have you considered both good effects and bad (advantages and disadvantages)—and have you distinguished clearly between them?

❑ Have you supported all your points with specifics—examples, short narratives, facts, step-by-step explanations?

❑ Have you arranged this information clearly and effectively?

❑ Have you concluded the essay effectively? Have you explained whether or not you think the advantages outweigh the disadvantages? Or have you suggested ways we might enjoy the good effects and avoid the bad?

❑ Have you proofread the essay carefully?

Passages

A. Here is the revised version of the essay seen in the last exercise. Notice how the writer has greatly expanded his introduction and conclusion, broken up his body paragraphs, and provided specific support for main points.

Learning at a Distance

The huge television monitors in the front of the room were the first sign that Education 200 would not be an ordinary college class. As I settled into my seat in Carroll 201, alongside a dozen or so other students, I was startled to see that we were all self-consciously staring back at ourselves on the left-hand monitor. In the monitor to the right, a pleasant-looking woman was smiling at us. "Good morning, Statesboro, Brunswick, and Camden," she said, "this is Dr. Cosgrove in Savannah. Welcome to distance learning class Education 200. We're on the air."

Though before that moment I had never even heard of distance learning (or "teleconferencing," as it's sometimes called), I have since found out that this high-tech method of taking college classes on live TV is becoming more and more common all over the country. By means of two-way interactive video, students sitting in a classroom at one college are able to participate in a class that is being taught at another college dozens or even hundreds of miles away. Ask a question in Brunswick, get a response from an instructor in Savannah, and hear a wisecrack from a student in Camden. Through a combination of new technologies (computers, remote-controlled cameras, wireless microphones, thirty-five-inch monitors, VCRs, and fax machines), distance learning classes are transmitted over telephone lines across the state. Within a few years, thousands of sites (including schools, hospitals, and libraries as well as colleges and universities) are expected to be linked in this fashion. The prospects are exciting— and a little bit scary, too.

That first day in Education 200 I was convinced that this distance learning business was a bad deal for those of us watching television screens in the so-called "remote" sites. I wondered how Dr. Cosgrove would ever get to know our names or grade us fairly on class participation or hold conferences with us outside of class if we were having problems. I imagined students ducking out of camera range to sneak out of class early or to cheat on examinations. Though Dr. Cosgrove made a point of calling out the names of the students at all four sites as their faces appeared on the screen (my uncombed hair looked like a rat's nest!), I left that first class feeling pretty certain that distance learning was a dead-end street running off the information superhighway.

Within a week or so, however, my attitude changed for the better. Dr. Cosgrove soon called on us all by name and even seemed to know when we were dozing off. She kept the class interesting with photographs that she placed on a graphics camera and with slides and videos that she beamed magically to all four sites. Our class discussions were unusually lively, involving students who ordinarily would never have met. After a few classes, I almost forgot that I was staring at a TV screen and not at a "live" person. Handouts were faxed to us in the classroom, and a graduate assistant always visited the class to supervise tests and exams. Most importantly, Dr. Cosgrove made a habit of staying after class to answer any questions we might have, and she gave us her e-mail address and office telephone number so that we could stay in touch. If you have a good teacher, I decided, you can have a good distance learning class.

Everything was going along fine until about the third week of term. It started with a little static and ended without any sound at all. While we tried reading Dr. Cosgrove's lips, a frustrated technician scrambled around the huge, black teleconferencing unit, pushing buttons and turning knobs without any success. Distance learning works well, I discovered, until it stops working. Dr. Cosgrove finally held up a sign saying that we could go home but that a "make-up class" would be ready the next day. The "make-up" turned out to be a videotape of the class we had missed. Though the tape was a poor substitute for actually participating in the class, at least we didn't miss any important information.

I doubt if anyone knows for sure just where distance learning is headed and what effects it will have on the way we learn. Will teleconferencing put some professors out of work, or will more people simply have more opportunities to take a wider range of college courses closer to home? Will distance learning save colleges (and students) money? Right now, the telephone line charges are expensive (over $2,000 a month, according to Dr. Cosgrove), and technicians and graduate students must be paid to keep the system running. Perhaps the biggest concern of all is that students might begin to feel more and more cut off from their professors—a situation that would trouble some and please others.

According to the AT&T commercials, before long we will be able to select courses not only from local campuses but from colleges and universities that may be thousands of miles away. If you choose, you will still be able to take a history course the usual way—traveling to campus two nights a week. But you will also have the option of taking the course in your living room (through Mind Extension University on cable, for instance) or in your home office (via Internet on your computer). For students who work full time, live far away from a college campus, or are busily engaged in raising a family, the value of distance learning is indisputable. Without it, many would not have any chance at all to go to college.

So is distance learning a good thing or a bad thing—a way of providing new educational opportunities or just further evidence that the one-eyed monster, television, has taken over the world? Easy answers can be found on either side of the issue: the technocrats argue that new technologies and increased competition will lead to more effective instruction and smarter citizens; their opponents fear that distance learning signals the defeat of higher education at the clicker-clutching hands of telemorons. The real answer is probably a lot more complicated than either of these views. Like it or not, distance learning is not very far away. Are you ready?

(Jason Walker)

B. In the following essay, author Nora Ephron explains why she hates her VCR—and why she is addicted to it.

Living with My VCR

When all this started, two Christmases ago, I did not have a videocassette recorder. What I had was a position on videocassette recorders. I was against them. It seemed to me that the fundamental idea of the VCR—which is that if you go out and miss what's on television, you can always watch it later—flew in the face of almost the only thing I truly believed—which is that the whole point of going out is to miss what's on television. Let's face it: part of being a grown-up is that every day you have to choose between going out at night or staying home, and it is one of life's unhappy truths that there is not enough time to do both.

Finally, though, I broke down, but not entirely. I did not buy a videocassette recorder. I rented one. And I didn't rent one for myself—I myself intended to stand firm and hold to my only principle. I rented one for my children. For $29 a month, I would tape *The Wizard of Oz* and *Mary Poppins* and *Born Free*, and my children would be able to watch them from time to time. In six months, when my rental contract expired, I would reevaluate.

For quite a while, I taped for my children. Of course I had to subscribe to Home Box Office and Cinemax in addition to my normal cable service, for $19 more a month—but for the children. I taped *Oliver* and *Annie* and *My Fair Lady* for the children. And then I stopped taping for the children—who don't watch much television, in any case—and started to tape for myself.

I now tape for myself all the time. I tape when I am out, I tape when I am at home and doing other things, and I tape when I am asleep. At this very moment, as I am typing, I am taping. The entire length of my bedroom bookshelf has been turned over to videocassettes, mostly of movies; they are numbered and indexed and stacked in order in a household where absolutely nothing else is. Occasionally I find myself browsing through publications like *Video Review* and worrying whether I shouldn't switch to chrome-based videotape or have my heads cleaned or upgrade to a machine that does six or seven things at once and can be set to tape six or seven months in advance. No doubt I will soon find myself shopping at some Video Village for racks and storage systems especially made for what is known as the "the serious collector."

How this happened, how I became a compulsive videotaper, is a mystery to me, because my position on videocassette recorders is very much the same as the one I started with. I am still against them. Now, though, I am against them for different reasons: now I hate them out of knowledge rather than ignorance. The other technological breakthroughs that have made their way into my life after my initial pigheaded opposition to them—like the electric typewriter and the Cuisinart—have all settled peacefully into my home. I never think about them except when I'm using them, and when I'm using them I take them for granted. They do exactly what I want to them to do. I put the slicing disk into the Cuisinart, and damned if the thing doesn't slice things up just the way it's supposed to. But there's no taking a VCR for granted. It squats there, next to the television, ready to rebuke any fool who expects something of it.

A child can operate a VCR, of course. Only a few maneuvers are required to tape something, and only a few more are required to tape something while you are out. You must set the time to the correct time you wish the recording to begin and end. You must punch the channel selector. You must insert a videotape. And, on my set, you must switch the "on" button to "time record." Theoretically, you can then go out and have a high old time, knowing that even if you waste the evening, your old videocassette recorder will not.

Sometimes things work out. Sometimes I return home, rewind the tape, and discover that the machine has recorded exactly what I'd hoped it would. But more often than not, what is on the tape is not at all what I'd intended; in fact, the moments leading up to the revelation of what is actually on my videocassettes are without a doubt the most suspenseful of my humdrum existence. As I rewind the tape, I have no idea of what, if anything, will be on it; as I press the "play" button, I have not a clue as to what in particular has gone wrong. All I know for certain is that something has.

Usually, it's my fault. I admit it. I have mis-set the timer or channel selector or misread the newspaper listing. I have knelt at the foot of my machine and methodically, carefully, painstakingly set it—and set it wrong. This is extremely upsetting to me—I am normally quite competent when it comes to machines—but I can live with it. What is far more disturbing are the times when what has gone wrong is not my fault at all but the fault of outside forces over which I have no control whatsoever. The program listing in the newspaper lists the channel incorrectly. The cable guide inaccurately lists the length of the movie, lopping off the last ten minutes. The evening's schedule of television programming is thrown off by an athletic event. The educational station is having a fund-raiser.

You would be amazed at how often outside forces affect a videocassette recorder, and I think I am safe in saying that videocassette recorders are the only household appliances that outside forces are even relevant to. As a result, my videocassette library is a raggedy collection of near misses: *The Thin Man* without the opening; *King Kong* without the ending; a football game instead of *Murder, She Wrote*; dozens of PBS auctions and fundraisers instead of dozens of episodes of *Masterpiece Theater*. All told, my success rate at videotaping is even lower than my success rate at buying clothes I turn out to like as much as I did in the store; the machine provides more opportunities per week to make mistakes than anything else in my life.

Every summer and at Christmastime, I reevaluate my six-month rental contract. I have three options: I can buy the videocassette recorder, which I would never do because I hate it so much; I can cancel the contract and turn in the machine, which I would never do because I am so addicted to videotaping; or I can go on renting. I go on renting. In two years I have spent enough money renting to buy two video-cassette recorders at the discount electronics place in the neighborhood, but I don't care. Renting is my way of deluding myself that I can still some day reject the machine in an ultimate way (by sending it back)—or else forgive it (by buying it)—for all the times it has rejected me.

In the meantime, I have my pathetic but ever-expanding collection of cassettes. "Why don't you just rent the movies?" a friend said to me recently, after I finished complaining about the fact that my tape of *The Maltese Falcon* now has a segment of *Little House on the Prairie* in the middle of it. Rent them? What a bizarre suggestion. Then I would have to watch them. And I don't watch my videotapes. I don't have time. I would virtually have to watch my videotapes for the next two years just to catch up with what my VCR has recorded so far; and in any event, even if I did have time, the VCR would be taping and would therefore be unavailable for use in viewing.

So I merely accumulate videocassettes. I haven't accumulated anything this mindlessly since my days in college, when I was obsessed with filling my bookshelf, it didn't matter with what; what mattered is that I believed that if I had a lot of books, it would say something about my intelligence and taste. On some level, I suppose I believe that if I have a lot of videocassettes, it will say something—not about my intelligence or taste, but about my intentions. I intend to live long enough to have time to watch my videotapes. Any way you look at it, that means forever.

(Nora Ephron)

Questions

1. Define the following words as they are used in Ephron's essay: *fundamental, compulsive, rebuke, revelation, methodically, deluding, virtually.*
2. Based on your reading of this essay, list both the advantages and disadvantages of owning (or renting) a VCR.
3. Toward the end of the essay, Ephron admits that she has deluded herself into thinking that she has "some control" over the VCR. Find examples of self-delusions throughout the essay.
4. Ephron's essay is both *personal* and *informal* (see Chapter Nine). Point out specific features of her writing that mark it as informal.

Postscript

In your other college courses you may also be called on to measure and evaluate the effects of something—of air pollution, for example, or a Supreme Court decision or a particular marketing strategy. Whatever the subject may be, you can follow the same writing strategies that you used here. Different assignments call for different information, but the fundamental principles of good writing remain unchanged. An introduction that makes a clear point, body paragraphs that support that point with specific details, and a conclusion that reinforces the main point—these are the basic parts of any good essay.

CHAPTER ELEVEN

Reasons
(CAUSES)

Preview

"Why do we do what we do?" Here you will turn this broad question into a topic that can be developed with reasons and examples. You will start by *brainstorming*—working with others to explore ideas. You will then incorporate some of these ideas in rough drafts of three or four paragraphs. Finally, you will revise these paragraphs as you organize them into a coherent essay.

Step 1

Brainstorm

College writing assignments often call on us to explain *why*: Why did a certain event in history occur? Why does an experiment in biology produce a particular result? Why do people behave the way they do? This last question is the starting point of this assignment. Your job is to identify just one of the things people do, so that you can go on to develop an essay explaining why people behave in this way.

Why do we do what we do? It's up to you to define the *we* (it could be everybody or a particular group or even, as far as you know, just you) and the *what* (anything from blushing to wearing ties, smoking to whistling in the dark). Through listing or freewriting (or both), fill up a page with possible topics—both the silly and the serious. At the top of the page write, "Why do we . . ." and then let your imagination go free as you consider some of the many things that people do. Don't reject any idea that comes to mind.

Once you have come up with a number of possible topics, you are ready to begin answering some of your questions. But rather than trying to answer them alone, join with three or four other students for a brainstorming session. In this session, each of you will, in turn, introduce a particular question (such as "Why do we own handguns?" or "Why do we eat junk food?") and then invite the others to suggest reasons. Either during the session or right afterwards, you should jot down the various reasons that are offered. These you can use later when you prepare a draft.

Following are the notes one student took during a brainstorming session:

Why Do We Smoke Cigarettes?

habit	hobby
advertising—Joe Camel, Kool sax player	everybody else does
peer pressure	like the taste
parents say not to smoke	suicide
nerves	keep the hands busy
addiction	rebellion
kill appetite—lose weight	excuse not to talk
look cool	boredom

Some of the points in this list may seem to you more important than others, and certainly a number of them appear to be saying the same thing in different ways. But during the brainstorming session itself, such judgments don't matter. Jot down all the ideas that tumble out, and evaluate them later. Keep in mind that those ideas which at first sound foolish or outlandish may eventually lead you to some of the most significant reasons.

EXERCISE PRACTICE IN BRAINSTORMING

You may want to practice brainstorming as a class before breaking into groups of four or five. If so, this exercise might give you some ideas for a topic of your own as you practice the strategy of sharing ideas without criticizing or passing judgments. Your class should spend a few minutes brainstorming each one of the following topics. Don't stop to discuss the responses; just let one idea lead to another.

1. Why do we exercise?
2. Why do the sciences attract more men than women?
3. Why do we go to college?
4. Why are we attracted to certain people?
5. Why do we watch television?
6. Why do people drink alcohol?
7. Why do we tell lies?
8. Why do we take writing courses in college?
9. Why do we stop at red lights?
10. Why do we keep pets? ■

Step 2 *Draft Reason Paragraphs Developed with Explanations and Examples*

Now that you have discovered some ideas about your topic in a brainstorming session, you can pause to evaluate those ideas. Eliminate points that you think are repetitious or unimportant, and select the three or four most significant ideas—that is, reasons that respond clearly to your question and are distinctly different from one another. Put each reason in a complete sentence, as shown in the following example:

Why Do We Exercise?

Reason 1   Some people, the ones in designer jump suits, exercise simply because keeping in shape is trendy.

Reason 2   Many people exercise to lose weight and thus appear more attractive.

Reason 3   Other people exercise for their health.

These sentences may serve as topic sentences for the paragraphs that you will now draft.

Once you are satisfied that you have found three or four distinct reasons, explore each one in a paragraph developed with explanations and examples. You may draw on your own experiences and observations for supporting material or use information and examples provided by your classmates in a follow-up brainstorming session. In any case, back up your main points with *specific* details that explain your reasons clearly and keep your readers interested.

One way to support a main point is with a series of brief examples. Consider, for instance, how a student has used a number of illustrative details to support one of her reasons for owning a revolver:

Reason

Example 1

Example 2

Example 3

Knowing that a Smith & Wesson .38 caliber five-shot revolver lies nestled among the tissues and romance books in my nightstand drawer gives me a sense of security. I think of my revolver when watching news reports of break-ins and murders and rapes. I think of it sometimes when dressing my baby, so helpless in a city occupied by armed drug addicts who would stop at nothing to make off with my cheap stereo and broken VCR. And sometimes in the dead of night, when creaking floorboards or a car's backfire startles me awake, I reach into the drawer and squeeze the handle of the revolver as if it were the hand of a friend. Though I hope that I never have cause to fire the revolver in self-defense, simply knowing that it's nearby—and that I know how to use it—tempers my fears and helps me sleep at night.

The examples in this paragraph show not only *when* the student thinks about the revolver in the drawer but, more importantly, *why.*

On the other hand, you may choose to explore a reason in a paragraph developed with one extended example, as shown below:

Reason

Extended
Example

The primary reason that some people go away to college is to escape the rules and restrictions of home and to enjoy living—and partying—with thousands of people their own age. My sister Tonya is a typical escapee. Tired of "the General's" curfews and my mother's constant fussing, Tonya had just one goal when she graduated from high school: to get out of the house as quickly as she could. Though she had no academic ambitions or career goals at the time (except to quit waitressing at the Shrimp House), she chose a college two hundred miles away as her party route. For nine months she danced and dated and watched TV, along the way earning a fractional grade point average that finally sent her straight back home.

As you can see, an extended example involving just one individual may help to explain a reason that applies to many.

When you have completed this step, you should have drafts of three or four paragraphs in support of your various reasons. You will have an opportunity to revise these paragraphs in the next step as you organize them into an essay.

EXERCISE EVALUATING REASON PARAGRAPHS

The paragraphs drafted in Step 2 of this assignment should be developed with specific details that explain your reasons clearly and keep your readers interested. To determine the effectiveness of the student drafts below, read each paragraph carefully and then respond to the questions that follow.

A.   *from* **Why We Keep Pets**

In some homes, pets serve to amuse children while also offering them lessons in responsibility. While I was growing up, my cat Stinky entertained me by pouncing at empty paper bags and by scampering after peppermint candies skipped along the kitchen floor. But entertainment had its price. "Change Stinky's water every morning," my mother was always reminding me, "or else she will die." What we didn't know at the time was that Stinky had a serious heart condition. She was only three years old when she died, and I thought my own heart would break.

1. Which details in this paragraph clearly support the topic sentence?

2. What information in this paragraph does *not* appear to be relevant to the reason contained in the topic sentence?

B.   *from* **Why We Drink Coffee**

For many of us, drinking coffee is a way to recharge our mental batteries between meals. Adult Americans consume, on average, 3.4 cups of coffee every day. Between breakfast and lunch and then again between lunch and dinner, a cup of coffee can perk us up. Coffee has a way of waking us up when we get drowsy, particularly after eating. When we take up someone's invitation to "talk awhile over a cup of coffee," we are probably more interested in the talk than we are in the brew.

1. Does the statistic provided in the second sentence clearly support the reason contained in the topic sentence?

2. Is adequate *specific* support for the topic sentence provided in this paragraph? Explain your response.

3. Does the observation contained in the final sentence support the reason provided in the topic sentence? How might this final sentence be used more effectively? ■

Step 3 *Draft an Essay*

You will now revise the three or four paragraphs that you drafted in the last step as you turn them into the body paragraphs of an essay. The essay will begin with an introductory paragraph that attempts to capture the interest of your readers while identifying the behavior you are attempting to explain. In revising the body paragraphs, you will concentrate on providing specific support and establishing clear connections between examples and ideas. Finally, in a concluding paragraph, you will emphasize a key observation about your subject or admit to questions that may still remain.

To catch the interest of your readers, there are various strategies that you might follow in developing an introduction. Beginning with an observation, a fact, a quotation, or a description may all serve to attract their attention. Consider, for instance, these four different openings to the same topic: "Why Are So Many Adults Riding Bicycles?":

Observation   Just a few years ago, bicycles were strictly for kids, but today they are a common form of transportation for adults as well. Whether traveling to work in city traffic or riding through the countryside for relaxation, men and women of all ages have forsaken their cars and returned to the bicycles of their younger days. Why are so many grownups riding bikes?

Fact   Last year, over ten million bicycles were sold to (and for) Americans over the age of seventeen, and this year that figure is expected to increase. Indeed, bicycle manufacturers have been showing healthier profit margins recently than American auto makers. There are several reasons why more and more adults are leaving their cars in the garage and hopping on bikes.

Quotation   "I love to ride my bicycle; I love to ride my bike!" For various reasons, increasing numbers of adults these days are singing this tune as they peddle their way down highways, back country roads, and city streets.

Description   He wears a Christian Dior herringbone suit, totes a black leather Pierre Cardin attaché case, keeps time by a gold-plated Gucci watch—and travels to his job on a ten-speed bicycle. This businessman is one of millions of American adults who have recently forsaken their automobiles for the trusty, non-polluting bicycle. But why?

In drafting your introductory paragraph, experiment with various attention-getters, and then select the one that you think is most interesting and appropriate.

As you revise the three or four body paragraphs that you drafted in the previous step, make sure that your examples are specific and that your points are logically organized. Your reasons may proceed from those that are less common to those that are better known—or the other way around. You might begin with a fairly trivial reason and proceed to more serious ones. Whatever approach you take, try to guide your readers from one paragraph to the next. You may find it helpful to use one or more of the common *reason* and *addition signals:*

also	in the first place, in the
a more important reason	second place
at times	more importantly
besides	moreover
in addition	most importantly
for this reason	next
furthermore	to begin with

Along with the time, place, and example signals listed in earlier chapters, these reason and addition signals help to make our writing easier to follow and understand.

In your concluding paragraph, you may want to emphasize what you consider to be the most important reason that you have discussed. Or you may choose to demonstrate how people are motivated by a combination of various reasons. In some cases, as in the conclusion to the following student essay, the most appropriate response might be to comment on the difficulty of ever achieving a complete understanding of your subject.

Attractions

Without the benefit of hair spray or a snappy line of patter, the male roadrunner courts a prospective mate by offering her a mouse or a baby rat that he has pounded into a state of shock. For the same purpose, peacocks display their plumage and bullfrogs croak loudly for hours. In the human world, mating rituals may seem even more outlandish than those carried out in the animal kingdom, but the secret of attraction is far more complicated and mysterious. Why we are attracted to some people and not to others is a question that most of us have pondered at one time or another.

In our commercial culture, it is no surprise that the most obvious cause of attraction is physical appearance. The television camera has taught our eyes how to zoom in on smooth complexions, fashionably coifed hair, and a predictable assortment of correctly proportioned body parts. Of course, sexual attraction predates the Flintstones, but these days physical appeal can be enhanced in countless ways. Elegantly trimmed nails, bodies sculpted by intensive aerobics, and fashionable make-up that disguises "flaws" certainly do manage to attract attention. Not everyone likes to admit that such cosmetic qualities control our emotional responses, but they do.

Nevertheless, the nature of attraction is not always so obvious or superficial: a feature that seems unremarkable or even odd to one person may appeal deeply to another. A tangled mop of curly hair or an eruption of freckles may be almost comical-looking to some and powerfully appealing to others. One friend of mine claims that he fell in love with a woman at the first sight of her tiny ears and lopsided grin. Even subtle, often unintentional movements, unnoticed by most people, may be a source of attraction. Legs swinging carelessly, eyes blinking nervously, or a slight twitch of the nose may send strong signals to an observer's heart.

In determining the secret of what attracts people to one another, we need to consider what we say as well as how we look. Though we may occasionally be impressed by someone who brags about his accomplishments, we are more often attracted to people who express genuine interest in us. A simple compliment or a shared joke about a goofy professor may signal the sort of interest that enhances our sense of self-esteem. For instance, my current boyfriend first caught my attention by telling me how much he liked my handwriting. That innocent remark led to light-hearted conversation about a lab instructor—a conversation that we continued during our first lunch together. On the other hand, not all remarks are so inviting. Grunts, wolf whistles, and obscene comments, for example, are more likely to repulse than to endear.

Though some degree of self-deception is probably involved in most human attractions, evidence of finer personality traits may also be found. Many people find comedians attractive, even ones that aren't good-looking. Laughter can be an emotional spark. Some are attracted to dynamic and energetic people, while others prefer quieter, more studious types. My sister Ann claims that she fell immediately in love with a young man whom she saw for the first time sitting alone on a park bench. What attracted her was not his face or his body, the way he laughed or anything he said. What she noticed was that he was diligently reading a novel by one of her favorite authors, Don DeLillo. The attraction was so sudden and so strong that for the first time in her life she found herself introducing herself to a strange man.

In the end, the nature of human attraction remains mysterious. Until recently, I had always imagined that my ideal mate would be tall, dark, and quiet; yet my boyfriend is short, fair-skinned, and extremely sociable. I suspect that most of us are surprised by many of the people we are attracted to and by many who are attracted to us. The wonderful news is that sometimes the attractions are mutual.

A careful reading of this student essay should give you a number of ideas on ways to organize and develop your own essay effectively: the attention-getting facts in the introductory paragraph; the arrangement of the body paragraphs from the most obvious reason to the most subtle; the use of brief, specific examples in each body paragraph; the reliance on signal words and phrases throughout the essay; and a conclusion that uses a personal example to dramatize the "mysterious" nature of human attraction.

EXERCISE EVALUATING ESSAYS

Carefully read this draft of an essay, and then respond to the questions that follow it.

Why I Hate Mathematics

I hated arithmetic back in third grade because I didn't want to memorize the times tables. Unlike learning how to read, there didn't seem to be any point to studying math. The alphabet was a code that could tell me all kinds of secrets after I had puzzled it out. Multiplication tables just told me how much six times nine was. There wasn't any pleasure in knowing that.

I really began to hate math when Sister Celine forced us to play counting contests. This old nun would make us stand up in rows, and then she would shout out problems. The ones who called out the correct answers fastest would win; those of us who answered wrong would have to sit down. Losing never bothered me that much; rather, it was that feeling in the pit of my stomach before and right after she called out the numbers. You know, that math feeling. Somehow, not only did mathematics seem irrelevant and dull, it also became associated in my mind with speed and competition. Math just got worse as I got older. Negative numbers, I thought, were insane. You either have some or none, I figured—not negative some. My brother would try to talk me through the steps when helping me with my homework, and eventually I would puzzle things out (long after the rest of the class had moved on to something else), but I never understood the point of the puzzle. My teachers were always too busy to explain why any of this mattered. They couldn't see the point of explaining the point of it all. I started to cause problems for myself in high school by skipping homework. With geometry, of course, that means death. My teachers would punish me by making me stay after school to do—what else?—more math problems. I came to associate the subject with pain and punishment. Though I'm through with math classes now, math still has a way of making me ill. Sometimes at work or on line at the bank, I get that old nervous feeling again, as if Sister Celine is still out there shouting out problems. It's not that I can't do the math; it's just that it *is* math.

I know I'm not the only one who has grown up hating math, but that doesn't make me feel any better. The funny thing is, now that I don't have to study math any more, I'm beginning to get interested in what it all means.

1. The introductory paragraph lacks a clear thesis sentence. Based on your reading of the rest of the draft, compose an appropriate thesis.

2. Point out where the single, long body paragraph might be divided to create three or four shorter paragraphs.

3. Show where signal words and phrases might be added to establish clearer connections between examples and ideas.

4. The concluding paragraph is rather abrupt. To improve this paragraph, what question might the student try to answer?

5. What is your overall evaluation of this draft, its strengths, and its weaknesses? What recommendations would you make to the student writer? ■

Step 4 ▸ **Revise and Proofread**

Now let someone else read and evaluate your essay. Then, taking your reader's comments into consideration, revise the essay once again. Use the following checklist as a guide.

REVISION CHECKLIST

❏ In your introductory paragraph, have you made an effort to gain the attention of your reader with an observation, fact, quotation, or description that will attract interest in your topic?

❏ In your introduction, have you clearly stated or implied your question?

❏ Have you offered at least three or four clear, distinct reasons in separate body paragraphs?

❏ Does each body paragraph begin with a clear topic sentence?

❏ Is each body paragraph developed with relevant explanations and examples?

❏ Have you used *reason* and *addition signals* to guide your readers from one point to the next?

❏ Does your concluding paragraph effectively draw together the key observations in your essay?

❏ Have you proofread the essay carefully?

Passages

A. The essay that follows is a carefully revised version of the draft that you evaluated in the last exercise, "Why I Hate Mathematics." Compare the specific revisions made by the student with those that you recommended when evaluating the draft.

Learning to Hate Mathematics

I started dreading arithmetic back in the third grade because I didn't want to memorize the multiplication tables. Unlike learning how to read, studying math seemed to have no purpose other than to give me massive headaches and shattered nerves. The alphabet was a wonderful code that, when deciphered, entertained me with stories and revealed all kinds of secrets about the world. Multiplication tables, on the other hand, just told me how much six times nine was. There was no joy in knowing that. Although even in third grade I understood that I shared with many other students a terrible fear and hatred of mathematics, I drew little comfort from that fact. Since then, I have struggled with math for a number of reasons.

I especially began to hate math when Sister Celine forced us to participate in her sadistic counting contests. Having ordered us to stand in rows, side by side, this jolly nun would shout problems at us: "Forty-eight divided by three? . . . Nine times twelve? . . . Three times eight divided by two?" The students who called out the correct answers fastest would win; those of us who answered wrong or not at all would have to sit down. To be honest, losing never bothered me that much. Rather, it was that feeling in the pit of my stomach before and right after she called out the numbers. You know, that awful math feeling. Not only did mathematics seem irrelevant and dull, it also became forever associated in my mind with speed and competition. During the counting contests, I would deliberately give an incorrect answer early on so that I could escape the game quickly.

As I grew older, math grew worse, like a persistent headache that makes you want to scream to relieve the pain. Negative numbers, I thought, were simply insane. You either have *some* or *none*, I figured—not *negative some*. Patiently, my older brother would try to talk me through the steps when helping me with my homework. Oh, eventually I would puzzle things out (long after the rest of the class had moved on to something else), but I never understood the point of the game. My teachers were always too busy droning out formulas to explain how and why any of these calculations mattered. Who on earth *cared* about determining the departure times of trains or figuring how long it would take Arthur to walk to the playground? Constantly frustrated by the sheer meaningless of it all, I even grew to hate the people and places mentioned in word problems: I imagined trains crashing in the dead of night and little Arthur becoming hopelessly lost on his way home from the playground.

After years of hating math and only barely passing my classes, I started to compound my difficulties in high school by skipping homework. With geometry, of course, that means death. My teachers would punish me by making me stay after school to do—what else?—more math problems. In anger and frustration, I broke pencils and tore paper as I dutifully filled page after page with utterly meaningless calculations. Not surprisingly, I came to associate mathematics with nothing more nor less than pain and heartless punishment. In my recurring nightmares, my head was fractured by fractions and crushed by multiplication signs.

Though I'm through with math classes now and carry a calculator in my purse, math still has a way of making me queasy. Sometimes at work or on line at the bank, I get that old nervous feeling again, as if Sister Celine is still out there barking out problems. It's not that I can't do the math; it's just that it *is* math.

Recently, however, a strange thing has happened. All those curious (probably maddening) questions that my teachers ignored have begun to crop up again. On a whim the other day, I bought a book called *Mathematics for People Who Hate Math*, and even though parts of it seem to have been written in a foreign language, I've actually been enjoying the book. In architecture and engineering, in physics and electronics, even in art and music, mathematics does have a purpose and a meaning. Like the letters of the alphabet, numerical signs *can* tell stories and reveal secrets about the world. Now, without sadistic teachers conducting drills or staging competitions, I think I might even enjoy learning more about math—on my own terms, at my own pace. But don't you dare throw any problems at me when I'm not looking, because I still get that math feeling in my stomach sometimes.

(Anne Miller)

B. In the following essay, science writer K. C. Cole suggests a number of reasons why relatively few women have been drawn to (or encouraged to pursue) careers in mathematics and science. As you read Cole's essay, consider whether your own experience supports the notion that mathematic and scientific skills depend in part on social circumstances and the attitudes of others.

Women and Science

I know few other women who do what I do. What I do is write about science, mainly physics. And to do that, I spend a lot of time reading about science, talking to scientists and struggling to understand physics. In fact, most of the women (and men) I know think me quite queer for actually liking physics. "How can you write about that stuff?" they ask, always somewhat askance. "I could never understand that in a million years." Or more simply, "I hate science."

I didn't realize what an odd creature a woman interested in physics was until a few years ago when a science magazine sent me to Johns Hopkins University in Baltimore for a conference on an electrical phenomenon known as the Hall effect. We sat in a huge lecture hall and listened as physicists talked about things engineers didn't understand, and engineers talked about things physicists didn't understand. What *I* didn't understand was why, out of several hundred young students of physics and engineering in the room, less than a handful were women.

Some time later, I found myself at the California Institute of Technology reporting on the search for the origins of the universe. I interviewed physicist after physicist, man after man. I asked one young administrator why none of the physicists were women. And he answered: "I don't know, but I suppose it must be something innate. My 7-year-old daughter doesn't seem to be much interested in science."

It was with that experience fresh in my mind that I attended a conference in Cambridge, Massachusetts, on science literacy, or rather the worrisome lack of it in this country today. We three women—a science teacher, a young chemist and myself—sat surrounded by a company of august men. The chemist, I think, first tentatively raised the issue of science illiteracy in women. It seemed like an obvious point. After all, everyone had agreed over and over again that scientific knowledge these days was a key factor in economic power. But as soon as she made the point, it became clear that we women had committed a grievous social error. Our genders were suddenly showing; we had interrupted the serious talk with a subject unforgivably silly.

For the first time, I stopped being puzzled about why there weren't any women in science and began to be angry. Because if science is a search for answers to fundamental questions then it hardly seems frivolous to find out why women are excluded. Never mind the economic consequences.

A lot of the reasons why women are excluded are spelled out by the Massachusetts Institute of Technology experimental physicist Vera Kistiakowsky in a recent article in *Physics Today* called "Women in Physics: Unnecessary, Injurious and Out of Place?" The title was taken from a 19th-century essay written in opposition to the appointment of a female mathematician to a professorship at the University of Stockholm. "As decidedly as two and two make four," a woman in mathematics is a "monstrosity," concluded the writer of the essay.

Dr. Kistiakowsky went on to discuss the factors that make women in science today, if not monstrosities, at least oddities. Contrary to much popular opinion, one of those is *not* an innate difference in the scientific ability of boys and girls. But early conditioning does play a stubborn and subtle role. A recent Nova program, "The Pinks and the Blues," documented how girls and boys are treated differently from birth—the boys always encouraged in more physical kinds of play, more active explorations of their environments. Sheila Tobias, in her book, *Math Anxiety,* showed how the games boys play help them to develop an intuitive understanding of speed, motion and mass. The main sorting out of the girls from the boys in science seems to happen in junior high school. As a friend who teaches in a science museum said, "By the time we get to electricity, the boys already have had some experience with it. But it's unfamiliar to the girls." Science books draw on boys' experiences. "The examples are all about throwing a baseball at such and such a speed," said my step-daughter, who barely escaped being a science drop-out.

The most obvious reason there are not many more women in science is that women are discriminated against as a class, in promotions, salaries and hirings, a conclusion reached by a recent analysis by the National Academy of Sciences.

Finally, said Dr. Kistiakowsky, women are simply made to feel out of place in science. Her conclusion was supported by a Ford Foundation study by Lynn H. Fox on the problems of women in mathematics. When students were asked to choose among six reasons accounting for girls' lack of interest in math, the girls rated this statement second: "Men do not want girls in the mathematical occupations."

A friend of mine remembers winning a Bronx-wide mathematics competition in the second grade. Her friends—both boys and girls—warned her that she shouldn't be good at math: "You'll never find a boy who likes you." My friend continued nevertheless to excel in math and science, won many awards during her years at the Bronx High School of Science, and then earned a full scholarship to Harvard. After one year of Harvard science, she decided to major in English.

When I asked her why, she mentioned what she called the "macho mores" of science. "It would have been O.K. if I'd had someone to talk to," she said. "But the rules of comportment were such that you never admitted you didn't understand. I later realized that even the boys didn't get everything clearly right away. You had to stick with it until it had time to sink in. But for the boys, there was a payoff in suffering through the hard times, and a kind of punishment—a shame—if they didn't. For the girls it was O.K. not to get it, and the only payoff for sticking it out was that you'd be considered a freak."

Science is undeniably hard. Often, it can seem quite boring. It is unfortunately too often presented as laws to be memorized instead of mysteries to be explored. It is too often kept a secret that science, like art, takes a well developed esthetic sense. Women aren't the only ones who say, "I hate science." That's why everyone who goes into science needs a little help from friends. For the past ten years, I have been getting more than a little help from a friend who is a physicist. But my step-daughter—who earned the highest grades ever recorded in her California high school on the math Scholastic Aptitude Test—flunked calculus in her first year at Harvard. When my friend the physicist heard about it, he said, "Harvard should be ashamed of itself."

What he meant was that she needed that little extra encouragement that makes all the difference. Instead, she got that little extra discouragement that makes all the difference. "In the first place, all the math teachers are men," she explained. "In the second place, when I met a boy I liked and told him I was taking chemistry, he immediately said: 'Oh, you're one of those science types.' In the third place, it's just a kind of social thing. The math clubs are full of boys and you don't feel comfortable joining."

In other words, she was made to feel unnecessary, and out of place.

A few months ago, I accompanied a male colleague from the science museum where I sometimes work to a lunch of the history of science faculty at the University of California. I was the only woman there, and my presence for the most part was obviously and rudely ignored. I was so surprised and hurt by this that I made an extra effort to speak knowledgeably and well. At the end of the lunch, one of the professors turned to me in all seriousness and said: "Well, K. C., what do the women think of Carl Sagan?" I replied that I had no idea what "the women" thought about anything. But now I know what I should have said: I should have told him that his comment was unnecessary, injurious and out of place.

(K. C. Cole)

Questions

1. Define each of the following words as they are used in Cole's essay: *askance, grievous, frivolous, innate, comportment.*

2. Cole suggests a number of reasons why relatively few women have been drawn to (or encouraged to pursue) careers in mathematics and science. Briefly summarize these reasons.

3. How convincing is the evidence that Cole presents in support of her ideas?

4. Consider to what extent your own mathematic and scientific ability has been affected by social circumstances and the attitudes of others.

5. Compare Cole's essay with the student essay "Learning to Hate Mathematics" (passage *A*). Judging by Cole's observations, do you think that the student's particular experiences are typical of the problems faced by female students?

Postscript

In this essay assignment, you gained further practice in applying strategies that were introduced earlier in the text: brainstorming; creating topic sentences; drafting paragraphs with examples and explanations; organizing paragraphs into a coherent essay; developing introductions and conclusions; using signal words and phrases; and revising and editing.

CHAPTER TWELVE

Approaches
(*CLASSIFICATION*)

Preview

In this assignment, you will classify a group of people according to their way of doing something—their approach to a particular activity. First, you will select an activity that you are familiar with and list some of the ways people carry it out. Then, guided by your classification plan, you will explain and describe each approach in a paragraph. Next, you will incorporate these paragraphs in a complete essay. Finally, you will revise and proofread your essay.

Step 1

List Approaches to an Activity

Rarely is there just one way of doing anything, whether it be hanging wallpaper, studying for a test, or fishing for bass. The way we work, study, or play depends on various factors—our experience and ability, our attitudes and goals. Still, we can usually identify certain *types* of approaches to any activity. You will begin this assignment by considering some of the activities you have participated in or observed. Then you will select one activity and classify people according to the way they approach it.

Spend five or ten minutes just listing some of the things you frequently do or have observed others doing. You might start with common, everyday activities (eating, walking, working, talking) and then go on to consider more specific or unusual subjects (eating an ice-cream cone, playing soccer, delivering mail, singing in a church choir). For instance, a general activity such as "going to college" can be broken down into any number of more particular activities:

participating in class	using the library
studying for an exam	writing an essay
scheduling classes	dissecting a frog in biology lab
selecting a major	using computers

You should be able to fill a page or two with dozens of different activities.

Once you have plenty of potential subjects at hand, you can begin thinking about classifying approaches to one of them. Pick an activity from your list and ask the question, "What are some of the different ways people do this?" For example, what are some of the different ways people drive, shop, jog, bathe a cat, repair a muffler, or compose an essay? Then answer the question, briefly describing the different approaches. Here, for example, is how we might classify the ways people cope with a cold:

1. Some people are stoics: they dope themselves with medicine and bravely try to carry out their usual routines.

2. Some people are whiners: sniffling and moaning, they go to their classes hoping to get some sympathy from others.

3. Some people are hermits: they lock themselves up in their rooms and feel miserable all on their own.

Your aim is to identify approaches that will help your readers either understand an uncommon activity or look at a common activity in a new light. What you want to avoid, therefore, are dull stereotypes and obvious classifications (good drivers, bad drivers, and average drivers, for instance).

See if you can identify *three* or *four* distinct approaches—a number that can be discussed adequately in a short essay. With some subjects, such as "Writing an Essay," you may come up with more than three or four approaches. If so, narrow the subject—to "Getting Started on an Essay," for example:

1. Some students make detailed outlines, trying to plan their essays carefully from the start.

2. Some spend a lot of time just thinking, trying to imagine that perfect opening sentence.

3. Some scribble like mad, gradually focusing their approach as they jot down whatever thoughts come to mind.

Look for the three or four most significant approaches, and make sure each one can be distinguished clearly from the others. At this stage, you might want to try classifying several activities before settling on one.

The activity you choose and the three or four approaches you identify will serve as your *classification plan*, a simple outline that will guide you in drafting an essay in later steps. Of course, you can always alter this plan as you go on to develop your ideas. But before proceeding to the next step, evaluate the sample classification plans in the following exercise, and then evaluate your own plan.

EXERCISE EVALUATING CLASSIFICATION PLANS

In a good classification plan, each approach you describe should be clearly relevant to your subject and distinct from the other approaches. In each of the three sample plans below, one approach needs to be eliminated because it fails to meet these criteria. Identify which approach should be eliminated and explain why.

1. The unsuccessful dieters in my office can be classified according to the ways that they avoid losing weight.
   a. The fad dieter switches from the Rotation Diet to the Guaranteed Grapefruit Diet to NutriSystem to the Jenny Craig Diet with astonishing regularity.
   b. The fake dieter enjoys boasting about her remarkable self-control almost as much as she enjoys dipping furtively into her desk drawer for Cheez Balls and Zagnut bars.
   c. The purgers, who usually deny that they are losing weight, maintain their emaciated forms through self-destructive behavior.
   d. The dietitian bores us all with information about Vitamin E, the rewards of bran, and the evils of cholesterol—and then orders a deluxe, double-cheese pizza for lunch.

2. Obnoxious moviegoers can be classified according to the way they behave in the theater.
   a. Some are party people, who travel in large boisterous gangs.
   b. Some are homebodies, who play rented films on their VCRs and never go out to the movies at all.
   c. Some are amateur critics, who deliver their reviews out loud during the movie.
   d. Some are repeaters—people who let you know they have seen the movie before by echoing dialogue and laughing *before* the punch line.

3. College students can be classified according to the way they behave during lectures.
   a. Some are scribblers, constantly taking notes without pausing to really listen.
   b. Some are sleepers, who have mastered the art of dozing with their eyes open.
   c. Some are attentive listeners, who follow the lecture carefully and take notes on key points.
   d. Some are stenographers, writing down every word the professor utters. ■

Step 2 *Explain and Describe Each Approach*

Once you have decided on a classification plan, you are ready to explain and describe each approach in a paragraph. Your aim is to *show* the approach to your readers, making clear what distinguishes it from other approaches. You may also want to comment on the advantages and disadvantages of the approach. Here we will look at some of the ways you can develop these explanations and descriptions in three or four paragraphs.

Begin each paragraph with a topic sentence that identifies a type of individual and the approach that person follows. To help your readers recognize and remember the approach, try making up a short descriptive label or nickname for each type. These identifying tags are underlined in the sample topic sentences below:

The <u>do-nothings</u> come to college to escape their parents and avoid hard work. . . .

<u>Tom Toucher</u> is the sort of conversationalist who just can't keep his hands off you while he talks. . . .

The <u>responsible hunter</u> is one who respects nature as much as he enjoys the sport of hunting. . . .

Don't be concerned if at first you have trouble coming up with an appropriate label or nickname: start working on the rest of the paragraph and soon a suitable tag should come to mind.

One way to support your topic sentence is with examples of the type you have identified. Briefly describe two or three individuals who represent the type. Consider this paragraph from a classification of relief pitchers in baseball:

<u>Fastball relievers</u> attempt to overpower batters, not trick them with surprise pitches. Ryne Duren, a reliever for the New York Yankees in the late 1950s, was one of the wildest as well as one of the fastest pitchers of all time. Firing one crazy bullet after another, he frightened batters into swinging at impossible pitches. Now and then a lucky hitter would connect for a home run, but far more often he would strike out swinging. Steve Bedrosian, a contemporary fastball reliever, has more control than Duren but can be just as intimidating. His speedballs have been clocked at just under one hundred miles an hour. Because fastball relievers tire quickly, they are usually called on to break up a rally, not carry a team through several innings.

Using two or three brief examples lets you show slight variations of a single approach.

Another way to develop a classification paragraph is to describe the approach of one typical character. Here is an example:

To the <u>Marathon Man</u>, jogging is more than just an exercise: it is a way of life. At six o'clock every morning and again at six in the evening, he is out pounding the pavement, always striving to increase his distance and decrease his time. Nothing can stop him. He misses meals, cancels dates, and skips classes to maintain his daily quota of miles. He jogs in searing heat and icy blizzards. Even a sprained ankle or damaged knee will only slow him down, not keep him indoors. On those rare occasions when he is not running, Marathon Man is either reading about his hobby (the late James Fixx is still his idol) or talking about it (with Marathon Woman, if he's lucky).

Unless you are deliberately exaggerating for humorous effect, make sure that the character you describe illustrates accurately the approach you have identified. As in any well-developed paragraph, the supporting details should clarify—not confuse— the point made in the topic sentence.

In addition to describing each approach in a paragraph, you may also want to interpret or evaluate it. That is, you may want to point out the good or bad effects of the approach, its advantages or disadvantages. Here is an example of a paragraph that both describes and interprets a certain way of behaving during a conversation:

> The bashful, darting glances of Mr. Shy-Eyes make conversation with him very unnerving. He looks over your shoulder, above your head, and at your feet, but never at your face. Sometimes you find yourself ducking and bobbing to meet his eyes, but he always manages to avoid making contact. The way he glances at his watch or looks up to the ceiling gives the impression that he wants to escape, but it's usually Mr. Shy-Eyes himself who prolongs the conversation. The truth is he is extremely self-conscious, and his darting glances are a sign of insecurity. Knowing this should make you more patient and sympathetic, but not any less uncomfortable.

Whether or not you choose to comment on the approach you describe will depend on both your subject and your purpose. In some cases, you may prefer to postpone your interpretations until the end of the paper. Or you may choose not to comment at all, letting your descriptions speak for themselves. Whichever strategy you choose, you should follow the same general pattern in developing all three or four of the paragraphs in this step.

No doubt, these paragraphs will be rough (you will have a chance to rework them as you compose a full draft in the next step), but they should let you see whether or not your classification plan is on course. Look over your paragraphs and make sure that each approach can be distinguished clearly from the others. If you find that your descriptions overlap or that you have wandered away from your subject, you will need to reconsider your plan and revise your paragraphs accordingly.

EXERCISE CLASSIFYING DETAILS

This exercise has been adapted from a student's classification of the ways people cope with a cold. First you will find short definitions of the three types of cold sufferer: *the stoic, the whiner,* and *the hermit.* Next are some descriptions of the three types, listed out of order. Match each description with one of the three types by filling in the outlines at the end of the exercise.

Coping with the Common Cold

Refusing to let a little cold get her down, the stoic numbs herself with Comtrex and tries to carry out her normal daily routine. . . .

The whiner also brings her cold to work, but not because she is tough: she is looking for sympathy. . . .

The hermit figures that the best cure for a cold is to stay home and coddle herself. . . .

1. She ends up sniffling in front of the television set all day, bored to tears and feeling guilty about having missed work.
2. When someone asks how she is feeling, she describes every symptom in detail: the nasal congestion, the watery eyes, and the aching bones.

3. Should a friend ask if she is feeling all right, she manages a brave smile and whispers, "I'll be just fine."
4. At lunchtime, she sneaks into a broom closet and falls asleep for the rest of the afternoon.
5. The worst part is that nobody seems to care: after all, as she is frequently reminded, "There's a lot of that going around."
6. She arrives at the office wearing sunglasses to hide her bleary, bloodshot eyes.
7. She shuts off the alarm, takes the phone off the hook, and pulls the covers over her head, but inevitably the daytime noises keep her awake.
8. Waiting for compassionate noises from her coworkers, she sits behind a row of medicine bottles and a big box of tissues on her desk.
9. She goes into the kitchen for a little treat, perhaps a chocolate doughnut or a few strawberries, but all she finds is an egg and a jar of pickles.
10. She spends the day sneezing and sniffling, moaning and groaning, and manages to accomplish not a jot of work.
11. Feeling as if her head has been stuffed with cotton, she finds it impossible to concentrate on her work or maintain a conversation.

Put the *number* of each example under its appropriate heading below.

The Stoic	*The Whiner*	*The Hermit*
a. _____	a. _____	a. _____
b. _____	b. _____	b. _____
c. _____	c. _____	c. _____
d. _____	d. _____	■

Step 3 | *Draft an Essay*

You are now ready to draft an essay made up of an introduction, at least three body paragraphs, and a conclusion. Following are some suggestions on how to develop and organize the different parts of your essay.

Your introduction, as in any essay, should clearly identify your subject—in this case, the group you are classifying. If you have narrowed your subject in any way (*bad* drivers, *professional* bowlers, *obnoxious* moviegoers), you should make this clear from the start. You may also want to provide some specific descriptive or informative details that will attract the interest of your readers and suggest the purpose of the essay. Finally, be sure to include a thesis sentence (usually at the end of the introduction) that briefly identifies the main types or main approaches you are about to examine. Here is an example of a short but effective introduction:

Thesis
It's a warm evening in July, and all across the country Americans are gathering to watch a game of professional baseball. Armed with hot dogs, they hurry to their seats, some in domed stadiums, others in small, minor-league parks. But no matter

where the game is played, you will find the same three types of baseball fan: the Party Rooter, the Sunshine Supporter, and the Diehard Fan.

Notice how this introduction creates certain expectations in the reader: the specific details provide a setting (a ballpark on "a warm evening in July") in which we expect to see the various fans described; the labels assigned to these fans (the *Party Rooter*, the *Sunshine Supporter*, and the *Diehard Fan*) lead us to expect descriptions of each type *in the order they are given*. A good writer will go on to fulfill these expectations in the rest of the essay.

Use the paragraphs you composed in the last step as the bases for the body paragraphs in your draft. Identify each approach in a topic sentence, and then go on to describe and explain it. Arrange the paragraphs in whatever order seems most clear and logical: from the least effective approach to the most effective; from the least common approach to the most familiar, or the other way around. Just make sure that the arrangement of your body paragraphs matches the arrangement promised in your thesis sentence. Here, in the body of the essay on baseball fans, you can see that the writer has fulfilled the expectations set up in his introduction:

Topic sentence   The Party Rooter goes to games for the hot dogs, the gimmicks, the giveaways, and the companionship; he is really not that interested in the ballgame itself. He is the sort of fan who shows up on a dime-a-brew night, often with a gang of fellow rooters. He tells jokes, hurls popcorn at the team mascot, applauds the exploding scoreboard, blasts an electronic horn whenever he pleases—and occasionally nudges a companion and asks, "Hey, who's winning?" The Party Rooter often wanders out of the park in the sixth or seventh inning to continue his celebrations with the gang in the car on the way home.

Topic sentence   The Sunshine Supporter, fortunately a more common type than the Party Rooter, goes to the park to cheer on a winning team and bask in its glory. When the home side is on a winning streak and still in contention for a playoff spot, the stadium will be packed with this sort of fan. As long as his team is winning, the Sunshine Supporter will be roaring at every play, waving his pennant and shouting out the names of his heroes. However, as his name implies, the Sunshine Supporter is a fickle fan, and his cheers quickly turn to boos when a hero strikes out or drops a line drive. He will stay around until the end of the game to celebrate a victory, but should his team fall behind he is likely to slip out to the parking lot during the seventh inning stretch.

Topic sentence   The Diehard Fan, although a strong supporter of the local team, goes to the park to watch good baseball, not just to root for a winner. More attentive to the game than other fans, the Diehard will study the stance of a power hitter, note the finesse of a quick fielder, and anticipate the strategy of a pitcher who has fallen behind in the count. While the Party Rooter is devouring a hot dog or dropping wisecracks, the Diehard may be filling in a scorecard or commenting on a player's RBI tally over the past few seasons. And when a Sunshine Supporter boos an opposing player for stealing a home run from a local hero, the Diehard may be quietly applauding the expert fielding of this "enemy" outfielder. No matter what the score is, the Diehard Fan remains in his seat until the last batter is out, and he may still be talking about the game hours after it is over.

Notice how the writer uses comparisons to unify the body of his essay. The topic sentences of the second and third paragraphs refer to the preceding paragraph. Likewise, in the third paragraph the writer draws explicit contrasts between the Diehard and the other two types of baseball fans. Such comparisons not only provide smooth transitions from one paragraph to the next but also reveal the sympathies of the writer: he begins with the fan he likes least and ends with the one he most admires. We now expect the writer to justify his attitudes in the conclusion.

Your conclusion gives you an opportunity to draw together the various types and approaches you have been discussing. You may want to offer a final brief comment on each one, summarizing its value or its limitations. Or you may want to recommend one approach over the others and explain why. Just make sure that your conclusion clearly reveals the purpose or value of your classification. Consider how successful the author of "Baseball Fans" has been in tying together his observations:

> Professional baseball would have difficulty surviving without all three types of fans. The Party Rooters provide much of the money that owners need to hire talented players. The Sunshine Supporters bring a stadium to life and help boost the morale of a talented team. But only the Diehard Fans maintain their support all season long, year in and year out. By late September in most ballparks, enduring chilly winds, rain delays, and humiliating losses, only the Diehards remain.

Notice how the writer hooks his conclusion back to the introduction by contrasting the chilly night in September with the warm evening in July. Connections such as this unify an essay and give it a sense of completeness.

Experiment with different strategies as you develop and organize your draft, but keep in mind this basic format: an introduction that identifies your subject and the different approaches; body paragraphs that describe and explain these approaches; and a conclusion that draws your points together and makes clear the purpose of the classification. As usual, you will have an opportunity to revise your draft in the next step.

EXERCISE EVALUATING ESSAYS

Read each of the essays below, and respond to the questions that follow.

Happy Feet

Dancing, like music, is a universal form of self-expression, but there can be no doubt that some people express themselves better than others. On a Friday night in Costa Rica, everyone seems to be dancing: young and old, natives and tourists, city folks and country folks. Though they all dance to the same Latin American music, they do not all dance in the same way.

To Maye, a city dancer, Friday night is the perfect time to go out to a disco to show off her dancing abilities. Starting early in the afternoon, she gets prepared by looking for a contemporary yet revealing outfit that will match her bright, colorful make-up, accessories, and high-heeled shoes. After spending three hours getting ready, she goes to the house of her friend, where all the girls set off to the disco together. Once they arrive, Maye and her friends look for a table located close to the dance floor. Because Maye's attractive presence cannot go unnoticed, she does not have any problems finding opportunities to dance. By the second song, Maye's fluent body and smiling face turn a simple way of dancing into a very sensual and provocative exhibition.

To Jamie, the American tourist, Friday is the day to go out to a disco to experiment dancing to the Latin music. She keeps on the same sweaty clothes that she has been wearing for a couple of days: sandals, a pair of faded jeans, and a Pearl Jam tee-shirt. Before leaving for the disco, she stops at the hotel lobby to see if any other tourists want to join her. Once Jamie and her new-found friends arrive at the disco, they head directly for the bar and order a round of Imperials. After downing a bottle or two of liquid courage, she proceeds to the middle of the dance floor and begins dancing alone. Because of her stiffness and inexperience, she spends the night stumbling over her feet like a helicopter spinning out of control. Looking greatly pained, Jamie turns dancing into an arduous chore.

Flor, the country dancer, spends Friday night with her boyfriend. Early in the morning, she hangs her disco clothes out on the clothesline. Her outfit consists of a polyester skirt, a cotton shirt with lace on the collar, a pair of boots, and a wide-brimmed hat. She needs little time to prepare. Early in the evening, Flor's long-time boyfriend arrives at her house and, after a polite conversation with her parents, escorts her to the disco. When they arrive, they head for an inconspicuous corner table under a low light. Throughout the evening, Flor allows her boyfriend to lead her through the intimate dance steps accompanying the most romantic songs.

No matter what group you are in, the contagious rhythm of the Latin music will surely move your feet.

1. (a) Does the introductory paragraph clearly suggest the purpose and direction of the essay? Explain your answer.
   (b) Compose a specific thesis sentence that could be added to improve the introduction.

2. Give at least three examples of the direct comparisons made between the approaches described in the body paragraphs.

3. Does the student provide enough specific details in the three body paragraphs? Explain your answer.

4. Is the concluding paragraph effective? Explain why or why not.

5. Offer an overall evaluation of the essay, identifying its strengths and weaknesses.

Shoppers

Working part-time at the Piggly Wiggly has given me a great opportunity to observe the way different human beings behave. I like to think of the shoppers as rats in a lab experiment, and the aisles as a maze designed by a psychologist. Most of the customers follow a dependable route, walking up and down the aisles, checking through my chute, and then escaping through the exit door. But not everyone is so dependable.

The first type of unusual shopper is one I call the amnesiac. He always seems to be heading down the aisles against the normal flow of traffic. He mutters things to himself, like "Peaches or potatoes? Doughnuts or Ding Dongs?" Of course, he has left his shopping list at home. When he finally makes it to my register and starts unloading the cart, he suddenly remembers the one item of food that brought him here in the first place. He then resumes his trip around the store while the customers waiting in line start to grumble impatiently. Inevitably, when it comes time to pay for the goods, the amnesiac discovers that he has left his checkbook at home. I don't say a word. I just void his receipt and tell him to have a nice day.

Even more annoying is someone I call the super shopper. You can tell that she plans her shopping trip days in advance. She enters the store with a pocketbook on her arm and a calculator in her hip pocket, and she carries a shopping list that makes the Dewey decimal system look downright chaotic. Like a soldier marching in a parade, she struts from one sale item to another, carefully organizing things in her basket by size, weight, and shape. Of course, she is the biggest complainer: something she wants always seems to be missing or mispriced or out of stock. Often the manager has to be called in to settle her down and set her back on course. Then, when she reaches my lane, she begins barking orders at me: "Twelve cents off on Jell-O! Put the ice cream in a plastic bag!" In the meantime, she stares at the prices on the register, just waiting to jump on me for making an error. If my total doesn't match the one on her calculator, she insists on a complete recount. Sometimes I make up the difference myself just to get her out of the store.

Senior citizens mean well, but they can also try my patience. One man stops by several times a week, more to visit than to shop. He wanders around the aisles slowly, pausing to read a box of cereal or squeeze a roll or sniff one of those lemon-scented room fresheners. But he never buys very much. When he finally comes up to the checkout, this old man likes to chat with me—about my hair style, his bunions, or that nice tune tinkling out of the ceiling speakers. Although the people waiting behind him in line are usually fuming, I try to be friendly. I don't think this man has anywhere else to go.

These are the three major types of unusual people I have encountered while working as a cashier at the Piggly Wiggly.

1. (a) Does the introductory paragraph clearly suggest the purpose and direction of the essay? Explain your answer.
   (b) Compose a specific thesis sentence that could be added to improve the introduction.

2. Does the student provide enough specific details in the three body paragraphs? Explain your answer.

3. (a) Suggest how the concluding paragraph might be improved.
   (b) Compose a more effective conclusion for this essay.

4. Offer an overall evaluation of the essay, identifying its strengths and weaknesses. ■

Step 4   *Revise and Proofread*

Let someone else read your essay and suggest ways you might improve it. Then revise the essay, using the following checklist as a guide.

REVISION CHECKLIST

❑ In your introduction, have you clearly identified the group you are classifying and your purpose in doing so?

❑ In your introduction, have you made an effort to attract the interest of your readers?

❑ Does your introduction contain a clear thesis that identifies the main approaches you will be considering?

❑ Does each body paragraph begin with a topic sentence that identifies and briefly explains a particular approach?

❑ Have you supported each topic sentence with specific informative and descriptive details?

❑ Have you drawn clear distinctions between different approaches?

❑ Have you arranged the body paragraphs according to a clear, logical plan?

❑ In your conclusion, do you emphasize the value of your classification or recommend one approach over the others?

❑ Have you proofread the essay carefully?

Passages

A. Here is the revised version of "Shoppers," an essay that you evaluated in the last exercise. Identify the numerous changes that have been made in this revision, and consider to what extent the essay has been improved as a result.

Shopping at the Pig

Working part-time as a cashier at the Piggly Wiggly has given me a great opportunity to observe human behavior. Sometimes I think of the shoppers as white rats in a lab experiment, and the aisles as a maze designed by a psychologist. Most of the rats—customers, I mean—follow a routine pattern, strolling up and down the aisles, checking through my chute, and then escaping through the exit hatch. But not everyone is so dependable. My research has revealed three distinct types of abnormal customer: the amnesiac, the super shopper, and the dawdler.

The amnesiac stops his car in the unloading zone, leaves the engine running with the keys locked inside, and tries to enter the store by crashing into the exit door. After dusting himself off and slipping through the entrance, he grabs a cart and begins hurtling down the aisles against the normal flow of traffic. "Peaches or potatoes?" he mutters to himself. "Doughnuts or Ding Dongs?" He has, of course, left his shopping list at home. When he finally makes it to my register and starts unloading the cart, he suddenly remembers the quart of milk or the loaf of bread that brought him here in the first place. He then resumes his race around the store while the customers waiting in line begin to grumble, tap their feet, and rattle the rack of *National Enquirers*. Inevitably, of course, when it comes time to pay for the goods, the amnesiac discovers that he has left his wallet and checkbook at home. Without saying a word, I void his receipt and lend him a coat hanger.

The super shopper has been planning her assault for days. She enters the store with a pocketbook on her arm, a coupon purse around her neck, a calculator in her hip pocket, and in her hand a shopping list that makes the Dewey decimal system look downright chaotic. With military-like efficiency, she trundles her cart from one sale item to another, carefully organizing them in her basket by size, weight, and shape. Rarely, however, does she make it through the store without a breakdown: either the Charmin has been moved to a different shelf or else some poor stockboy has forgotten to replenish a supply of Crunch-a-Munch. Usually the manager has to be called in to settle her down and set her back on course. Then, when she reaches my lane, she begins barking orders: "Twelve cents off on Jell-O! Put the ice cream in a plastic bag! Don't put the grapes in with the Ho-Ho's!" In the meantime, she stares at the prices blinking on the register, just waiting to pounce on me for making an error. If my total doesn't match the one on her calculator, she insists on a complete recount. Sometimes I make up the difference myself just to get her out of the store.

The dawdler wanders in as if he had been looking for the library and arrived here by mistake. He tours the aisles slowly, pausing frequently to read a box of Fruit Loops, squeeze a dinner roll, or sniff one of those lemon-scented rubber blobs of room freshener. However, he seldom ends up buying many of the things he picks up. When he finally strolls up to the checkout, the dawdler likes to settle in for a chat—about my hair style, his bunions, or that nice Johnny Mathis tune tinkling out of the ceiling speakers. Although the people waiting behind him in line are fuming, I try to be friendly, knowing that this must be the major social event of the dawdler's week.

To be truthful, most of the people who pass through my checkout are quietly efficient and polite—and a little bit boring. Though the abnormal ones may try my patience, they also help to make a dull job interesting. So, for your own amusement, keep an eye out for them the next time you pull into the parking lot of the Piggly Wiggly: a fellow trying to unlock his car with a coat hanger, a woman fussing at the bag boy for squashing a grape, and a sweet old man who may try to tell you about the arthritis in his knees or the expiration date of buttermilk.

(Diane Esposito)

B. In the following essay, Canadian journalist Enid Nemy illustrates some of the different ways that people eat some very common foods. Consider what Nemy's seemingly trivial examples may reveal about human attitudes and behaviors.

You Are How You Eat

There's nothing peculiar about a person walking along a Manhattan street, or any other street for that matter, eating an ice cream cone. It's the approach that's sometimes a little strange—ice-cream-cone-eating is not a cut-and-dried, standardized, routine matter. It is an accomplishment with infinite variety, ranging from methodical and workmanlike procedures to methods that are visions of delicacy and grace.

The infinite variety displayed in eating ice cream isn't by any means unique; it applies to all kinds of food. The fact is that although a lot of research has been done on what people eat and where they eat it, serious studies on the way food is eaten have been sadly neglected.

Back to ice cream, as an example. If five people leave an ice cream store with cones, five different methods of eating will likely be on view. There are people who stick out their tongues on top of a scoop, but don't actually eat the ice cream. They push it down into the cone—push, push, push—then take an intermission to circle the perimeter, lapping up possible drips.

After this, it's again back to pushing the ice cream farther into the cone. When the ice cream has virtually disappeared into the crackly cone, they begin eating. These people obviously don't live for the moment; they plan for the future, even if the future is only two minutes away. Gobble up all the ice cream on top and be left with a hollow cone? Forget it. Better to forgo immediate temptation and then enjoy the cone right to the end.

On the other hand, there are the "now" types who take great gobby bites of the ice cream. Eventually, of course, they get down to an empty cone, which they might eat and, then again, they might throw away (if the latter, one wonders why they don't buy cups rather than cones, but no point in asking).

The most irritating of all ice cream eaters are the elegant creatures who manage to devour a whole cone with delicate little nibbles and no dribble. The thermometer might soar, the pavement might melt, but their ice cream stays as firm and as rounded as it was in the scoop. No drips, no minor calamities—and it's absolutely not fair, but what can you do about it?

Some of the strangest ice cream fans can be seen devouring sundaes and banana splits. They are known as "layer by layer" types. First they eat the nuts and coconut and whatever else is sprinkled on top. Then they eat the sauce; then the banana, and finally the ice cream, flavor by flavor. Some might feel that they are eating ingredients and not a sundae or a split, but what do they care?

As for chocolate eaters, there are three main varieties, at least among those who like the small individual chocolates. A certain percentage pop the whole chocolate into their mouths, crunch once or twice and down it goes. Others pop the whole chocolate into their mouths and let it slowly melt. A smaller number hold the chocolate in hand while taking dainty little bites.

Peanuts and popcorn are a completely different matter. Of course, there are always one or two souls who actually pick up single peanuts and popcorn kernels, but the usual procedure is to scoop up a handful. But even these can be subdivided into those who feed them in one at a time and those who sort of throw the handful into the open mouth, then keep on throwing in handfuls until the plate, bag or box is empty. The feeders-in-one-at-a-time are, needless to say, a rare breed with such iron discipline that they probably exercise every morning and love it.

Candies like M & M's are treated by most people in much the same way as peanuts or popcorn. But there are exceptions, among them those who don't start eating until they have separated the colors. Then they eat one color at a time, or one of each color in rotation. Honestly.

A sandwich cookie is a sandwich cookie, and you take bites of it, and so what? So what if you're the kind who doesn't take bites until it's pulled apart into two sections. And if you're this kind of person, and an amazing number are, the likelihood is that the plain part will be eaten first, and the one with icing saved for last. Watch Oreo eaters.

A woman who seems quite normal in other respects said that although she considers her eating habits quite run-of-the-mill, she has been told that they are, in fact, peculiar.

"If I have meat or chicken and a couple of vegetables on a plate, I go absolutely crazy if they don't come out even," she said. "I like to take a piece of meat and a little bit of each vegetable together. If, as I'm eating I end up with no meat and a lot of broccoli, or no potatoes and a piece of chicken, it drives me mad."

A man listening to all this rolled his eyes in disbelief. Peculiar is putting it mildly, he said. He would never eat like that.

How does he eat?

"One thing at a time," he said. "First I eat the meat, then one of the vegetables, then the other. How else would you eat?"

(Enid Nemy)

Questions

1. Explain how the introductory paragraph establishes Nemy's *attitude* toward her topic as well as the purpose of the essay. What do you think *is* the purpose of Nemy's essay?

2. Does Nemy adequately prepare the reader for the change in subject from ice cream to chocolate?

3. Based on your own observations, provide some additional examples of different approaches to eating particular foods.

Postscript

Classification is a basic way of organizing our lives as well as our writing. Just as we rely on certain classification plans to arrange the clothes in our bedroom and the food in our kitchen, we can use classification to break down any large subject into types or parts. Used carelessly, classification is just a form of stereotyping—a lazy substitute for examining the way people and things really are. But used thoughtfully, classification can help us achieve a better understanding of the subjects we study and the people we know. In our writing, classification is a way of presenting these insights clearly.

CHAPTER THIRTEEN

Issues
(Argument)

Preview

In this assignment, you will explain and defend your position on some controversial issues. First, you will explore your topic, considering both sides of the issue before preparing your essay plan. Then, guided by this simple outline, you will draft three or four paragraphs in support of your argument. Next, you will incorporate these paragraphs in a complete essay. Finally, you will revise and proofread your essay.

Step 1 | ## *Explore Both Sides of the Issue*

What are the important issues now being discussed on your campus or in your community—a change in the drinking laws? a revision of the honor code? a proposal to construct a new gymnasium or close a notorious nightspot? Consider issues being debated by columnists in the local paper or by your friends over lunch. And then prepare to explore one of these issues, examining both sides of the argument before you outline your own position.

Probably the best way to get started, either on your own or with others, is to list several possible topics for this assignment. Jot down any number of current issues, whether or not you have formed strong opinions on them. Just make sure that they *are* issues—matters open to discussion and debate. For example, "Cheating on College Examinations" is hardly an issue: few would dispute that cheating is wrong. More controversial, however, would be a proposal that students caught cheating should automatically be dismissed from college.

As you list possible topics, keep in mind that your eventual aim is not simply to vent your feelings on an issue but to support your views with valid information. Therefore, it would be wise to avoid topics that are highly charged with emotion or just too complicated to be dealt with in a short essay—topics such as abortion or capital punishment or a freeze on nuclear weapons. Now, this doesn't mean you must limit yourself to trivial issues or ones you care nothing about. Rather, it means you should consider topics you *know* something about and are prepared to deal with thoughtfully in a short paper. A well-supported argument on the need for a campus day-care center, for instance, would be much more effective than a collection of vague opinions on the need for a world government.

Once you have listed several possible topics, select one that appeals to you, and freewrite on this issue for ten or fifteen minutes. Put down some background information, your own views on the issue, and opinions you have heard from others. You might then join a few other students in a brainstorming session: invite ideas on *both* sides of the issue, and list them in separate columns. As an example, here are some notes taken during a discussion of a proposal that students should not be required to take physical-education courses:

Pro (Support Proposal)	Con (Oppose Proposal)
1. PE grades unfairly lower the grade-point averages of some good students.	1. Physical fitness is an important part of education: "A sound mind in a sound body."
2. Students should exercise on their own time outside of college.	2. Students need an occasional break from lectures, textbooks, and exams.
3. College is for study, not for play.	3. A few hours of PE courses never hurt anybody.
4. One gym course can't turn a poor athlete into a good one.	4. What good is improving your mind if your body is falling to pieces?
5. Do taxpayers realize they are paying for students to bowl and play badminton?	5. PE courses teach some valuable social skills.
6. PE courses can be dangerous.	6. Most students enjoy taking PE courses.

As you can see, some of these points are repetitious, and some appear more convincing than others. As in any good brainstorming session, ideas have been proposed, not evaluated. By first exploring your topic in this way, considering both sides of the issue, you should find it easier to focus and plan your argument.

Focusing your argument means taking a stand on the issue. Express your point of view in a one-sentence proposal, such as the following:

Proposal: Students should (*or* should not) be required to pay for a campus parking permit.
Proposal: Students should (*or* should not) be required to take physical-education courses.

Of course, as you develop your paper in the next few steps, you are likely to reword your proposal or even change your position on the issue. For now, though, this simple statement will guide you in planning your approach.

Planning the argument means deciding on the three or four points that best support your proposal. You may find these points in the lists you have already drawn up, or you may combine certain points from these lists to form new ones. Compare the points below with the ones given earlier on the issue of required physical-education courses:

Proposal: Students should not be required to take physical-education courses.

1. Although physical fitness is important for everyone, it can be achieved better through extracurricular activities than in required physical-education courses.

2. Grades in physical-education courses may have a detrimental effect on the GPAs of students who are academically strong but physically weak.

3. For students who are not athletically inclined, physical-education courses can be humiliating and even dangerous.

Notice how the writer has drawn on both of his original lists, "pro" and "con," to create this three-point plan. Likewise, you may support a proposal by arguing *against* an opposing view as well as by arguing *for* your own.

As you draw up your list of key arguments, you should also be thinking ahead to the next step, in which you must support each of these observations with specific facts and examples. In other words, you must be prepared to prove your points. If you are not ready to do that, you should explore your topic further, either with the help of other students in another brainstorming session or by researching your topic in the library. Remember that feeling strongly about an issue does not necessarily enable you to argue about it effectively. If, at this point, you don't know enough about the issue to develop an argument, you need to gather more information or find another topic that you are more familiar with.

EXERCISE EXPLORING BOTH SIDES OF THE ISSUE

Either on your own or in a brainstorming session with others, explore at least five of the issues below. Jot down as many supporting points as you can, both in favor of the proposal and in opposition to it.

1. A year of national service, with low pay, should be required of all eighteen-year-olds in America.

2. College students should have complete freedom to choose their own courses.

3. A student convicted of cheating on an exam or an outside assignment should be automatically dismissed from college.

4. All states should follow Nevada's lead and legalize prostitution.

5. Americans should be required by law to vote.

6. Grades given in physical-education courses should not be figured into a student's grade point average.

7. The production and sale of cigarettes should be made illegal.

8. Letter grades should be abolished in all college courses and replaced by grades of pass or fail. ■

Step 2 *Draft Paragraphs in Support of Your Argument*

Now, guided by the plan you drew up in the last step, you will draft three or four paragraphs in support of your proposal. These paragraphs need to be developed with information that is specific, accurate, and relevant to your argument.

Use each sentence in your argument plan as the basis for the topic sentence of a paragraph. Then support this topic sentence with specific facts or examples. Here, for instance, a writer has used statistics to support her argument:

Proposal: A mandatory seat-belt law should be enacted by the state legislature.

> According to a study cited in the *AMA News* of January 1986, traffic fatalities have been reduced in all states that have passed a seat-belt law. In New York and Michigan, for example, the number of fatalities has dropped twenty-eight percent since the laws went into effect in early 1985. In Illinois, there was a twenty-seven percent drop in traffic fatalities in August and September of 1985 as compared to those same months, before the law took effect, in 1984. Even the smallest improvement, a thirteen percent decline in fatalities in New Jersey, has been remarkable (Lesky 27–28).

If you rely on books or magazine articles for supporting information, as this writer has done, be sure to identify your sources and present the information accurately.

Sometimes the best way to support your own argument is to refute—or show the weaknesses of—an opposing argument. In this paragraph, for example, a writer uses historical facts to discredit a view contrary to his own:

Proposal: "America the Beautiful" should not replace "The Star-Spangled Banner" as our national anthem.

> People who dismiss "The Star-Spangled Banner" as "un-American" because its tune derives from an English drinking song must be unaware of the anthem's genuine American roots. During the War of 1812, Washington lawyer Francis Scott Key heard that a friend had been captured by the British navy, which was anchored off Baltimore's coast. Bravely, he sailed out to obtain a promise of release, but the British were about to bombard Fort McHenry, and so Key and his companions were detained for a week. During the night of September 13, 1814, Key watched o'er the ramparts expecting the fort to fall. At dawn, to his surprise and joy, the giant flag was still there, and he began to write his heroic poem. It was published as a handbill, paired with the English melody, and so became popular throughout the new nation.

Be fair when you refute an opposing argument: use facts to bolster your case, not insults or sarcasm.

In some cases, the most effective support for your argument may be examples drawn from your own observations or experience. In the following paragraph, the writer mentions her own experience not to complain about a personal problem but to illustrate her argument:

Proposal: The college Writing Center should be open in the evening as well as during the day.

For many students, evening is the only time they are free to visit the Writing Center. My schedule, I think, is a typical one. I am in classes from eight through twelve every morning, and then I must dash off to work, which keeps me busy until six. Some students, such as my sister, keep an opposite schedule (work in the morning, classes in the afternoon), and they, too, are unable to visit the center during its current operating hours. Opening the Writing Center in the evening would benefit many of the students who hold part-time jobs.

Although one or two examples such as we have here do not necessarily *prove* an argument, they can help to demonstrate and clarify a point. The more specific your facts and examples are, the more convincing your argument is likely to be.

In addition to being specific, the support you provide in each paragraph should be accurate and clearly related to your proposal. You risk undermining your argument if the information you give is false or irrelevant. Consider, for example, what makes this paragraph ineffective:

Proposal: Students should not be required to take physical-education courses.

Activity courses such as volleyball, wrestling, and tennis often lead to serious physical injuries. My roommate, for instance, suffered a sprained ankle last semester while diving for a tennis ball. Similarly, I have heard of a student whose arm was broken in a wrestling match. Why, even dining in the cafeteria can be dangerous: I cracked my knee once when I slipped on a puddle of milk. Studies have shown that over half of the students enrolled in American colleges end up with some sort of physical disability as a result of their participation in physical-education courses.

It's unlikely that anyone would be convinced by this argument. One sprained ankle and the rumor of a broken arm do not support the observation that activity courses "*often* lead to *serious* physical injuries." In fact, the writer fails to make clear whether or not these injuries even occurred in class. And, certainly, the cafeteria accident is altogether irrelevant to the argument. Finally, the studies referred to in the last sentence sound very suspicious indeed. If the writer cannot be more specific about who conducted the studies and where they were reported, we must conclude that they exist only in his imagination.

Your aim in this step is to draft three or four paragraphs on separate points in support of your proposal. You will, of course, have a chance to revise these paragraphs in the next step. Before proceeding, however, make sure that you have developed your paragraphs with information that is accurate, specific, and relevant to your argument.

EXERCISE EVALUATING SUPPORT IN PARAGRAPHS

As you have just seen, each point given in support of an argument needs to be developed with information that is *accurate, specific,* and *relevant* to the argument. Guided by these standards, decide whether each paragraph below is effective or ineffective, and explain why.

1. *Proposal:* College students should be required to study at least one foreign language.

Students who graduate from college without having learned a foreign language will be severely handicapped in the job market. Few companies today will even consider hiring an applicant who knows no language other than English. Whether a person wants to be an engineer with AT&T, a systems analyst with Xerox, or an inventory clerk at Rose's Discount Emporium, he or she must be able to read, write, and speak fluently at least one foreign language. The vast majority of graduates who lack this knowledge end up on welfare and must be serviced by the state for the rest of their days.

2. *Proposal:* Armstrong State College should sponsor a day-care center on campus.

A campus day-care center would benefit not only parents who attend Armstrong but also students who are in the Department of Education. Dr. Battiste, a senior professor in the Department of Education, points out that such a center would be a valuable training ground for students majoring in elementary education. By giving students an opportunity to observe child development and participate in the actual teaching of the children, a day-care center would be well worth the expense. "Such a service," she argues, "would help us to prepare prospective teachers for the difficult job of working day in and day out with young children."

3. *Proposal:* The United States government should not legalize marijuana.

The legalization of marijuana would have disastrous effects on our country's well being. It would rip apart our moral fibers. It would be harmful to people of all ages, young and old. Legalizing marijuana would be damaging to white and black, rich and poor, Democrat and Republican. Certainly, it would have a serious effect on our school systems, which are already in a sorry state of decline. In addition, the economy would suffer.

4. *Proposal:* The college should not withdraw its support of fraternities.

The fraternity system actively supports worthwhile causes throughout the community. In the past few months alone, it has raised over $23,000 for the Leukemia Society, and its members have spent many afternoons raking leaves for the elderly in town. Fraternity members have held carnivals for homeless children, supported a fund-raising drive for the Special Olympics, and helped clear land at the local Boys Club. There are now plans to build a playground for children in a community housing project and provide tutors for the local literacy program.

5. *Proposal:* Sex education should be taught at all levels in the public schools.

Sex education would be a very informative class for many young students. The human body is such a fascinating subject. We pay so much attention to our appearance, and yet very few of us really know what is going on inside. Sex is interesting to people of all different ages, and most students would enjoy the class more than arithmetic, for example. Sex education would give young people a much better understanding of sex. ■

Step 3	# Draft an Essay

You are now ready to draft an essay made up of an introduction, at least three body paragraphs, and a conclusion. Following are some suggestions on how to develop and organize the different parts of your essay.

Briefly yet clearly, your introduction should provide whatever background information your readers will need in order to understand the issue and the position you are taking. If you are arguing against a particular policy, you should let your readers know what that policy is. If you are recommending a course of action, you should explain the circumstances that make such action necessary. You might also find it helpful to explain one or more key terms in your argument. If, for instance, you are arguing that "Cheating should be grounds for dismissal from college," you ought to explain what you mean by *cheating*. Above all, your introduction should contain a thesis that clearly states your position. The following introduction moves smoothly from an explanation of a current policy to a thesis advocating a change in that policy:

> Students living in the college residence halls are currently required to purchase a meal plan from one of the three cafeterias on campus. The only choice these students have is between a five-day meal plan costing $1,071 per academic year and a seven-day plan costing $1,275. For students who are able to eat all of their meals at the cafeteria, this arrangement is quite fair: the food is adequate and the prices are
> **Thesis** reasonable. <u>However, the meal-plan policy discriminates against the many students in the residence halls who are unable or who do not want to take full advantage of the cafeteria's services, and therefore, the current policy should be abolished.</u>

You may also want to include in the introduction a brief statement of your qualifications in regard to the issue. If you have had experience that gives you some claim to authority on your subject, it may strengthen your argument to say so from the start. On the other hand, if you feel that revealing your involvement in the issue might prejudice readers against your position, you may want to withhold this information until you have had an opportunity to argue your case.

Use the paragraphs you composed in the last step as the bases for the body paragraphs in your draft. In a topic sentence, identify each of your main points— whether in support of your own position or in refutation of an opposing position— and then go on to develop the point with specific facts, explanations, or examples. Arrange the paragraphs in whatever order seems most clear and logical. You may choose to refute your opponents' arguments first and then proceed to support your own, or vice versa. In any case, your last point will probably be your strongest one, thus providing a strong lead-in to your conclusion. Here, in the body of the essay on the meal-plan policy, notice how the writer moves from exceptional cases to more common ones:

Topic sentence <u>The current policy is unfair to students on restricted diets.</u> My roommate, for instance, has an allergy to soy products that prevents her from enjoying such cafeteria staples as Swedish meatballs, burgers, meatloaf, and shepherd's pie. Likewise, an Indian friend of mine, who is a vegetarian, has had great difficulty in adapting to the all-American menu at the cafeteria. And hundreds of fee-paying students who are watching their weight must avoid the calorie-rich foods that are regularly served. All of these people have to spend additional money to prepare their own meals in the dorm kitchen.

Topic sentence

The mandatory meal-plan policy also discriminates against students whose work or class schedules conflict with the serving hours at the cafeteria. This term, for instance, my work-study job at the library runs from 4:00 to 8:00 every evening, while dinner at the cafeteria runs from 5:00 to 7:00. Although I have already been forced to pay for dinners at the dining hall, I do not get to enjoy them. Instead, I pick up a sandwich from the Sub Shop or make do with a snack in my room. My boyfriend has a similar problem at lunchtime. Because his chemistry lab runs from 11:00 to 1:45 every Tuesday and Thursday, he has to sustain himself on those days with candy bars from the vending machines in the union building. Many students are in this position of having to pay for meals they are not free to eat.

Topic sentence

Finally, even some of the students who are able to eat most of their meals at the cafeteria are unhappy about having to do so. According to a survey reported in last Tuesday's *Inkwell*, close to forty percent of students living in the residence halls would not eat most of their meals at the cafeteria if they were not required to purchase a meal plan. Most would prefer to have the option of eating at one of the fast-food restaurants in town or preparing their own meals in the dormitory. Certainly, even a date at Burgerland is more intimate than one at the cafeteria. However, because these students have already invested in a meal plan, they are reluctant to pass up what they have already paid for to spend additional money elsewhere.

Notice that the writer uses examples in the first two body paragraphs to demonstrate how the policy discriminates against particular students. Then, in the third paragraph, she broadens the argument, citing a survey from the college newspaper to show that a large number of students are displeased with the policy. We now expect her to state in the conclusion just how the policy should be changed.

Use your concluding paragraph to drive home the main point of your argument. You may reemphasize points you have already made or explain briefly how a recommendation should be carried out, but above all, be sure to end with your main idea. In the concluding paragraph of the meal-plan essay, the writer first deals with an opposing argument and then restates her key point:

I understand the reasoning behind the mandatory meal-plan policy: cafeteria prices can be kept low only if all students are made to participate. In practice, this means that students who do not eat all of their meals at the cafeteria are supporting those who do. This situation is obviously unfair. Therefore, the current policy should be abolished, even if it means raising the cost of meals. Students living in the residence halls should be given several meal-plan options, among them the option not to dine at the cafeteria at all.

By conceding a point to your opponents (as the writer has done here in stating that meal prices may rise), you can strengthen the force of your own argument. You will show that you have thought about the issue carefully and weighed both sides before delivering your point of view.

As you draft your essay, experiment with different ways of developing and arranging your material until you find an approach that is clear, logical, and convincing. But, as always, be guided by the basic essay format: an introduction that identifies your position on the issue; body paragraphs that provide specific, relevant support for your main points; and a conclusion that reemphasizes your central idea. In the next step, you will have an opportunity to revise your draft.

EXERCISE EVALUATING ARGUMENT ESSAYS

Respond to the questions that follow the essay below.

Time for a New National Anthem

Francis Scott Key was a Washington lawyer who witnessed the bombardment of Fort McHenry by the British in September 1814. The fort withstood the attack, and the sight of the American flag still waving "in dawn's early light" inspired Key to write the four verses of "The Star-Spangled Banner." He set the words to the tune of an eighteenth-century English drinking song. Over a century later, on March 3, 1931, an act of Congress designated "The Star-Spangled Banner" as our national anthem. Ever since then, people have been complaining about both the words and the music of our anthem. Some are bothered that the first stanza ends in a question. Others are troubled by all the depressing references to war, such as, "Their blood has washed out their foul footsteps' pollution." A lot of people don't even know what the lyrics are about. On top of that, the song is very difficult to sing. The low notes are too low, and the high notes are too high. For all of these reasons, people have recently been talking about replacing "The Star-Spangled Banner" with a new national anthem. Many different songs have been considered, but the best choice is "America the Beautiful."

"America the Beautiful" would make an excellent national anthem. Already it is very popular in our ball parks, school assemblies, and official state functions. The music is simple, dignified, and easy to sing. The lyrics celebrate our heroes, our future, and our land. The song expresses pride in America, but it is not warlike. It is idealistic, like the American people themselves.

Certainly, "America the Beautiful" is more popular than "The Star-Spangled Banner." "The Star-Spangled Banner" is hard even for professional singers to sing. It has a range of twelve notes, three more than "America the Beautiful." No matter what key it starts in, it ends up going too high or too low for most people. The lyrics are all about war, and they are very confusing in places. I doubt if anyone knows what these lines mean:

> No refuge could save the hireling and
>   slave
> From the terror of flight or the gloom of
>   the grave.

And does anybody really believe that red rockets and bursting bombs express the true spirit of America?

Other songs have been suggested as replacements for "The Star-Spangled Banner," but clearly "America the Beautiful" is the best choice. There is "The Battle Hymn of the Republic," but that is also all about war, and "The Stars and Stripes Forever" doesn't have any lyrics to accompany it. I suppose "My Country 'Tis of Thee" is nice enough, but the British have already used the music for their national anthem. Some people would like to see a more modern song adopted, such as "Born in the U.S.A.," by Bruce Springsteen. But can you imagine what it would be like to start a ballgame with the line, "You end up like a dog that's been beat too much"!

1. (a) The introductory paragraph of "Time for a New National Anthem" could be improved through revision. Point out the problems you see in this introduction.
   (b) Based on your reading of the whole essay, revise the introduction to "Time for a New National Anthem." You may add important information and eliminate any unnecessary details.

2. Are you satisfied that the author of "Time for a New National Anthem" has arranged the body paragraphs clearly and logically? (Briefly explain your response.)

3. Provide an overall evaluation of this essay by responding to the following questions. Is the argument convincing? Are the main points adequately supported? Does the conclusion emphasize the writer's central idea? (You may include suggestions on ways to improve the essay.)

4. Based on your reading of the whole essay, write a new conclusion to "Time for a New National Anthem," one that emphasizes the main point of the writer's argument. ■

Step 4　Revise and Proofread

Let someone else read your essay and comment on the effectiveness of your argument. Then revise the essay, using the checklist below as a guide.

REVISION CHECKLIST

❑ In your introduction, have you clearly identified the issue and provided any background information your readers might need?

❑ If you need to explain any key terms in your argument, have you done so in your introduction?

❑ Does your introduction contain a thesis that clearly states your position?

❑ Does each body paragraph begin with a topic sentence that identifies a main point—either in support of your own position or in refutation of an opposing position?

❑ Have you supported each topic sentence with information that is accurate, specific, and relevant to the argument?

❑ Have you arranged the body paragraphs clearly and logically, using signal words and phrases to guide your readers?

❑ Does the concluding paragraph emphasize the main idea of your essay?

❑ Have you proofread the essay carefully?

Passages

A. Following is a revised version of an essay you worked with in the last exercise. Notice how the writer has shortened the introduction, rearranged the body paragraphs, provided more detailed support, and added a new conclusion. Consider the extent to which these changes are consistent with the revisions and recommendations you made in the exercise.

Time for an Anthem the Country Can Sing

The music was composed as a drinking song for an eighteenth-century London social club. The words were written in 1814 by Francis Scott Key to commemorate a battle. And on March 3, 1931, "The Star-Spangled Banner" officially became our national anthem. Ever since then, people have been complaining that the tune is unsingable and the lyrics are offensive. In response to these complaints, a bill was recently filed in Congress to replace "The Star-Spangled Banner" with "America the Beautiful" as our national anthem. For a number of reasons, this bill deserves wide support.

"The Star-Spangled Banner" is as painful to listen to as it is difficult to sing. Even professional singers have difficulty with its twelve-note span, rumbling at "Oh! say, can you see" and screeching at "the rockets' red glare." In a way, however, such rumbles and screeches are fitting, for the lyrics are bloody, confusing, and war-stained. Does anyone really believe that red rockets and bursting bombs express the true spirit of America? And all that talk of "the foe's haughty host," "the gloom of the grave," and "the war's desolation" is far from being rousing and inspirational.

Over the years, other songs have been recommended as replacements, but most of these are just as inappropriate as the present anthem. "The Battle Hymn of the Republic," for instance, is also a war tune, and John Philip Sousa's stirring march "The Stars and Stripes Forever" has no lyrics at all. "My Country 'Tis of Thee" is sweet and dignified, but the music belongs to the British national anthem, "God Save the Queen." And finally, among recent contenders, Bruce Springsteen's "Born in the U.S.A." has a terrific beat, but its lyrics are better suited to a requiem than to an anthem. Just imagine how disconcerting it would be to start a ball game with the line, "You end up like a dog that's been beat too much."

Clearly, "America the Beautiful" deserves to be our national anthem. For years now, it has been gaining popularity in school assemblies, at official state functions, and even in our ball parks. The music is simple, dignified, and—most important—easy to sing. The lyrics celebrate our history ("O beautiful for pilgrim feet . . ."), our land ("For purple mountain majesties above the fruited plain"), our heroes ("Who more than self their country loved"), and our future ("That sees beyond the years"). It is proud but not warlike, idealistic without sounding silly.

Oh! say, it's time "The Star-Spangled Banner" was put to rest. Surely our flag will continue to wave "O'er the land of the free and the home of the brave" without benefit of this windy tune. Let us have at last a national anthem that the whole country can sing. Let us sing, with pride, "America the Beautiful."

(Shelby Wilson)

B. In the following essay, author and educator Tertius Chandler seriously challenges the value of formal education. As you read, consider *how* Chandler supports his arguments, and consider whether or not your own educational experiences match those described in the essay.

Education—Less of It!

Will Durant in his *Lessons of History* claimed that the greatest hope of the human race is increased education.

I venture to wonder why? School is unfree, rather like a jail with a term lasting twenty years, if you're able to stick the course. Childhood and youth are sacred times when innate curiosity is intense and health and zest tend to be strong. Those years are too important to be frittered away memorizing irrelevant trivia in herded mobs under the heavy hand of compulsion. Ben Franklin had just two years in school and flunked both times—yet he went on to make himself the ablest and best-rounded leader in our history. Pascal and Petrie had no schooling at all. So learning can occur outside school as well as in—perhaps even better, and especially now, when there are fine libraries open to all as well as television, bookstores, newspapers, and magazines. Think of the *National Geographic*!

Here on the other hand are arguments for education:

1. *Older people know more, so the young can learn from them.* Parental teaching might be preferable (and does increasingly occur), but in many families both parents are away at work. Anyway, teachers are specialists in particular subjects. These arguments are valid, and, it must be conceded, some learning does occur in schools.

2. *Money!* A school diploma is virtually useless on the job market, and so is a college degree. But school prepares for college, which prepares for postgraduate school, which prepares for entry into well-paid professions. In 1981 the average high school graduate made $18,138, whereas the average for those with five or more years of college was $32,887. Lifetime earnings for the high school graduates averaged $845,000, compared with $1,503,000 for five-year collegians.[1] Yet an underlying flaw vitiates the comparison, for college draws people of higher intelligence and those from richer families. Their lifelong earnings largely reflect these particular factors.

3. *The rah-rah spirit.* A person likes to say he or she has been to such-and-such college. It's the "in" thing.

4. *High ambition.* In this country of open opportunity parents naturally push their children all they can. It is refreshing to recall, however, that Washington, Lincoln, and Truman were among those who made it to president without going to college—and they were unusually good presidents.

5. *Culture.* The claim is often made that if culture wasn't rammed into the young, they would never come to appreciate literature, art, and fine music. Frankly, that's ridiculous.

6. *Meeting friends.* There are, of course, other places to meet people, and most of them allow more leisure to enjoy the friendship. Nevertheless it must be said that college is a fine place to make interesting acquaintances. Students are easily met in the dining halls and on campus. Eventually one may make friends even among the professors.

To sum up, education does pass on some learning and introduces a person to many out-of-town folks, while being the only way to enter some professions. But it takes a long, long time!

Conditioned Robots

Raymond Moore observes that: "The biggest shortcoming of mass education is the fact that students end up completely turned off to learning."[2] Or as Bertrand Russell ruefully concluded: "We are faced with the paradox that education has become one of the chief obstacles of intelligence and freedom of thought."

The educational profession has become geared to the College Board Examinations, which give it an awesome amount of rigidity. As a result, elective courses are rather few, and are becoming fewer even in college.

The number of school years is also prescribed. If a child masters mathematics in one year, so much the worse for him. Conversely, someone of low IQ has to suffer year after year with subjects that baffle him. Insofar as school is adjusted to anybody, it is adjusted to the mediocre student, and he, hopelessly unable to lead the class or win any prize, just drones on, loathing the whole procedure.

All that keeps the system from destroying the students altogether is that most of them instinctively rebel inwardly against it and cooperate only enough to get by, reserving as much energy and time as they can manage for other activities. Indeed, the most unruly boys in class sometimes tend to do better later on in life. Unfortunately some rebellious activities, such as smoking, heavy drinking, and fast driving, are not healthy, yet by a discreet degree of rebelliousness and shirking a boy can remain spiritually alive.

As Agatha Christie put it: "I suppose it is because nearly all children go to school nowadays, and have things arranged for them, that they seem so forlornly unable to produce their own ideas."[3]

Kahlil Gibran's great passage is relevant here: "Your children are not your children. They are the sons and daughters of life's longing for itself . . . you may give them your love but not your thoughts, for they have their own thoughts. You may house their bodies but not their souls. Their souls dwell in the house of to-morrow, which you may not visit, even in your dreams."

Gibran was not looking for conditioned robots.

A Shorter School Year

Some sadist must have written the law requiring 180 annual school days. They begin in August, when berries are still ripening, and last into the sweltering heat of June. Fall and spring, by their nature gorgeous seasons, become fixed in young minds as symbols of the agony of school.

It was when I was about halfway through prep school that teachers thought up a way to cut into the summer vacation—our only prolonged free time. They began assigning compulsory reading of novels. This was a grief and an indignity I will not easily forget. I had been reading the finest sort of literature on my own in the summers. After that I read the minimum—and hated it. Liberty dies hard in the human soul.

Change should be in the other direction: toward less schooling.

How Early?

Jean Piaget noticed stages in children's capacity to learn. To impose reading and mathematics on them before their minds are ready is to puzzle and torment them. School by its nature is force-feeding and, when children are very young, not only their bodies but also their feelings are very tender. To separate them from their parents and to inflict cold drill in seemingly pointless subjects on them can drive their feelings inward and make them feel unwanted and lonely, even in a crowded room. All this Piaget understood. Indeed, it is perfectly obvious.

But, Piaget added, give the students those same subjects a few years later, and they can grasp them rather quickly, because their minds have become equal to the techniques needed and because they have reached the stage where they can see a purpose in what they are doing.

Raymond Moore in his book *School Can Wait*[4] suggests delaying school to the age of eight or ten and in a recently published letter[5] opposes giving any exams before the age of ten. The idea is not new. A century ago Robert Owen withheld books from children in his famous school until their tenth year. Montessori, likewise, set the young to playing games. These are the real heroes for the cause of children.

Puberty

School treats pupils alike year after year. Yet somewhere in their teens boys notice girls. They are never the same again. School carries on as if the children were still just that. In the school where I went, aside from a warning to "stay pure," nothing changed. The hard drill on useless scholasticism to get us into college continued. We were to think college and nothing but college so that success in life would be automatic.

I got the message. When I was seventeen I met a girl I liked on a ski trip. I deliberately dropped her and by a hard effort, managed to forget her, since I still had five years before I'd be clear of college (actually nine, but I didn't know about postgraduate study then). That was a romance that should have gotten off the ground and didn't. Looking back, I see that I could probably have worked in the girl's father's factory. The father and mother liked me. I was past the compulsory school-age, which was then sixteen in my state—but nobody told me things like that. College was a fixation for my parents and my teachers, and therefore for me, too.

I was not unique. Bernard DeVoto told us in a talk at Harvard around 1935, "No one marries his first love." He meant among the highly educated, for of course some dropouts do marry their first choice. It was, anyway, a chilling remark, an unpleasant commentary on how the educational system impacts on youth. The trade-off of love for a series of degrees is a poor deal.

Lately, private schools have done a sudden about-face and flung the boys and girls together. They are aroused to love earlier and so have longer to agonize. Education and puberty thus now clash head-on, but they still haven't come to terms.

On Teaching English

English can be dropped altogether. Charles W. Eliot of Harvard and others put English into our schools in 1900 by making it a requirement for the College Board Examinations. Eliot's idea was that pupils can be compelled to present ideas clearly and to enjoy literature. He would drill these skills into them. The sheer quantity of disciplined effort would get results and turn our 18-year-olds into incisive, clear, witty writers.

The result of all this massive drill over nearly a century has been to make our youths somewhat duller than before. Our few famous writers now are notable for their gloom, their insobriety, and their utter inability to come up with answers to our problems. It would seem that English was made a required subject to no purpose whatsoever.

The correct way to teach English fundamentals—grammar, spelling, sentence structure—is to teach them as a part of other subjects. That way, English has a chance of being interesting. Just in this way, one teaches the use of a hammer in the process of teaching carpentry; one does not take a special course in hammering. It would be fiendishly dull if one did.

Mathematics

Ever since the Russians put Sputnik into orbit in 1957 there have been spasmodic efforts to increase the mathematics load of *all* U.S. schoolchildren, including future janitors, nurses, maids, and ditch diggers. While I respect those occupations, they do not require higher mathematics. Actually any useful computations for war or business will be made by a very few experts—perhaps by one-hundredth of 1 percent of the population—and they will be using computers.

Underwood Dudley of DePauw University, himself a mathematics teacher, believes that we teach mathematics not to solve problems or inculcate logical thinking but simply because we always have done so. As he puts it: "Practical? When was the last time you had to solve a quadratic equation? Was it just last week that you needed to find the volume of a cone? Isn't it a fact that you never need any mathematics beyond arithmetic? . . . Algebra? Good heavens! Almost all people never use algebra, ever, outside of a classroom."[6]

He rightly adds that mathematical talent is very easy to spot early in life. Surely he is right that a special annual test should be held to see which students should be allowed to take mathematics beyond arithmetic—as an honor, not a requirement! The motivated proud few would then accomplish more than the slave-driven multitude.

Any School at All?

Once the need for school was clear. Back around 1800 schools were few and didn't take long, only four to six years. They taught basics and were almost the only place for the young to get books. Nowadays, alternative means of learning are plentiful. As already mentioned, they include public libraries, television, bookstores, newspapers, and magazines. These actually represent an overabundance.

If some state dropped schooling altogether, I wouldn't oppose it. (I would not wish this change to be imposed by the federal government however.)

Self-Reliance

Adult life calls for decision making and responsibility. These arise naturally at home but not in the educational system, where teachers make the decisions. A student, moreover, is competing against all the others, a self-centered attitude he will have to drop when he goes on to a job or into marriage.

Required Reading

In British colleges (but not schools!) the students pick their own reading. Here in the United States, students are told what to read and when to read it. Recoiling against this conformity, Professor Carl Sauer told us in his class at the University of California in 1939: "The required book list defeats its own purpose. Books should enable you to meet ideas, meet other personalities, if you like, appropriating from them what you can use, what you need. I don't think I remember a single thing I had to read as required reading for any professor in college. I think if I had had any share in the discovery of something, a few ideas would have stuck. . . . Doing things for instructors is basically not doing anything at all."

Do Universities Broaden Minds?

Does university training help or hinder in developing intellectual capacity to do highly original work? Among highly creative modern thinkers the following were formally educated: Montesquieu, Jefferson, Goethe, Macaulay, Marx, Freud, Schweitzer, Proskouriakoff, Champollion, and Gandhi. These did not go to college: Voltaire, Hume, Owen, Austen, Balzac, Jairazbhoy, Gibran, Tolstoy, Twain, and Shaw.

Bright people can teach themselves. As Henry Adams said, "No one can educate anyone else. You have to do it for yourself." There should, of course, be equivalency exams for the self-taught, as well as on-the-job training, for most professions.

Some would claim that if the youthful were encouraged to act freely, their initiative would be too great; that they would go berserk. But I think not: Most would marry, others would travel, invent, and carry on original work on all sorts of lines.

Early marriage could balance many of them so they could work better. It is worth remembering in this connection that among the young, idealism and faith are uncommonly strong.

Those destined for ordinary jobs don't need to learn anything taught in college, and many of them know it. They attend college because it's the thing to do. They tend to take "snaps" such as English literature or sociology. I see no objection to letting them enjoy themselves at private colleges if they want to.

Public universities should, I think, confine themselves to serious training. The number entering should be preset as in Sweden, so as to train the quantity of people needed to fit the estimated number of openings in each profession, always allowing for the rise of some persons via equivalency exams.

College represents now too much of a good thing. There are too many learned professors and section leaders to adjust to, too many books to hasten through at a set speed, too many years to plod away on the treadmill. A Ph.D. in history is now expected to take four to eight years—on top of the twelve in school and four in college. Perhaps, worst of all, the Ph.D. subject is deliberately kept small, so that the student will be able to claim mastery of something. Four to eight years of deliberate narrowing can have the effect of incapacitating him from ever taking a broad view of anything. The result of all this mental drill tends to be a mashed human, an eviscerated person. Only a very sturdy soul, such as a Freud or a Schweitzer, can come through all this and still retain the ability to think for himself. University study could, with no intrinsic loss, be shortened from eight years to four, and school could be limited to ages ten to fifteen.

These suggested reductions in compulsory education would have another powerful advantage: They might set our people's minds largely free, a result surely to be wished.

References

1. *Digest of Education Statistics.* Washington, D.C.: National Center for Education Statistics, 1982. P. 181–82.

2. Raymond Moore, *Parent Educator & Family Report*, August 1984. P. 6.

3. Agatha Christie, *Autobiography.* New York: Doubleday, 1978. P. 59.

4. Raymond Moore, *School Can Wait.*

5. Raymond Moore, correspondence cited in *Parent Educator & Family Report*, January 24, 1985.

6. Underwood Dudley, article in *San Francisco Chronicle*, April 28, 1984.

(Tertius Chandler)

Questions

1. Define each of the following words as they are used by Chandler in this essay: *zest, frittered, vitiates, prescribed, discreet, shirking, forlornly, compulsory, indignity, fixation, incisive, spasmodic, inculcate, eviscerated, intrinsic.*

2. Summarize Chandler's chief arguments against formal education, and then

(either on your own or with the rest of the class) evaluate each of those arguments.

3. Chandler supports a number of his points with brief quotations from a diverse group of authors. How convincing and effective is this method of support?

4. Which of Chandler's observations do you agree with? Which do you disagree with? In both cases, explain why.

Postscript

The basic strategies involved in writing a good argument essay are the same ones you have been following throughout this book: identify your topic, state your position, support that position with specific information, and arrange that information clearly and logically. You should now have confidence in your ability to write essays on a variety of topics and of various lengths. By keeping in mind the strategies you have learned here and by applying the skills you have practiced, you should be able to handle any writing assignments your college professors may give you.

CHAPTER FOURTEEN

Additional Essay Assignments

Preview

The essay assignments in this chapter offer variations on some of the topics and writing strategies introduced in earlier chapters. Although you are not given step-by-step instructions for each assignment, the guidelines provided should help you to apply techniques you have already practiced.

1. Daily Log (Description and Narration)

In a chronologically organized essay, compose a detailed report on your activities and observations during the course of a typical day.

Guidelines

This assignment calls for an expanded version of the report that you composed in Chapter One (*Observations*). Write a detailed report on what you did and what you observed during a set period of time—say, from waking up in the morning to going home at the end of the day. As you draft and revise your report, you may discover certain patterns to your activities and observations, which you may choose to highlight in the body of the essay and comment on in the conclusion. Although in some ways this assignment resembles an extended journal entry, put some effort into revising and editing your report so that it can be clearly understood by another reader.

The essay that follows takes us through one day in the life of a homeless woman, Collette H. Russell. Consider how the details in the first part of Russell's essay contribute to the force of her conclusion.

A Day in the Homeless Life

"Good morning, ladies. It's 5 A.M. Time to get up." Ceiling lights were suddenly ablaze. This message boomed repeatedly until nearly everyone was out of bed.

Two toilets and three sinks for 50 women; no toilet paper in the morning, invariably. Three tables with benches bordered by beds on two sides were our day room, dining room, and lounge.

Breakfast usually arrived at 5:45 A.M., too late for those who were in the day-labor van pools. They went to work on empty stomachs, and they were the ones needing food the most.

Breakfast generally consisted of rolls and sausage and juice until it ran out. The coffee was unique: It didn't taste like coffee, but that's what we had to drink.

At 6:30 A.M. we were ordered to go down to the lobby, where we joined 50 other women either standing or sitting on wooden benches awaiting the light of day. Some talked to themselves. Some shouted angrily. Some sat motionless. Some slept sitting up. Some jumped up and down, walking away and then returning. Some chain-smoked.

All of us had our belongings with us. Carrying everything every step of the way every day was hard on the arms, and I felt it was a dead giveaway that I was homeless.

At 7:30 A.M. the clothing room opened. It was shocking to be told "Throw away what you're wearing after you get a new outfit." No laundry, just toss out yesterday's garments. We were allotted five minutes to paw through racks looking for articles that fit.

I was always happy to see 8:30 A.M. roll around. Grabbing my bags, I headed down Berkeley Street away from the jam-packed, smoke-filled "holding cell." Always I felt guilty at not going to work like everyone else who hurried by as I approached the business district.

The main library was my daily stop. I positioned myself at a table where I could watch the clock: We had to return to the shelter before 4 P.M. to get in line for a bed, otherwise we might miss out.

Reading was the high point of the day. Escape into a book. There was relative privacy at a library table. It was heavenly. I hated to leave.

The clock signaled the task of trudging back, at 3:45 P.M., with even heavier bags. The bags, of course, were no heavier; they just seemed heavier.

Back in the "yard" I joined the group already assembled. Some women never left the grounds, staying all day in the small yard by the building. God forbid. With the appearance of a staff member we would form a line as the staffer prepared a list of our names and bed requests.

I was always glad when the lights went out at 9 P.M. and I could climb into bed (a bottom sheet and a blanket—no top sheet) and close my eyes and pretend I wasn't there but back in my apartment on the West Coast.

Twice I was robbed. Once a bag was taken. Another time my new blue underpants disappeared out of one of my bags. Who knew they were there?

Even if I were to do day labor at $4 per hour and clear $28 or so a day, how many weeks would it take to save enough for first and last months' rent on an apartment plus deposit and enough to pay for initial utilities? I was too depressed to even try to work and took frequent breaks to sit down while doing kitchen volunteer work. I was tired all the time.

The true stories I heard were heartbreaking. Which was the sadder?

One young woman with no skills and no job training had been OK financially until her CETA job ended—the program was abolished—and the YWCA raised its weekly room rate. She couldn't afford a room and couldn't find a job. She'd been in shelters for three or four years. I marveled that she was still sane. She did crossword puzzles while waiting everywhere.

Another older lady had held the same job for 10 years and would still have been working had not the corporation, without notice, closed up shop. She was 59 years old and out of a job, with a little severance pay and no help to find new work. She tried but was unsuccessful in finding a new job. She exhausted her savings after her unemployment ran out. One June day in 1987 she found herself homeless. No money for rent.

Both of these women are intelligent, honest, pleasant, clean, and neatly dressed. And both are penniless and homeless. How will they escape the shelters? Will they?

I got by, all right, by keeping my mouth shut around the staff and talking only with two or three women whom I knew to be sane and sociable. I was lucky. Two and a half months after I'd first gone into a shelter my son rescued me. I was on the verge of madness, so hungry for a little privacy and peace that I was afraid I'd start screaming in my sleep and be shunted off to a mental ward.

Now I've got a job paying more than I've ever earned. But I remember those days and nights.

No one should have to live like that. Too many do. And will, I fear, unless and until we who do have homes and jobs help them end their eternal, living nightmare.

(Collette H. Russell)

Questions

1. Define each of the following words as they are used in Russell's essay: *invariably, allotted, severance, shunted*.

2. How would you describe the *tone* of Russell's report? Does she seem to invite the reader's sympathy or is the essay marked by self-pity?

3. Within eighteen months after writing this report, Russell had lost her job and was back living in the streets. Nine months later she died alone in a motel room. Does this information alter in any way your response to her essay?

---

2. Mementos (Description and Narration)

In an essay, describe an item that reminds you of a particular event or experience from your past.

Guidelines

This assignment invites you to combine the strategies of description (from Chapter Two) and narration (from Chapter Five). Like the paragraph you composed for *Belongings*, this essay will include a description of an item that holds some personal significance. And like the paragraph you composed for *Growing*, the essay will also include the story of how the item became important to you. Following the example of the student essay below, you might describe the item in your introduction and then proceed in the body of your paper to relate the story that lies behind it.

My Superman Suit

There it hangs, my orange football jersey, worn and faded with spots of blood and paint. The smell of freshly cut grass intermixes with the salty smell of sweat— gentle reminders of its previous uses. Once I wore it as if it were a suit of armor, the orange color my coat of arms. I wore it in every game I played, whether it was football, stickball, or soccer. Now I wear it only when I'm mowing the lawn. But I can still remember how awkward I felt before I owned this magical jersey.

When I was twelve years old, living in Tampa, Florida, I began playing football on an open field across the street where the larger and older kids played. They were like giant redwoods towering over me, growling. I knew that these sixteen-year-olds could rip me to shreds. In fact, they often ripped my old school shirts to shreds. The fabric, almost as thin and weak as I was, would tear as easily as unbaked pie crust. After going through several shirts in just a few days, I felt like giving up.

Then, for Christmas, my sister Jacklyn sent me an official orange football jersey. It was love at first sight. Modeled after professional jerseys, it was made of the toughest fibers. Even the meatiest hand couldn't rip it. Just as important, its extra-large size gave the impression that I was much bigger than I really was. Putting on that jersey made me feel like Superman.

Under the afternoon sun, the orange jersey would shine as if the fabric had been threaded with gold. I could feel the adrenalin rushing through my body, my heart beating as if trying to pop out of my chest. Wearing that jersey, I was unstoppable. When I played football or any other sport, I became quicker, stronger, more aware of everything around me. I wasn't just a little twelve-year-old trying to keep from getting killed by the big guys. I was Superman.

I guess everybody has a lucky coin or a security blanket. But my jersey is much more than that now: it's part of my past. It represents my character, my willing-ness to do anything to win. Today I approach problems as challenges, overcoming them with either aggressiveness or finesse. So, when my friends ask me why I hold on to that old, worn-out jersey, I say, "That's not just a jersey. That's part of me." It is my past, every thread intertwined with my past accomplishments. The spots of blood represent the price I paid for victory, the spots of paint my clumsiness. So it hangs, seldom worn but never forgotten, my superman suit.

(Adam B. Butcher)

Questions

1. Why does the student refer to his football jersey as his "superman suit"?

2. What common needs and feelings experienced by adolescents are revealed in Butcher's narrative?

3. Show how Butcher blends specific descriptions of the jersey with explanations of its significance to him.

3. Experiences (Narration)

In an essay, relate an experience that led to a deeper understanding of yourself or others.

Guidelines

This assignment calls for a longer version of the sort of paper you wrote in Chapter Five (*Growing*). You will relate a particular incident, explaining where and when it occurred, who was involved, and exactly what happened. In your introduction, you should identify the experience and provide the necessary background information. In the body paragraphs, explain what happened in the order the events occurred. Use descriptive details to make your narrative vivid and interesting, and use time signals to guide your readers clearly through the sequence of events. In your conclusion, explain the effect the experience had on you.

In the following essay, the student has used precise details and an unusual number of short sentences in her recreation of a painful personal experience.

The Closet

It has been a long hot morning. Now, at two in the afternoon, the Santa Anas are blowing, and the air begins to cool our desert home. He's getting ready for work. He'll be gone for eight hours, and, if the baby's quiet, I will have eight hours of peace.

I've been in the kitchen preparing an early dinner. His four-to-midnight shift makes it impossible to sit and eat a "family dinner." I'm in a hurry again. Trying to make a four-course meal and a snack for his break is no easy task. Everything with him has to be perfect. Even his snack has to be a complete meal and yet altogether different from the dinner. I'm cooking chicken with rice and vegetables today. The salad is in the fridge, and for dessert we'll have some chocolate ice cream. For his snack, I'm making a ham and cheese sandwich. I add a pickle, a bag of chips, and some oatmeal cookies, and the snack is ready to place in the lunch pail.

While I'm right in the middle of frying the chicken, the baby starts crying. She's hot and wet. I take her to her room and change her. Then, while fastening a fresh diaper on Katie, I notice the burning smell coming from the kitchen. Tonight won't be as good as I'd wished. I hurry to the kitchen with my daughter clinging to my neck. In my panic, I've disturbed my other baby, the one yet unborn. The kicking seems anxious and tense. It's almost as if the child knows it's going to get rough. I put Katie into the high chair and turn to the stove, opening a pot. "Oh no, it's the rice again." He'll be furious. He's still in the shower; maybe there's time to make more rice.

The more I rush the harder things get. I tear open the bag, and the rice goes flying all over the stove, the floor, and even Katie's high chair. Unable to understand my distress, my daughter laughs at the sight of the explosion and mess. As if matters could get any worse, she throws down the uncooked rice as fast as I can sweep it up. The water in the shower shuts off. He's running ahead of schedule, but maybe he'll take his time getting dressed.

I can't help myself. I feel tears building up in my eyes, but I fight them. My face feels hot, and it's probably red. My face always turns red when I start to cry. "Don't cry," I say to myself. "You'll never get it right." So I close my eyes and try to regain my focus, my purpose. Hands shaking and sweat forming across my forehead, I try to continue. At this point my nerves are shot.

The new pot of rice isn't nearly ready. He comes around the corner expecting to see a complete meal sitting on the table. I can tell by the expression on his face (his eyebrows meet in the middle when he's angry) that he has caught the lingering scent of burnt rice. Without a word (I don't even have time to brace myself) with one swift movement of his arm, he hits me with the back of his fist. I can feel something trickling down my cheek—maybe tears. No, it's blood: tears are warm and taste salty. Even through the ringing in my ears, I can hear him yelling Spanish with a few derogatory English words, as if to be sure I understand. The anger in his tone is as painful as his physical contact. "¡Ay Dios mio, que gringa estupida, que puta!" ("Oh my God you stupid white bitch! Can't you get anything right?") I'm down on the floor as far into the corner of the cabinets as I can get. I hear him, but my numbness mode has been activated, enabling me to go to a place in my head where nothing he does or says can penetrate.

I'm feeling hands and boots. I know his anger is increasing by the intensity of the blows. "I'm not really here," I tell myself. I don't cry, and this seems to aggravate him even more. My next memory is that of being tugged at and then pulled down the hallway by my hair and an arm. The closet door slams shut. The lock turns.

The minutes seem like hours. Then he is opening the door. He places the baby chair on the floor, then the baby in it. Next to the chair he sets down three bottles in a large bowl of ice, and a box of diapers. Then one last blow to my head. I'm not sure if the next thud I hear is the door slamming again or my head hitting the wall behind me.

I wake up and think, "Thank God for walk-in closets." This one is about ten feet by five feet and has an exposed light bulb with a pull chain affixed to the ceiling. I've hidden some pillows and a blanket behind some boxes. I look at my sweet, beautiful daughter and wonder how long she's been asleep. There's no concept of time in here. I can't tell if the sun is still up, and I have no watch. Soon I hear the baby stirring. I change and feed her. She doesn't seem to mind the closet. I guess by now this has become just another part of the day for us. I'm hungry.

It must be twelve thirty in the morning: I can hear the door of the Blazer shut and then the keys unlocking the front door. I know he's in the kitchen (the refrigerator door squeaks) probably getting a beer. He must be smoking a cigarette, winding down before he decides whether or not to set me free.

The closet door opens. As if I'm not even there, he turns to Katie and lifts her from the chair. As he walks down the long hallway, he talks so sweetly to her, tossing and tickling her. The Spanish language can sound so soothing, and his tone has changed so much. "Mi niña, qui linda. Catalina es mi niña." ("My beautiful daughter. Katie is my baby.") He sounds loving and sweet toward her. I can only dream of the day that he speaks this way to me. He has no words for me now. I get up and follow him to the family room where he continues to play with Katie on the brown leather sofa. Then, as I turn to go into the kitchen, I see on the table a red rose and some Mexican take-out food. "He's sorry," I think to myself. "He'll never say it. He just tries to show it. He never says he won't do it again. We both know better."

I figure I lived in the closet for approximately one year and six months. My son was five and a half months old when I finally worked up the nerve to leave. I decided that the closet was no place in which to raise two beautiful children.

(Student's name withheld by request)

Questions

1. Although the student is recounting an experience from her past, she writes consistently in the present tense. What effect is created by her reliance on the present tense?

2. What purpose is served by the numerous precise details provided in the first four body paragraphs?

3. Many of the sentences in this essay are short, often abrupt. What effect is created by the student's reliance on so many short, simple sentences?

4. The experience recounted here is extremely personal and clearly painful. How would you characterize the *tone* of this essay—objective, self-pitying, regretful?

---

4. Rules (Explanation and Examples)

In an essay, list a number of rules or guidelines for others to follow when they are in your company.

Guidelines

At work, in class, and at home, we are all guided by certain rules of behavior: "No smoking," "No late papers," "Feed the cat." In this assignment, you will have an opportunity to provide advice or create rules for others to follow—rules to make life easier, more enjoyable, or less stressful.

Focus the topic by considering your audience. You may devise rules or guidelines for your coworkers or a supervisor, for your instructors or fellow students, for your roommates, friends, or family members. Identify your audience in the introduction to the essay, and explain the circumstances under which the rules will apply. In the body of your essay, explain each rule or piece of advice in a separate paragraph. Be as specific as you can. The basic organizing principle is the list form that you first practiced in Chapter One. You might conclude your essay by considering just how the rules you have drawn up could be enforced.

In the essay that follows, humorist Roy Blount, Jr., provides some advice for college students. As you read, consider the ways in which Blount's comic writing conveys, in places, some serious recommendations.

Gather Round, Collegians

Generally my advice to young people is, Don't listen to advice. I say that not only because it is something young people will listen to. I say it also because questionable advice ("Hey, organic chemistry will take care of itself") is always so much more appealing than sound advice ("Worry about everything").

But this year I am a sophomore parent. That is, my daughter Ennis is a sophomore at Stanford. That is, I believe she is. Since Stanford's policy is not to send grades, comportment ratings, or even bills, as such, to parents, her only connection with the university may be that she has a room, a mailing address, and a number of college-age-looking friends there. Of these things I have personal knowledge. (One of the friends, Chuck Gerardo, a gymnast, feels that he has invented a dance step called the Goober, which entails moving exactly counter to the beat. In point of fact I stumbled upon a subtler and rather more complex version of that step myself, quite a few years ago, and by now it has become more or less second nature—give or take a half-sh'boom—to me. You young people today aren't necessarily the first people in history to be hup. Hep.) And every so often I receive word from Ennis that she has made five more A-pluses and needs another $47,000 for gasoline, incidentals, and felt-tip pens. (We didn't have felt-tips in my day. We improvised: Q-tips and our own blood. We parents want to spare you all that—in fact, *don't bleed*.)

So I know, as surely as I know most things, that I am a sophomore parent. And it may be that there is no one who knows more about anything, aside from a sophomore student about life outside college, than a sophomore parent about life inside college. It may also be that I am being incredibly unassuming and gracious, as parents are, as you will realize when you are parents.

So if you would just stop darting your eyes around for one moment, please.

❑ Eat pizza. (See, you thought I was going to come down hard. Not at all. Parents do not come down nearly as hard as they have every right to, because parents came *up* hard, and are tired.) Chuck Noll, the head coach of the Pittsburgh Steelers, once told me that pizza contains every element of the human body. For a while this put me off pizza. But the Steelers won the Super Bowl that year, so Noll must have been right: There is no more perfect food. Even *gigot de français* (leg of Frenchman), say, does not contain *every* element of the human body. I don't think. You could check me on that, with your School of Medicine. Or Romance Languages. Oh, the banquet of knowledge that is spread out before you.

❑ Learn a trade. Even if it is something so highly technical that of course it makes us very proud of you, but perhaps is not the most considerate field you could have gone into, since how can we tell whether you are doing it right? Every moment that you aren't learning a trade, worry about why you aren't. This is known as pure thought. Or "unadulterated" thought, so called because adults cannot afford to indulge in it. By *trade* I mean something that will support aging parents, suitably, before you know it.

❑ Save mailing tubes. Those cardboard tubes. I tried to buy one recently, in which to mail someone something, and looked all over everywhere. I could have bought an expensive fancy plastic art-supply deal with caps on the ends, suitable for shipping a Caravaggio to the Vatican, but I didn't want that. I wanted just a regular cardboard tube, the kind you receive in the mail with something noninvaluable rolled up in it. I could not buy one for love or money. I had to learn this the hard way. You don't.

❑ Finish up in four years. Maximum. Every extra day after four years means another three months off your parents' lives. There has been a study on this. By a university. Whose bursar suppressed the findings.

❑ Don't keep small, gnawing pets, such as hamsters, in your room. Hamsters get loose and eat money. This is why college costs so much. *Why does college cost so much?* Oh, you want to change the subject! You want to know how my generation has managed to run up a $2,000,000,000,000 debt. Well, how else can we send you through college in 100 percent natural-fiber clothes? The natural-fiber money ran out! I'll tell you this: My college roommate insisted on keeping a hamster, and one night it got into my wallet and ate everything. It was a valuable lesson. There are some things we can't control. *But we can do without insidious little animals out there in the darkness gnawing.*

❏ Cling to eternal verities. This is all recent, you know, all these post-hyphen-you-name-it-isms. Post-modernism, post-vandalism, whatever. We didn't have any of them in my day, and we didn't exactly come to town on a load of rutabagas. Mark my words: These things will blow over.

❏ So will everything else. Except parents. Who will just get pitiful and die. But you let us worry about that. You just worry about how bad you are going to feel—too late.

❏ If some fad like riding five to a motorcycle backward or watching insect-monster movies for seventy-two hours straight while wearing nothing but feelers arises, hey, you're only young once. But think what it will do to your parents. They are only going to be middle-aged once, which is all they have left, and perhaps not for long. Call your parents. Talk to them— *about something else*— until the urge passes.

❏ On the other hand, what makes you feel the need to take sixteen courses in accounting? We're sending you to college so you can learn everything there is to know about the bottom line? You want to know about the bottom line? Call your parents.

❏ *Drugs.* Young people don't need to get high. Young people are already, *qua* young people, higher than they will ever be again, even tomorrow. Wait until you are seventy. There is no one more tickled with himself or herself than a seventy-year-old college graduate who *feels* seventy but who has not yet developed a tolerance for killer Nepalese mushrooms.

❏ *Politics.* I fully realize that the point of collegiate political activity is to make all the blood drain out of your parents' faces. Fine. Fair enough. But if anything involving heavy explosives ever comes back in style, remember that you will be alumni soon. For every $100,000 in damage done to campus property, you may count on receiving two dozen solicitations to contribute to the building fund. In demolitions, as in economics, there is no such thing as a free boom. On the other hand, before you plunge headlong into your Campus Young Arch-Reactionary Club, stop and think. Shouldn't *some* gratifications be deferred until you can no longer enjoy anything else?

❏ *Plagiarism.* This above all, to thine own self be true.

❏ *Extramarital relations.* Never marry your relatives. See? Parents can laugh about these things. As long as we are sure your heads are on straight. Once we realize that they aren't, we can never laugh again.

❏ Excuse me. Will you please stop doing that with your corneas when I am talking to you? Yes, your corneas. You know what I mean.

❏ Yes, you do.

❑ And don't expect to remember any of this, unless you write it all down. Right now. The older you get, the less you remember, even tomorrow.

❑ Any of what?

(Roy Blount, Jr.)

Questions

1. Define the following words as they are used in Blount's essay: *comportment, unassuming, insidious.*

2. Receiving advice from a parent is not always one of life's most enjoyable experiences. What particular strategies does Blount use in his first two paragraphs to maintain our interest in what he has to say?

3. Although many of Blount's recommendations are comical, what serious points does he succeed in delivering during the course of the essay?

5. *Profiles (Description, Examples, Narration)*

Write an essay-length study of a person you know well.

Guidelines

This assignment calls for an essay-length sketch of someone you know—or have known—quite well. Freewriting about the character should help you to get started. You might begin by describing the person's physical appearance and go on to give examples of certain outstanding character traits. In addition, provide some biographical information (such as age, occupation, and hometown) and include at least one short narrative that reveals some aspect of the person's character. Keep in mind that you are writing this essay for someone who has never met the person you are describing.

In the student essay that follows, notice how the introductory paragraph prepares us for the key qualities that are brought out in the rest of the paper.

The Tough Old Bird

"Genesis, Exodus, Leviticus, Riter Faye, gets on ta other side, so's we can gets 'em in betwenched us an' tha fence." I can still hear these words being bellowed at me by my grandma. She was a scrawny, whiteheaded little lady with a fiery temper, flour-sack dress, corncob pipe, and a still full of moonshine.

As kids, my brother and I would visit our Grandma Cornelison at her old country house. Really it was more of a shack, though we never had the courage to let Grandma hear us saying such a thing. Visiting was always an adventure: bathing outside in old metal washtubs, lighting kerosene lamps instead of flicking a switch, hand-pumping water in the kitchen, and going to an outhouse rather than a bathroom. We would lie in bed at night and watch through the cracks in the board walls as the fireflies darted to and fro, and finally, into the blackness. It was like stepping back a hundred years.

My most vivid memories are of motion. Grandma, at almost five feet tall, moving: running after a hog, chasing loose chickens, or chopping firewood. She was nicknamed "the little blast," and she lived up to every inch of the name.

Once, when I was about seven, we were having chicken and dumplings, my favorite meal. Before Grandma "readied it," she asked me to help get the chicken. I thought she meant get it out of the freezer; where else do you get a chicken? Heading out the squeaking back door and down the dusty dirty path, I wondered where we were going. The freezer couldn't be out here. Arriving at the ramshackle old chicken coop, with its rusting, sagging wire fence, I was breathless and no wiser to the location of the freezer. Grandma, with hands on hips and a sly smile, told me to go to the other side and we would corner Old Blue, the rooster. Now I was not only wondering about where the freezer was, but why in Grandma's name did we need a live chicken? But I did as I was told. You always did as Grandma said, if you knew what was good for your backside.

Slowly creeping toward the old rooster, we backed him into the corner with no trouble. A couple of steps more, and Old Blue began to dance. A little more, and he was squawking and prancing, looking for an escape route. Knowing that this was my chance to impress Grandma, I lunged for him. Amid the molted feathers and enraged clucks, I sprawled face first, just in time to have Old Blue jump lightly on my head, tiptoe down my back, and spur my rear-end. Getting to my feet, and wiping the egg from my face, I sighted my ornery little grandma sprinting around the deformed coop. She was bellowing the books of the Bible, and yelling for me to get to the other side "so's we can gets 'em in betwenched us an' tha fence." I knew from experience that her Irish temper was riled.

"Numbers, Deuteronomy, stupid ol' cock, ain't no good for nothin'. Joshua, Judges, when I gets my hans on ya, ya'll be good fur somethin', tha stew pot!"

Fifteen minutes and a lot of sweating, tumbling, and Bible-calling went by before we snagged him. Grandma proudly held him by his feet. His wings were flapping wildly, his feathers flying, and he was squawking idiotically. Grandma puffed her pipe in satisfaction. Then she strutted back toward the house. With prize in hand and a smirk on her face (she always did like a challenge), Grandma did a little jig up the wooded path.

Coming to the clearing, Grandma went directly to the old tree stump, calling over her shoulder, "Fetch my hatch."

Excited by the game and still not suspicious, I ran to the shed. When I returned, Grandma had old Blue stretched across the stump. I looked down to follow the instructions Grandma was giving on the art of holding chicken feet. Then, looking up, I saw the rusted metal hatchet swinging down in slow motion. Suddenly, I knew what was happening. I closed my eyes. My hands jerked. I heard a dull thud and felt something warm and thick splash onto my arms. But before the nausea could overcome me, the impossible happened. The headless rooster jumped to the ground. Feathers still flying and severed neck flopping, blood spurting everywhere, he raced down the dirt path, with Grandma right behind.

That night, I wasn't very hungry, but Grandma dug in with gusto.

My grandma raised eight kids on bootlegging money. She smoked a corncob pipe until the day she died and made her clothes out of flour sacks. She spoke her mind wherever she was and had an Irish temper to match the devil's own, but she was a good, strong woman. Maybe soft city living keeps us from being tough old birds.

(Rita Black)

Questions

1. In what ways does the student's description of her grandmother's "old country house" contribute to our understanding of this woman?

2. How does the incident involving the capture of the rooster help further our understanding of the student's grandmother?

3. What is the significance of the title of the essay?

---

6. Outsiders (Description, Narration, Examples)

In an essay, relate and interpret the experience of being an outsider—a stranger in an unfamiliar or even an unfriendly place.

Guidelines

Moving to a new town, arriving at a new school or college, trying to adapt to the routines of a place where the dominant culture is not your own—all of these are common, disorienting experiences. In this essay, you will recount one particular experience of this kind, whether it happened to you or to someone you have known. Describe the circumstances that contributed to the sense of strangeness, isolation, or alienation, and relate at least one particular incident that illustrated this condition.

In the essay that follows, a student recalls the way that she and her classmates once treated a girl who "was different from the start."

The Playground Pariah

In every classroom in every school, there is a child who stands out as the misfit. This child by unfortunate circumstance is the object of ridicule and the butt of jokes. Junior high school is teeming with prepubescent savages who hunger for the acceptance of their peers, at any cost. My own school was no exception. We were herd-like creatures determined to be as much like everyone else as possible. If you were different, you were doomed. And Doris Wash was different from the start.

Doris Wash was the grossest girl in my school. She wore hand-me-down, yellowed uniforms and cheap, used vinyl saddle oxfords, and it was rumored that the Wash household had only just received hot running water the summer before. She had long greasy hair, which she parted on the side and secured with two tarnished silver barrettes. When one of these aged clips chanced to break, her hairstyle changed to a bare rubber-banded ponytail to accommodate the loss. The only thing that Doris Wash had that the rest of us truly wanted was her substantial bosom. The fact that she was a year older and had failed first grade slightly diminished the significance of this important step towards womanhood. She was taller and plumper than most seventh grade girls, and we despised her slow and awkward presence. In reading class, Doris was a "Minnow"; we were "Dolphins." During math, Doris left our class to receive instruction from Miss Lucy, who taught the "dummy" math class. We frequently reminded Doris of this.

It was widely known that Doris and her younger brother "Tater" were attending school on a "scholarship." Tuition fees were waived, and we tolerated their presence out of the Christian charity we were learning in parochial school. The sisters there did their best to shield Doris from the various cruelties we threw her way. During recess and lunch, Doris was often asked to stay inside and help the teachers clap erasers or straighten desks or decorate bulletin boards. Doris was always glad to oblige, and she basked in self-importance as she helped the teachers inside. The blacktop was a hazardous place for Doris, because over the years a horrible sort of game had developed. Some brave soul would sneak up behind Doris, touch her quickly, and shriek, "I've got Doris's cooties! Who wants Doris's cooties?" The idea was to infect unsuspecting schoolmates who had not been prudent enough to inoculate themselves against the dreaded Doris cooties. (For the uninformed, simply tracing one's index finger on one's arm and chanting, "Circle, circle; dot, dot—now I've got my cootie shot!" was the preferred method of preventing the cooties from taking hold.) But Doris never cried. She never shed one tear, nor did she react in any visible way to the daily verbal blows. On St. Valentine's Day, we snubbed her heartlessly. Doris received only a few token Valentines from lads whose parents insisted they leave no one out, which rendered the cards worthless. But Doris hoarded her precious small stash of Valentines as if they were diamonds, arranging and rearranging them until their order suited her. Doris was gloating, and we were gagging at the sight of it.

A couple of months later it was Doris herself who provided the opportunity we were hoping for. We had assembled ourselves as usual on the grass beside the jungle gym. We, undeniably the coolest girls in the seventh grade, sat in a lopsided circle to discuss boys, make-up, boys, and other closely related subjects. We were several smaller cliques really that convened separately on the weekends at the shopping malls or via extended phone conversations; but during recess and lunch the smaller circles opened and formed this larger, more powerful sphere. Here we sunned ourselves and applied mascara on the sly (out of Sister Mary of the Angels' bionic eyesight). Here the scents of Love's Baby Soft and Sweet Honesty colognes collided head-on in the air around us. On that ordinary day in May, Doris Wash approached our circle carrying a crumpled brown lunch bag. She stood there for a moment, smiled broadly, and announced, "It's my birthday this weekend, and I'm having a slumber party." She reached grandly into the grease-spotted lunch bag and extracted a stack of neat white note cards, and gave one to each of us. Then she smiled, as if encouraging us to smile back, and left.

We were stunned. Shocked. Outraged! A couple of the cockier girls laughed aloud, obviously overcome by the hilarity of what had just transpired. The very idea of Doris Wash throwing a slumber party! And actually expecting us to come! The nerve! The circle snorted indignantly about the impending sleep-over and its unsuspecting hostess for the rest of the week, and then dismissed it as forgotten. And as the school bell rang announcing the end of class that fateful Friday, we each knew with unmerciful certainty that none of us would go.

Doris did not come back to school until Wednesday of the following week. Had it not been for the party that wasn't, I doubt we would have missed her. Her desk stood empty and alone, much like Doris herself. We could hardly contain our satisfaction. We passed smug, knowing glances across the room. We all knew she wasn't sick; we all knew she hadn't broken any bones. We all knew Doris had cried and, possibly, was still crying. And in knowing that, we were satisfied.

(Jill S. Girard)

Questions

1. What does the student reveal about the "Dolphins"—the group, referred to in the essay as "we," who took such pleasure in ostracizing Doris Wash?
2. Why was Doris Wash treated as an outsider?
3. How effective is the conclusion to this essay? Do you think that further explanation or interpretation of the experience is needed?

7. Neighborhood (Description, Explanation, Persuasion)

Write a letter, in essay form, in which you describe your neighborhood for the benefit of someone who is trying to decide whether or not to move there.

Guidelines

Imagine that friends of yours from out of town are thinking of moving to your neighborhood (this might be a city block, a college dormitory, an apartment complex, a trailer park, a suburb—whatever you call "home"). Write them a letter in which you identify some of the important characteristics of the neighborhood. Provide the sort of information that will help them decide whether or not to move.

To write an effective letter, you will have to put yourself in the position of your readers. Consider what your friends already know about the neighborhood and what they need to know. Consider what *particular* things these individuals would be interested in. You may slant the letter, emphasizing either the favorable or the unfavorable aspects of your neighborhood, or you may attempt to be objective, leaving the decision up to your friends.

In the following essay, novelist and essayist Ishmael Reed provides a detailed description of his neighborhood in North Oakland, California. Observe how Reed attempts to paint a picture of everyday life in the neighborhood while identifying both its negative and positive qualities.

My Oakland

My neighborhood, bordered by Genoa, Market Street, and 48th and 55th streets in North Oakland, is what the media refer to as a "predominantly black neighborhood." . . . We've lived on 53rd Street for three years now. Carla's dance and theater school, which she operates with her partner, Jody Roberts—Roberts and Blank Dance/Drama—is already five years old. I am working on my seventh novel and a television production of my play *Mother Hubbard*. The house has yet to be restored to its 1906 glory, but we're working on it.

I've grown accustomed to the common sights here—teenagers moving through the neighborhood carrying radios blasting music by Grandmaster Flash and Prince, men hovering over cars with tools and rags in hand, decked-out female church delegations visiting the sick. Unemployment up, one sees more men drinking from sacks as they walk through Market Street or gather in Helen McGregor Plaza, on Shattuck and 52nd Street, near a bench where mothers sit with their children, waiting for buses. It may be because the bus stop is across the street from Children's Hospital (exhibiting a brand-new antihuman, postmodern wing), but there seem to be a lot of sick black children these days. The criminal courts and emergency rooms of Oakland hospitals, both medical and psychiatric, are also filled with blacks.

White men go from door to door trying to unload spoiled meat. Incredibly sleazy white contractors and hustlers try to entangle people into shady deals that sometimes lead to the loss of a home. Everybody knows of someone, usually a widow, who has been gypped into paying thousands of dollars more than the standard cost for, say, adding a room to a house. It sure ain't El Cerrito. In El Cerrito the representatives from the utilities were very courteous. If they realize they're speaking to someone in a black neighborhood, however, they become curt and sarcastic. I was trying to arrange for the gas company to come out to fix a stove when the woman from Pacific Gas and Electric gave me some snide lip. I told her, "Lady, if you think what you're going through is an inconvenience, you can imagine my inconvenience paying the bills every month." Even she had to laugh.

The clerks in the stores are also curt, regarding blacks the way the media regard them, as criminal suspects. Over in El Cerrito the cops were professional, respectful—in Oakland they swagger about like candidates for a rodeo. In El Cerrito and the Berkeley Hills you could take your time paying some bills, but in this black neighborhood if you miss paying a bill by one day, "reminders" printed in glaring and violent typefaces are sent to you, or you're threatened with discontinuance of this or that service. Los Angeles police victim Eulia Love, who was shot in the aftermath of an argument over an overdue gas bill, would still be alive if she had lived in El Cerrito or the Berkeley Hills.

I went to a bank a few weeks ago that advertised easy loans on television, only to be told that I would have to wait six months after opening an account to be eligible for a loan. I went home and called the same bank, this time putting on my Clark Kent voice, and was informed that I could come in and get the loan the same day. Other credit unions and banks, too, have different lending practices for black and white neighborhoods, but when I try to tell white intellectuals that blacks are prevented from developing industries because the banks find it easier to lend money to communist countries than to American citizens, they call me paranoid. Sometimes when I know I am going to be inconvenienced by merchants or creditors because of my 53rd Street address, I give the address of my Berkeley studio instead. Others are not so fortunate.

Despite the inconveniences and antagonism from the outside world one has to endure for having a 53rd Street address, life in this neighborhood is more pleasant than grim. Casually dressed, well-groomed elderly men gather at the intersections to look after the small children as they walk to and from school, or just to keep an eye on the neighborhood. My next-door neighbor keeps me in stitches with his informed commentary on any number of political comedies emanating from Washington and Sacramento. Once we were discussing pesticides, and the man who was repairing his porch told us that he had a great garden and didn't have to pay all that much attention to it. As for pesticides, he said, the bugs have to eat, too.

There are people on this block who still know the subsistence skills many Americans have forgotten. They can hunt and fish (and if you don't fish, there is a man who covers the neighborhood selling fresh fish and yelling, "Fishman," recalling a period of ancient American commerce when you didn't have to pay the middleman). They are also loyal Americans—they vote, they pay taxes—but you don't find the extreme patriots here that you find in white neighborhoods. Although Christmas, Thanksgiving, New Year's, and Easter are celebrated with all get-out, I've never seen a flag flying on Memorial Day, or on any holiday that calls for the showing of the flag. Blacks express their loyalty in concrete ways. For example, you rarely see a foreign car in this neighborhood. And this 53rd Street neighborhood, as well as black neighborhoods like it from coast to coast, will supply the male children who will bear the brunt of future jungle wars, just as they did in Vietnam.

We do our shopping on a strip called Temescal, which stretches from 46th to 51st streets. Temescal, according to Oakland librarian William Sturm, is an Aztec word for "hothouse," or "bathhouse." The word was borrowed from the Mexicans by the Spanish to describe similar hothouses, early saunas, built by the California Indians in what is now North Oakland. Some say the hothouses were used to sweat out demons; others claim the Indians used them for medicinal purposes. Most agree that after a period of time in the steam, the Indians would rush en masse into the streams that flowed through the area. One still runs underneath my backyard—I have to mow the grass there almost every other day.

Within these five blocks are the famous Italian restaurant Bertola's, "Since 1932"; Siam restaurant; La Belle Creole, a French-Caribbean restaurant; Asmara, an Ethiopian restaurant; and Ben's Hof Brau, where white and black senior citizens, dressed in the elegance of a former time, congregate to talk or to have an inexpensive though quality breakfast provided by Ben's hardworking and courteous staff.

The Hof Brau shares its space with Vern's market, where you can shop to the music of DeBarge. To the front of Vern's is the Temescal Delicatessen, where a young Korean man makes the best po' boy sandwiches north of Louisiana, and near the side entrance is Ed Fraga's Automotive. The owner is always advising his customers to avoid stress, and he says goodbye with a "God bless you." The rest of the strip is taken up by the Temescal Pharmacy, which has a resident health advisor and a small library of health literature; the Aikido Institute; an African bookstore; and the internationally known Genova deli, to which people from the surrounding cities travel to shop. The strip also includes the Clausen House thrift shop, which sells used clothes and furniture. Here you can buy novels by J.D. Salinger and John O'Hara for ten cents each.

Space that was recently occupied by the Buon Gusto Bakery is now for rent. Before the bakery left, an Italian lady who worked there introduced me to a crunchy, cookie-like treat called "bones," which she said went well with Italian wine. The Buon Gusto had been a landmark since the 1940s, when, according to a guest at the New Year's Day Hoppin' John supper, North Oakland was populated by Italians and Portuguese. In those days a five-room house could be rented for $45 a month, she said.

The neighborhood is still in transition. The East Bay Negro Historical Society, which was located around the corner on Grove Street, included in its collection letters written by nineteenth-century macho man Jack London to his black nurse. They were signed, "Your little white pickaninny." It's been replaced by the New Israelite Delight restaurant, part of the Israelite Church, which also operates a day care center. The restaurant offers homemade Louisiana gumbo and a breakfast that includes grits.

Unlike the other California neighborhoods I've lived in, I know most of the people on this block by name. They are friendly and cooperative, always offering to watch your house while you're away. The day after one of the few whites who lives on the block—a brilliant muckraking journalist and former student of mine—was robbed, neighbors gathered in front of his house to offer assistance.

In El Cerrito my neighbor was indeed a cop. He used pomade on his curly hair, sported a mustache, and there was a grayish tint in his brown eyes. He was a handsome man, with a smile like a movie star's. His was the only house on the block I entered during my three-year stay in that neighborhood, and that was one afternoon when we shared some brandy. I wanted to get to know him better. I didn't know he was dead until I saw people in black gathered on his doorstep.

I can't imagine that happening on 53rd Street. In a time when dour thinkers view alienation and insensitivity toward the plight of others as characteristics of the modern condition, I think I'm lucky to live in a neighborhood where people look out for one another.

A human neighborhood.

(Ishmael Reed)

Questions

1. Define the following words as they are used in Reed's essay: *curt, antagonism, emanating, subsistence, alienation.*

2. Identify the negative elements in Reed's description of his neighborhood, and explain what these elements have in common. Then identify the positive qualities. Which view—negative or positive—appears to dominate the essay?

3. At the end of the essay, Reed observes, "I think I'm lucky to live in a neighborhood where people look out for one another." How has this observation been supported by evidence provided earlier in the essay?

8. *Rituals and Procedures (Process Analysis)*

In an essay, describe and explain the steps involved in carrying out some activity.

Guidelines

This assignment is an extension of the one described in Chapter Eight (*Skills*). Here, instead of telling your readers how to do something, you will explain how something is (or was) done. In other words, instead of writing a how-to-do-it paper that *directs* your readers, you will write a how-it's-done essay that *informs* them. You may explain how birds fly, how Eskimos hunt, how presidents get elected, or how rock groups produce a video. Choose a topic that interests you and that you know a good deal about. Then follow the advice in Chapter Eight on organizing information in step-by-step fashion. Be sure to explain each step clearly and define any terms that might be unfamiliar to your readers.

Before you begin to write, you may find it helpful to research your topic, either by visiting the library or by interviewing an expert. The writer of the following essay, for example, learned about Chinese marriage customs through an important conversation with her future mother-in-law.

The Red Wedding Dress

Before marrying into my fiance's Oriental family, I agreed to listen well to my prospective mother-in-law and learn as much about Chinese customs as I could. The Chinese people, I found out, hold on to many traditions that are both interesting and perplexing. For instance, women customarily walk behind their husbands, old people are held in great reverence, and often three or four generations live together in the same house. None of these customs troubled me, however, until the day I found out that my wedding dress was to be red.

The prospect of wearing a red dress at my wedding was more than I could bear. This is America, I thought to myself, not China, and I am not going to make myself look silly by wearing that dress. What would my friends and family think? No, I thought defiantly, I am not wearing that red dress!

My future mother-in-law soon caught wind of my reluctance to wear the dress and came to visit me. She arrived with a package under her arm and a determined look on her face. After making small talk for awhile, she approached the real reason for her visit.

"I know it is difficult for you to accept wearing a red wedding dress," she said. "I would like to help you understand our marriage customs, but first you must listen to my own story.

"It was not easy for me to come to America," she began. "I could not speak the language and the food was not edible, but I had no say in the matter. My husband had been chosen for me, and I did not dare go against the wishes of my father. I was thinking just as you are today: those old ways are not for me. Yet here I am, imposing those same old traditions on the next generation. Why do I hold on to them? It is because I am reminded of another world, a world that I left behind so long ago."

She leaned forward to take a breath of air, and I knew that the part about the dress was coming next.

"All Chinese women marry in a red dress because this color symbolizes great happiness, good luck, and a bright future. To marry in a white dress would bring very bad luck, for white represents mourning and deep sorrow. When I came here, my own mother sent a package that was to remain unopened until my wedding day. It contained a red silk dress that had been worn by many brides coming into my family. Since my mother knew that I would never be able to come back home, she had made a great sacrifice by giving me the dress. Now the other brides entering our family would not have the opportunity to wear such a lovely costume.

"Along with the dress," my future mother-in-law continued, "came an embroidered pouch, trimmed in gold. This attaches to the sleeve. Tiny red envelopes filled with gifts of money will be given to you on your wedding day by family and friends. These are to be stored in the pouch and worn the entire day. The fuller the pouch becomes, the more 'face' and respect our family will gain."

She sat back for a moment and then quietly handed me the package. There was no way that I could refuse to wear that dress, for it was so precious and dear to this lady. As I took out the dress, she broke into a contented smile. The gown was so beautiful that a princess would gladly have worn it.

"Of course," she reminded me, "you must promise to pass on this particular tradition to your own daughter one day." She was still smiling. "Old ways should never be forgotten."

On my wedding day, I wore that beautiful dress, never giving the color a second thought. My gift pouch grew so full that a second one had to be borrowed. My new parents gained great "face" on that account. To this very day, they still tell their old friends just arriving from China, "Yes, our son married an American girl. But she wore the red dress!" And for some reason that makes everything all right.

So many years have passed since that day, and as I have gotten older, I have changed my mind about holding on to some of the old ways. Some things never change, though, and one of them is the attitude of people growing up in a new generation. I had to smile after I told my own daughter the history of the red dress. Her reply? "I'm not wearing that dress!"

(Dee Wu)

Questions

1. How do Chinese wedding customs, as described in this essay, differ from those followed by the majority of Americans?

2. Why do you think that the student chose to convey almost half of this essay in the words of her prospective mother-in-law?

3. In what ways does the concluding paragraph hook back to the opening paragraphs of the essay?

9. Sales (Persuasion)

Combine descriptive and informative details in a short essay that advertises a product you have for sale.

Guidelines

In this assignment, you will combine strategies introduced in Chapter Two (*Belongings*) and Chapter Seven (*Complaints*). Begin by selecting one of your belongings—large or small, valuable or worthless, something you would be willing to sell. Draft a detailed description of the item, and then respond to the questions in the following *audience analysis*. Ignore questions that appear irrelevant, and add questions that you feel are more appropriate.

AUDIENCE ANALYSIS

❑ This item would probably appeal most to a person in what age group?

❑ Would this item appeal more to a man or to a woman?

❑ Would this item appeal more to a single person or to a married person?

❑ This item would probably appeal most to a person in what income bracket?

❑ Would a person be more likely to purchase this item for his or her own use or as a gift for someone else?

❑ Would this person be interested more in what the item does or in what it looks like?

❑ What needs or desires would this item satisfy for such a person?

❑ What aspect(s) of this item would most interest a potential buyer?

❑ Would a potential buyer be interested more in the cost or in the quality of the item?

❑ What sort of technical information about this item would a potential buyer need or want to know before making a decision?

Guided by your answers to the audience analysis, expand your descriptive paragraph into a short essay. Your *introduction* should identify the item for sale and attract the interest of your audience. The *body paragraph(s)* should contain particular information about the item and specific descriptions of it. The *conclusion* should summarize the chief attraction(s) of the item (its value, quality, attractiveness, or whatever), state its cost, and explain where and how it can be purchased. You will find all of this information clearly arranged in the student essay that follows.

Tressel Toaster

Do you just love those New Wave hairstyles but can't afford the costly services of a professional hairdresser? Then it's time you freaked out with the new Tressel Toaster from Zappew International. It's fun, it's fast, and it's foolproof.

Made of sturdy bakelite, available in white or mocha, the Tressel Toaster will keep you in fashion for years to come. Just pop the handy steel comb into the toaster, wait sixty seconds, and then run the hot comb through your hair: instant punk. The Tressel Toaster lets you frizz, fluff, flip, or flatten your hair into the latest style. And you can change styles instantly with the help of the free bottle of Un-Do Shampoo that's provided with every Tressel Toaster. If you get tired of your Medusa cut or want to transform a wedge into a conehead in time for that big date, this clinically tested de-punking shampoo will instantly restore the luster of your hair and condition it for another Tressel Toaster treatment.

Now, how much would you expect to pay for the marvelous new Tressel Toaster and bottle of Un-Do? As much as a hundred dollars, perhaps? Well, for a limited time only, you can buy the amazing new Tressel Toaster, with free bottle of Un-Do Shampoo, for only $19.95. You heard right: only $19.95. So, have your credit card handy and call our toll-free number now: 1-800-555-1891.

(Ruth Norris)

Questions

1. How would you characterize the *tone* of this short essay—that is, the student's attitude toward her subject and her audience?

2. Clearly, this essay is a parody of a certain kind of product and the television commercials that promote such products. What specific qualities and techniques are being parodied here?

10. Choices (Comparison)

In an essay, compare two related subjects in order to guide your readers in making a choice between them.

Guidelines

This assignment offers a variation on the writing strategy of *comparison*, which was introduced in Chapter Nine (*Changes*). The topic you select should come out of your own interests, knowledge, and experience, but keep in mind that your primary aim is to inform others, not just to recount your own experience. Begin by considering some of the decisions you have made that might interest others—a choice between two colleges, two jobs, two social organizations, or two types of housing, for instance. Think about some of the purchasing decisions you have recently made—between two types of automobile, stereo, running shoe, or even frozen pizza. You might compare two different strategies or techniques—for saving money, perhaps, or growing tomatoes or administering artificial respiration. Or you might compare two people who perform similar jobs but who represent different philosophies or approaches: two politicians, for example, or two coaches, athletes, or performers. Just be sure to *narrow* your topic: two *specific* colleges, for instance, not "A Big College and a Small One."

Explore several topics before deciding on one. You might start by freewriting, jotting down all the information and ideas that come to mind. You might also get together with a few others for a brainstorming session. Exchange ideas for topics, and invite suggestions on how to focus and develop the topic you choose. Make sure from the start that your topic is neither too personal (nobody has to choose between your brother and your sister, for example) nor too broad (potential defectors might be interested in a comparison between the United States and Russia, but the topic is too large to be covered adequately in a short essay). You may also need to do some basic research, though this does not necessarily mean long hours in the library. If you decide to compare two sandwich shops, for instance, visit them both: note the prices, the selections, and the quality of the service, and then taste the sandwiches. Keep in mind that your readers will need specific information if they are to make an intelligent choice.

Once you have decided on two subjects to compare and have spent some time exploring these subjects, you are ready to plan your approach to the essay. Begin, simply enough, by identifying the two subjects:

> **Topic:** A comparison between eyeglasses and extended-wear contact lenses

Next, in a sentence or two, explain the purpose of your comparison and identify the audience you are addressing:

> **Purpose and Audience:** This essay will help eyeglass-wearers decide whether or not they should switch to contact lenses.

After you have done this, list at least three main points of comparison. Draw a line down the center of your paper, and write down corresponding facts, descriptions, and examples for your two subjects.

Use this list as a guide when writing your rough draft. The draft should include an introductory paragraph, at least three body paragraphs, and a conclusion. In the introduction, identify your two subjects, suggest who should be interested in the topic (and why they should be interested), and mention the main points you are about to consider. Each body paragraph should be built around one main point and contain specific information supporting that point. Make sure that your comparisons are *balanced*—that you have provided corresponding details for both subjects. Finally, in your conclusion, bring together the main points of your comparison. Here you may recommend one subject over the other, or merely remind your readers that the choice is theirs to make.

Afterwards, perhaps guided by the advice of a fellow student who has read your draft, revise the essay. At this point, check to see that you have made smooth transitions from one subject to the other throughout your paper. You may want to use some of the following *comparison signals* to improve the coherence of your essay:

To introduce similarities:	*To introduce differences:*
also	by (*or* in) comparison
by the same token	however
in like manner	in contrast
in similar fashion	instead
in the same way	nevertheless
likewise	on the contrary
similarly	on the other hand
	rather

The following essay uses a number of these signals to guide the reader clearly from one point to the next.

Still Making a Spectacle Out of Yourself?

Over ninety percent of the people who now wear eyeglasses could correct their vision problems just as effectively with contact lenses. In fact, since the arrival of extended-wear contacts in 1981, over sixteen million people have switched from spectacles to these soft slips of plastic. If you suffer from a common vision problem, such as nearsightedness, farsightedness, or astigmatism, you may be thinking about making the switch yourself. Before you do, however, there are some important factors to consider in regard to comfort, maintenance, and cost.

Are contact lenses less comfortable than a pair of eyeglasses? Back in the days of hard lenses (about ten years ago), the answer would probably be yes, but not anymore. After just a few days behind soft lenses, you should hardly be aware of them at all. You can blink, wink, weep, and sleep behind contacts without any discomfort. For most people, in fact, contacts are now more comfortable than eyeglasses. After all, spectacles do have some annoying habits: when they aren't slipping down the nose, they try to bore into the face, often irritating the skin around the ears, under the eyes, and along the bridge of the nose.

Nevertheless, eyeglasses are still easier to maintain and more durable than contact lenses. Whereas glasses can be kept clean with the occasional wipe of a tissue, extended-wear contacts need to be soaked every thirty days in a special solution. Likewise, a pair of modern eyeglasses can be sat on, dropped in a parking lot, and walloped with a fly ball, and still come out unharmed. In contrast, a contact lens can easily be scratched or torn by careless handling. And because even a slightly damaged lens can irritate the eye, the contact must be replaced. Even when handled most delicately, contact lenses must be replaced every one or two years. In that time, the lenses tend to stretch out of shape and turn an unhealthy shade of yellow. A pair of eyeglasses, on the other hand, may last for several years, as long as your prescription stays the same and your frames are in fashion.

The fact that contacts need to be replaced more often than glasses should be kept in mind when considering the relative cost of the two. Extended-wear lenses and a pair of fashionable eyeglasses now fall within the same general price range, anywhere from $60 to $150, not including the cost of the eye examination. If you are now in the habit of changing your glasses every year or so, because of changes in your vision or the novelty of new frames, then there is no significant difference in cost. However, if you count on a pair of glasses to last you a number of years, you will end up paying at least twice as much for contacts over that same period. Failing to replace your contacts regularly would be false economizing, for your eyes could suffer permanent damage.

So, should you stop making a spectacle out of yourself and exchange your eyeglasses for contact lenses? If you do, you won't see any worse, and you will probably look much better. Nonetheless, you should be prepared to take good care of your contacts, and be aware that over the long run they may be more expensive than glasses. Of course, before deciding anything, you should turn to your ophthalmologist or optometrist for professional advice. Then, when you go shopping at the optician's, make sure you keep your eyes open, no matter what you decide to put over them.

(Roz Evans)

Questions

1. In simple outline form, identify the specific qualities of eyeglasses and contact lenses that are compared and contrasted in this student essay.

2. Underline the *comparison signals* used by the student to help give the essay a sense of coherence.

3. Does it appear that the student has objectively presented fair and accurate information throughout the essay? Explain your response.

11. Problem Solving (Explanation and Argument)

Write an essay in which you identify a problem, explain why it is a problem, propose a solution, and explain why your solution is the best one available.

Guidelines

In this assignment, you will combine strategies introduced in Chapters Seven (*Complaints*) and Thirteen (*Issues*). Begin by selecting a problem from everyday life—in the place you live or work, in your college or community. Here are some topics to start you thinking:

a problem with a roommate, family member, or neighbor

the problem of maintaining a social life without any money

the problem of television addiction

the problem of paying for a college education

a problem with a particular college course or instructor

a problem concerning a pet

the problem of how to cope with stress in a particular situation

Choose a problem that you have experienced and thought about—one that you have solved or are in the process of solving. Then, in the essay itself, you may use your own experience to illustrate the problem. However, don't focus all the attention on yourself and *your* problem. Instead, direct the paper at others who are experiencing a similar problem. In other words, don't write an *I* essay ("How I Cure the Blues"); write a *you* essay ("How You Can Cure the Blues").

How do you organize a problem-solution paper? To some extent this depends on your topic, but do make sure you include the following information:

Introduction: Identify the problem in a nutshell. Explain why this is a problem, and mention who should be concerned about it.

Problem Paragraph(s): Explain the problem clearly and specifically. Demonstrate that this is not just a personal complaint, but a genuine problem that affects many.

Solution Paragraph(s): Offer a concrete solution to the problem, and explain why this is the best one available. You may want to point out why other possible solutions are inferior to yours. If your solution calls for a series of steps or actions to be followed, present these steps in a logical order.

Conclusion: Reemphasize the importance of the problem and the value of your solution.

Consider how all of this information is organized in the following essay by freelance writer Mike Brake. Combining personal experience with factual observations, Brake proposes a controversial solution to a major problem—alcoholism.

Needed: A License to Drink

We buried my cousin last summer. He was 32 when he hanged himself from a closet coat rack in the throes of alcoholism, the fourth of my blood relatives to die prematurely from this deadly disease. If America issued drinking licenses, those four men—including my father, who died at 54 of liver failure—might be alive today.

Addiction to alcohol is one of the primary public-health problems in the United States. It causes more than 19,000 auto fatalities each year; it is responsible for more than a third of deaths from drowning and fire. Booze is a central factor in divorce. It can trigger incest, child and spousal abuse, suicide, homicide, assault and other crimes. It can kill by the liver, the kidneys, the heart, the pancreas, the central nervous system. The total cost, from increased jail time to workplace injuries and lost productivity, is impossible to measure, but a conservative estimate is as high as $90 billion per year. As ways to trim health-care costs are considered we must recognize that alcoholism is a big contributor to hospital admissions.

I spent two years working as a counselor in a chemical-dependency treatment center and met these "statistics" on a daily basis. I remember the bright young man who, because he passed out while smoking, lost both legs to terrible burns; the nurse with a master's degree who lost her license and became a prostitute; and there was the cheerful grandmother dying of liver failure, with only a few weeks to live. Their families cared about them but could do nothing. I've seen the helplessness in my own family.

About two thirds of adolescent and adult Americans drink alcohol. Of those, from 8 to 12 percent will become alcoholics or problem drinkers. Much is being done to confront this huge public-health crisis as judges increasingly sentence drunk drivers and other alcohol-related offenders to treatment programs and participation in Alcoholics Anonymous. I propose that a national system of licensing, with appropriate penalties, would do more.

Drivers are licensed by every state. There are licenses for fishing and for hunting—hunters are often required to attend gun-safety classes before they venture afield. These licenses are revocable; if you fail to keep to accepted norms the state suspends your right to drive, hunt or fish and imposes criminal penalties should you violate that suspension.

Although this might seem a farfetched idea, I believe drastic measures are needed. Licensing drinking would acknowledge the growing medical consensus that roughly one drinker in 10 has a genetic predisposition for addiction. In many cases, future alcoholics are dangerously unaware of their internal time bomb. They don't aspire to become drunks, but once trapped in the disease they can do enormous harm to others and themselves.

Because some potential alcoholics would not bother to apply for a drinking license, licensing would act as a screen—preventing a small percentage of the misery up-front. Those who do seek a license would follow a path similar to existing driver's licensing procedures.

Applicants would be required to study a manual containing basic information about alcohol and the law, much like the driver's manual we all memorized in high school. How many drinks will it take to intoxicate a 150-pound man? What is the penalty for drunk driving? Have any of your blood relatives been treated for alcoholism or chemical dependency? If they have, you need to know that you're at increased risk for developing addiction.

The next step would be to pass a written test. License holders would then be able to buy alcoholic beverages (including beer). A liquor store or bar caught selling to an unlicensed drinker would forfeit its license.

The 90 percent of us who do not have a problem with alcohol would simply show our licenses at the counter, bar or restaurant—in much the same way as driving to and from work each day with a driver's license.

Most of the problem 10 percent would at some point face arrest on an alcohol-related offense. Once convicted they'd lose their license. From that point on, attempting to buy or possess alcohol or being found with a detectable blood level of booze would subject them to a misdemeanor charge—with penalties comparable to those for drunk driving. Unlicensed drinkers who got drunk could be referred to treatment and to Alcoholics Anonymous.

Doctors are required to report cases of syphilis, gonorrhea, AIDS and tuberculosis as public-health hazards. They should also be required to report the medical diagnosis of alcoholism. If a patient is admitted to a chemical-dependency treatment center, his drinking license would be suspended. Physicians would report people who show signs of alcoholism after having their licenses rescinded, just as social agencies report parole violators. The objective would be treatment. If the offenders refuse to seek sobriety, they would be unable to get their licenses renewed.

A commonly accepted canon of civilized society is that when the public health is threatened, privacy rights must be compromised. Americans rarely die of typhoid, cholera or plague because we have identified their sources. Infectious carriers are quarantined when necessary and offered compassionate and lifesaving treatment.

The same criteria should apply to alcoholism, a disease that is the third leading cause of preventable death in this country. The costs inflicted by 18 million drunks, on themselves and on our social fabric, is unacceptable. Congress and the states should cooperate by instigating national drinking licenses, encouraging treatment for those afflicted and imposing firm penalties on violators. It's not such a crazy idea.

(Mike Brake)

Questions

1. Define each of the following words as they are used in Brake's essay: *venture, revocable, consensus, predisposition, rescinded, canon, quarantined.*

2. Why do you think Brake chose to begin his essay with a brief account of his cousin's suicide?

3. How effective do you think Brake's proposed solution would be?

4. Who do you think might oppose Brake's proposed solution? What sort of opposing arguments might be made?

12. Values (Definition)

In an essay, use examples and comparisons to define a value.

Guidelines

This assignment calls on you to combine writing strategies introduced in various earlier assignments, including those in Chapters Four (*Virtues and Vices*), Nine (*Changes*), and Thirteen (*Issues*). Your central purpose in this essay is to identify the essential characteristics of a *value*—some principle or quality that you consider to be important. You may select a topic from the list below:

honor	friendship	humility
modesty	happiness	privacy
self-assurance	maturity	loyalty
respect	courage	sportsmanship
ambition	gumption	self-respect
individualism	responsibility	pride
a sense of humor	strength	integrity
patriotism	heroism	charm
success	idealism	dedication
persistence	common sense	trust
generosity	honesty	freedom

Feel free, of course, to write on a topic not included in this list. Indeed, you may choose to invert one of these values and write on a topic such as dishonor, immodesty, or disrespect.

There are various ways to develop and organize this sort of essay, as the following student paper demonstrates. You should use comparisons to distinguish between related values. And be sure to use examples to make your abstract ideas clear and concrete.

Compassion

The young volunteer from Denver was sweating in the Indian heat, planting seeds with twenty local villagers. She was there not for money or fame or even adventure, but because she wanted to help the people in this small village, help them raise food and keep their population in check. In short, she had compassion, the feeling that sparks within us a desire to help others. Whether we are trying to improve the quality of life of villagers halfway around the world or tending to the needs of an older person in our own neighborhood, we may be motivated by compassion. It is that special human quality that adds dignity to our lives.

Almost everyone has felt compassion at one time or another. The compassion we feel, however, is just a concept. What we do with that feeling is reality. When we see a CARE commercial on television, it is easy to feel compassion, but most people find it much harder to sacrifice their pocket money to actually help those who have nothing. I know I am guilty of this hypocrisy. When I went to dinner this evening, I had my mind on this essay, thinking about starving people in India, Ethiopia, and Appalachia. But I was halfway through my steak and mashed potatoes before I got around to being thankful for what I had.

Still, with effort, we can translate compassionate feelings into actions. An experience last weekend showed me this is true. I work part-time in a drugstore across from an apartment complex for the elderly. These old people are our main customers, and it's not hard to lose patience over their slowness and confusion. But last Sunday, one aged gentleman appeared to teach me a valuable lesson. This unkempt man walked up to my register with a box of crackers and a jar of pimento cheese spread. He said he was out of cash, had just moved into his apartment, and had not yet stocked his cupboards. Offering a dirty, worn-out polyester jacket as collateral, he asked if we could let him have the food on trust. He promised to repay me the next day.

I couldn't help staring at him. I wondered what kind of person he had been ten or twenty years before, how he had come to be all alone, what he would be like if luck had gone his way. I had a hurt in my heart for this kind human soul, all alone in the world. And I told him that I was very sorry, but store policy prohibited me from making credit transactions. I felt foolish and stupid and unkind saying this, but I valued my job. How else would I make those payments on my Toyota?

Just then, another man, standing behind the first, spoke up. If anything, he was more ragged and destitute-looking than the man with the pimento cheese. He spoke softly. "Charge it to me," was all he said.

What I had been feeling was pity, and compassion is not the same as pity. Pity is soft and safe and easy. Compassion, on the other hand, is caring in action.

Compassion means making sacrifices. I thanked the second man but told him that store policy also prohibited such loans. Then I reached into my pocket and paid for the crackers and cheese spread myself. I reached into my pocket because these two men had reached into my heart and taught me compassion.

(April Scott)

Questions

1. In defining *compassion*, the student distinguishes this virtue from another, related quality. What is that quality, and what distinction does she make?

2. Explain how the example involving "the young volunteer" in the introductory paragraph prepares the reader for the extended example in the second half of the essay.

---

13. *Holidays (Explanation and Argument)*

In an essay, argue in favor of adding to the calendar a new regional or national holiday whose purpose and customs you have devised.

Guidelines

After reading the following essay, in which editor and essayist Frederick Turner advocates the creation of a new holiday, Blushing Monday, consider what holiday you would like to add to the calendar. It might honor a particular person or group of people, an historical event or a natural occurrence. Or, following Turner's lead, you may want "to celebrate a mystery or call humanity to some new self-awareness." A brainstorming session with a few of your classmates should help you to discover a number of potential topic ideas. Whether you decide to take a serious approach or a humorous one, be sure to include in your essay the following information: the name of the holiday, the day on which it is to be observed, a justification for adding this holiday to the calendar, and a detailed description of how it is to be celebrated.

Blushing Monday:
A day set aside to revel in shame

The holidays that divide our calendar year were meant to remind us of something important, something we shouldn't forget. The word, after all, means "holy day." The oldest holidays—those around spring and fall—date back to pagan rituals of thanksgiving for the arrival of the growing season or for the harvest to come. Religious holidays such as Passover and Easter seek to transmute the memory of ancient suffering into the promise of better times. At the center of ritual is sacrifice, whereby we acknowledge by some smaller act of voluntary loss the great gifts that enable us to exist at all.

From time to time civilization demands the creation of a new holiday—to celebrate a mystery or call humanity to some new self-awareness. We need a new holiday today because we need to be reminded that the great works of humanity, the very best that we do, entail a heavy cost not only to ourselves but also to the world we inhabit. As a species, we cringe at the thought of the price we pay to live in civilization: We kill animals for food; we raze forests to provide shelter and print our books; our thirst drains rivers; our wastes create dreary landfills; our cars and factories darken the air. Our very existence depends on the loss of other species, extinct or never allowed to evolve. As individuals, our freedom is achieved at the cost of other people's choices, our personhood at the cost of our parents' plans and sacrifices. We are creative and loving only in the shadow of our own embarrassing childhoods, of our accepted shame.

Because in our minds we have uncoupled the costs implicit in human activities from the resulting benefits, we have become a nation divided into two kinds of unpleasant people: scolds, who, in an eternal search for moral purity, sourly demand suffering and guilt; and debauchers, who scorn any accounting that interferes with their pillaging. Without acknowledging the heavy price we pay, we cannot truly enjoy the rewards. And without enjoying the rewards, we cannot truly lament the cost.

This simplest of human contradictions derives from the presence of a reflective mind in a smelly, sexed, appetite-driven body. Both as a society and as individuals, we are compelled to commit certain acts that make us ashamed after we have thought about them. Shame, which is nothing other than the discovery of self, figures in the foundational myth of nearly every culture on earth. Self-knowledge is humankind's most distinguishing attribute, and our bodies inform us, in a way that no other animal knows, when we are caught in the ludicrous contradiction of our competing selves: the blush—that hot feeling around your neck and cheeks at the memory of something you said or did last night, or twenty years ago. We blush about many things: when we are seen naked or in the wrong clothes; when a homeless beggar asks us for a dollar; or when our own sexual feelings are made obvious to others. We are shamed by the gifts that we give and the gifts that we receive because they always seem too paltry or too generous. We are shamed by economic injustice and the carnage of war, shamed by the daily slaughter in our abattoirs and by the killing done by our police and our soldiers on behalf of the poor conceptions of justice we have achieved.

Yet the hot flush of shame, when recognized and accepted, can serve as the prelude to a strange, fresh moment of transformation and epiphany, both for individuals and communities. For this we require some ritual that enlarges upon the essential paradox of humanity. I propose the creation of a new festival, to be observed on the first Monday in August, a month without a national holiday despite the fact that it is the one month all Americans associate with vacations and time off. Thus, on this first weekday of August, before we set off on our family trips or month-long leaves, we will celebrate this new holiday. Its name will be Blushing Monday. On this day we will recognize our destructive nature and celebrate our creativity and our lunacy.

As with other important holidays, Blushing Monday will have a culinary dimension. The first meal, served in midmorning, about 10:30 A.M., will be somber, penitential. It will prepare us for the morning ritual of sacrifice. Each region, city, neighborhood, or family will be encouraged to invent its own sacrifice—specific to its own circumstances and values. Thus, in the forests of the Northwest, the people might gather to cut down a 500-year-old tree. In the Southwest, they might publicly butcher a cow. In the Midwest, the ceremony might involve the display of sports injuries; in the cities of the East, the burning of money. We will parade—unhidden and unexcused—all the costs of our existence and our civilization. This ritual will serve as a recognition of our mortal needs and desires.

The remainder of the day will be marked by increasingly clownish disorder. In the evening, a grand and hilarious feast will acknowledge our astonishing human gifts of consciousness and beauty that accompany our faults and absurdities. We will make bonfires of virgin timber. Bloody steaks will be barbecued. Expensive gifts will be exchanged. Splendid works of charity and low-cost housing projects will be dedicated. Major sports events will take place. Grand scientific projects and symphony halls will be inaugurated. Comedians will anchor the network news, and the evening will be given over to the consummation of midsummer-night's romances.

The mood of the day will be shockingly mixed—deadly serious, comically manic, cynical, idealistic, horrified, and joyful. We will accuse ourselves, forgive ourselves, and celebrate the absurd joy of mortal conscious life. Everybody has to dress, and act, in the most embarrassing way that he or she can imagine, indulging the same concealed desire to put on silly clothes that we see expressed by transvestites, football mascots, and Shriners. The laws against indecent exposure will be relaxed. Everyone must say the most embarrassing thing that comes into one's head—the thing that everybody thinks but nobody says.

The mythical figure—the Easter Bunny or Santa Claus who will personify Blushing Monday—will be that singular primate, the mandrill. With its multicolored genitalia and its embarrassing social and anatomical resemblance to ourselves, the mandrill is the perfect representative for us, the triumphant yahoo species. The mandrill of Blushing Monday shall be called "Pinky."

Toward the end of the day, we will celebrate—on television, in our newspapers, and at public gatherings—the highest reaches of achievement in art, science, and the work of charity; and do it all in a burlesque, giddy, and high-spirited way. Either civilization is worth the cost or humanity is obliged to purge itself from the earth. Because we have not chosen the latter option, we owe it to the world to give thanks for its sacrifices.

(Frederick Turner)

Questions

1. Define the following words as they are used in Turner's essay: *transmute, debauchers, pillaging, ludicrous, prelude, paradox, culinary, manic, purge.*

2. What is the key point regarding human behavior that Turner appears to be making in this essay? Explain whether or not you agree with this central observation.

3. In what ways do the particular rituals and festivities that mark Blushing Monday correspond to the purpose of the holiday as described by Turner?

14. Reviews (Summary and Evaluation)

Write an essay in which you review a particular book, movie, or television program.

Guidelines

Generally, a review contains a summary, an evaluation, and a recommendation.

Begin with a concise *summary* of the plot: identify the major characters and explain what happens to them. If you're reviewing a weekly television series, summarize a typical plot. Also, tell what type of book, movie, or television program this is—comedy, mystery, romance, soap opera, or whatever.

The longest part of your essay should be the *evaluation*: identify what you particularly like or dislike, and explain why. Point out specific strengths or weaknesses. Discuss to what extent the book, movie, or television program fulfills what it apparently set out to do. For example, don't criticize a comedy because it's not great drama; it doesn't pretend to be. You may criticize it, however, for not being the least bit funny. In your evaluation, you may also compare the book, movie, or television program to a similar work or to a previous work by the same writer or producer.

End your review with a *recommendation*. Is the book worth reading? Is the movie or television program worth seeing? What type of audience would like it? What type probably wouldn't?

You are writing this review for someone who has not read the book or viewed the movie or television program. Whether or not your reader takes the time to do so will depend on what you say. Therefore, be sure to support all your observations. It's not enough to say that the work is "great" or "terrible"; you need to explain what makes it so.

The following essay offers a review of the controversial MTV cartoon series *Beavis and Butt-head*. Compare your own attitudes to the program with those expressed by professional critic James Wolcott.

An Airhead Exercise in Aimless Activity

Watching certain programs is like having a TV inside your TV. They act as framing devices—a box within a box. They repackage the original show, placing ironic quotation marks around content that would otherwise be too sordid or tedious to watch. . . .

MTV's "Beavis and Butt-head," created by Mike Judge, represents a non-advance in the art of animation. If anything, it beats a ragged retreat. Their heads filling the screen like a pair of potato chips, Beavis and Butt-head share a bumpy sofa, stare at a non-stop circular of infomercials, game shows, and rock videos, and offer their own critical remarks. Vegetating without any parental supervision, they lead a lowest-common-denominator existence. They live in a generic suburb, attend a generic high school, and flip burgers at a generic fast-food outlet. They change their T-shirts about once every six months.

Because of their vast pockets of ignorance (advanced geometry is "triangles and stuff"), idiot pranks, and insipid wordplay, Beavis and Butt-head have been nominated by *Newsweek, The Nation*, and Joe Queenan in *Playboy* as the official pet rocks of the New Stupidity, a movement that includes Howard Stern and the "Wayne's World" movies. I think the dumb surface is deceptive. The show practices a shrewd primitivism. Now that the furor has died down over the series' animal-torture and firebug tendencies, it's clear that "Beavis and Butt-head" is a makeshift addictive classic, like *Mad* and "Louie, Louie"—a random virus that infects the entire pop culture.

Although "Beavis and Butt-head" satirizes psychobabble and political correctness, the show is mostly an airhead exercise in aimless activity. Like Laurel and Hardy, Beavis and Butt-head idle sideways through an endless sunny afternoon. The best episodes are those in which they set out for adventure, their Popsicle-stick legs leading them straight into disaster. A local hood squires them around in the trunk of his car; a tornado tears through a trailer park, interrupting their chance to score with some trailer chicks. In perhaps the prize episode, their attempt to buy a jockstrap has them trying on smaller and smaller sizes (Butt-head: "I'm no Don Johnson"), until they end up wearing eye patches as athletic supporters, only to be pictured on the front page of the school paper under the headline "THE THONG HAS ARRIVED!" Although the setbacks they suffer are at least as bad as those inflicted on Jay Sherman in "The Critic," there's no sticky trace of masochism in their exploits, because they have such a deadpan disregard for their own dignity. They rotate inside a dryer just to make themselves dizzy. They're at that age when any new sensation (fear, nausea, and even pain) is a trip, because it gives them something to talk about afterward.

Beavis and Butt-head have a binary system when it comes to evaluating experience. Either things are cool or they suck, though some things overlap. The conceptual coup of "Beavis and Butt-head" is the crosscut between the overproduced, hyperactive rock videos they watch—loaded with explosions, black leather, tattooed flesh, computer graphics—and the fishy reaction shots of the two, their casual sarcasm undercutting the lavish outlay of rock-star ego. Butt-head accuses George Michael of making eyes at Beavis. The band Kiss, who wear whiteface, are "pretty cool, for a bunch of mimes." Beavis and Butt-head compare a broody black-and-white video starring Chris Isaak to those ads by that perfume guy Alvin Klein. Like Mel Brooks' critic, they're baffled by abstract explorations. An especially atmospheric video by U2 moves Butt-head to ask, "Is this art?" (Beavis: "This means something.") When Yoko Ono pops onto the screen, Butt-head exclaims, "What the *hell* is *this* crap?" The more you watch Beavis and Butt-head, the more you're struck by how apt, beautifully timed, and effortlessly funny their backtalk is. It's true that reruns of the show have been in rotation for so long on MTV that these two characters are in danger of becoming historical figures, but their effect is so contagious that regular rock videos seem incomplete without the yellow "Beavis and Butt-head" sticker on the corner of the screen.

As television expands into more channels, more niche categories, there will be more mutations to monitor what's on those channels. TV will become a mall jammed with copycat boutiques. On E!, "Talk Soup" has already spawned "Pure Soap," a digest of daytime drama. It's probably only a matter of time before there's a program keeping tabs on the network news-magazine shows, folding stories from "20/20," "Dateline," and "PrimeTime Live" into one handy video volume. Such meta-TV seems to cater to our condescension toward TV per se. We watch and withdraw at the same time, telling ourselves that this focal shift is deconstructive. I wonder how long viewers will be able to maintain their superior attitude watching used clips in new folders. If we're so superior to what we're watching, why aren't we doing something else? It's easy to fake being a critic when you're only looking down. It's looking up, or even looking straight ahead, that's hard.

(James Wolcott)

Questions

1. Define the following words as they are used in Wolcott's essay: *insipid, primitivism, psychobabble, binary, condescension.*

2. What aspects of *Beavis and Butt-head* appeal to Wolcott? Explain whether or not you share his enthusiasm.

3. In his final paragraph, Wolcott moves beyond *Beavis and Butt-head* to criticize the general trend toward "meta-TV." Summarize what you think is the main point of this final paragraph, and explain why you agree or disagree with Wolcott's observations.

15. Responses (Critical Analysis and Evaluation)

In response to the short story that follows, write an essay in which you examine the attitudes and conflicts of Sylvia, the young girl who recalls a particular trip to a Manhattan toy store.

Guidelines

Your practice in analyzing and evaluating paragraphs and essays in earlier assignments has prepared you for this exercise in critical analysis. Begin by reading—and enjoying—"The Lesson," a short story by the African-American author Toni Cade Bambara. Then, after studying the questions at the end, *re*read the story. Mark what you think are key passages, and take notes on your reactions to particular things that Sylvia says and does. A brainstorming session with a few of your classmates should help you to focus your thoughts about Sylvia's attitudes and conflicts. Organize your notes into a rough draft in which each body paragraph comments on and illustrates a particular aspect of Sylvia's character. Finally, revise your essay, making sure that you have expressed your responses clearly and supported all of your observations with specific references to details in the story.

The Lesson

Back in the days when everyone was old and stupid or young and foolish and me and Sugar were the only ones just right, this lady moved on our block with nappy hair and proper speech and no makeup. And quite naturally we laughed at her, laughed the way we did at the junk man who went about his business like he was some big-time president and his sorry-ass horse his secretary. And we kinda hated her too, hated the way we did the winos who cluttered up our parks and pissed on our handball walls and stank up our hallways and stairs so you couldn't halfway play hide-and-seek without a goddamn gas mask. Miss Moore was her name. The only woman on the block with no first name. And she was black as hell, cept for her feet, which were fish-white and spooky. And she was always planning these boring-ass things for us to do, us being my cousin, mostly, who lived on the block cause we all moved North the same time and to the same apartment then spread out gradual to breathe. And our parents would yank our heads into some kinda shape and crisp up our clothes so we'd be presentable for travel with Miss Moore, who always looked like she was going to church, though she never did. Which is just one of the things the grownups talked about when they talked behind her back like a dog. But when she came calling with some sachet she'd sewed up or some gingerbread she'd made or some book, why then they'd all be too embarrassed to turn her down and we'd get handed over all spruced up. She'd been to college and said it was only right that she should take responsibility for the young ones' education, and she not even related by marriage or blood. So they'd go for it. Specially Aunt Gretchen. She was the main gofer in the family. You got some ole dumb shit foolishness you want somebody to go for, you send for Aunt Gretchen. She been screwed into the go-along for so long, it's a blood-deep natural thing with her. Which is how she got saddled with me and Sugar and Junior in the first place while our mothers were in a la-de-da apartment up the block having a good ole time.

So this one day Miss Moore rounds us all up at the mailbox and it's puredee hot and she's knockin herself out about arithmetic. And school suppose to let up in summer I heard, but she don't never let up. And the starch in my pinafore scratching the shit outta me and I'm really hating this nappy-head bitch and her goddamn college degree. I'd much rather go to the pool or to the show where it's cool. So me and Sugar leaning on the mailbox being surly, which is a Miss Moore word. And Flyboy checking out what everybody brought for lunch. And Fat Butt already wasting his peanut-butter-and-jelly sandwich like the pig he is. And Junebug punchin on Q. T.'s arm for potato chips. And Rosie Giraffe shifting from one hip to the other waiting for somebody to step on her foot or ask her if she from Georgia so she can kick ass, preferably Mercedes'. And Miss Moore asking us do we know what money is, like we a bunch of retards. I mean real money, she say, like it's only poker chips or monopoly papers we lay on the grocer. So right away I'm tired of this and say so. And would much rather snatch Sugar and go to the Sunset and terrorize the West Indian kids and take their hair ribbons and their money too. And Miss Moore files that remark away for next week's lesson on brotherhood, I can tell. And finally I say we oughta get to the subway cause it's cooler and besides we might meet some cute boys. Sugar done swiped her mama's lipstick, so we ready.

So we heading down the street and she's boring us silly about what things cost and what our parents make and how much goes for rent and how money ain't divided up right in this country. And then she gets to the part about we all poor and live in the slums, which I don't feature. And I'm ready to speak on that, but she steps out in the street and hails two cabs just like that. Then she hustles half the crew in with her and hands me a five-dollar bill and tells me to calculate 10 percent tip for the driver. And we're off. Me and Sugar and Junebug and Flyboy hangin out the window and hollering to everybody, putting lipstick on each other cause Flyboy a faggot anyway, and making farts with our sweaty armpits. But I'm mostly trying to figure how to spend this money. But they all fascinated with the meter ticking and Junebug starts laying bets as to how much it'll read when Flyboy can't hold his breath no more. Then Sugar lays bets as to how much it'll be when we get there. So I'm stuck. Don't nobody want to go for my plan, which is to jump out at the next light and run off to the first bar-b-que we can find. Then the driver tells us to get the hell out cause we there already. And the meter reads eighty-five cents. And I'm stalling to figure out the tip and Sugar say give him a dime. And I decide he don't need it bad as I do, so later for him. But then he tries to take off with Junebug foot still in the door so we talk about his mama something ferocious. Then we check out that we on Fifth Avenue and everybody dressed up in stockings. One lady in a fur coat, hot as it is. White folks crazy.

"This is the place," Miss Moore say, presenting it to us in the voice she uses at the museum. "Let's look in the windows before we go in."

"Can we steal?" Sugar asks very serious like she's getting the ground rules squared away before she plays. "I beg your pardon," say Miss Moore, and we fall out. So she leads us around the windows of the toy store and me and Sugar screamin, "This is mine, that's mine, I gotta have that, that was made for me, I was born for that," till Big Butt drowns us out.

"Hey, I'm goin to buy that there."

"That there? You don't even know what it is, stupid."

"I do so," he say punchin on Rosie Giraffe. "It's a microscope."

"Whatcha gonna do with a microscope, fool?"

"Look at things."

"Like what, Ronald?" ask Miss Moore. And Big Butt ain't got the first notion. So here go Miss Moore gabbing about the thousands of bacteria in a drop of water and the somethinorother in a speck of blood and the million and one living things in the air around us is invisible to the naked eye. And what she say that for? Junebug go to town on that "naked" and we rolling. Then Miss Moore ask what it cost. So we all jam into the window smudgin it up and the price tag say $300. So then she ask how long'd take for Big Butt and Junebug to save up their allowances. "Too long," I say. "Yeh," adds Sugar, "outgrown it by that time." And Miss Moore say no, you never outgrow learning instruments. "Why, even medical students and interns and," blah, blah, blah. And we ready to choke Big Butt for bringing it up in the first damn place.

"This here costs four hundred eighty dollars," says Rosie Giraffe. So we pile up all over her to see what she pointin out. My eyes tell me it's a chunk of glass cracked with something heavy, and different-color inks dripped into the splits, then the whole thing put into a oven or something. But for $480 it don't make sense.

"That's a paperweight made of semi-precious stones fused together under tremendous pressure," she explains slowly, with her hands doing the mining and all the factory work.

"So what's a paperweight?" asks Rosie Giraffe.

"To weigh paper with, dumbbell," say Flyboy, the wise man from the East.

"Not exactly," say Miss Moore, which is what she say when you warm or way off too. "It's to weigh paper down so it won't scatter and make your desk untidy." So right away me and Sugar curtsy to each other and then to Mercedes who is more the tidy type.

"We don't keep paper on top of the desk in my class," say Junebug, figuring Miss Moore crazy or lyin one.

"At home, then," she say. "Don't you have a calendar and pencil case and a blotter and a letter-opener on your desk at home where you do your homework?" And she know damn well what our homes look like cause she nosys around in them every chance she gets.

"I don't even have a desk," say Junebug. "Do we?"

"No. And I don't get no homework neither," says Big Butt.

"And I don't even have a home," say Flyboy like he do at school to keep the white folks off his back and sorry for him. Send this poor kid to camp posters, is his specialty.

"I do," says Mercedes. "I have a box of stationery on my desk and a picture of my cat. My godmother bought the stationery and the desk. There's a big rose on each sheet and the envelopes smell like roses."

"Who wants to know about your smelly-ass stationery," say Rosie Giraffe fore I can get my two cents in.

"It's important to have a work area all your own so that . . ."

"Will you look at this sailboat, please," say Flyboy, cuttin her off and pointin to the thing like it was his. So once again we tumble all over each other to gaze at this magnificent thing in the toy store which is just big enough to maybe sail two kittens across the pond if you strap them to the posts tight. We all start reciting the price tag like we in assembly. "Handcrafted sailboat of fiberglass at one thousand one hundred ninety-five dollars."

"Unbelievable," I hear myself say and am really stunned. I read it again for myself just in case the group recitation put me in a trance. Same thing. For some reason this pisses me off. We look at Miss Moore and she lookin at us, waiting for I dunno what.

"Who'd pay all that when you can buy a sailboat set for a quarter at Pop's, a tube of glue for a dime, and a ball of string for eight cents? It must have a motor and a whole lot else besides," I say. "My sailboat cost me about fifty cents."

"But will it take water?" say Mercedes with her smart ass.

"Took mine to Alley Pond Park once," say Flyboy. "String broke. Lost it. Pity."

"Sailed mine in Central Park and it keeled over and sank. Had to ask my father for another dollar."

"And you got the strap," laugh Big Butt. "The jerk didn't even have a string on it. My old man wailed on his behind."

Little Q. T. was staring hard at the sailboat and you could see he wanted it bad.

But he too little and somebody'd just take it from him. So what the hell. "This boat for kids, Miss Moore?"

"Parents silly to buy something like that just to get all broke up," say Rosie Giraffe.

"That much money it should last forever," I figure.

"My father'd buy it for me if I wanted it."

"Your father, my ass," say Rosie Giraffe getting a chance to finally push Mercedes.

"Must be rich people shop here," say Q. T.

"You are a very bright boy," say Flyboy. "What was your first clue?" And he rap him on the head with the back of his knuckles, since Q. T. the only one he could get away with. Though Q. T. liable to come up behind you years later and get his licks in when you half expect it.

"What I want to know is," I says to Miss Moore though I never talk to her, I wouldn't give the bitch that satisfaction, "is how much a real boat costs? I figure a thousand'd get you a yacht any day."

"Why don't you check that out," she says, "and report back to the group?" Which really pains my ass. If you gonna mess up a perfectly good swim day least you could do is have some answers. "Let's go in," she say like she got something up her sleeve. Only she don't lead the way. So me and Sugar turn the corner to where the entrance is, but when we get there I kinda hang back. Not that I'm scared, what's there to be afraid of, just a toy store. But I feel funny, shame. But what I got to be shamed about? Got as much right to go in as anybody. But somehow I can't seem to get hold of the door, so I step away from Sugar to lead. But she hangs back too. And I look at her and she looks at me and this is ridiculous. I mean, damn, I have never ever been shy about doing nothing or going nowhere. But then Mercedes steps up and then Rosie Giraffe and Big Butt crowd in behind and shove, and next thing we all stuffed into the doorway with only Mercedes squeezing past us, smoothing out her jumper and walking right down the aisle. Then the rest of us tumble in like a glued-together jigsaw done all wrong. And people lookin at us. And it's like the time me and Sugar crashed into the Catholic church on a dare. But once we got in there and everything so hushed and holy and the candles and the bowin and the handkerchiefs on all the drooping heads, I just couldn't go through with the plan. Which was for me to run up to the altar and do a tap dance while Sugar played the nose flute and messed around in the holy water. And Sugar kept givin me the elbow. Then later teased me so bad I tied her up in the shower and turned it on and locked her in. And she'd be there till this day if Aunt Gretchen hadn't finally figured I was lyin about the boarder takin a shower.

Same thing in the store. We all walkin on tiptoe and hardly touchin the games and puzzles and things. And I watched Miss Moore who is steady watchin us like she waitin for a sign. Like Mama Drewery watches the sky and sniffs the air and takes note of just how much slant is in the bird formation. Then me and Sugar bump smack into each other, so busy gazing at the toys, specially the sailboat. But we don't laugh and go into our fat-lady bump-stomach routine. We just stare at that price tag. Then Sugar run a finger over the whole boat. And I'm jealous and want to hit her. Maybe not her, but I sure want to punch somebody in the mouth.

"Watcha bring us here for, Miss Moore?"

"You sound angry, Sylvia. Are you mad about something?" Givin me one of them grins like she tellin a grown-up joke that never turns out to be funny. And she's lookin very closely at me like maybe she planning to do my portrait from memory. I'm mad, but I won't give her that satisfaction. So I slouch around the store bein very bored and say, "Let's go."

Me and Sugar at the back of the train watchin the tracks whizzin by large then small then getting gobbled up in the dark. I'm thinkin about this tricky toy I saw in the store. A clown that somersaults on a bar then does chin-ups just cause you yank lightly at his leg. Cost $35. I could see me askin my mother for a $35 birthday clown. "You wanna who that costs what?" she'd say, cocking her head to the side to get a better view of the hole in my head. Thirty-five dollars could buy new bunk beds for Junior and Gretchen's boy. Thirty-five dollars and the whole household could go visit Granddaddy Nelson in the country. Thirty-five dollars would pay for the rent and the piano bill too. Who are these people that spend that much for performing clowns and $1000 for toy sailboats? What kinda work they do and how they live and how come we ain't in on it? Where we are is who we are, Miss Moore always pointin out. But it don't necessarily have to be that way, she always adds then waits for somebody to say that poor people have to wake up and demand their share of the pie and don't none of us know what kind of pie she talking about in the first damn place. But she ain't so smart cause I still got her four dollars from the taxi and she sure ain't gettin it. Messin up my day with this shit Sugar nudges me in my pocket and winks.

Miss Moore lines us up in front of the mailbox where we started from, seem like years ago, and I got a headache for thinkin so hard. And we lean all over each other so we can hold up under the draggy-ass lecture she always finishes us off with at the end before we thank her for borin us to tears. But she just looks at us like she readin tea leaves. Finally she say, "Well, what did you think of F. A. O. Schwarz?"

Rosie Giraffe mumbles, "White folks crazy."

"I'd like to go there again when I get my birthday money," says Mercedes, and we shove her out the pack so she has to lean on the mailbox by herself.

"I'd like a shower. Tiring day," say Flyboy.

Then Sugar surprises me by sayin, "You know, Miss Moore, I don't think all of us here put together eat in a year what that sailboat costs." And Miss Moore lights up like somebody goosed her. "And?" she say, urging Sugar on. Only I'm standin on her foot so she don't continue.

"Imagine for a minute what kind of society it is in which some people can spend on a toy what it would cost to feed a family of six or seven. What do you think?"

"I think," say Sugar pushing me off her feet like she never done before, cause I whip her ass in a minute, "that this is not much of a democracy if you ask me. Equal chance to pursue happiness means an equal crack at the dough, don't it?" Miss Moore is beside herself and I am disgusted with Sugar's treachery. So I stand on her foot one more time to see if she'll shove me. She shuts up, and Miss Moore looks at me, sorrowfully I'm thinkin. And somethin weird is goin on, I can feel it in my chest.

"Anybody else learn anything today?" lookin dead at me. I walk away and Sugar has to run to catch up and don't even seem to notice when I shrug her arm off my shoulder.

"Well, we got four dollars anyway," she says.

"Uh hunh."

"We could go to Hascombs and get half a chocolate layer and then go to the Sunset and still have plenty money for potato chips and ice cream sodas."

"Un hunh."

"Race you to Hascombs," she say.

We start down the block and she gets ahead which is O.K. by me cause I'm going to the West End and then over to the Drive to think this day through. She can run if she want to and even run faster. But ain't nobody gonna beat me at nuthin.

(Toni Cade Bambara)

Question

1. Explain what you think is the significance of the story's title. Has Sylvia learned any lessons? Are there any lessons that she seems to resist learning?

2. What appears to be Sylvia's attitude toward the authority figures in her life? Why do you think that she feels this way?

3. What appears to be Sylvia's attitude toward the other children? Why do you think that she feels this way?

4. Try rewriting the first paragraph of "The Lesson" in standard ("correct") English. How does this exercise in revision help to demonstrate the importance of Sylvia's language to our understanding of her character?

5. For all the humor in Bambara's story, the author delivers some serious social observations. What social commentary do you find in the story, and how is it presented?

6. What do you think Sylvia means when she says at the end of the story, "But ain't nobody gonna beat me at nuthin." Is she referring only to Sugar?

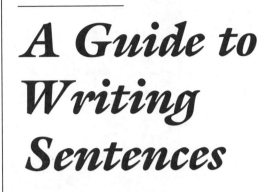

PART TWO

A Guide to Writing Sentences

CHAPTER FIFTEEN

Basic Sentence Structures

Preview

This chapter will give you practice in building and combining basic sentence structures. You will learn to identify and use subjects and verbs, which together form the basic sentence unit. You will then expand simple sentences by adding adjectives, adverbs, and prepositional phrases. Finally, you will practice connecting words, phrases, and clauses through coordination. An understanding of these basic sentence structures will help you as you revise your writing for clarity and correctness. This chapter will also prepare you for the rest of the work you will be doing in Part Two.

15.A Basic Sentence Parts

You do not need a thorough knowledge of formal English grammar to be a good writer. However, knowing a few basic grammatical terms will help you to follow the exercises here and in later chapters, exercises that provide opportunities to *apply* the principles of good writing. Therefore, the brief definitions and explanations below are for you to use, not simply memorize.

15.A¹ Subjects and Verbs

A sentence is commonly defined as "a complete unit of thought." Normally, a sentence expresses a relationship, conveys a command, voices a question, or describes someone or something. It begins with a capital letter and ends with a period, question mark, or exclamation point.

The basic parts of a sentence are the **subject** and the **verb**. The subject is usually a noun—a word that names a person, place, or thing. The verb usually follows the subject and identifies an action or state of being. See if you can identify the subject and verb in each of the following sentences:

> The crow flies.
> The teachers weep.
> My daughter is a wrestler.
> The children are tired.

In each of these sentences, the subject is a noun: *crow, teachers, daughter, children*. The verbs in the first two sentences—*flies, weep*—show action and answer the question, "What does the subject do?" The verbs in the last two sentences—*is, are*—are called *linking verbs* because they link the subject with a word that renames it (*wrestler*) or describes it (*tired*). (You can find more information about the different verb forms in Chapters Eighteen and Nineteen.)

EXERCISE IDENTIFYING SUBJECTS AND VERBS

For each of the following sentences, underline the subject and circle the verb.

1. The dog shivered.
2. An owl shrieked.
3. The moon disappeared behind the clouds.
4. We waited.
5. For a moment, nobody even breathed.
6. A light rain fell on our heads.
7. The leaves trembled.
8. Our hearts beat faster and faster.
9. Then the black sky opened up.
10. Furious flames lit up the night. ■

15.A² Pronouns

Pronouns are words that take the place of nouns in a sentence. In the second sentence below, the pronoun *she* stands for *Merdine*:

Merdine danced on the roof of her trailer during the thunderstorm.
She was waving an American flag.

As the second sentence demonstrates, a pronoun, like a noun, may serve as the subject of a sentence. The common subject pronouns are *I, you, he, she, it, we*, and *they*. (You can find more information on pronouns in Chapter Twenty.)

15.A³ Objects

In addition to serving as subjects, nouns may also serve as **objects** in sentences. Instead of *performing* the action, as subjects usually do, objects *receive* the action and usually follow the verb. See if you can identify the objects in the sentences below:

The girls hurled rocks.
Melissa swigged coffee.
Victor dropped the casserole.

The objects—*rocks, coffee, casserole*—all answer the question *what*: What was hurled? What was swigged? What was dropped?

As the following sentences demonstrate, pronouns may also serve as objects:

Before drinking the carrot juice, George sniffed it.
Because I had no money to give the tramp, I kissed him instead.

The common object pronouns are *me, you, him, her, it, us,* and *them.*

15.A⁴ The Basic Sentence Unit

You should now be able to identify the main parts of the basic sentence unit: SUBJECT plus VERB, or SUBJECT plus VERB plus OBJECT. Remember that the subject names what the sentence is about, the verb tells what the subject does or is, and the object receives the action of the verb. Although many other structures can be added to this basic unit, the pattern of SUBJECT plus VERB (or SUBJECT plus VERB plus OBJECT) can be found in even the longest and most complicated structures.

EXERCISE IDENTIFYING SUBJECTS, VERBS, AND OBJECTS

On the line to the right of each sentence below, identify the underlined word as a *subject*, a *verb*, or an *object*.

1. The shopping mall is a common experience for the majority of American youth. _____

2. They have probably been going there all their lives. _____

3. Some bought their first toy in a mall. _____

4. Some read their first book in a mall. _____

5. Some may have smoked their first cigarette—or turned it down—in a mall. _____

6. Many of today's teenagers experienced their first kiss in the mall parking lot. _____

7. Young Americans now spend more time in the mall than anywhere else but home and school. _____

8. They spend so much time at the mall partly because their parents encourage them to go there. _____

9. The mall appears safe, after all, and doesn't seem to harbor any unsavory activities. _____

10. For working parents, in particular, the temptation is to let the mall serve as their babysitter. _____

■

> **Writing Suggestion**
>
> In a paragraph, describe some of the particular activities typically carried out by people at a shopping mall. When you are done, underline the subject(s) and circle the verb(s) in each of your sentences.

15.B Adjectives and Adverbs

A common way of expanding the basic sentence is with *modifiers*—words that add to the meaning of other words. The simplest modifiers are **adjectives** and **adverbs**. Adjectives modify nouns, while adverbs modify verbs, adjectives, and other adverbs. For instance, in the sentence below the adjective *sad* modifies the noun *smile* (the subject of the sentence):

The clown's sad smile touched us deeply.

In the same sentence, the adverb *deeply* modifies the verb *touched*. Used carefully, adjectives and adverbs make our writing clearer and more precise.

EXERCISE ADDING ADJECTIVES

Many adjectives are formed from nouns and verbs. The adjective *thirsty*, for instance, comes from *thirst*, which may be either a noun or a verb. For each pair of sentences below, fill in the blank with the adjective form of the underlined noun or verb. Use your dictionary as a guide.

Example:
We <u>enjoyed</u> the concert. We <u>had a</u> very *enjoyable* evening.

1. Martha's job requires <u>patience</u> and skill. She is a _____ negotiator.

2. All through high school, Jeremy <u>rebelled</u> against his parents and his teachers. Now he has three _____ children of his own.

3. Your suggestion makes a great deal of <u>sense</u>. You have a very _____ idea.

4. Professor Legree views students only as an <u>irritation</u>. He is a very peevish and _____ old man.

5. The parson was <u>scandalized</u> by Merdine's singing and dancing. He thought her behavior was _____.

6. Telling jokes that will not <u>offend</u> others is difficult. Some comedians are deliberately _____ . ■

EXERCISE ADDING ADVERBS

Many adverbs are formed by adding *-ly* to an adjective. The adverb *softly*, for instance, comes from the adjective *soft*. Note, however, that not all adverbs end in *-ly*. *Very, quite, always, almost,* and *often* are some of the common adverbs not formed from adjectives.

For each pair of sentences below, fill in the blank with the adverb form of the underlined adjective. Use your dictionary as a guide.

Example:
By nature, I am a <u>patient</u> man. However, I can't listen *patiently* to any more of your excuses.

1. This morning Gus had an <u>accidental</u> encounter with the Good Humor man. Gus _____ backed his pick-up truck into an ice cream van.

2. This is a <u>dangerous</u> road. We are driving _____ close to the shoulder.

3. Howard is a <u>graceful</u> dancer. He moves _____ .

4. Paula made a <u>generous</u> contribution to the Independent Order of Odd Fellows. She gives _____ every year.

5. I ordered a <u>manual</u> transmission. Are the windows operated _____ ?

6. The lecture was <u>brief</u>. The dentist spoke _____ about the importance of flossing after every meal. ■

15.B¹ *Arranging Adjectives*

Adjectives most often appear just in front of the nouns they modify:

Several <u>confused</u>, <u>weary</u> pensioners waited patiently in the hallway.

Note that when two or more adjectives precede a noun they are usually separated by commas. But occasionally adjectives *follow* the nouns that they modify:

Several pensioners, <u>confused</u> and <u>weary</u>, waited patiently in the hallway.

Notice here that the commas appear outside the pair of adjectives, which are joined by *and*. Putting the adjectives after the noun is a way of emphasizing them.

Adjectives sometimes appear in a third position in the sentence: after a linking verb such as *am, are, is, was,* or *were*. As their name implies, these verbs link adjectives with the subjects they modify. See if you can identify the adjectives in the sentences below:

His skin was rough.
Your children are cruel.

In each of these sentences, the adjective (*rough, cruel*) modifies the subject but follows the linking verb (*was, are*).

15.B² *Arranging Adverbs*

Adverbs usually follow the verbs they modify:

I study occasionally.

However, an adverb may also appear directly in front of the verb or at the very beginning of a sentence:

I occasionally study.
Occasionally I study.

Because not all adverbs are this flexible in all sentences, you should try them out in different positions until you find the clearest arrangement.

EXERCISE IDENTIFYING ADJECTIVES AND ADVERBS

For each of the following sentences, underline any adjectives and circle any adverbs.

1. The small dog shivered fearfully.
2. Somewhere in the dark trees, an owl shrieked.
3. Suddenly, the moon disappeared behind wispy clouds.
4. We waited silently.
5. For a long moment, nobody even breathed.
6. A light rain fell softly on our heads.
7. The fragile leaves trembled.
8. Our anxious hearts beat quickly.
9. Then the black sky opened up.
10. Furious fires lit up the night. ■

Writing Suggestion

In a paragraph or short essay, recount an experience that was particularly fearful or exciting. When you are done, underline any adjectives and circle any adverbs that you have used in your report.

15.B³ *Combining Sentences with Adjectives and Adverbs*

Many of the exercises that follow in this chapter and the next will call on you to practice the technique of sentence combining. This technique will help you to create various kinds of clear and effective sentences. Consider, for instance, how the two sentences below might be combined:

The lions crept back into their cages.
The cages were dark.

Because the only new information provided by the second sentence is the adjective *dark*, we can attach this detail to the first sentence:

The lions crept back into their <u>dark</u> cages.

Sentence combining allows us to cut out needless repetition and make clear connections between related ideas.

In similar fashion, we can combine details from three or more sentences:

The lions crept back into their cages.
The cages were dark.
The cages were small.
The lions crept angrily.

In addition to placing the adjectives *small* and *dark* in front of the noun *cages*, we can also place the adverb *angrily* in front of the verb *crept*:

The lions <u>angrily</u> crept back into their <u>small, dark</u> cages

Or we may prefer to put the adverb at the beginning of the sentence:

<u>Angrily</u>, the lions crept back into their small, dark cages.

As practice in sentence combining will show you, there are often many ways to build and arrange sentences. The aim of sentence combining, therefore, is not to find the one correct combination of words, but the best combination.

To determine which combination of sentences is the best, you may want to compare your sentences with those created by other students. Read your sentences aloud when you evaluate them: how they sound can be just as revealing as how they look. And keep these six qualities in mind:

Meaning: As far as you can determine, have you accurately conveyed the idea intended by the original author?

Clarity: Is the sentence clear? Can it be understood on the first reading?

Coherence: Do the various parts of the sentence fit together logically and smoothly?

Emphasis: Are key words and phrases put in emphatic positions (usually at the very end or the very beginning of a sentence)?

Conciseness: Does the sentence clearly express an idea without wasting words?

Rhythm: Does the sentence flow, or is it marked by interruptions? Do the interruptions help to emphasize key points (an effective technique), or do they merely distract (an ineffective technique)?

Repeated practice will help you decide which combinations are the clearest and most effective.

You will find two kinds of sentence combining exercises in this chapter and the next. In the first type—*Sentence Building*—you will combine sets of two or more shorter sentences into a single longer sentence, just as we did above. Experiment with different combinations on your own paper, and then copy what you think is the best combination on the lines below the set. In *Paragraph Building* exercises, the second type, you will not only combine sets of short sentences but also arrange these sentences into a paragraph. Use your own paper for the *Paragraph Building* exercises.

The combining exercises that follow will give you practice in building sentences with adjectives and adverbs. They will also prepare you for the more challenging exercises to come later.

EXERCISE SENTENCE BUILDING WITH ADJECTIVES AND ADVERBS

Combine the sentences in each set into a single clear sentence containing at least one adjective or adverb (or both). You should omit words that are needlessly repeated, but do not leave out any important details. Experiment with different combinations on your own paper, and then copy what you think is the best combination on the lines below each set.

Example:
A hobo guarded his bottle of wine.
The hobo was drunk.
The hobo was dirty.
He guarded the bottle jealously.
Combination 1: A drunk, dirty hobo jealously guarded his bottle of wine.
Combination 2: A hobo, drunk and dirty, guarded his bottle of wine jealously.

1. Willie had a beard and a moustache.
   The beard was bushy.
   The beard was long.
   The moustache was droopy.

   _____

   _____

2. The man handed me a photograph of a woman.
   He did this silently.
   The man was old.
   The woman was beautiful.

   _____

   _____

3. The man handed me a photograph of a woman.
   The photograph was torn.
   The photograph was faded.
   The woman was young.

   _____

   _____

4. The photograph brought back memories.
   The memories were brought back instantly.
   The memories were fine.
   The memories were old.

   _____

   _____

5. The photograph of the woman brought back memories.
   The memories were brought back instantly.
   The woman was beautiful.
   The woman was young.
   The photograph was torn.
   The photograph was faded.
   The memories were fine.
   The memories were old.

   _____

   _____

■

EXERCISE PARAGRAPH BUILDING WITH ADJECTIVES AND ADVERBS

On your own paper, combine the sentences in each set into a single clear sentence with at least one adjective or adverb (or both). Then arrange your new sentences into a paragraph.

Martha's Departure

1. Martha waited on her front porch.
   She waited patiently.

2. She wore a bonnet and a calico dress.
   The bonnet was plain.
   The bonnet was white.
   The dress was long.

3. She watched the sun sink beyond the fields.
   The fields were empty.

4. Then she watched the light in the sky.
   The light was thin.
   The light was white.
   The sky was distant.

5. She listened for the sound.
   She listened carefully.
   The sound was soft.
   The sound was familiar.

6. A ship descended through the evening air.
   The ship was long.
   The ship was silver.
   The ship descended suddenly.
   The evening air was warm.

7. Martha picked up her purse.
   The purse was small.
   The purse was black.
   She picked it up calmly.

8. The spaceship landed in the field.
   The spaceship was shiny.
   It landed smoothly.
   The field was empty.

9. Martha walked toward the ship.
   She walked slowly.
   She walked gracefully.

10. Minutes later, the field was silent again.
    The field was dark again.
    The field was empty again. ■

Writing Suggestion

In a paragraph or short essay, recount a particular departure of your own—leaving home, quitting a job, or saying goodbye to a close friend. When you are done, underline any adjectives and circle any adverbs that you have used in your report.

15.C Prepositional Phrases

Acting like adjectives and adverbs, **prepositional phrases** add meaning to the nouns and verbs in a sentence. There are two prepositional phrases in the following sentence:

The spaceship <u>from Venus</u> landed <u>in the field</u>.

The first prepositional phrase, *from Venus*, modifies the noun *spaceship*; the second, *in the field*, modifies the verb *landed*. The two phrases provide information that helps us to understand the sentence.

15.C¹ Prepositions

A prepositional phrase has two parts: a preposition plus a noun or pronoun. Some of the common prepositions appear in the following list.

about	between	of
above	beyond	off
across	by	on
after	despite	outside
against	down	over
along	during	past
among	except	through
around	for	to
at	from	under
before	in	until
behind	inside	up
below	into	with
beneath	near	without
beside		

EXERCISE IDENTIFYING PREPOSITIONAL PHRASES

Underline each prepositional phrase in the following report.

The Burglar Who Went Too Far

A trail-blazing burglar broke into a vast mansion on millionaire's row in June 1982 at Bel Air, Los Angeles. While on a sack-filling tour of this palatial structure, he went through the ballroom into the hall, down the escalators to the swimming arbor, up to the library across from the dining room, out of the annex and into the conservatory containing sixty-three varieties of tropical plants and a cageful of sulphur-crested parrots.

Deciding that now was the time to make a quick exit, he went back through the dining room, up to the gymnasium, across the indoor tennis court, down a spiral staircase to an enclosed patio with synchronized fountains, out to the cocktail lounge through junior's sound-proofed drum studio and back into the room full of increasingly excited parrots who normally see nobody from one day to the next.

Panicking slightly, he ran back toward the library, through the swinging doors into a gallery containing the early works of Jackson Pollock, out through the kitchen across a jacuzzi enclosure and up two flights of stairs, at which point he became hysterical, ran outside along the balcony around the circular corridors, up more stairs, down the landing into the master bedroom and woke the owners to ask them how to get out.

In order to spare him further distress, they arranged for a local policeman to escort him from the premises.

(Adapted from *Cannibals in the Cafeteria and Other Fabulous Failures*, by Stephen Pile)

■

15.C² *Arranging Prepositional Phrases*

As we saw earlier, a prepositional phrase is often placed after the word it modifies:

The spaceship from Venus landed in the field.

However, like adverbs, prepositional phrases that modify verbs can also be found at the very beginning or very end of a sentence:

Before breakfast every morning, Vera jogs ten miles.
Vera jogs ten miles every morning before breakfast.

The prepositional phrase *before breakfast* modifies the verb *jogs* in both of the above sentences.

Be careful that you don't confuse your reader by misplacing a prepositional phrase:

Vera jogs for ten miles before breakfast in the park every morning.

This arrangement gives the idea that Vera enjoys her breakfast in the park. If this is not the case, shift the prepositional phrase:

Before breakfast every morning, Vera jogs for ten miles in the park.

The best arrangement is one that is clear and uncluttered.

EXERCISE EXPANDING SENTENCES WITH PREPOSITIONAL PHRASES

Expand each sentence below by adding one or more prepositional phrases that answer the question(s) in parentheses.

Example:
The cat jumped and pounced.
(What did the cat jump off of? What did the cat pounce on?)
The cat jumped off the stove and pounced on the gerbil.

1. The candles flickered.
   (Where were the candles?)

   _____

   _____

2. Merdine sat down.
   (With whom did she sit? Where did she sit?)

   _____

   _____

3. The professor lectured.
   (To whom did he lecture? What did he lecture on?)

   _____

   _____

4. Visitors arrived yesterday.
   (Where were the visitors from? Where did they arrive?)

   _____

   _____

5. Jenny stood, raised her shotgun, aimed, and fired.
   (Where did she stand? What did she fire at?)

   _____

   _____

■

EXERCISE SENTENCE BUILDING WITH PREPOSITIONAL PHRASES

Combine the sentences in each set into a single clear sentence containing at least one prepositional phrase. You should omit words that are repeated needlessly, but do not leave out any important details. Experiment with different combinations on your own paper, and then copy what you think is the best combination on the lines below each set.

Example:
The women collect periwinkles.
They collect them down by the shore.
They collect them at dawn.
The women are in Romney.
Combination 1: At dawn in Romney, the women collect periwinkles down by the shore.
Combination 2: At dawn, the women in Romney collect periwinkles down by the shore.

1. A mouse darted.
   It darted across the salad bar.
   This happened during the luncheon.

   _____

   _____

2. We traveled this summer.
We traveled by train.
We traveled from Biloxi.
We traveled to Dubuque.

_____

_____

3. The convertible swerved, crashed, and caromed.
It swerved off the road.
It crashed through the guardrail.
It caromed off a maple tree.

_____

_____

4. Dick planted seeds.
He planted them in his garden.
He did this after his quarrel.
The quarrel was with Mr. Rogers.

_____

_____

5. Grandpa dropped his teeth.
His teeth were false.
His teeth dropped into a glass.
There was prune juice in the glass.

_____

_____

■

EXERCISE PARAGRAPH BUILDING WITH PREPOSITIONAL PHRASES

The following exercise has been adapted from Annie Dillard's memoir, *An American Childhood*. One December afternoon, seven-year-old Annie and friend Mikey hit a driver's windshield with a volley of snowballs. The driver got out of his car and headed after the children. This passage describes the chase.

On your own paper, combine the sentences in each set into a single clear sentence with at least one prepositional phrase. Then rearrange your sentences into a paragraph.

The Chase

1. The man ran after us, and we ran away from him.
   We ran up the sidewalk.
   The sidewalk was snowy.

2. He chased Mikey and me.
   He chased us around the yellow house.
   He chased us up a backyard path we knew by heart.
   He chased us under a low tree.
   He chased us up a bank.
   He chased us through a hedge.
   He chased us down some snowy steps.
   And he chased us across the grocery store's delivery driveway.

3. We smashed through a gap.
   The gap was in another hedge.
   We entered a backyard and ran.
   The backyard was scruffy.
   We ran around its back porch.
   And we ran tight between houses to Edgerton Avenue.

4. We ran across Edgerton.
   We ran to an alley.
   And we ran up our own sliding woodpile to the Halls' front yard.

5. We ran up Lloyd Street.
   And we wound through mazy yards.
   We wound toward the hilltop at Willard and Lang.
   The hilltop was steep.

6. He chased us silently.
   He chased us block after block.

7. He chased us silently.
   He chased us over picket fences.
   He chased us through thorny hedges.
   He chased us between houses.
   He chased us around garbage cans.
   And he chased us across streets.

8. He chased us through the backyard labyrinths of ten blocks.
   He chased us before he caught us.
   He caught us by our jackets. ■

Writing Suggestion

In a paragraph or short essay, provide clear directions for someone who needs to travel from your classroom building to your home. When you are done, underline any prepositional phrases that you have used in your report.

15.D Coordinating Words, Phrases, and Clauses

A common way to connect related words, phrases, and even entire sentences is to *co-ordinate* them—that is, connect them with a word such as *and* or *but*. The following short paragraph contains several coordinated words and phrases:

> Omar is <u>both</u> a good athlete <u>and</u> a good student. He jogs five miles every morning <u>and</u> swims across the lake every afternoon. Often he lifts weights <u>or</u> does calisthenics after dinner. He <u>neither</u> smokes <u>nor</u> drinks, <u>yet</u> he does find time to attend all his classes <u>and</u> study hard.

The underlined words are *coordinators*—short linking words. The simple coordinators are *and, but, yet, or, nor, for*, and *so*.

Similar to these simple coordinators are the *paired coordinators: both . . . and; either . . . or; neither . . . nor; not . . . but; not . . . nor; not only . . . but (also); whether . . . or*. The paired coordinators serve to emphasize the two items being connected. Consider, for example, the sentence below, which contains two adjectives joined by *and*:

> Gus is mean <u>and</u> ugly.

We can rewrite this sentence with paired coordinators to give emphasis to the adjectives:

> Gus is <u>not only</u> mean <u>but</u> ugly.

We frequently use simple and paired coordinators in our writing to connect related ideas.

15.D¹ Punctuating Coordinated Words, Phrases, and Sentences

When just two words or phrases are joined by a coordinator, no punctuation is needed:

> Sam's job offers poor pay <u>but</u> good benefits.

However, when two or more items are listed *before* a coordinator, those items should be separated by commas:

> Dick's job offers poor pay, no benefits, <u>and</u> miserable working conditions.

Similarly, when two complete sentences (called *main clauses*) are joined by a coordinator, place a comma before the coordinator:

> Most people regard the computer as an electronic marvel, <u>yet</u> the principle on which it operates is relatively simple.

Chapter Twenty-one offers additional advice and exercises on punctuating words, phrases, and clauses.

EXERCISE SENTENCE BUILDING WITH COORDINATED WORDS, PHRASES, AND CLAUSES

Combine the sentences in each set into a single clear sentence by coordinating words, phrases, or clauses. Use an appropriate simple or paired coordinator. You should omit words that are needlessly repeated, but do not leave out any important details. Experiment with different combinations on your own paper, and then copy what you think is the best combination on the lines below each set.

Example:
Papa would sit on the front porch.
Papa would sit after supper.
Papa would sit on summer nights.
The nights were warm.
Papa would tell us stories.
The stories were about ghosts.
The stories were about witches.
Combination: On warm summer nights after supper, Papa would sit on the front porch and tell us stories about ghosts and witches.

1. The dancer was not tall.
   The dancer was not slender.
   She was very, very elegant.

   _____

   _____

2. The winds dispersed.
   The rain slackened to a drizzle and a mist.
   The clouds fell apart.
   The sun shone through.

   _____

   _____

3. The pickpocket moved through the crowd.
   He moved quickly.
   He paused beside a policeman.
   He stole the policeman's wallet.
   The pickpocket slipped away.

   _____

   _____

4. The waitress tugged the pencil out of her hair.
Her hair was lacquered.
She licked the pencil point.
She flicked over her bill pad.
She asked if she could take our order.

_____

_____

5. Fenton's brother had a moustache.
The moustache was long.
The moustache was ragged.
Fenton's brother wore a felt hat.
The hat was shapeless.
The hat was battered.
Fenton's brother kept a towel tucked into his waistband.

_____

_____

■

EXERCISE PARAGRAPH BUILDING WITH COORDINATION

The following exercise has been adapted from a chapter in John Steinbeck's novel *The Grapes of Wrath*. This passage describes the arrival of rain after a long drought.

On your own paper, use appropriate coordinators to combine the sentences in each set into a single clear sentence. Arrange your new sentences into a coherent paragraph.

The Coming of Rain

1. The clouds marched in from the ocean.
The clouds were gray.
The clouds marched over the high coast mountains.
The clouds marched over the valleys.

2. The wind blew fiercely.
The wind blew silently, high in the air.
The wind swished in the brush.
The wind roared in the forests.

3. The clouds came in brokenly.
The clouds came in puffs.
The clouds came in folds.
The clouds came in gray crags.

4. The clouds piled in together.
   The clouds settled low over the west.

5. And then the wind stopped.
   The wind left the clouds deep.
   The wind left the clouds solid.

6. The rain began with showers.
   The showers were gusty.
   The rain began with pauses.
   The rain began with downpours.
   Then gradually it settled to a single tempo.
   It was a tempo with small drops.
   It was a tempo with a steady beat.

7. The earth drank the rain until the earth was full.
   The earth drank for two days. ■

Writing Suggestion

In a paragraph or short essay, describe some particularly memorable encounter (either pleasant or unpleasant) that you have had with nature: a blizzard, a sun shower, a flood, a drought, a walk through the woods, an earthquake, a hurricane. When you are done, underline any coordinators that you have used in your report.

Postscript

In this chapter, you have learned to identify these basic sentence parts: *subjects, verbs, objects, adjectives, adverbs, prepositional phrases,* and *coordinators.* More importantly, you have practiced building and combining sentences using these basic sentence parts in a variety of ways. The next chapter will introduce you to some additional sentence structures.

CHAPTER SIXTEEN

Additional Sentence Structures

Preview

This chapter will give you further practice in building and combining sentences. You will work with various structures that can be added to the basic sentence unit. Some of these structures (adjective clauses, appositives, participle phrases) add information about nouns. Others (adverb clauses and absolutes) add information to verbs or entire sentences. The sentence and paragraph building exercises in this chapter, similar to those in Chapter Fifteen, will help you to use these structures effectively in your own writing.

16.A Adjective Clauses

As we saw in the last chapter, coordination is a useful technique for connecting ideas that are roughly equal in importance. Often in our writing, however, we need to show that one idea is more or less important than another. On these occasions we use *subordination* to indicate that one part of a sentence is secondary (or subordinate) to another part. One common form of subordination is the *adjective clause*—a word group that modifies a noun.

Consider, for instance, how the following pair of sentences might be combined:

My father is a superstitious man.
He always sets his unicorn traps at night.

One option, as we saw in Chapter Fifteen, is to coordinate the two sentences:

My father is a superstitious man, and he always sets his unicorn traps at night.

When the sentences are coordinated in this fashion, each main clause is given equal emphasis.

However, what if we wanted to place greater emphasis on one statement than on the other? Then we have the option of reducing the less important statement to an adjective clause. For example, to emphasize the fact that father sets his unicorn traps at night, we can turn the first main clause into an adjective clause, as follows:

My father, who is a superstitious man, always sets his unicorn traps at night.

As you can see, the adjective clause functions as an adjective and immediately follows the noun it modifies—*father*. Like a main clause, an adjective clause contains a subject (in this case, *who*) and a verb (*is*); but unlike a main clause it cannot stand alone: it must follow a noun in a main clause. For this reason, an adjective clause is considered to be subordinate to the main clause.

16.A¹ *Identifying Adjective Clauses*

The most common adjective clauses begin with one of these relative pronouns: *who, which, that*. All three pronouns must refer to a noun, but *who* refers only to people and *which* refers only to things. *That* may refer to either people or things. The sentences below show how these pronouns are used to begin adjective clauses:

> Mr. Clean, who hates rock music, smashed my electric guitar.
> Mr. Clean smashed my electric guitar, which had been a gift from Vera.
> Mr. Clean smashed the electric guitar that Vera had given me.

In the first sentence, the relative pronoun *who* refers to *Mr. Clean*, the subject of the main clause. In the second and third sentences, the relative pronouns *which* and *that* refer to *guitar*, the object of the main clause.

EXERCISE IDENTIFYING ADJECTIVE CLAUSES

Only some of the sentences below contain adjective clauses. Underline any adjective clauses that you find.

1. In the early years of my boyhood, my parents coped very well in America.
2. My father, who had steady work, and my mother, who managed at home, were nobody's victims.
3. Ambition led them to purchase a house that was many blocks from the poor side of Sacramento.
4. This home, which they had worked so hard to own, was only a block from the biggest, whitest houses in town.
5. Despite their achievements, the confidence of "belonging" in public was withheld from them both.
6. They regarded the people at work, the faces in crowds, as very distant from us.
7. They were the others, *los gringos*, who always spoke too rapidly.
8. The English that my parents spoke in public was hesitant, accented, not always grammatical.
9. The Spanish language of their Mexican past, which they spoke at home, sounded in counterpoint to the English of public society.
10. The Spanish that they spoke with ease was a pleasing, soothing, consoling reminder of home.*   ■

*Adapted from a paragraph in *Hunger of Memory* by Richard Rodriguez, 1982.

16.A² *Punctuating Adjective Clauses*

Here are three guidelines that should help you to decide when you need to set off an adjective clause with commas:

1. Adjective clauses beginning with *that* are never set off from the main clause by commas.

   > Food <u>that has turned green in the refrigerator</u> should be thrown away.

   The basic meaning of the sentence would be changed if we omitted the *that* clause, and so commas should not be used.

2. Adjective clauses beginning with *who* or *which* should not be set off by commas if omitting the clause would change the basic meaning of the sentence.

   > Students <u>who turn green</u> should be sent to the infirmary.

   The basic meaning of the sentence would be altered if we omitted the *who* clause, and so commas should not be used.

3. Adjective clauses beginning with *who* or *which* should be set off by commas if omitting the clause would not change the basic meaning of the sentence.

   > Last week's pudding, <u>which has turned green in the refrigerator,</u> should be thrown away.

   The *which* clause provides added, not essential, information, so it is set off from the rest of the sentence by commas.

EXERCISE PUNCTUATING ADJECTIVE CLAUSES

In the sentences below, use commas to set off only those adjective clauses that provide added, but not essential, information. Do not add commas if the adjective clause affects the basic meaning of the sentence.

1. I refuse to live in any house that Jack built.
2. John Wayne who appeared in over two hundred films was the biggest box-office attraction of his time.
3. It is time for an open debate on smoking which many have called the nation's number one health problem.
4. Healthy, intelligent people who refuse to work should not be given government assistance.
5. Students who have young children are invited to use the free day-care center.
6. I left my son at the campus day-care center which is free to all full-time students.
7. Jack who gave Amy a bouquet of ragweed has been exiled to the storm cellar for a week.
8. A physician who smokes and overeats has no right to criticize the personal habits of his patients. ■

16.A³ Adjective Clauses Beginning with the Pronouns Whose *and* Whom

Whose (the possessive form of *who*) and *whom* (the object form of *who*) are also pronouns used to begin adjective clauses. *Whose* begins adjective clauses that describe something that belongs to or is a part of someone or something mentioned in the main clause, as in the sentence below:

I lent some money to Earl, whose house was destroyed in the flood.

Whom stands for the noun that receives the action of the verb in the adjective clause:

Diane, whom we visited last summer in Boise, is moving to Detroit.

Whose and *whom* clauses are far less common than those beginning with *who*, *which*, or *that*.

EXERCISE ADDING PRONOUNS TO ADJECTIVE CLAUSES

Complete each adjective clause below by adding an appropriate pronoun: *who, which, that, whose,* or *whom.*

1. Joan DiNitto is the lawyer _____ handled my case.
2. A lawyer, _____ first responsibility is to her client, should nevertheless have respect for the law.
3. Pandora, _____ had recently celebrated a birthday, opened the big box of gifts.
4. My first car was a ten-year-old Pacer, _____ once was considered "the car of the future."
5. The creek beds, _____ in May are usually swollen to bursting, are no more than a summer trickle.
6. Sun City Center is an unincorporated town of about 8,500 people, almost all of _____ are over the age of sixty.
7. Professor Legree, _____ dissertation on toadstools has been published by Vanity Press, has agreed to be the keynote speaker at the next meeting.
8. The green liquid _____ you gave me is not cough syrup. ■

16.A⁴ Combining Sentences with Adjective Clauses

Consider how the following two sentences can be combined:

My running shoes fell apart after the first hundred yards.
My running shoes cost over fifty dollars.

By substituting the pronoun *which* for the subject of the second sentence, we can create a single sentence containing an adjective clause:

My running shoes, <u>which cost over fifty dollars</u>, fell apart after the first hundred yards.

Or, we may choose to substitute *which* for the subject of the first sentence:

My running shoes, <u>which fell apart after the first hundred yards</u>, cost over fifty dollars.

Put what you think is the main idea in the main clause, the secondary idea in the adjective clause.

Another way to combine sentences is to replace the *object* of one of the sentences with a relative pronoun. Try combining the following pair of sentences by replacing the object *umbrella* in the second sentence with *which*:

Professor Legree lost his umbrella.
He has owned his umbrella for over twenty years.

Here is how the sentences can be combined:

Professor Legree lost his umbrella, <u>which he has owned for over twenty years</u>.

Whichever method is appropriate, keep in mind that the adjective clause is usually placed directly after the noun it modifies. The following exercises will give you practice in combining sentences with adjective clauses.

EXERCISE SENTENCE BUILDING WITH ADJECTIVE CLAUSES

Combine the sentences in each set by turning the underlined sentence into an adjective clause. Begin the adjective clause with an appropriate pronoun: *who, which, that, whose,* or *whom.*

Example:
The space shuttle is a rocket.
The rocket is manned.
<u>This rocket can be flown back to earth.</u>
<u>This rocket can be re-used.</u>
Combination: The space shuttle is a manned rocket <u>that can be flown back to earth and re-used.</u>

1. John Reed helped found the Communist Labor party in the United States.
   John Reed is the only American buried at the Kremlin in Moscow.

   _____

   _____

2. Clarence Birdseye got the idea of selling frozen food after dining on caribou.
   <u>The caribou had been frozen in the Arctic ice.</u>

   _____

   _____

3. A series of baffling fires in an Ohio rubber factory was traced to a young woman.
<u>The young woman's body was found to carry an electrostatic charge of 30,000 volts.</u>

_____

_____

4. <u>Merdine was born in a boxcar.</u>
<u>Merdine was born somewhere in Arkansas.</u>
Merdine grows homesick every time she hears the wail of a train whistle.

_____

_____

5. <u>Oxygen is colorless.</u>
<u>Oxygen is tasteless.</u>
<u>Oxygen is odorless.</u>
Oxygen is the chief life-supporting element of all plant life.
Oxygen is the chief life-supporting element of all animal life.

_____

_____

6. Sammy has curly blond hair.
<u>He wears his hair very long.</u>*
Sammy has hazel eyes.
<u>The eyes reveal a lively and ironic wit.</u>*

(*Create _two_ adjective clauses as you combine these sentences.)

_____

_____

■

EXERCISE PARAGRAPH BUILDING WITH ADJECTIVE CLAUSES

The following exercise has been adapted from _The Water Is Wide_, by Pat Conroy. In this passage the author describes the island of Yamacraw, where he worked for a year as a teacher.

On your own paper, combine the sentences in each set into a single clear sentence, and arrange your new sentences into a paragraph. Sentences that can be turned into adjective clauses are underlined.

Yamacraw

1. Yamacraw is an island.
   The island is off the South Carolina mainland.
   The island is not far from Savannah, Georgia.

2. The twentieth century has basically ignored the presence of Yamacraw.

3. The island is populated with black people.
   These people depend on the sea for a living.
   These people depend on their small farms for a living.

4. Thus far, no bridge connects Yamacraw with the mainland.
   Anyone who sets foot on the island comes by water.

5. The roads of the island are unpaved.
   The roads are rutted by the passage of ox carts.
   Ox carts are still a major form of transportation.

6. The hand pump serves up water to the residents.
   The water is questionable.
   The residents are black.
   The residents live in their small familiar houses.

7. Sears, Roebuck catalogues perform their classic function.
   They perform this function in the privies.
   The privies are crudely built.
   The privies sit, half-hidden, in the grasses.
   The grasses are tall.
   The grasses are behind the shacks.

8. Electricity came to the island several years ago.
   There are no telephones.

9. To call the island you must go to the Beaufort Sheriff's Office.
   You must talk to the man.
   The man works the radio.

10. Otherwise, Yamacraw remains aloof.
    Yamacraw remains apart from the world.
    The world is beyond the river. ■

Writing Suggestion

In a paragraph or short essay, describe a particular place (a town, a house, even a single room) that contains reminders of the past. When you are done, underline any adjective clauses that you have used in your report.

16.B Appositives

An *appositive* is a word or group of words that identifies or renames another word in a sentence.

Like an adjective clause, an appositive provides more information about a noun. In fact, one may think of an appositive as a simplified adjective clause. Consider, for instance, how the following sentences can be combined.

Elkie Fern is a famous botanist.
Elkie Fern led the children on a nature hike.

One way to combine these sentences is to turn the first into an adjective clause:

Elkie Fern, who is a famous botanist, led the children on a nature hike.

We also have the option of reducing the clause in this sentence to an appositive. All we need to do is omit the pronoun *who* and the verb *is*:

Elkie Fern, a famous botanist, led the children on a nature hike.

The appositive *a famous botanist* identifies the subject, *Elkie Fern*. Not all adjective clauses can be shortened to appositives in this way: only those that contain a form of the verb *to be (is, are, was, were)*. The appositive almost always appears directly after the noun it identifies or renames, where it is usually set off by commas.

EXERCISE IDENTIFYING APPOSITIVES

Some of the sentences below contain adjective clauses; others contain appositives. For each sentence, underline the adjective clause or appositive, and then write **C** (for clause) or **AP** (for appositive) on the line at the left.

_____ **1.** Jimbo Goldberg, who is a professional magician, entertained at my daughter's birthday party.

_____ **2.** Jimbo Goldberg, a professional magician, entertained at my daughter's birthday party.

_____ **3.** Rosa Coldfield, a good country woman, recently decided to move to the city.

_____ **4.** Og, the King of Bashan, was saved from the flood by climbing onto the roof of the ark.

_____ **5.** My sister, who is a supervisor at Union Camp, drives a company car.

_____ **6.** The dog, a sturdy black animal with an idiotic love of life, always followed her to school. ■

EXERCISE SENTENCE BUILDING WITH APPOSITIVES

Combine the sentences in each set by turning the underlined sentence(s) into an appositive. Place the appositive directly after the noun it identifies or renames, and set it off with commas.

Example:
Pan was the pastoral god of fertility.
Pan was depicted as a merry man.
Pan was depicted as an ugly man.
Pan was depicted as a man with a goat's horns, ears, and legs.
Combination: Pan, the pastoral god of fertility, was depicted as a merry, ugly man with a goat's horns, ears, and legs.

1. St. Valentine is the patron saint of lovers.
   St. Valentine was never married.

   _____

   _____

2. Monroe and I strolled through the graveyard.
   The graveyard is the most peaceful spot in town.

   _____

   _____

3. William Faulkner is one of the greatest writers of this century.
   William Faulkner failed freshman composition and left college after two semesters.

   _____

   _____

4. I read a biography of Disraeli.
   Disraeli was a British statesman.
   Disraeli was a novelist of the nineteenth century.

   _____

   _____

5. Paul Revere was a silversmith.
   Paul Revere was a soldier.
   Paul Revere was immortalized in Longfellow's poem for his "midnight ride" to warn the minutemen.

   _____

   _____

6. Jackie Robinson was a fierce competitor.
   <u>Jackie Robinson was a daring base runner.</u>
   <u>Jackie Robinson was a solid hitter.</u>
   Jackie Robinson led the Dodgers to six World Series in his ten years with the team.

_____

_____

■

EXERCISE PARAGRAPH BUILDING WITH APPOSITIVES

The following exercise has been adapted from an article by syndicated columnist Carl T. Rowan. In it, he reminisces about Mrs. Bessie Taylor Gwynn, his high school English teacher. On your own paper, combine the sentences in each set into a single clear sentence, and arrange your new sentences into a paragraph. Sentences that can be turned into appositives are underlined.

1. Born in 1895, in poverty, Bessie grew up in Athens, Alabama.
   There was no public school for blacks in Athens, Alabama.
   (Use *where* to join these two sentences.)

2. She attended Trinity School.
   <u>Trinity School was a private institution for blacks.</u>
   This institution was run by the American Missionary Association.

3. In 1911, she graduated from the Normal School.
   <u>The Normal School was a "super" high school.</u>
   <u>The Normal School was at Fisk University in Nashville.</u>

4. In later years, Mrs. Bessie Taylor Gwynn never talked about her years in Athens.
   <u>Mrs. Bessie Taylor Gwynn was the essence of pride and privacy.</u>

5. She had never attended Fisk University itself because she could not afford the four-year course.
   Only in the months before her death did she reveal that.

6. At Normal School she learned a lot about Shakespeare.
   Most of all she learned about the profound importance of education—especially for a people trying to move up from slavery.

7. Mrs. Gwynn taught hundreds of youngsters during her forty-four-year career.
   Her career was remarkable.
   The youngsters were economically deprived.
   The youngsters were black.

8. These youngsters included my mother, my brothers, my sister, and me.*
   (*You may want to try combining this sentence with those in set 7.)

9. Miss Bessie was an example of an informed, dedicated teacher.
   <u>She was a blessing to children.</u>
   <u>She was an asset to the nation.</u> ■

> **Writing Suggestion**
>
> In a paragraph or short essay, describe a particular teacher who has influenced your life. When you are done, underline any appositives that you may have used in your report.

16.C Adverb Clauses

Adverb clauses are subordinate structures that show the relationship and relative importance of ideas in sentences. They can explain such things as *when, where*, and *why* about an action stated in the main clause. Consider the two sentences below:

A Los Angeles school board tried to ban Tarzan books.
The hero lives with Jane in a tree house, and they aren't married.

What is the connection between these two statements? By turning the second sentence into an adverb clause and combining it with the first sentence, we can make the connection clear:

A Los Angeles school board tried to ban Tarzan books because the hero lives with Jane in a tree house, and they aren't married.

Here the adverb clause (beginning with the adverb *because*) offers a reason for the action stated in the main clause. Notice that an adverb clause cannot stand alone; like an adjective clause, it must be attached to a main clause. But whereas an adjective clause modifies a noun, an adverb clause (like a simple adverb) can modify a verb, an adjective, an adverb, or even the rest of the sentence in which it appears.

An adverb clause begins with an adverb that shows how the clause relates to the rest of the sentence. This adverb may signify time, place, cause, or condition. Adverbs commonly used to begin clauses are listed below.

Time		
after	once	when
as soon as	since	whenever
as long as	till	while
before	until	
Place		
where	wherever	
Cause		
as	in order that	so that
because	since	
Condition		
although	if	though
as	in case	unless
as though	just as	whereas
even if	provided that	while
even though		

EXERCISE IDENTIFYING ADVERB CLAUSES

Only some of the sentences below contain adverb clauses. Underline any adverb clauses that you find.

1. You can register for the course in demonology if you first obtain the permission of the professor.
2. You can register for a course in demonology, but you must first obtain the permission of the professor.
3. Cinderella left the reception early because she was tired.
4. Wherever you go, I will follow.
5. Although the forest looks peaceful, it supports incessant warfare.
6. We gave away our dog so that we could get some sleep at night. ■

16.C¹ *Arranging Adverb Clauses*

Adverb clauses are more flexible than adjective clauses: they may be placed at the beginning, at the end, or occasionally even in the middle of a sentence.

> After the party was over, Mr. Buck took a shortcut home.
> Mr. Buck took a shortcut home after the party was over.
> Mr. Buck, after the party was over, took a shortcut home.

An adverb clause at the beginning of a sentence is usually separated from the main clause by a comma. An adverb clause in the middle of the sentence (usually between the subject and the verb) is often set off by a pair of commas. However, a comma is usually not necessary when the adverb clause follows the main clause.

EXERCISE SENTENCE BUILDING WITH ADVERB CLAUSES

Combine the sentences in each set by turning the underlined sentence(s) into an adverb clause. Begin the adverb clause with an appropriate adverb from the lists on page 246.

Example:
Sailors wear earrings.
The earrings are made of gold.
Sailors always carry the cost of a burial.
They carry the cost on their bodies.
Combination 1: So that they always carry the cost of a burial on their bodies, sailors wear gold earrings.
Combination 2: Sailors wear gold earrings so that they always carry the cost of a burial on their bodies.

1. It is unlikely that Cleopatra actually committed suicide with an asp.
   The species is unknown in Egypt.

   _____

   _____

2. My parents and I watched in awe.
   We watched on a hot mid-August evening.
   Erratic bolts of lightning from a distant storm illuminated the sky.

   _____

   _____

3. Women are ill more frequently than men.
   Women recover from illnesses more easily than men.
   Women recover from illnesses more frequently than men.

   _____

   _____

4. Natural rubber is used chiefly to make tires and inner tubes.
   It is cheaper than synthetic rubber.
   It has greater resistance to tearing when wet.

   _____

   _____

5. A Peruvian woman finds an unusually ugly potato.
   She runs up to the nearest man.
   She smashes it in his face.
   This is done by ancient custom.

   _____

   _____

6. One scarcely ever sees a sailboat in these waters.
   One scarcely ever sees a hardy swimmer in these waters.
   These waters are icy.
   One does occasionally spot a seal.
   One does occasionally spot an otter.
   One does occasionally spot a sperm whale.

   _____

   _____

   _____

EXERCISE PARAGRAPH BUILDING WITH ADVERB CLAUSES

The following exercise has been adapted from the article "How Teachers Make Children Hate Reading," by John Holt.

On your own paper, combine the sentences in each set into a single clear sentence, and arrange your new sentences into a paragraph. Sentences that can be turned into adverb clauses are underlined. Begin each adverb clause with an appropriate adverb from the list on page 246.

Learning to Hate Reading

1. We make books and reading a constant source of possible failure.
   We make books and reading a constant source of public humiliation.
   We do this from the very beginning of school.

2. We make children read aloud.
   We do this when children are little.
   We make them read before the teacher.
   We make them read before other children.
   We do this so that we can be sure of something.
   We can be sure that they "know" all the words they are reading.

3. Here is what this means.
   They are going to make a mistake.
   They make a mistake when they don't know a word.
   They make a mistake right in front of everyone.

4. They have done something wrong.
   Instantly they are made to realize this.

5. "Are you sure?"
   Perhaps the teacher will say this.
   Perhaps the teacher will ask someone else what he thinks.

6. Or perhaps the teacher will just smile.
   It will be a sweet smile.
   It will be a sad smile.
   The teacher will smile if she is kindly.
   This is often one of the most painful punishments.
   It is one of the punishments a child suffers in school.

7. In any case, the child knows he has made the mistake.
   The child who has made the mistake knows this.
   The child feels foolish.
   The child feels stupid.
   The child feels ashamed.
   Any of us would feel the same way in his shoes.

8. Many children associate books and reading with mistakes and penalties and humiliation.

The mistakes may be real.
The mistakes may be feared.
Children do this before long.

9. Books may cause children humiliation and pain.
If so, children are likely to decide something.
They will decide to leave all books alone.
They will decide that this is the safest thing. ■

Writing Suggestion

In a paragraph or short essay, recount how a parent, a friend, or a teacher introduced you to the pleasure (or chore) of reading. When you are done, underline any adverb clauses that you have used.

16.D Participle Phrases

Certain verb forms—called *participles*—can be used in phrases that modify nouns or pronouns. Notice, for example, that the sentence below contains three verbs:

My father's hair, <u>streaked</u> with gray and <u>receding</u> on both sides, <u>is combed</u> straight back to his collar.

Is combed is the main verb of the sentence. The other two verbs begin participle phrases that modify the subject, *hair.* In other words, *streaked* (a past participle) and *receding* (a present participle) are verbs that function as adjectives. The exercises in this section will give you practice in building sentences with present and past participle phrases.

16.D¹ Present and Past Participles

The following sentence contains both a present and a past participle:

The children, <u>crying</u> and <u>exhausted</u>, were guided out of the mine shaft.

Crying is a present participle, formed by adding *-ing* to the present form of the verb (*cry*). *Exhausted* is a past participle, formed by adding *-ed* to the present form of the verb (*exhaust*). Both participles modify the subject, *children.*

All present participles end in *-ing.* And the past participles of all regular verbs end in *-ed.* However, irregular verbs have various past participle endings (for instance, throw*n*, ridd*en*, deal*t*, go*ne*). A list of the common irregular verbs appears in Chapter Nineteen (*Verb Tenses*).

EXERCISE FORMING PRESENT AND PAST PARTICIPLES

A. Complete each sentence below by adding -ing to the verb in parentheses to form a present participle.

1. Let _____ dogs lie.   (sleep)

2. The _____ telephone kept Jim awake all night.   (ring)

3. Bob coached the _____ team.   (lose*)

4. Joy's smart remark deserves a _____ reply.   (sting)

B. Complete each sentence below by adding the past participle form of the verb in parentheses.

1. Mrs. Barrows laughed at the _____ little man.   (frighten)

2. The _____ quarterback was carried off the field.   (injure)

3. By mistake, I purchased a _____ television set.   (steal)

4. Professor Legree demanded a _____ apology.   (write)

(*In most cases, drop the final e before adding -ing to the verb.)   ■

16.D² *Building and Combining Participle Phrases*

A participle phrase consists of a participle and its modifiers. A participle may be followed by an object, an adverb, a prepositional phrase, an adverb clause, or any combination of these. In the following sentence, for example, the participle phrase consists of a present participle (*holding*), an object (*the torch*), and an adverb (*steadily*):

Holding the torch steadily, the woman stood a few feet away from the monster.

In the next sentence, the participle phrase consists of a present participle (*making*), an object (*a great ring*), and a prepositional phrase (*of white light*):

The woman waved the torch over her head, making a great ring of white light.

Now consider some of the ways sentences can be combined with participle phrases. First, try turning the first sentence below into a present participle phrase, and then attach it to the second sentence:

Victor smiled shyly.
Victor accepted the bowling trophy.

We can create a present participle phrase by omitting the subject (*Victor*) and changing *smiled* to *smiling*:

Smiling shyly, Victor accepted the bowling trophy.

Next, turn the first sentence below into a past participle phrase, and then attach it to the second sentence:

> The cat was abandoned by its owner.
> The cat wandered aimlessly through the streets.

Here, we need to omit not only the subject (*the cat*) but also the helping verb (*was*):

> <u>Abandoned by its owner,</u> the cat wandered aimlessly through the streets.

Helping verbs such as *is, are, was, were, had been,* and *have been* need to be omitted when reducing a sentence to a participle phrase.

EXERCISE IDENTIFYING PARTICIPLE PHRASES

Underline the participle phrase in each sentence below, and on the line at the left, state whether the participle phrase is present or past. Remember that a participle phrase cannot stand alone: it must be attached to a main clause.

_____ **1.** Joan's house, built in 1837, is the oldest in the city.

_____ **2.** Feeling like death warmed over, Merdine dragged herself to work.

_____ **3.** Last night I relaxed at home, sipping mint tea and watching TV.

_____ **4.** Humming along with the mechanical music, I pushed my cart down the supermarket aisles.

_____ **5.** Encouraged by the polite applause of the audience, Professor Legree repeated his favorite joke.

_____ **6.** Byron's essay, written in just ten minutes, deserves to win this month's freewriting award.

_____ **7.** Rod Stewart, wearing very tight, striped pants, looked like a bifurcated squash.

_____ **8.** Pushing my cart down the supermarket aisles, I hummed along with the mechanical music. ■

16.D³ *Arranging Participle Phrases*

A participle phrase is a flexible structure, one that may appear at the beginning, in the middle, or at the end of a sentence. It is usually set off by a comma or a pair of commas. Even though a participle phrase can be shifted to different positions, it should not be placed too far from the noun it modifies. For instance, the participle phrase is positioned clearly in both of the following sentences:

Written in just ten minutes, Byron's essay deserves to win this month's freewriting award.

Byron's essay, written in just ten minutes, deserves to win this month's freewriting award.

However, shifting the phrase to the end of this sentence would result in an awkward and confusing construction:

Byron's essay deserves to win this month's freewriting award, written in just ten minutes.

Here, the participle phrase appears to modify *award*, not *essay*.

In a sentence beginning with a participle phrase, the subject of the main clause is presumed to be the subject of the participle phrase as well. Consider the following sentence:

Pushing my cart down the supermarket aisles, I hummed along with the mechanical music.

In this sentence, the subject of the main clause (*I*) also serves logically as the subject of the participle phrase: *I* did the pushing. The following sentence, however, is not so logical:

Pushing my cart down the supermarket aisles, mechanical music played out of the loudspeakers overhead.

Here, the subject of the main clause (*music*) does not make sense as the subject of the participle phrase: how could mechanical music push the cart? This sentence is faulty and must be corrected either by changing the subject of the main clause (as in the original version) or by turning the participle phrase into an adverb clause:

As I pushed my cart down the supermarket aisles, mechanical music played out of the loudspeakers overhead.

Be careful to construct and arrange participle phrases so that they refer clearly and logically to a word in the main clause.

EXERCISE ADDING PARTICIPLE PHRASES

Rewrite each sentence below, adding the participle phrase given in parentheses. Be sure to position the participle phrase so that it refers clearly and logically to a noun in the main clause.

1. The children gazed at the monkeys.
   (hanging by their tails from the branches)

   _____

   _____

2. Stella vowed that she would never marry again.
(haunted by the memory of her first husband)

_____

_____

3. I watched the sun rise over the ridge.
(blazing over houses, farms, and fields)

_____

_____

4. The first baseman bobbled the line drive.
(distracted by an ostrich in the dugout)

_____

_____

5. Little Danny waited for the thunderstorm to pass.
(hiding inside the clothes hamper)

_____

_____

■

EXERCISE SENTENCE BUILDING WITH PARTICIPLE PHRASES

Combine the sentences in each set by turning the underlined sentence(s) into a participle phrase and attaching it clearly and logically to the main clause.

Example:
When mother made fruitcakes, I was allowed to blanch the almonds.
I pinched the scalded nuts so that they sometimes hit the ceiling or bounced across the room.
Combination: When mother made fruitcakes, I was allowed to blanch the almonds, pinching the scalded nuts so that they sometimes hit the ceiling or bounced across the room.

1. I took small sips at the Coke.
I was sitting on the ground in a shady corner.
I was sitting with my back against the wall.

_____

_____

2. The house sat stately upon a hill.
The house was weather-worn.
The house was gray.
The house was surrounded by barren tobacco fields.

_____

_____

3. The sun shot through the tree tops.
The sun bounced off the water.
The sun imprinted a beauty stain on the flowers.
The flowers lined the edge of the creek.

_____

_____

4. I was sitting on the window ledge.
The ledge overlooked the narrow street.
I watched the children.
The children were frolicking in the first snow of the season.

_____

_____

5. The medieval peasant was distracted by war.
The medieval peasant was weakened by malnutrition.
The medieval peasant was exhausted by his struggle to earn a living.
The medieval peasant was an easy prey for the dreaded Black Death.

_____

_____

6. He eats slowly.
He eats steadily.
He sucks the sardine oil from his fingers.
The sardine oil is rich.
He sucks the oil with slow and complete relish.

_____

_____

EXERCISE PARAGRAPH BUILDING WITH PARTICIPLE PHRASES

On your own paper, combine the sentences in each set into a single clear sentence, and arrange your new sentences into a paragraph. Sentences that can be turned into participle phrases are underlined.

A Slippery Thief

1. In September 1979, Carlo Colodi parked his car outside a bank in Milan, Italy, and then dashed inside.
   He dashed inside with a revolver in his hand and a scarf.
   The scarf was hiding his face.
2. He hit his foot on the corner of the mat.
   He slid across the marble floor.
3. His scarf dropped off, and, as he fell, he accidentally fired his revolver.
   When his scarf dropped off, his face was revealed.
4. He scrambled hastily to his feet.
   He ran to the cashier's desk, skidded wildly, and grabbed at a counter.
   He grabbed at a counter to keep his balance.
5. He dropped his gun in the process.
   The entire bank rocked with laughter.
6. He was offended by this lack of appreciation.
   The man turned, ran, slipped again, and finally crawled out of the bank.
7. Outside he found a police officer.
   The police officer was writing out a ticket for his car.
   His car was parked in a no-waiting zone.
   (Suggestion: Convert this last sentence into an adjective clause.) ■

Writing Suggestion

In a paragraph or short essay, describe a particularly disastrous occasion (for example, a date, a party, a day at work) when everything that could go wrong did go wrong. When you are done, underline any participle phrases that you have used.

16.E Absolutes

An absolute is a word group that modifies an entire sentence. It consists of a noun plus at least one word, as shown in the following sentence:

The hunters rested for a moment in front of the shack, their breaths white in the frosty air.

The noun (their *breaths*) that begins this absolute is followed by an adjective (*white*) and a prepositional phrase (*in the frosty air*). In addition to adjectives and prepositional phrases, adverbs and participles can also follow the noun in an absolute. As the sentence above demonstrates, an absolute allows us to move from a description of a *whole* person, place, or thing to just one or more parts: from *hunters* to *their breaths*.

16.E¹ Building and Arranging Absolutes

Consider how the sentence just seen might be broken down into two sentences:

> The hunters rested for a moment in front of the shack.
> Their breaths were white in the frosty air.

The second sentence, then, is turned into an absolute by simply omitting the linking verb *were*. As we have already seen, the absolute may appear at the end of the sentence:

> The hunters rested for a moment in front of the shack, their breaths white in the frosty air.

The absolute may also appear at the beginning of the sentence:

> Their breaths white in the frosty air, the hunters rested for a moment in front of the shack.

And the absolute is occasionally positioned between the subject and verb:

> The hunters, their breaths white in the frosty air, rested for a moment in front of the shack.

Note that an absolute, like a participle phrase, is usually set off from the rest of the sentence by a comma or a pair of commas.

EXERCISE SENTENCE BUILDING WITH ABSOLUTES

Combine the sentences in each set by turning the underlined sentence(s) into one or more absolutes. Remember to omit the linking or helping verb (*is, are, was, were*) when you reduce a sentence to an absolute. Position the absolutes clearly and logically.

Example:
The paperboy stood shivering in the cold, dark doorway.
His teeth were chattering.
His palm was extended.
Combination 1: His teeth chattering, his palm extended, the paperboy stood shivering in the cold, dark doorway.
Combination 2: The paperboy, his teeth chattering and his palm extended, stood shivering in the cold, dark doorway.

1. The engineers stared back at me.
   <u>Their faces were blank.</u>

   _____

   _____

2. Ed and the little man climbed the stairs together.
   <u>Each was in his own strange world.</u>

   _____

   _____

3. I sat on the highest limb of a big, sturdy oak tree.
   <u>Its branches were reaching to the clouds.</u>
   <u>The branches were reaching as if to claim a piece of the sky.</u>

   _____

   _____

4. The raccoon goes down on all fours and strides slowly off.
   <u>Her slender front paws are reaching ahead of her to the limit.</u>
   <u>Her slender front paws are like the hands of an experienced swimmer.</u>

   _____

   _____

5. The wolf trots away.
   <u>His head and tail are erect.</u>
   <u>His hips are slightly to one side and out of line with his shoulders.</u>

   _____

   _____

6. They were holding hands in the New York City subway train.
   <u>Their faces were old.</u>
   <u>Their faces were beautifully lined.</u>
   <u>Their gray heads were almost touching.</u>

   _____

   _____

■

EXERCISE PARAGRAPH BUILDING WITH ABSOLUTES

The following exercise has been adapted from Leonard Gardner's novel _Fat City_. This passage describes the morning run of Ernie Munger, a boxer in training for a fight.

On your own paper, combine the sentences in each set into a single clear sentence, and arrange your new sentences into a paragraph. Sentences that can be turned into absolutes are underlined.

1. He was zipped up in his leather jacket.
   Each fist was squeezing a small rubber ball.
   He ran along the dirt road.
   He ran past burst mattresses, water heaters, fenders, sodden cartons, worn-out tires, and rusty cans strewn down the deep bank.

2. Ernie was opposite the warehouses.
   By this time he was hot and sweaty.

3. His breathing was fixed to the plopping of his long black tennis shoes.
   He pounded past the port.

4. Larks rose with flashes of yellow from the dead weeds and wild grass.
   He came unflaggingly on.
   He was feeling he would never tire.

5. The oaks of Dad's Point stood ahead in the distance.
   Their trunks were painted white.

6. His mouth was gaping.
   His damp hair was in his eyes.
   His body was like a fired-up furnace.
   Ernie held his stride opposite Rough and Ready Island.
   Rows of mothballed warships were there.
   They were moored three abreast for the future.
   Their gun mountings were sealed in protective pods.

7. He was gagging on a dry throat.
   He chose some object as his finish line.
   He plodded up to it on weighted legs.
   He plodded right on past.

8. His head was back.
   His heaving chest was shot with pains.
   He strained on to a farther landmark.

9. He did not quit there either.

10. He fought on with himself to the edge of the park.
    He stumbled over the lawn past picnic tables and barbecue pits.
    He careened with flailing arms farther and farther under the trees.
    At last he stood gasping on the muddy bank of the point with nowhere else to run. ■

Writing Suggestion

In a paragraph or short essay, describe a particular athletic activity or event that you have either observed or participated in. When you are done, underline any absolutes that you have used.

16.F Further Practice in Building Paragraphs

The sentence combining you have done so far has helped you to become a more versatile writer. You should now feel comfortable experimenting with a variety of structures as you look for the most effective way of arranging your ideas in sentences and paragraphs. The final exercises in this chapter will give you an opportunity to apply all the combining strategies you have been practicing.

Remember that no one particular sentence structure is automatically superior to another. We should try to vary the length and structure of our sentences to convey ideas clearly, concisely, logically, and smoothly. Repeating a single structure too frequently can make our writing monotonous. Likewise, too many long sentences in succession can be just as boring and confusing to the reader as too many short ones.

The first exercise has been adapted from the first three paragraphs of George Orwell's essay "A Hanging." Orwell's eyewitness account is based on an experience he had while serving with the Indian Imperial Police in the 1920s. On your own paper, combine the sentences in each set into a single clear sentence, and arrange your sentences (sets 1–6, 7–14, 15–19) into three paragraphs.

A Hanging

1. It was in Burma, a morning of the rains.
   The morning was sodden.

2. A sickly light was slanting over the walls into the jail yard.
   The light was like yellow tinfoil.
   The walls were high.

3. We were waiting outside the condemned cells.
   The cells were a row of sheds fronted with double bars, like small animal cages.
   (Suggestion: Convert the underlined sentence into an appositive.)

4. Each cell measured about ten feet by ten.
   Each cell was quite bare within except for a plank bed and a pot for drinking water.
   (Suggestion: Coordinate the two sentences.)

5. In some of them men were squatting at the inner bars.
   The men were brown.
   The men were silent.
   The men were squatting with their blankets draped around them.

6. These were the condemned men.
   The condemned men were due to be hanged within the next week or two.

7. One prisoner had been brought out of his cell.

8. He was a Hindu.
   He was a puny wisp of a man.
   He was a man with a shaven head and vague liquid eyes.
   (Suggestion: Convert the underlined sentence into an appositive.)

9. He had a moustache, absurdly too big for his body, rather like the moustache of a comic man on the films.
   The moustache was thick.
   The moustache was sprouting.

10. Six Indian warders were guarding him.
    The warders were tall.
    The warders were getting him ready for the gallows.

11. Two of them stood by with rifles and fixed bayonets.
    <u>The others handcuffed him.</u>
    <u>The others passed a chain through his handcuffs and fixed it to their belts.</u>
    <u>The others lashed his arms tightly to his sides.</u>
    (Suggestion: Convert the underlined sentences into an adverb clause beginning with <u>while</u>.)

12. They crowded very close about him, with their hands always on him, as though all the while feeling him.
    Their hands were always on him in a careful, caressing grip.
    They were feeling him to make sure he was there.

13. It was like men handling a fish.
    <u>The fish is still alive and may jump back into the water.</u>
    (Suggestion: Convert the underlined sentence into an adjective clause.)

14. But he stood quite unresisting.
    <u>He yielded his arms limply to the ropes.</u>
    It was as though he hardly noticed what was happening.
    (Suggestion: Changing <u>yielded</u> to <u>yielding</u>, convert the underlined sentence into a present-participle phrase.)

15. Eight o'clock struck and a bugle call, thin in the air, floated from the barracks.
    The bugle call was desolately thin.
    The air was wet.
    The barracks were distant.

16. The superintendent of the jail raised his head at the sound.
    <u>The superintendent was standing apart from us.</u>
    <u>The superintendent was moodily prodding the gravel with his stick.</u>
    (Suggestions: Convert the first underlined sentence into an adjective clause; convert the second underlined sentence into a present-participle phrase.)

17. He was an army doctor.
    <u>He had a gray toothbrush moustache.</u>
    <u>He had a gruff voice.</u>
    (Suggestion: Convert the two underlined sentences into a prepositional phrase beginning with the preposition <u>with</u>.)

18. "For God's sake, hurry up, Francis," he said irritably.

19. "The man ought to have been dead by this time. Aren't you ready yet?"

Because there are no sets in the remaining exercises, you will need to group the sentences logically before you combine them. Vary the length as well as the structure of your sentences.

Clipper Ships

1. The clipper was one of the great sailing ships.
2. It was the fastest of these ships.
3. It was the most beautiful of these ships.
4. It was the most short-lived of these ships.
5. The clipper was developed in the 1820s.
6. It was developed in the United States.
7. It reached the height of its fame in the 1850s and 1860s.
8. It was obsolete by the end of the century.
9. The clipper was built primarily for speed.
10. The clipper was slim and light.
11. The clipper had a limited cargo space.
12. The clipper carried an enormous area of canvas.
13. The clipper fulfilled a variety of needs.
14. The Californian gold rush was served by the clippers.
15. The China tea trade was served by the clippers.
16. The Australian wool trade was served by the clippers.
17. There was competition between shipping companies.
18. There was competition in the race to make fast passages.
19. There was competition in the race to make high profits.
20. This competition produced crews of the highest quality.
21. Several factors made the clippers obsolete.
22. Steamships made the clippers obsolete.
23. The opening of the Suez Canal made the clippers obsolete.
24. The transcontinental railroads made the clippers obsolete.
25. The clippers were replaced by other ships.
26. The clippers were replaced first by windjammers.
27. The clippers were replaced later by steamships.
28. The days of the great sailing ships are gone.
29. The clipper remains as a symbol.
30. It is a symbol of craftsmanship.
31. It is a symbol of efficiency.
32. It is a symbol of beauty.

The Gramercy Gym

1. The Gramercy Gym is two flights up some stairs.
2. The stairs are littered.
3. The stairs are lightless.
4. The stairs look like a mugger's paradise.
5. Undoubtedly they are the safest stairs in New York.
6. Two dozen bodies are inside.
7. They are chopping up and down.
8. They are self-clocked.
9. Each fellow is cottoned in his dreams.
10. Some are skipping rope.
11. They are turbaned in towels.
12. They are wrapped in robes.
13. They are dressed this way in order to sweat.
14. These are white-looking figures, whereas the men who are about to spar have on dark headguards.
15. The headguards close around the face.
16. They close grimly.
17. They close like an executioner's hood.
18. There are floor-length mirrors.
19. There are mattresses.
20. These are for exercising.
21. These are for rubdowns.
22. There are two speedbags.
23. They bang like drums.
24. There are three heavy bags.
25. They swing even between the rounds.
26. They swing with the momentum of more than a decade of punches.
27. The bell is loud.
28. The fighters jerk like eating and walking birds.
29. The fighters hiss through their teeth as they punch.
30. Their feet sneaker the floor with shuffly sounds.
31. They wear red shoelaces in white shoes.
32. They wear gloves.
33. The gloves are peanut-colored.
34. They are learning to move their feet.
35. They move to the left.

36. They move to the right.

37. They are learning to move in and out.

38. They are learning to punch over an opponent's guard.

39. Then they punch under an opponent's guard.

40. They are learning other repetitive skills.

41. Without these skills a man in the ring becomes a man of straw.

42. The speedbags teach head-punching.

43. The heavy bags teach body work.

44. There is one big bag pinned to the wall.

45. Both a head and a torso are diagrammed on the bag.

46. The diagram is complete with numbers.

47. This is so the trainer can shout out what punches his fighter should throw.

48. "Bounce, bounce" the trainers yell. ■

Postscript

In this chapter, you have practiced building and combining sentences using various kinds of subordinate structures: *adjective clauses, appositives, adverb clauses, participle phrases,* and *absolutes.* Your work in this chapter should not only prepare you for the editing exercises in the rest of the text but should also help you to use a variety of sentence structures effectively in your own writing.

CHAPTER SEVENTEEN

Clear, Complete Sentences

Preview

As we have seen in the last two chapters, an effective sentence expresses a complete thought, and its parts are clearly connected. Therefore, in building and combining sentences we must be careful to avoid writing *fragments* (incomplete sentences) and *run-ons* (two sentences incorrectly run together as one). This chapter will give you additional practice in sentence combining as you work to eliminate fragments and run-ons.

17.A Sentence Fragments

The basic parts of the sentence, as we saw in Chapter Fifteen, are the subject and the verb. Thus, a complete sentence may consist of just two words:

George sneezed.

Here, *George* is the subject and *sneezed* is the verb. Either word by itself would not make a complete sentence. Generally, a subject without a verb is a fragment, as is a verb without a subject. Because a fragment does not express a complete thought, it is likely to distract and even confuse the reader. Thus, we should be careful to write complete sentences, not fragments.

The length of a word-group does not determine whether it is a fragment or a complete sentence. As we have just seen, a sentence may be as short as two words. A fragment, on the other hand, may consist of a long chain of phrases and subordinate clauses (structures discussed in Chapters Fifteen and Sixteen):

X Trying hard not to laugh while his sister, who was hiding under the table, tickled his toes.*

Lengthy as this statement is, it does not express a complete thought. The reader is left asking, "Whom are you talking about?" (in other words, what is the subject?) and "What happened?" (where is the verb?). Such phrases and subordinate clauses must be made part of a sentence:

Felix was trying hard not to laugh while his sister, who was hiding under the table, tickled his toes.

*Throughout this text, examples of incorrect sentences are preceded by an **X** to remind you that they are faulty.

265

By adding a subject (*Felix*) and a helping verb (*was*), we have turned this fragment into a sentence. The exercises that follow will give you practice in recognizing and correcting sentence fragments.

17.A[1] Recognizing Phrase Fragments

Don't confuse a phrase with a sentence. As we saw in the sections on prepositional phrases, appositives, participle phrases, and absolutes in Chapters Fifteen and Sixteen, a phrase is a group of words that lacks a subject or a verb (or both). A phrase cannot stand alone as a complete unit of thought: it must be attached to a sentence. Therefore, any phrase not connected to a sentence is a fragment.

Below you will find phrases used incorrectly as fragments (in the column on the left) and correctly as parts of sentences (in the column on the right):

Fragments	*Corrected*
X At the sight of a pig in a tuxedo.	Gloria laughed heartily at the sight of a pig in a tuxedo.
X Gloria, my sister.	Gloria, my sister, laughed heartily.
X Squinching her eyes and flapping her hands.	Squinching her eyes and flapping her hands, Gloria laughed heartily.
X Her eyes leaking tears of joy.	Her eyes leaking tears of joy, Gloria laughed heartily.

If you read aloud each of the fragments, you should be able to hear that something is missing. As the sentences on the right make clear, the missing elements are a subject (*Gloria*) and a verb (*laughed*).

Two types of phrases, in particular, are often mistaken for sentences. These are example phrases and participle phrases. Be especially careful with phrases that introduce examples: *for example, for instance, in addition to, including, such as*. Make sure that your examples appear in a complete sentence, not in a fragment:

Fragment	*Corrected*
X Family comedies such as *Roseanne* and *Home Improvement*.	My favorite television programs are family comedies such as *Roseanne* and *Home Improvement*.

An example phrase must be attached to a complete sentence; otherwise, it is a fragment.

Participle phrases, also, should not be confused with complete sentences. Although a participle phrase does contain a verb form (usually ending in *-ing, -ed,* or *-en*), it lacks a subject and a helping verb, and it does not express a complete thought. Thus, if unattached to a sentence, a participle phrase is a fragment:

Fragments	*Corrected*
X Driving through the nature park.	Driving through the nature park, we spotted an orangutan hiding behind a sycamore.
X Trapped inside the laundry basket for hours.	Trapped inside the laundry basket for hours, the cat finally cried itself to sleep.

Being able to distinguish between phrases and sentences will help you to eliminate phrase fragments from your writing.

EXERCISE RECOGNIZING PHRASE FRAGMENTS

Some of the word-groups below are complete sentences: they contain a subject and a verb, and they express a complete thought. Others are fragments: they lack a subject or a verb (or both) and do not express a complete thought. Put an **S** in front of each sentence, an **F** in front of each fragment.

_____ 1. Such as spaghetti and chocolate pudding.

_____ 2. Some foods, such as spaghetti and chocolate pudding, do not go well together.

_____ 3. Katie laughed.

_____ 4. A bearded man wearing gold-rimmed spectacles and one tiny diamond earring.

_____ 5. I was introduced to the prophet, a bearded man wearing gold-rimmed spectacles and one tiny diamond earring.

_____ 6. The bus stopped suddenly.

_____ 7. Running wildly through the crowded city streets.

_____ 8. Seared by the sun and beaten by the wind and rain.

_____ 9. On the bottom shelf, next to the Oreos and under the saltines.

_____ 10. Famous American writers, for example, Cather, Faulkner, and Twain. ■

17.A² Correcting a Phrase Fragment

There are two methods for correcting a phrase fragment: either combine the phrase with an adjacent sentence or turn the phrase itself into a sentence by adding a subject and a verb. The first method is usually the more effective one.

In most cases, as we have already seen, a phrase fragment can be corrected by attaching it to the sentence that precedes or follows it. In the passage below, the underlined word-groups are fragments:

X After visiting the museum. We will have lunch at the Chinese restaurant. Next to the library.

We can correct both of these fragments by attaching them to the sentence:

After visiting the museum, we will have lunch at the Chinese restaurant next to the library.

Remember, to avoid confusion, place the phrases close to the words they modify.

The other way to correct fragments is to turn the phrases into complete sentences. Here, for instance, is how we might add a subject and a verb to each of the fragments just seen:

> First, we will visit the museum. Then we will have lunch at the Chinese restaurant. It is next to the library.

Although correct, such short, choppy sentences could soon bore the reader, and thus the first method is usually the more effective one. However, if you want to use one or two short sentences for emphasis or if you want to avoid making another sentence overly long, turn the fragment into a sentence by adding a subject and a verb.

EXERCISE CORRECTING PHRASE FRAGMENTS

In each set below, correct the fragment(s) in two different ways:

(a) Combine the sentences and fragments to make one clear, complete sentence.
(b) By adding a subject or a verb (or both), turn each phrase into a complete sentence.

Example:
In my travels throughout the world.
I have climbed many tall mountains.
Including Mount Elbert, Electric Peak, and the Transylvanian Alps.

(a) In my travels throughout the world, I have climbed many tall mountains, including Mount Elbert, Electric Peak, and the Transylvanian Alps.
(b) I have traveled throughout the world. I have climbed many tall mountains.
These include Mount Elbert, Electric Peak, and the Transylvanian Alps.

1. Boogie-woogie is the most physical piano rhythm.
In the world of jazz.

(a) _____

_____

(b) _____

_____

2. The word *boogie* comes from African-American slang and means to dance very rhythmically.
Using the whole body as opposed to only the feet and legs.

(a) _____

_____

(b) _____

_____

3. It is possible that *boogie* derives from the West African Kongo word *mbugi*. Meaning "devilishly good."

(a) _____

_____

(b) _____

_____

4. Over the repeated, rocking left-hand rhythm. The right hand plays percussive phrases and chords.

(a) _____

_____

(b) _____

_____

5. The style probably grew out of early blues accompaniments. On banjo, guitar, or piano.

(a) _____

_____

(b) _____

_____

6. Considered low-class during the first few decades of this century. Boogie-woogie was generally confined to barrelhouses, dance halls, and houses of ill-repute.

(a) _____

_____

(b) _____

_____

7. In a Chicago dance hall brawl over a woman. It was there that Clarence "Pine Top" Smith (1904–1929) was shot dead only three months after he had recorded "Pine Top's Boogie-Woogie."

(a) _____

_____

(b) _____

_____

8. "Pine Top's Boogie-Woogie" gave the whole genre its name.
And also defined the main characteristics of the rocking style.

(a) _____

_____

(b) _____

_____

■

Writing Suggestion

In a paragraph or short essay, identify the distinctive characteristics of a particular kind of music that you enjoy. When you are done, check to make sure that all of your sentences are clear and complete.

17.A³ Recognizing and Correcting Subordinate-Clause Fragments

Adjective and adverb clauses (discussed in Chapter Sixteen) are called *subordinate* clauses because they cannot stand alone: they must be attached to a main clause to express a complete thought. An adjective clause or an adverb clause by itself is a fragment.

We can recognize an adjective clause by the relative pronoun that introduces it— *who, which, that, whose, whom.* Below you will find adjective clauses used incorrectly as fragments (in the column on the left) and correctly as parts of sentences (in the column on the right):

Fragments	*Corrected*
X Mrs. Grummidge, *who will be ninety-five on her next birthday.*	I delivered a Christmas parcel to Mrs. Grummidge, who will be ninety-five on her next birthday.
X The book *that Maria lent me.*	The book that Maria lent me was lost in the fire.

As you can see, an adjective clause (unlike a phrase) does contain its own subject and verb. However, because each clause begins with a relative pronoun (*who, that*), we know that these clauses cannot stand alone. Thus, we have corrected each fragment by attaching the adjective clause to a complete sentence.

Although subordinating an adjective clause to a main clause is usually the best method of correcting this type of fragment, there is another way. We can drop the relative pronoun and turn the adjective clause itself into a sentence:

Fragments	Corrected
X Mrs. Grummidge, *who will be ninety-five on her next birthday.*	Mrs. Grummidge will be ninety-five on her next birthday.
X The book *that Maria lent me.*	Maria lent me the book.

We have turned the first fragment into a sentence by replacing the relative pronoun (*who*) with a new subject (*Mrs. Grummidge*). And we have turned the second fragment into a sentence by dropping the relative pronoun (*that*) and adding a direct object (*the book*). Just be careful not to overwork this strategy: it can lead to choppy writing.

Like an adjective clause, an adverb clause can be recognized by the word that introduces it—in this case, an adverb such as *when, if, although, as,* or *because* (see section 16.C for a full list). Below you will find adverb clauses used incorrectly as fragments (in the column on the left) and correctly as parts of sentences (in the column on the right):

Fragments	Corrected
X *Although Heidi was exhausted after her long drive.*	Although Heidi was exhausted after her long drive, she volunteered to take the kids to the shopping mall.
X *Because he was denied financial aid.*	George had to withdraw from college because he was denied financial aid.

Although the adverb clause does contain its own subject and verb, the adverb itself (*although* in the first example, *because* in the second) is a signal that the word-group cannot stand alone and express a complete thought. We have corrected each fragment by attaching the adverb clause to a main clause. Again, we also have the option of changing the subordinate clause itself into a main clause, simply by dropping the adverb:

Heidi was exhausted after her long drive.
He was denied financial aid.

As we have already noted, however, this approach can easily lead to choppy, disconnected writing.

In summary, then, neither a phrase nor a subordinate clause can stand alone as a complete unit of thought. Usually the best approach to correcting a fragment of any sort is to attach it to an adjacent sentence. Occasionally, however, we may want to turn the fragment itself into a sentence: either by adding a subject and verb to a phrase or by removing the initial relative pronoun or adverb from a subordinate clause.

EXERCISE RECOGNIZING SUBORDINATE-CLAUSE FRAGMENTS

Some of the word groups below are complete sentences: they contain a subject and a verb and they express a complete thought. Others are fragments—subordinate clauses (beginning with a relative pronoun or adverb) that do not express a complete thought. Put an **S** in front of each sentence, an **F** in front of each fragment.

_____ **1.** Although many people are convinced that the tarantula's bite is deadly.

_____ 2. If a woman is sufficiently ambitious, determined, and gifted.

_____ 3. Nobody answered when I knocked on the door.

_____ 4. The Sphinx, which was a monster with the head of a woman, the body of a dog, and the tail of a serpent.

_____ 5. He answered the riddle of the Sphinx.

_____ 6. When my brother was preparing to leave home for college.

_____ 7. After I had studied frantically to meet a deadline for a psychology assignment.

_____ 8. Our Western Civilization class listened intently as the professor recounted the sad tale of Pheidippides, a hero of ancient Greece.

_____ 9. A cynic, who knows the price of everything and the value of nothing.

_____ 10. A man whose arrogance is exceeded only by his ignorance. ■

EXERCISE CORRECTING SUBORDINATE-CLAUSE FRAGMENTS

In each set below, correct the fragment(s) in two different ways:

(a) Combine the sentences and fragments to make one clear, complete sentence.
(b) By removing the initial adverb or by replacing the relative pronoun with a new subject, turn each subordinate clause into a complete sentence.

Example:
Uncle Fred, who claims to be a descendant of Thomas Edison.
He invented a gadget.
That automatically empties ashtrays and freshens the air.

(a) Uncle Fred, who claims to be a descendant of Thomas Edison, invented a gadget that automatically empties ashtrays and freshens the air.
(b) Uncle Fred claims to be a descendant of Thomas Edison. He invented a gadget. It automatically empties ashtrays and freshens the air.

1. The international craze for boogie-woogie began in the late 1930s.
When record executive John Hammond teamed Meade "Lux" Lewis with two other pianists for a performance at Carnegie Hall.

(a) _____

_____

(b) _____

_____

2. Lewis, whose father was a Pullman porter.
Lewis was washing cars for a living in a Chicago garage when Hammond discovered him.

(a) _____

_____

(b) _____

_____

3. The most poetic of the boogie pianists was Jimmy Yancey (1898–1951).
Who often played at a leisurely and contemplative tempo with great emotional
eloquence.

(a) _____

_____

(b) _____

_____

4. The popularity of boogie-woogie lasted through the Forties and into the
Fifties.
As vocal and big band versions of the music extended its popularity.

(a) _____

_____

(b) _____

_____

5. Though there were some fine later performances from Count Basie, Jay
McShann, and Sam Price.
Blandness and sterility set in.
As the art became reduced to a commercial formula.

(a) _____

_____

(b) _____

_____

6. However, the boogie rhythm, which is found in rock music, in the soul music of the Sixties, and in the jazz-rock-fusion music of the Seventies.
The boogie rhythm has had a dynamic influence on various musical forms.

(a) _____

_____

(b) _____

_____

7. The boogie rhythm also permeates the work of many major jazz musicians, including Thelonius Monk.
Whose beautiful slow blues "Misterioso" recalls the music of Jimmy Yancey.

(a) _____

_____

(b) _____

_____

8. Because the best work of the great originators has been reissued in recent years.
Boogie-woogie remains fresh and dynamic, to be enjoyed by future generations.

(a) _____

_____

(b) _____

_____

Writing Suggestion

In a paragraph or short essay, describe the rise and decline in popularity of some particular fad (in music, fashion, or television, for instance) that you have witnessed or even participated in. When you are done, check to make sure that all of your sentences are clear and complete.

EXERCISE PROOFREADING FOR FRAGMENTS

Each paragraph that follows contains three sentence fragments. Slowly and carefully, read each paragraph aloud and underline each fragment. Then, on your own paper, correct each fragment either by attaching it to an adjacent sentence or by turning the fragment itself into a sentence.

Anthony

My five-year-old son Anthony is built like a little wind-up toy. His black curly hair, bushy eyebrows, cute button nose, and chubby cheeks, which people can't resist pinching. These make him look like a life-size teddy bear. Anthony loves to wear his favorite black leather jacket with the picture of the Skoal Bandit on the back. And jeans with patches on the knees as a result of the holes he puts in them while crawling on the floor, pushing his toy cars around. Indeed, he is a very energetic little boy. In one afternoon, he will ride his bicycle, play video games, complete a 200-piece jigsaw puzzle, and, of course, play with his toy cars. In fact, his energy scares me sometimes. For example, that time on the roof. He shinnied up a tree and jumped onto the roof. However, he wasn't energetic (or bold) enough to climb back down, and I had to rescue my wonderful little wind-up toy.

Why Do We Keep Pets?

Most American families have at least one member who never works, seldom speaks, and spends most of the day either eating or sleeping. No, I'm not talking about your brother or crazy Uncle Carl, but our pets—our dogs, cats, hamsters, turtles, and fish. Why do so many Americans keep these apparently lazy and unproductive creatures? Most would agree that pets are ideal companions for young and old alike. Studies demonstrating that pets give the elderly a sense of security and companionship. Which may help them overcome loneliness. In some cases, the enthusiasm and devotion of a pet dog actually make the sick feel better. At times, feeding the fish, walking the dog, or putting the cat out at night. These activities can teach young children a sense of responsibility. Our pets may not contribute to the family income, but I know from experience that they give us a great deal in terms of comfort and companionship.

The Handbag

Three years ago at a flea market, I bought a small white-beaded handbag. Which I have never since carried in public, but which I would never dream of giving away. The purse is small, about the size of a paperback bestseller. And thus totally unsuited for lugging around such paraphernalia as a wallet, comb, compact, checkbook, keys, and all the other necessities of modern life. Hundreds of tiny pearl-colored beads dot the outside of the handbag, and on the front, woven into the design, is a starburst pattern formed by larger, flat beads. Creamy white satin lines the inside of the bag and forms a small pocket on one side. At the bottom of the purse is a silver coin, which reminds me of my teenage days. When my mother warned me never to go out on a date without a dime in case I had to telephone home for help. In fact, I think that's why I like my white-beaded handbag: it reminds me of the good old days when men were men and women were ladies. ■

EXERCISE PARAGRAPH BUILDING

The passage below consists of short sentences and sentence fragments. On your own paper, compose a coherent paragraph by combining the short sentences and fragments into several clear and complete sentences. Vary the length as well as the structure of your sentences.

A Fish Story

1. While many people fish for food.
2. A great number of us, sport fishermen, trophy-hunters, and Saturday trollers.
3. We fish simply for entertainment.
4. Because most of us are gentle, harmless creatures.
5. I can only conclude that if people realized the cruelty of sport fishing.
6. Then they would refrain from practicing it.
7. In an effort to increase the awareness of such people.
8. I ask you to put yourself in the fish's place.
9. Imagine that you are a hungry young trout.
10. Gliding silently through the cool waters of a salty creek.
11. You notice a faint, white blur drifting a short distance ahead of you.
12. A meal-sized shrimp.
13. Eager and unsuspecting, you grab it.
14. Planning to swallow the creature in a gulp.
15. Before it realizes what has happened.
16. When suddenly you feel an excruciating pain in your mouth.
17. And you find that you cannot swallow your would-be breakfast.
18. Fighting for all you are worth, you are nevertheless pulled toward the surface of the waters.
19. Toward that awful void in which the murderously hot, heavy winds blow.
20. The roof of your mouth is torn and bleeding.
21. But you still cannot free yourself.
22. At the surface you are hauled into the bright light.
23. Driven into frenzy when you leave the buoyancy of the water.
24. And your resulting weight increase redoubles the pain in your mouth.
25. And echoes it with an ache in your smothered gills.
26. A dry, rough blanket wraps around you, and you are lifted and turned over a few times.
27. And then the barb is twisted and snatched from your face.
28. You fall into the cold water again.

29. Feeling the salt bite ruthlessly at your wound.

30. As the subsequent days pass.

31. You cannot eat with your mangled mouth, and a white, prickly infection spreads across your sides.

32. In the places where that dry roughness touched your scales.

33. Whether or not you heal and live to chance another such experience.

34. Your body struggles to recover.

35. And your mind can only wonder, "Why?" ■

17.B Run-on Sentences

Whereas a fragment is a phrase or subordinate clause incorrectly treated as a complete sentence, a *run-on* is two sentences incorrectly treated as one. Because run-on sentences can be just as distracting and confusing in our writing as fragments, we need to be able to recognize and correct them.

17.B¹ Recognizing Run-ons

Distinctions are sometimes drawn between two types of run-on: the fused sentence and the comma splice. A fused sentence, as shown below on the left, runs two main clauses together with no punctuation or linking word between them:

Fused Sentences	*Corrected*
X I have seen pictures of the old church it was torn down years ago.	I have seen pictures of the old church. It was torn down years ago.

A fused sentence gives the reader no clue as to where one main clause ends and the next one begins. A comma splice, on the other hand, provides the reader with a misleading clue—a comma instead of a period, semicolon, or appropriate linking word:

Comma Splice	*Corrected*
X I have fond memories of Sunday dinner at Grandmother's house, her chicken and rice casserole was everyone's favorite dish.	I have fond memories of Sunday dinner at Grandmother's house. Her chicken and rice casserole was everyone's favorite dish.

The fused sentence and the comma splice share the same basic fault: two sentences are incorrectly run together as one.

In the sample run-on sentences just seen, notice that the second main clause in each begins with a pronoun—*it* and *her*. In fact, many run-on sentences result from confusion about the proper use of pronouns:

I, my	this, that, these, those
you, your	we, our
he, she, it, his, her	they, their

Because a pronoun refers to a person or thing already identified, we may sometimes presume mistakenly that a pronoun can connect two sentences. It can't. Be careful, then, not to make a run-on when you use a pronoun as the subject or the modifier of a subject in a main clause. (See Chapter Twenty for more practice in using pronouns.)

Later in this chapter you will practice four methods of correcting run-ons: with a period, a semicolon, coordination, and subordination. First, however, test your ability to recognize run-ons in the exercise that follows.

EXERCISE RECOGNIZING RUN-ON SENTENCES

Read aloud each word-group below to help determine whether it is a sentence or a run-on sentence. You will probably find that your voice drops slightly at the end of a main clause—that you pause after reading a complete thought. Put an **S** in front of each sentence and an **RS** in front of each run-on sentence.

_____ 1. My children will never go back to Showboat Pizza, they hated the food and were frightened by the big gorilla at the keyboard.

_____ 2. Laughing or crying is what a human being does when there is nothing else he can do.

_____ 3. I plan to visit Bimini over Christmas this is where I have always wanted to go.

_____ 4. Matthew is a skilled carpenter, he single-handedly built his own house.

_____ 5. Education is the ability to listen to almost anything without losing your temper or your self-confidence.

_____ 6. Some children are frightened by the violent antics of cartoon characters others are delighted.

_____ 7. We waited at the station all morning, the train never arrived.

_____ 8. I haven't heard from Annie in several years, perhaps she left her husband and moved to the Yukon.

_____ 9. A college professor is someone who talks in other people's sleep.

_____ 10. Remember to wear your safety goggles the sparks could blind you. ■

17.B² Correcting a Run-on with a Period or Semicolon

The simplest way to correct a run-on sentence is with a mark of punctuation—a period or a semicolon.

To make two separate sentences out of a run-on sentence, put a period at the end of the first main clause and begin the second main clause with a capital letter:

Run-on Sentence	*Corrected*
X A woman should never dangle a pocketbook from her shoulder instead she should clench it under her arm.	A woman should never dangle a pocketbook from her shoulder. Instead, she should clench it under her arm.

Placing a period at the end of the first main clause is often the best way to correct a long run-on sentence.

Another way to separate two main clauses is with a semicolon:

Run-on Sentence	*Corrected*
X A woman should never dangle a pocketbook from her shoulder instead she should clench it under her arm.	A woman should never dangle a pocketbook from her shoulder; instead, she should clench it under her arm.

Don't overwork the semicolon. It should be used between two main clauses that are closely related in meaning or grammatical form—or both.

Although a period or a semicolon will correct a run-on sentence, a mark of punctuation alone will not explain what relation the second main clause has to the first. If you want to make this relationship clear, you can follow the period or semicolon with a *conjunctive adverb*—a signal word that introduces a main clause. The common conjunctive adverbs show that you are continuing a thought (*furthermore, moreover*), offering a contrast (*however, nevertheless, still*), or showing a result (*accordingly, consequently, then, therefore, thus*). Unlike simple coordinators (discussed in section 15.D), conjunctive adverbs do not *join* main clauses; they do, however, guide your reader by linking ideas:

> I loathed my job more than I loved the paycheck; <u>consequently</u>, I quit work and returned to college.
> After three days of rain, I was tempted to abandon the hike. <u>Nevertheless</u> on the fourth morning I took bearings from my compass and set out due west toward Onandoga Bay.

Remember that a conjunctive adverb between two main clauses must be preceded by a semicolon or a period. It is usually followed by a comma.

EXERCISE **CORRECTING A RUN-ON WITH A PERIOD OR SEMICOLON**

Correct each run-on sentence below using either a period or a semicolon.

1. Fifty years ago parents were apt to have a lot of kids nowadays kids are apt to have a lot of parents.

   _____

   _____

2. A low blood-sugar level signals hunger a higher one tells the brain that you don't need to eat.

   _____

   _____

3. A lobotomy is a fairly simple operation however amateurs should not attempt it.

_____

_____

4. Mrs. Barbee never missed a day of school I think even the flu and the common cold were afraid of that lady.

_____

_____

5. Black magic is intended to harm or destroy white magic is intended to benefit the community or an individual.

_____

_____

6. A jump rope is the ultimate aerobic exercise it provides a top-notch daily workout for those without orthopedic or cardiovascular problems.

_____

_____

7. Open the can of soup carefully and be sure not to cut your fingers empty the contents of the can into the pot.

_____

_____

8. It's not enough to hear opportunity knock you must let him in, greet him, make friends, and work together with him.

_____

_____

■

17.B³ Correcting a Run-on through Coordination or Subordination

Writing nothing but short, simple sentences is not the solution to the problem of run-ons. In fact, this would be a step backwards, for run-on sentences often result when we first attempt to combine sentences in new ways. Rather than shy away from new methods, we should continue to practice combining sentences according to various strategies. In other words, often the best way to correct a run-on is through one of the techniques of coordination or subordination discussed in Chapters Fifteen and Sixteen.

If you have run together two main clauses that are roughly equal in importance, coordinate them to correct the run-on. Between the two clauses put a comma and a simple coordinator (*and, but, yet, or, nor, for, so*):

Run-on Sentence	Corrected
X Most feet aren't very good looking for ugliness mine have always been in a class by themselves.	Most feet aren't very good looking, <u>but</u> for ugliness mine have always been in a class by themselves.

For additional guidance, review section 15.D on "Coordinating Words, Phrases, and Clauses."

If the two main clauses in a run-on are not of equal importance, subordinate one of them. That is, turn the clause of lesser significance into an adjective or adverb clause:

Run-on Sentences	Corrected
X Last night I had my first taste of sake it is a Japanese beverage made from rice.	Last night I had my first taste of sake, <u>which is</u> a Japanese beverage made from rice.
X A Frenchman murdered two wives he didn't like their cooking.	A Frenchman murdered two wives <u>because</u> he didn't like their cooking.

Here we have used an adjective clause to correct the first run-on and an adverb clause to correct the second one. In fact, we can further reduce the adjective clause in the first sentence to an appositive:

Last night I had my first taste of sake, a Japanese beverage made from rice.

Thus, one of the most effective ways of correcting a run-on (and creating a clear, concise sentence in the process) is to turn one of the main clauses into a subordinate clause or phrase. For additional guidance, see Chapter Sixteen.

We have considered four basic ways of correcting run-on sentences. The two simplest methods involve *separating* the main clauses with a mark of punctuation (a period or a semicolon). The other two methods involve *joining* the two clauses correctly through coordination or subordination. If our writing is to be interesting and effective as well as simply correct, we should be adept at applying all four strategies.

EXERCISE CORRECTING RUN-ON SENTENCES

Correct each run-on sentence below in two different ways. For the first four run-ons, follow the instructions in parentheses. For the last four, decide for yourself how to correct the faulty sentences.

1. Most smoke detectors have a test button, this button may test only the sounding device and not the working components.
   (*Coordinate the two main clauses.*)

   (a) _____

   _____

(Turn the first main clause into an adverb clause beginning with <u>although</u>.)

(b) _____

_____

2. Sunlight flooded the room the pianos, all black, gleamed.
   (Coordinate the two main clauses.)

   (a) _____

   _____

   (Separate the two main clauses with a semicolon.)

   (b) _____

   _____

3. We walked back to the big house, it had been built by my great-grandfather
   almost a century ago.
   (Turn the second main clause into an adjective clause.)

   (a) _____

   _____

   (Turn the second main clause into a past participle phrase beginning with <u>built</u>.)

   (b) _____

   _____

4. I gave your paycheck to Butch he told me you had sent him.
   (Turn the second main clause into an adjective clause.)

   (a) _____

   _____

   (Turn the second main clause into an adverb clause beginning with <u>because</u>.)

   (b) _____

   _____

5. Don't carry your house keys in your wallet a pickpocket then has easy access
   to your house.

   (a) _____

   _____

   (b) _____

   _____

6. The gardens are dry the road to the shore is dusty.

(a) _____

_____

(b) _____

_____

7. Nobody knows for certain how many games Bull Cyclone won the best detective efforts put his record at 97–62–3.

(a) _____

_____

(b) _____

_____

8. For most of the passengers, the trip ended on a note of gloom for me, it ended on a note of triumph.

(a) _____

_____

(b) _____

_____ ■

EXERCISE PROOFREADING FOR RUN-ON SENTENCES

Each paragraph that follows contains three run-on sentences. Slowly and carefully, read each paragraph aloud and underline any run-on sentences. Then, on your own paper, correct each run-on by the method you think is most effective.

How to Give a Great Back Massage

Giving a great back massage can be just as much fun as receiving one, all you need is a towel, a bottle of baby oil, and a willing body. Once you have been assured that your friend has no serious back problems, you are ready to begin. Place the towel on any hard, flat surface. Then invite your friend to remove his shirt and lie down on the table with his arms relaxed at his sides. Tell your friend to take three deep breaths this should help him to relax. Now, squirt some baby oil into the palm of one hand, and rub your hands together. Then gently rub the oil all over your friend's back. After the back has been saturated, you can begin the actual massage. Gently but firmly, manipulate the skin and muscles with your fingertips, move from the neck line all the way down your friend's back. Add oil periodically to keep the skin soft and pliable. After kneading your friend's back for about twenty minutes, you should hand him these instructions so that now you can receive a great back massage.

Why I Had to Get Rid of Plato

Although I am a dog lover by nature, I recently had to give away my three-month-old retriever, Plato. I had several good reasons for doing so. A few months ago I picked up the dog at the Humane Society as a Christmas gift for my girlfriend. Alas, she dumped me on Christmas Eve I was left to console myself by caring for the dog. That's when my misery began. For one thing, Plato was not house broken. Throughout the apartment he left little mementoes, staining rugs and furniture and fouling the air, he would burrow under any newspapers I laid down for him. His untamed potty habits were supported by an insatiable appetite. Not content with a sack of Gravy Train every day, he would also gnaw the furniture and shred clothes, sheets, and blankets, one night he chewed up a friend's thirty-dollar pair of clogs. Finally, he simply was not happy cooped up by himself in a small apartment. Whenever I left, he would begin a whimpering that soon turned into furious barking. As a result, my neighbors were threatening to murder both me and the "monster," as I had unaffectionately dubbed him. So, after six weeks of life with Plato, I gave him away to my uncle in Baxley. Fortunately, he is quite accustomed to animal feed, waste, noise, and destruction.

Nervous Norman

Mr. Elmo Norman, my elementary school teacher, was the most nervous person I have ever known he was a short, pudgy man, always overdressed. His conventional uniform consisted of a neatly pressed pin-striped suit, a thin black tie over a starched white shirt, and a pair of brightly polished brown oxfords. His receding gray hair was always neatly trimmed, his shiny pink head always darted about like a radar blip on his neck. He paced the school hallways in a perpetual motion of twitching, fidgeting, and twiddling. In the space of a minute, he would wrinkle his little nose, scratch his plump chin, shrug his shoulders, straighten his tie, and glance at his watch, never once looking directly at the person he was with. As he spoke in his lackadaisical drawl, he would glance at the ceiling, inspect his knuckles, and check the floorboards for dust. When the conversation was over, he would dash back into his office like a frightened bunny, he was probably praying that he could lock himself in there forever. For all I know, he may still be hiding in his office today. ■

Writing Suggestion

In a paragraph or short essay, describe the most distinctive traits of a person you have known. When you are done, check to make sure that all of your sentences are clear and complete.

EXERCISE REVISING PARAGRAPHS TO ELIMINATE FRAGMENTS AND RUN-ONS

Each of the following paragraphs contains a number of fragments and run-ons as well as complete sentences. On your own paper, rewrite each paragraph, correcting all faulty sentences. Feel free to recombine the sentences and change the sentence order.

Divorce American Style

Divorce has become a fact of American life. There were one million last year, another million are expected this year. Divorce may be common it is never routine. Beneath the numbing statistics lie families in desperate circumstances. Couples, amid their pain and anger and guilt and confusion, asking courts to bridle the chaos they have unleashed. That task has always made the law uneasy, today it borders on the overwhelming. Of all the incompatible couples in America. Few can match the unhappiness of the family and the law.

William Booth

One hundred years ago, William Booth took to the streets of London's slums to preach to the poor. His message affected the husband drunk on beer, it affected the laundress. Who smelled of gin. His message affected the anemic charwoman, the unemployed chimney sweep, and the homeless waif. The waif living under a tarpaulin between bales in a warehouse. Booth's Salvation Army, growing from a few early converts to the thousands in his own lifetime. Booth's Salvation Army has left few corners of the world untouched.

The Stowe School

The Stowe School, tucked away in Vermont ski country. The Stowe School is one of the last outposts of the Woodstock generation. Students and faculty live communally. They live in a huge barn-red building or in cabins, they built the cabins in the forest behind the campus. Patched jeans, hiking boots, and down-the-back hair. These are standard for both sexes. Incense is as pervasive as the rock music, the music blares from the rooms. Jimi Hendrix, Janis Joplin, and Jim Morrison live on for the students, many of whom yearn for the late 1960s. A time when Stowe was transformed into a hang-loose alternative academy. "These students identify with the rebellious mood of the '60s," says the thirty-two-year-old headmaster. "They wish they had been there."

The Parishes of Bermuda

Each of Bermuda's nine parishes is unique. Hamilton, the capital and one of the world's smallest cities. It is a deep, land-locked harbor. Paget is understated and patrician. Pembroke is the most densely populated. Also the most modern. Warwick boasts much of the most dramatic coastal scenery in all Bermuda, it also boasts one of the best beaches. Southampton has two luxury holiday hotels.

Sandys is very nautical, it has the world's smallest drawbridge, a fine maritime museum, it houses some of the best ghosts in Bermuda. Devonshire, like its name, is a little stodgy but offers a variety of scenery. Several important historical sites there at Devonshire also. Smiths has Devil's Hole Grotto and Bermuda's prettiest church. St. Mark's Anglican Church. Finally, there is St. George. Unhurried, content, very pretty. Quite unwilling to undergo change for the sake of change.

Sexism in the Schoolhouse

In elementary school, researchers say, teachers call on boys much more often and give them more encouragement. Boys frequently need help with reading, remedial reading classes are an integral part of many schools. But girls, who just as often need help with math. They rarely get a similar chance to sharpen their skills. Boys get praised for the intellectual content of their work. While girls are more likely to be praised for neatness. Boys tend not to be penalized for calling out answers and taking risks, girls who do the same are reprimanded for being rude. Research indicates that girls learn better in cooperative settings, where students work together, while boys learn better in competitive settings. Yet most schools are based on a competitive model. Despite these problems, girls get better grades and are more likely to go on to college. Though even these successful girls have less confidence in their abilities than boys, have higher expectations of failure and more modest expectations. The result is that girls are less likely to reach their potential than boys. ■

Postscript

In this chapter, you worked on eliminating needless fragments and run-ons as you practiced building and editing sentences for clarity and completeness. In the chapters that follow, you will turn your attention to the correct and effective use of particular words.

CHAPTER EIGHTEEN

Subject-Verb Agreement

Preview

This chapter will give you practice in applying one of the most basic and also most troublesome rules of writing: *a verb must agree in number with its subject.* Put simply, this means we must remember to add an *-s* to the verb if its subject is singular and not to add an *-s* if the subject is plural. The exercises here will help you to recognize and eliminate any errors of subject-verb agreement in your own writing. At the same time, this chapter will give you additional practice in combining sentences and building paragraphs.

18.A The Principle of Agreement

Compare the underlined verbs in the sentences below:

> Edna sings the blues at the Rainbow Room.
> My brothers sing the blues at the Rainbow Room.

Both verbs describe a present or ongoing action (that is, they are in the *present tense*), but the first verb ends in *-s* and the second doesn't. Why this difference? Because both sentences correctly illustrate the basic principle of subject-verb agreement: we must add an *-s* to the verb (*sings*) if the subject is singular (*Edna*) and omit the *-s* from the verb (*sing*) if the subject is plural (*brothers*). This principle applies only to verbs in the present tense.*

If you are able to identify subjects and verbs in sentences, you should have no trouble understanding the rules of subject-verb agreement. You might find it helpful, therefore, to review section 15.A on basic sentence parts before studying the rules that follow.

18.B Rules of Subject-Verb Agreement

The following five rules of agreement should help you to apply the principle that a verb must agree in number with its subject.

*A detailed discussion of verb tense appears in Chapter Nineteen.

Rule 1

Add an *-s* to the verb if the subject is a singular noun—a word that names one person, place, or thing.

> Mona drives a hard bargain.
> England owns the Seychelles.
> Lightning strikes twice.

Rule 2

Add an *-s* to the verb if the subject is one of the third-person singular pronouns: *he, she, it, this, that.*

> He owns a boat.
> She drives a hard bargain.
> It strikes without warning.
> This beats me.
> That takes the cake.

Rule 3

Do not add an *-s* to the verb if the subject is not a singular noun or a third-person singular pronoun.

> The workers strike for higher pay.
> I make my own clothing.
> You drive a hard bargain.
> We take pride in our work.
> They beat us every year.

Rule 4

Do not add an *-s* to the verb if two subjects are joined by *and.*

> Gus and Merdine own a still on Holloway Hill.
> Linda and Jimbo drive like maniacs.

Rule 5

Do not add an *-s* to the verb if it is preceded by *to.*

> Lorna wants to strike up a conversation.
> He hopes to own a Mercedes some day.

Sometimes people's speech habits interfere with their ability to apply these rules of agreement. If you have a habit of dropping the final *-s* when you talk, you need to be particularly careful when you write. As you do the following exercises, read each sentence aloud and listen for the sound of the final *-s.*

EXERCISE MAKING VERBS AGREE WITH THEIR SUBJECTS

On the line at the left of each pair of sentences, write the correct form of the verb in parentheses. Keep to the present tense, and be guided by the five rules of agreement.

Examples:

_____rides_____   I ride the bus to work every morning. My wife never (ride) the bus.

_____begin_____   Gloria and Shyla begin new jobs today. They (begin) working at 9:00 A.M.

_____   **1.** Our ceiling leaks. Water (leak) onto the floor and loosens the tiles.

_____   **2.** The Mobil station closes at midnight. The other stations never (close).

_____   **3.** This old watch keeps perfect time. I (keep) it on a silver chain.

_____   **4.** My sisters play musical instruments. My brother (play) the radio.

_____   **5.** Your excuse sounds familiar. It (sound) like the one you gave last week.

_____   **6.** This water tastes like crankcase fluid. You (taste) it and tell me what you think.

_____   **7.** Omar complains about everything. He even (complain) about the color of the rain.

_____   **8.** My drink consists of V-8 and grenadine. Your drink (consist) of tomato juice and Sprite.

_____   **9.** Felix criticizes everyone at work. He never (criticize) himself.

_____ **10.** Edna lives by herself next door. Simon and Peter (live) downstairs.

_____ **11.** This machine sorts the mail. It (sort) envelopes according to size and weight.

_____ **12.** Helen seldom visits her mother. She never wants to (visit) anyone.

_____ 13. Merdine sings the children to sleep every night. Now the children (sing) barroom ballads to me.

_____ 14. Pete and Lorna sell eggs at the public market. Lorna also (sell) her homemade jams.

_____ 15. This device tests your ability to distinguish colors. It also (test) depth perception. ■

EXERCISE COMBINING SENTENCES WITH CORRECT VERB FORMS

This exercise has two steps:

1. On the line at the left of each sentence, write the correct form of the verb in parentheses. Keep to the present tense.
2. On your own paper, combine the sentences in each passage into a coherent paragraph. You may add, delete, or alter words in the interest of clarity and coherence.

See if you can combine the following sentences into a paragraph of three or four sentences.

Landlord

_____ 1. The landlord (come) here once a month.

_____ 2. The landlord (inspect) our apartment.

_____ 3. We (give) him a glass of iced tea.

_____ 4. We (tell) him our problems.

_____ 5. He (listen) politely.

_____ 6. He (drink) his iced tea.

_____ 7. He (leave) without fixing anything.

_____ 8. The faucet still (drip).

_____ 9. The pipes still (leak).

_____ 10. The roaches still (dance) all night in the kitchen.

See if you can combine the following sentences into a paragraph of three or four sentences.

Running in the Night

_____ **1.** Thunder (rumble) overhead.

_____ **2.** Lightning (crease) the sky.

_____ **3.** The old man (sit) quietly.

_____ **4.** He (watch*) the rain.

_____ **5.** The rain (rattle) against the windows.

_____ **6.** He (smile).

_____ **7.** He (remember) another storm.

_____ **8.** He begins to (drift) back into the past.

_____ **9.** He (dream).

_____ **10.** In his dream, he (race) the lightning.

_____ **11.** A woman (race) beside him.

_____ **12.** They (laugh).

_____ **13.** They (disappear) into the night.

_____ **14.** The old man never (wake) from his dream. ■

Writing Suggestion

In a paragraph or short essay, describe the precise actions of someone carrying out a simple task, such as making a cup of coffee, pumping gasoline, or kissing a child goodnight. Write in the present tense, and when you are done, check to make sure that all of your verbs agree with their subjects.

18.C *Making* **Have, Do,** *and* **Be** *Agree with Their Subjects*

Although all verbs follow the same basic rules of agreement, certain ones seem to be more troublesome than others. In particular, many agreement errors result from the misuse of the common verbs *have, do,* and *be.*

---

*Add *-es*, not just *-s*, to verbs that end in *-ch, -sh, -ss,* or *-x.*

Have

The verb *have* appears as *has* if the subject is a singular noun or a third-person singular pronoun:

> Gus has a broomstick in his bathroom.
> He has a problem with wombats.

If the subject is a plural noun or any other pronoun, use *have*.

Do

The verb *do* appears as *does* if the subject is a singular noun or a third-person singular pronoun:

> Silas does the housework.
> She does needlepoint.

If the subject is a plural noun or any other pronoun, use *do*.

Be

The verb *be* has three forms in the present tense: *is, am, are*. Use *is* if the subject is a singular noun or a third-person singular pronoun:

> Eloise is unhappy.
> It is very late.

Use *am* if the subject is the first-person singular pronoun *(I)*:

> I am not the person you think I am.

Finally, if the subject is a plural noun or any other pronoun, use *are*.

On occasion, a subject may follow, rather than precede, a form of the verb *have*, *do*, or *be*. As shown in the sentences below, this reversal of the usual order occurs in questions that require a helping verb. (Helping verbs are underlined; subjects are in italics.)

> Where has *Pete* put the flashlight?
> Where have the *flowers* gone?
> What does *Jenny* do for a living?
> What do *you* do in your spare time?
> Is *Artie* driving to work in the morning?
> Are *we* having a test tomorrow?

Here, the present forms of *have*, *do*, and *be* serve as helping verbs and appear in front of their subjects. Another case in which a form of the verb *be* precedes the subject is in sentences beginning with *there* or *here*:

> There is a *unicorn* in the garden.
> Here is an excellent *cookbook*.
> There are two *gerbils* on the ledge.
> Here are the *photocopies*.

Keep in mind that no matter where a verb appears in a sentence, it must still agree with its subject.

EXERCISE MAKING *HAVE*, *DO*, AND *BE* AGREE WITH THEIR SUBJECTS

On the line at the left of each pair of sentences, write the correct form of the verb in parentheses. Use *do, have,* or *be* in the present tense.

_____ 1. I have an electric saxophone. My wife (have) a headache.

_____ 2. I do my best to simplify things. Professor Legree (do) his best to make things complicated.

_____ 3. There are strange lights in the sky. There (be) a spaceship flying overhead.

_____ 4. What have the children been hiding in their rooms? Why (have) Rusty dug a deep hole in the garden?

_____ 5. There is sugar on my hamburger. There (be) onions in my coffee.

_____ 6. The children have an extra holiday. Why (have) the teachers gone on strike?

_____ 7. Do you know how to play croquet? The game (do) not require much athletic ability.

_____ 8. Here are my lost socks. Now, where (be) my favorite tie?

_____ 9. Why have you put papers on the floor? The cat and its kittens (have) a new litter box.

_____ 10. There is a roach on the wedding cake. Where (be) all the guests?
■

EXERCISE COMBINING SENTENCES WITH CORRECT VERB FORMS

This exercise has two steps:

1. On the line at the left of each sentence, write the correct form of the verb in parentheses. Keep to the present tense.

2. On your own paper, combine the sentences in each passage into a coherent paragraph. You may add, delete, or alter words in the interest of clarity and coherence.

See if you can combine these sentences into a paragraph of nine or ten sentences.

Fast Break

_____ 1. The kettle (whistle) furiously.

_____ 2. The toast (smolder).

_____ 3. The cat (nibble) the bacon.

_____ 4. There (be) a crash.

_____ 5. A juice glass (smash) against the wall.

_____ 6. The baby (start) to cry.

_____ 7. The other children (scream).

_____ 8. They (kick) one another.

_____ 9. Little Vera (have) an egg in her fist.

_____ 10. She (hurl) it.

_____ 11. The egg (splatter) against the wall.

_____ 12. Howie (do) his imitation of a police siren.

_____ 13. Godfrey (bang) his head against the refrigerator.

_____ 14. The children's mother (do) not hear anything.

_____ 15. She (sit) out on the front steps.

_____ 16. She (sip) tea.

_____ 17. There (be) planes flying overhead.

_____ 18. She (watch) them.

_____ 19. A taxi (pull) up to the curb.

_____ 20. The cab driver (honk) the horn.

_____ 21. The children's mother (climb) into the cab.

_____ 22. She (stare) straight ahead.

_____ 23. The cab (drive) off.

_____ 24. The woman (have) no intention of ever returning.

See if you can combine the following sentences into a paragraph of eight or nine sentences.

A Visit to the Dentist

_____ 1. I (lie) back in the chair.

_____ 2. I (be) whimpering.

_____ 3. Fat tears (be) dripping down my cheeks.

_____ 4. Soft music (play).

_____ 5. The music (come) out of the ceiling speakers.

_____ 6. There (be) an X-ray machine in one corner of the room.

_____ 7. The X-ray machine (hum) to itself.

_____ 8. Water (gurgle) in the bowl by my elbow.

_____ 9. The dentist (hurry*) into the room.

_____ 10. He (be) wearing a white mask.

_____ 11. Behind his mask, he (giggle).

_____ 12. He (tie) a bib around my neck.

_____ 13. A bright light (blind) me.

_____ 14. He (plant) cotton swabs around my gums.

_____ 15. The dentist (chuckle).

_____ 16. He (pick) up a Black & Decker drill.

_____ 17. He (wave) the drill in front of my face.

_____ 18. My eyes (spin) around in my head.

_____ 19. I (bolt) out of the chair.

_____ 20. I (dive) through the window.

_____ 21. I (tear) off down the road. ■

*To add an -s to a verb ending in -y preceded by a consonant (for example, *try, cry, hurry*), first drop the -y and then add *-ies (tries, cries, hurries)*.

> **Writing Suggestion**
>
> In a paragraph or short essay, describe a real or imagined "fast break" of your own—an escape from some troubling person, place, or situation. Write in the present tense, and when you are done, check to make sure that all of your verbs agree with their subjects.

18.D Words between the Subject and Verb

In determining subject-verb agreement, don't be confused by words that come between the subject and the verb. Compare these two sentences:

This box <u>belongs</u> in the attic.
This box of ornaments <u>belongs</u> in the attic.

In both sentences, the verb *belongs* agrees with its subject, *box*. Don't let the prepositional phrase in the second sentence confuse you into thinking *ornaments* is the subject. It is simply the object of the preposition *of* and does not affect the agreement of subject and verb.

As you saw in Chapters Fifteen and Sixteen, prepositional phrases (as well as adjective clauses, appositives, and participle phrases) often come between a subject and a verb. So, to make sure that a verb agrees with its subject and not with a word in the phrase or clause, mentally cross out the interrupting word-group.

One ~~of my sister's friends~~ <u>is</u> a coal miner.
The people ~~who survived the avalanche~~ <u>are</u> in an emergency shelter.
A man ~~selling peanuts~~ <u>is</u> on the terrace.

Remember, then, that the subject is not always the noun closest to the verb. It is the noun that names what the sentence is about, and it may be separated by several words from the verb.

EXERCISE MAKING VERBS AGREE WITH THEIR SUBJECTS

In each set of sentences below, cross out the words that come between the subject and the verb in the second sentence. Then, on the line at the left, write the correct form of the verb in parentheses.

_____ **1.** My hobbies are unusual. One of my hobbies (be) photographing unicorns.

_____ **2.** Stephen King's latest novel is terrifying. The last few chapters of the book (be) particularly scary.

_____ **3.** George makes breakfast for everyone in the apartment. The sight of bacon and eggs first thing in the morning (make) me sick.

_____ **4.** These magazines cost too much at the drugstore. A subscription to any one of these magazines (cost) less than ten dollars.

_____ **5.** Where is your roommate? Several pages from my journal (be) missing.

_____ **6.** There are plums in the refrigerator. There (be) a box of mints on the counter.

_____ **7.** My children never cry. The children who live in the downstairs apartment (cry) whenever they are left alone.

_____ **8.** The telephone in your office never rings. The telephones in my office (ring) constantly all day.

_____ **9.** The two girls playing house ignore the little boy. The boy, playing with his action toys, (ignore) the girls.

_____ **10.** One of the exchange students has nowhere to live. Two other students, a young couple from Finland, (have) a house to themselves.

_____ **11.** Two of my uncles fix television sets for a living. One of my brothers (fix) his hair.

_____ **12.** Wake me with a smile for a change. The odor of burnt toast and the sound of a raving disc jockey (wake) me every other morning.

_____ **13.** Professor Legree frequently goes out for long walks in the dark. The lights in his house (go) out whenever it rains.

_____ **14.** The editorial in today's newspaper contains nothing but wisecracks. The comic strips on the back page (contain) more wisdom.

_____ **15.** People who haven't seen the movie criticize it. Felix, who has seen the movie, (criticize) those who haven't seen it. ■

EXERCISE COMBINING SENTENCES WITH CORRECT VERB FORMS

This exercise has two steps:

1. On the line at the left of each sentence, write the correct form of the verb in parentheses. Keep to the present tense.

2. On your own paper, combine the sentences in the passage into a coherent paragraph. You may add, delete, or alter words in the interest of clarity and coherence.

See if you can combine these sentences into a paragraph of nine or ten sentences.

Youth for Sale

_____ 1. Commercials on television (celebrate) youth.

_____ 2. Commercials (make) us afraid of growing old.

_____ 3. One of these commercials (tell) us to "Think young."

_____ 4. Another commercial (invite) us to "Join the Pepsi generation."

_____ 5. Teenage actors on the screen (sell) soft drinks and jeans.

_____ 6. Little children (promote) cereals and candy.

_____ 7. Young people in commercials (act) like adults.

_____ 8. Older people in commercials (behave) like children.

_____ 9. The advertisers (appeal) to our vanity.

_____ 10. The advertisers (play) on our fears.

_____ 11. A soap commercial (promise) "younger-looking skin."

_____ 12. A commercial for hair-dye products (tell) us to "Wash away that gray."

_____ 13. There (be) an ad for a little yellow pill.

_____ 14. This pill is guaranteed to (make) you "feel alive."

_____ 15. Another pill (help) you to "be your young self again."

_____ 16. Such appeals to our vanity and fear obviously (work).

_____ 17. Americans (be) bamboozled into spending millions of dollars each year.

_____ 18. Americans (spend) this money in search of the Fountain of Youth.

_____ 19. Meanwhile, we still (grow) older, but no wiser. ■

> **Writing Suggestion**
>
> In a paragraph or short essay, describe two or three television commercials that particularly amuse or annoy you, and explain why. Write in the present tense, and when you are done, check to make sure that all of your verbs agree with their subjects.

18.E Agreement with Indefinite Pronouns as Subjects

Add an -s to the verb in the present tense if the subject is one of the indefinite pronouns listed below:

one	anyone	everybody	something
no one	anybody	everything	each
nobody	anything	someone	either
nothing	everyone	somebody	neither

Treat these words as third-person singular pronouns (*he* or *she* or *it*). In the following sentences, each subject is an indefinite pronoun and each verb ends in -s:

Nobody claims to be perfect.
Everybody plays the fool sometimes.
Each of the divers has an oxygen tank.

In the last sentence, note that *has* agrees with the subject *each*, not with *divers* (the object of the preposition).

EXERCISE MAKING VERBS AGREE WITH THEIR SUBJECTS

On the line at the left of each pair of sentences, write the correct form of the verb in parentheses. Keep to the present tense.

_____ **1.** Both candidates support increased defense spending. Neither of the two candidates (support) gun control.

_____ **2.** Everybody wants to take classes in the morning. Nobody (want) classes in the afternoon.

_____ **3.** Everyone has an essay to write. Nobody in the class (have) time to attend the lecture.

_____ **4.** The animal acts are not the main attraction at the circus. The main attraction at the circus (be) the clowns.

_____ **5.** Not one of those books belongs to me. One of those books (belong) to Amy.

_____ 6. Everything you do seems to work out perfectly. Nothing I do ever (seem) to work out at all.

_____ 7. All of the doors need to be painted. Every one of the windows (need) to be washed.

_____ 8. Those two science projects in the refrigerator are turning green. One of the projects (be) beginning to breathe.

_____ 9. There are many interesting people living in my neighborhood. One of the most eccentric (be) Sasha Hightest.

_____ 10. Gus and Merdine want a trial separation. Neither one (want) to move out of the trailer. ■

EXERCISE PROOFREADING FOR ERRORS IN SUBJECT-VERB AGREEMENT

In each paragraph below, some of the sentences contain verbs that do not agree with their subjects. Underline any verb that is used incorrectly, and write the correct form of the verb in the margin.

The following paragraph contains five errors in subject-verb agreement.

A Fluke of Luck?

The sheep-liver fluke is a parasitic flatworm with a very complex life cycle. The fluke start life by hatching inside a snail. The fluke is then ejected from the snail in a ball of slime. These balls of slime is eaten by ants. The fluke digs its way through the ant's body until it reach the ant's brain. There, the fluke takes control of the ant by manipulating its nerves, thus turning the ant into its personal robot. Under the command of the fluke, the ant climb to the tip of a blade of grass. If the fluke is in luck, the ant is eaten by a passing sheep. From the sheep's stomach, the fluke work its way home — to the liver.

The following paragraph contains six errors in subject-verb agreement.

Santa Claus

Santa Claus is a fat old man who visits every house on our planet in about eight hours on one of the worst nights of the year. Santa, according to tradition, stop for a glass of milk and a slice of pie at each house along the route. He prefer to work unnoticed, so he wears a luminous red suit and travel with a pack of bell-jangling reindeer. For reasons which common people does not understand, this jolly fat man enters each house not by the front door but through the chimney. He gives generously to children in wealthy families, and he remind poorer children that it's the thought that counts. Santa Claus is one of the earliest beliefs that parents try to instill in their children. After this absurdity, how can any child believes in anything again?

The following paragraph contains seven errors in subject-verb agreement.

Life Forms

Northgate Plaza, like all shopping plazas, were designed for automobiles, not human beings. All natural life has been extinguished; even the weeds along the curb appears artificial. But somehow, amidst all the plastic, steel, and concrete, a solitary shrub manage to survive. The shrub, not in vigorous bloom but certainly alive, stand a few yards from the entrance to Banyard's department store. It grows straight up through the concrete. Now and then a shopper pause to examine this curious life-form, not for sale in any of the sixty-seven stores. Occasionally, someone will glance around furtively and then break off a twig, slip it into a shopping bag, and hurry back to the parking lot. Why people do this are a mystery to me. Are such people intent on preserving life or destroying it? Whatever the case may be, the shrub have managed to survive all assaults.

The following paragraph contains eight errors in subject-verb agreement.

Contact Lenses

About four million people in this country wears soft contact lenses. These lenses, made of water-absorbing plastic, were developed in Czechoslovakia and were introduced into the United States in 1964. The first soft lens was approved by the FDA in 1971. In recent years, soft lenses has become more popular than hard lenses. There is several reasons for this increasing popularity. Many wearers find the soft lenses more comfortable. Also, unlike the case with hard lenses, no break-in period are necessary for soft lenses. But there is drawbacks as well. The soft lens cost more than the hard lens. In addition, the life of soft lenses are often measured in months compared to years for hard lenses. They tear easily and become worn by handling. Also, soft contact lenses corrects only a limited range of visual problems. Nevertheless, for those who can afford them, soft contact lenses are a safe, simple, and attractive solution to the problem of poor vision. ■

Postscript

In this chapter, you have practiced applying the basic principle that a verb must agree in number with its subject. In addition, you have gained further practice in combining sentences and in creating paragraphs of your own. You will continue working with various verb forms in the next chapter.

CHAPTER NINETEEN

Verb Tenses

Preview

The *tense* of a verb suggests the time of its action—present, past, or future. Different verb endings and different helping verbs suggest different times. In the last chapter, you worked with verbs in the present tense. Here, you will learn how to form other tenses and use them effectively. You will work with both *regular* verbs (those with *-ed* endings in the past tense) and *irregular verbs* (those that do not end in *-ed* in the past tense). And the exercises in this chapter will continue to give you practice in combining sentences and building paragraphs.

19.A Regular Verbs

Because all regular verbs in the past tense have the same *-ed* ending, these verb forms are the easiest to remember. Therefore, we will look at the various ways regular verbs indicate time before we consider the more troublesome irregular verbs.

19.A¹ Forming the Past Tense of Regular Verbs

We use the *past tense* to show that an action has already been completed. In the following sentences, the underlined verbs are in the past tense:

The Martins moved into their new house last Sunday.
Yesterday I visited the county jail.

Both *move* and *visit* are called *regular verbs* because they have the same past tense ending of *-ed*. If the present form of the verb ends in *-e*, we add *-d* to form the past tense:

The Martins move frequently.   (present tense)
The Martins moved into their new house last Sunday.   (past tense)

If the present form of the verb ends in a letter other than *-e*, we add *-ed* to form the past tense:

I visit my parole officer every Saturday.   (present tense)
Yesterday I visited the county jail.   (past tense)

Because all regular verbs have the same *-ed* ending in the past tense no matter what the subject is, subject-verb agreement is not a problem.

Don't let the *sound* of an *-ed* ending ever trick you into making a spelling error when you form the past tense. While we do hear a *d* sound at the end of some words (*visited, moved*), we hear a *t* sound at the end of others (*laughed, promised*). Also, if you have a habit of clipping off word endings when you speak, be careful not to do this when you write. So, no matter what sound you hear or fail to hear when you pronounce a regular verb in the past tense, be sure when you write to add *-d* or *-ed* at the end.

EXERCISE FORMING THE PAST TENSE OF REGULAR VERBS

The first sentence in each set below contains a verb in the present tense. Complete the second sentence in each set by adding *-d* or *-ed* to the verb in parentheses to form the past tense.

_____ 1. We rarely punish the children. However, we (punish) them yesterday for painting the cat.

_____ 2. Simon uses unusual props in his magic act. Recently he (use) a live cobra.

_____ 3. Halley's comet appears every seventy-six years. It last (appear) in 1986.

_____ 4. I usually purchase a season ticket from the box office. I (purchase) this ticket from a scalper.

_____ 5. Gina tries very hard to be helpful. Last night she (try*) too hard.

_____ 6. Please carry this piano upstairs for me. I (carry) it into the house.

_____ 7. The men in our family marry young. Doug was only sixteen when he (marry) Marlene.

_____ 8. I never study for more than an hour at a time. Last night Katie (study) for six hours straight.

_____ 9. Every day I receive invitations to different sales gatherings. Yesterday I (receive) an invitation to a Tupperware party.

_____ 10. Jonah separates the white of the egg from the yolk before making an omelet. Maybe that is why he and his wife (separate). ■

*If the present form of the verb ends in *-y* preceded by a consonant (for example, *try, cry, carry*), change the *y* to *i* and add *-ed* to form the past tense (*tried, cried, carried*).

EXERCISE COMBINING SENTENCES WITH VERBS IN THE PAST TENSE

Follow these two steps:

1. On the line at the left of each sentence, write the correct past form of the verb in parentheses.
2. On your own paper, combine the sentences in the passage into a coherent paragraph. You may add, delete, or alter words in the interest of clarity and coherence.

The Bum

_____ 1. Yesterday I (wait) in the park for my husband.

_____ 2. Half an hour (pass).

_____ 3. I (walk) in circles.

_____ 4. I (scatter) bread crumbs for the pigeons.

_____ 5. I (avoid) the stares of the vagrants.

_____ 6. Finally, I (rest) on one of the benches.

_____ 7. Out of the corner of my eye, I (watch) a middle-aged bum drinking wine.

_____ 8. He (wave) the bottle of wine in the air.

_____ 9. He (pour) the wine over his head.

_____ 10. I (laugh).

_____ 11. He (giggle).

_____ 12. He (start) to dance.

_____ 13. I (enjoy) his foolish antics.

_____ 14. Then the bum (stagger) over to my bench.

_____ 15. I (scream).

_____ 16. I (recognize) the bum: he was my husband.

See if you can combine these sentences into a paragraph of eight or nine sentences.

■

> **Writing Suggestion**
>
> **In a paragraph or short essay, record your observations at a particular place as you waited for someone to appear or for something to happen. Use the past tense, and, when you are done, check to make sure that all of your verb forms are correct.**

19.A² *Using* Has *or* Have *with the Past Participle*

In Chapter Sixteen, you saw how the past-participle form of a verb can function as an adjective. Coupled with the helping verb *has* or *have*, a past participle can also serve as the main verb in a sentence. Compare these two sentences:

Max worked here for twenty years.
Max has worked here for twenty years.

The first sentence is in the past tense: Max once worked here but no longer does. The second sentence carries a different meaning: Max still works here. We use *has* or *have* with a past participle to describe an action that started in the past and is (or may be) still going on. This construction is called the *present-perfect tense*.

The past-participle form of a regular verb is identical to the past form: it always ends in *-ed*.

Past	*Past Participle*
promised	(has or have) promised
finished	(has or have) finished
tried	(has or have) tried

The helping verb—*has* or *have*—changes to agree with its subject, but the past participle itself does not change.

Max has worked here for twenty years.
Max and Darlene have worked here for twenty years.

Use the past tense to show a completed action. Use the present-perfect tense (*has* or *have* plus the past participle) to show an action begun in the past but continuing up to the present.

EXERCISE FORMING THE PAST TENSE AND THE PRESENT-PERFECT TENSE

On the line at the left of each pair of sentences, write the correct form of the verb in parentheses. Use either the past tense or the present-perfect tense (*has* or *have* plus the past participle). The first sentence in each pair will help you decide which tense is needed in the second sentence.

_____ 1. Mr. Baggins lives in the house next door. He (live) there for the past twenty years.

_____ 2. We are still raising money for the scholarship drive. So far we (raise) over two thousand dollars.

_____ 3. I have gained five pounds since I started my diet. I also (gain) a craving for Mars bars.

_____ 4. I watched the news last night. Then I (watch) David Letterman's show.

_____ 5. I have called you several times this week. You (call) me once last September.

_____ 6. Felicia frequently uses the new word processor. George not (use*) it once.

_____ 7. Several years ago I stayed two weeks on a farm. I (stay) in the city ever since.

_____ 8. Carol shouted in my ear. I turned and (shout) right back.

_____ 9. Felix ordered one book from the club last year. He not (order) anything since.

_____ 10. I have never tried to raise chickens. Once I (try) to raise hogs.

■

EXERCISE COMBINING SENTENCES IN THE PRESENT-PERFECT TENSE

Follow these two steps:

1. On the line at the left of each sentence, put the verb in parentheses into the present-perfect tense—that is, use *has* or *have* with the past participle.

2. On your own paper, combine the sentences in the passage into a coherent paragraph. You may add, delete, or alter words in the interest of clarity and coherence.

Taxi Driver

_____ 1. I (work) for the G & M Cab Company the past six months.

_____ 2. In this time, I (locate) every back alley in the city.

*The negatives *not* and *never* often go between the helping verb and the past participle in the present-perfect tense.

_____ **3.** I (discover) every shortcut.

_____ **4.** I (learn) how to make a decent income.

_____ **5.** I (figure) out how to avoid trouble.

_____ **6.** A passenger never (rob) me.

_____ **7.** A passenger never even (refuse) to pay the fare.

_____ **8.** My passengers (appreciate) my good service.

_____ **9.** I (race) to the hospital with expectant mothers.

_____ **10.** I (carry) bags of groceries for older folks.

_____ **11.** I (load) huge sacks of potatoes into the trunk.

_____ **12.** I (tie) a wheelchair to the roof of the cab.

_____ **13.** In return, my passengers (reward) me handsomely.

_____ **14.** I (receive) some very generous tips.

_____ **15.** A few of my regular passengers (invite) me to their homes.

_____ **16.** They (fix) meals for me.

_____ **17.** They (offer) me something to drink.

_____ **18.** They (introduce) me to their daughters.

_____ **19.** I (learn) to love my job.

See if you can combine these sentences into a paragraph of nine or ten sentences.

■

Writing Suggestion

In a paragraph or short essay, identify some of the specific duties you performed at a job that you once held. Use the past tense, and, when you are done, check to make sure that all of your verb forms are correct.

19.A³ *Using* Had *with the Past Participle*

We use *had* with the past participle to show that one past action was completed before another. Compare the two verbs in the sentence below:

Everyone <u>had returned</u> home by the time Felix <u>arrived</u>.

Both verbs report past actions, but one action occurred before the other. The *past-perfect tense* (*had* with the past participle) reports the earlier action: *had returned*. The ordinary past tense reports the later action: *arrived*.

Don't confuse the past perfect with the present perfect. Remember that the present perfect (*has* or *have* plus the past participle) shows an action begun in the past but continuing up to the present:

The guests <u>have arrived</u>.

In contrast, the past perfect (*had* plus the past participle) shows that one past action was completed before another:

I <u>had arrived</u> a few minutes before the bomb exploded.

The helping verb *had* does not change its form in the past-perfect tense.

EXERCISE FORMING THE PAST TENSE AND THE PAST-PERFECT TENSE

Each sentence that follows contains two verbs: one should be in the ordinary past tense and the other in the past perfect (*had* plus the past participle). On the line at the left of each sentence, write the correct form of the verb in parentheses.

_____ 1. Although I had studied my notes carefully, I still (fail) the exam.

_____ 2. Although my boss often (promise) to give me a raise, he finally decided to fire me instead.

_____ 3. Jocko (move) his car just minutes before the tornado moved down Main Street.

_____ 4. We had completed our own audit before the bank examiners (arrive).

_____ 5. I remembered that Gus (lock) all the doors the week before.

_____ 6. Professor Legree realized that no one (complete) the assignment.

_____ 7. Bobo (type) his term paper before I even started mine.

_____ **8.** I (use) up all of my money by the time I reached Reno.

_____ **9.** She had just clobbered the burglar when I (show) up.

_____ **10.** Moose tried to call her, but she already (return) to Topeka. ■

19.A⁴ *Showing Future Time with* Will *and* Would

So far we have considered some of the ways verbs can show present and past time. On occasion, however, we need to report actions that have not yet occurred. In these instances we rely on the *future tense*. Compare the two sentences below:

I watch the stars at night.	(present tense)
I will watch the sun rise in the morning.	(future tense)

To form the future tense, use *will* in front of the *present* form of the verb.

Will signifies a *definite* future action. To indicate only a *possible* or *conditional* future action, use *would* in front of the present form of the verb:

I wash the car every Saturday.	(present tense)
I would wash the car if I had the time.	(future-conditional)

Neither *will* nor *would* changes form to agree with its subject.

EXERCISE **RECASTING A PARAGRAPH IN THE FUTURE TENSE**

On your own paper, rewrite the paragraph below changing the main verbs from the past tense to the future tense (*will* plus present form of the verb).

Example:
> **Original:** I traveled to London to visit the Queen of England.
> **Recast:** I will travel to London to visit the Queen of England.

Visiting Her Majesty

I traveled to London to visit the Queen of England. Being a clever fellow, I disguised myself as a prince and walked into Buckingham Palace as if I owned it. After receiving directions from the chambermaid, I stepped into the Queen's bedroom and surprised Her Royal Highness with a hearty slap on the back. Then, of course, I tipped my hat, bowed, and delivered the usual compliments. After uncorking a bottle of champagne, we exchanged pleasantries and talked about our families for over an hour. I showed her my photograph album and my stamp collection, and she showed me hers. After a thoroughly entertaining visit, I traded addresses with Her Majesty and then kissed her goodbye—on the fingertips of her white gloves, of course. ■

19.B Irregular Verbs

There are over one hundred irregular verbs—verbs that do not end in *-ed* in the past tense. Though their endings differ from those of regular verbs, irregular verbs rely on the same helping verbs to indicate present, past, and future time.

19.B¹ The Principal Parts of Irregular Verbs

We have seen how regular verbs have three basic forms: the present form, the past form (ending in *-ed*), and the past-participle form (also ending in *-ed*). These three forms are referred to as the *principal parts* of a verb. Here is how we might list the principal parts of the regular verb *laugh*:

Present	*Past*	*Past Participle*
laugh	laughed	laughed

Remember that the past-participle form works with different helping verbs (*has* or *have; had*) to form different tenses.

Irregular verbs also have three principal parts, though their endings differ from those of regular verbs. Consider these sentences:

I tell a joke.	(present)
I told a joke.	(past)
I have told a joke.	(past participle)

Some irregular verbs, such as *tell*, have the same form in the past and the past participle. Others, however, have different forms:

I wear a cap.	(present)
I wore a cap.	(past)
I have worn a cap.	(past participle)

With irregular verbs such as *wear*, we need to learn the different forms for the past and the past participle.

Just like regular verbs, irregular verbs are used with various helping verbs to form different tenses. For instance, we use *has* or *have* with the past participle of an irregular verb to form the present-perfect tense:

Bob has worn out his welcome.

Likewise, we use *had* with the past participle of an irregular verb to form the past-perfect tense:

I had never worn a seat belt before you told me why I should.

And we use *will* with the present form of an irregular verb to form the future tense:

I will wear a seat belt from now on.

In short, irregular verbs *work* the same way as regular verbs do; they just have different endings.

The list that follows contains the most common irregular verbs. Although you are probably familiar with many of them already, study the entire list and look for certain patterns that will help you remember the forms of all these verbs. For example, look for those verbs that change from a *-d* ending in the present (*send*) to a *-t* ending in the past (*sent*). Notice those that contain an *i* in the present (*ring*), an *a* in the past (*rang*), and a *u* in the past participle (*rung*). Pick out all those verbs whose past participle ends in *-n* (such as *beaten, blown,* and *frozen*). And group together those verbs that have the same form in the past and the past participle (such as *found, heard,* and *told*). The exercises that follow the list will give you an opportunity to review these various forms.

To find the correct past or past-participle form of a verb not included in the following list, check your dictionary. If the dictionary gives only the present form of the verb, then the verb is regular and forms the past and past participle by adding *-d* or *-ed*.

The Principal Parts of Irregular Verbs

Present (Now we . . .)	Past (Yesterday we . . .)	Past Participle (We have . . .)
arise	arose	arisen
be	were (*singular* was*)	been
beat	beat	beaten (*or* beat)
become	became	become
begin	began	begun
bend	bent	bent
bite	bit	bitten
bleed	bled	bled
blow	blew	blown
break	broke	broken
bring	brought	brought
build	built	built
burst	burst	burst
buy	bought	bought
cast	cast	cast
catch	caught	caught
choose	chose	chosen
cling	clung	clung
come	came	come
come	came	come
cost	cost	cost
cut	cut	cut
deal	dealt	dealt
dig	dug	dug
dive	dived (*or* dove)	dived
do	did	done
draw	drew	drawn
drink	drank	drunk
drive	drove	driven

*Be is the only verb whose past tense changes its form to agree with singular and plural subjects. See section 19.B².

Present	*Past*	*Past Participle*
(Now we . . .)	(Yesterday we . . .)	(We have . . .)
eat	ate	eaten
fall	fell	fallen
feed	fed	fed
feel	felt	felt
fight	fought	fought
find	found	found
fly	flew	flown
forget	forgot	forgotten (*or* forgot)
freeze	froze	frozen
get	got	got (*or* gotten)
give	gave	given
go	went	gone
grow	grew	grown
hang (*execute*)	hanged	hanged
hang (*suspend*)	hung	hung
have	had	had
hear	heard	heard
hide	hid	hidden (*or* hid)
hit	hit	hit
hold	held	held
hurt	hurt	hurt
keep	kept	kept
kneel	knelt (*or* kneeled)	knelt (*or* kneeled)
knit	knitted (*or* knit)	knitted (*or* knit)
know	knew	known
lay	laid	laid
leave	left	left
lend	lent	lent
let	let	let
lie (*recline*)	lay	lain
lie (*tell a falsehood*)	lied	lied
light	lighted (*or* lit)	lighted (*or* lit)
lose	lost	lost
make	made	made
mean	meant	meant
meet	met	met
mow	mowed	mowed (*or* mown)
pay	paid	paid
prove	proven	proved (*or* proven)
put	put	put
read	read	read
rid	rid (*or* ridded)	rid (*or* ridded)
ride	rode	ridden
ring	rang	rung
rise	rose	risen
run	ran	run
see	saw	seen
say	said	said
seek	sought	sought

Present	Past	Past Participle
(Now we . . .)	(Yesterday we . . .)	(We have . . .)
sell	sold	sold
send	sent	sent
sew	sewed	sewed (*or* sewn)
shake	shook	shaken
shine	shone	shone
shoot	shot	shot
show	showed	shown
shrink	shrank (*or* shrunk)	shrunk (*or* shrunken)
shut	shut	shut
sing	sang	sung
sink	sank (*or* sunk)	sunk (*or* sunken)
sit	sat	sat
sleep	slept	slept
slide	slid	slid
sling	slung	slung
slit	slit	slit
speak	spoke	spoken
speed	sped (*or* speeded)	sped (*or* speeded)
spin	spun	spun
split	split	split
spread	spread	spread
spring	sprang (*or* sprung)	sprung
stand	stood	stood
steal	stole	stolen
stick	stuck	stuck
sting	stung	stung
stink	stank (*or* stunk)	stunk
strike	struck	struck (*or* stricken)
string	strung	strung
swear	swore	sworn
sweep	swept	swept
swell	swelled	swelled (*or* swollen)
swim	swam	swum
swing	swung	swung
take	took	taken
teach	taught	taught
tear	tore	torn
tell	told	told
think	thought	thought
throw	threw	thrown
thrust	thrust	thrust
wake	woke (*or* waked)	woke (*or* waked *or* woken)
wear	wore	worn
weave	wove	woven
weep	wept	wept
win	won	won
wind	wound	wound
write	wrote	written

EXERCISE USING THE CORRECT PAST FORMS OF REGULAR AND IRREGULAR VERBS

Write the correct past or past-participle form of each verb in parentheses.

The Corner Store

One evening my mother (tell) _____ me that thereafter I would have to do the shopping for food. She (take) _____ me to the corner store to show me the way. I was proud; I (feel) _____ like a grownup. The next afternoon I looped the basket over my arm and (go) _____ down the pavement toward the store. When I (reach) _____ the corner, a gang of boys (grab) _____ me, (knock) _____ me down, (snatch) _____ the basket, (take) _____ the money, and (send) _____ me running home in panic. That evening I (tell) _____ my mother what had (happen), but she (make) _____ no comment; she (sit) _____ down at once, (write) _____ another list, (give) _____ me more money, and (send) _____ me out to the grocery again. I crept down the steps and (see) _____ the same gang of boys playing down the street. I (run) back into the house.

(Adapted from Chapter One of *Black Boy*, by Richard Wright)　　　■

Writing Suggestion

In a paragraph or short essay, recall a particular occasion when you were forced to avoid or retreat from a difficult situation. When you are done, make sure that all of your verb forms are correct.

EXERCISE USING THE CORRECT PAST FORMS OF REGULAR AND IRREGULAR VERBS

Write the correct past or past-participle form of each verb in parentheses.

Babe

He was (call) _____ the Sultan of Swat, the Wondrous Walloper, the Caliph of Crash. Hank Aaron hit more home runs lifetime, and Roger Maris (set)

_____ the record for a single season, but Babe Ruth's numbers remain magic: sixty home runs in 1927, 714 in all. While Aaron and Maris were quiet, methodical men who simply (do) _____ their jobs well, Ruth was the model for every brash athlete who boasted he could do the impossible. He (tell) _____ a dying boy that he would hit a home run and then delivered. He (make) _____ more money than the President of the United States and insisted that he deserved it. He may even have (point) _____ to the stands during the World Series and knocked the ball to the exact spot.

Off the field, Ruth also (swing) _____ for the fences. He (love) _____ steaks and booze, fast cars and beautiful women. In short, it (appear) _____ that the Babe could do anything. Though his round belly and skinny legs (recall) _____ an ice cream cone on drumsticks, he was an excellent outfielder with an outstanding arm. An aggressive base runner, he (steal) _____ home ten times. He (strike) _____ out often, but could adjust his style to a particular pitcher. Batting against a knuckleballer, he swung mightily twice and (miss) _____ both times. He then (choke) _____ up slightly and connected for a towering home run.

Ruth (star) _____ for the New York Yankees through the 1920s and enjoyed his last great moment against the Chicago Cubs during the 1932 World Series, when he hit a home run that no one knows if he predicted or not. Cub fans (spit) _____ on the Babe and threw lemons from the stands. The players (curse) _____ at him from the dugouts. When Ruth (come) _____ up to bat in the fifth inning of Game Three, he took a called strike and raised one finger. Two pitches later, he let another strike pass and (raise) _____ two fingers. He then hit a tremendous homer deep into the bleachers in center field, laughing to himself as he (run) _____ down the first base line.

After retiring in 1935, unable to convince any major-league owner that he deserved a shot at managing, Ruth (spend) _____ his remaining days golfing, hunting, and appearing at exhibition games. When he died in 1948, 100,000 people (stand) _____ silently in the rain outside St. Patrick's Cathedral to pay their respects to the greatest baseball player of all time. ■

19.B² *Using Forms of the Verb* Be

The irregular verb *be* is an important helping verb, both in the present tense and in the past. As we saw in section 18.C, *be* has three forms in the present:

I am.
You (We, They) are.
He (She, It) is.

And as we saw in the list of irregular verbs in this chapter, *be* has two forms in the past:

I (He, She, It) was.
You (We, They) were.

Be is the only verb whose past tense changes its form to agree with the subject.

A form of *be* may serve as a helping verb with the present participle of any other verb. The present participle, as you may remember from section 16.D, is made by adding *-ing* to the present form of a verb. A present form of *be* plus the present participle describes an action still in progress:

I am talking to Eva.
The Floyds are driving to Orlando.
Arnold is visiting me next week.

Each of these sentences shows continuous action in the present.

To show continuous action in the past, we use a past form of *be* with the present participle:

I was talking to Eva.
The Floyds were driving to Orlando.
Arnold was visiting me.

Remember to use *was* after singular subjects (singular nouns and the pronouns *I, he, she, it, this, that*) and *were* after plural subjects (plural nouns and the pronouns *you, we, they, these, those*).

We may also use a form of *be* with the past participle to express an idea in the *passive voice*. In the passive voice, the subject *receives* the action of the verb:

The Bulldogs are rated number one in the region.
The Bulldogs were beaten by the Schooners.

We use the passive voice when the performer of the action is unknown or is far less important than the receiver of the action. Otherwise, we should keep to the *active voice*, in which the subject performs the action of the verb:

The editors of *Sports Illustrated* rate the Bulldogs number one.
The Schooners beat the Bulldogs.

Don't overwork the passive voice. The active voice is usually more concise and forceful.

EXERCISE USING THE CORRECT FORM OF *BE*

On the line at the left of each sentence, write the correct form of the verb *be* in the tense given in parentheses.

_____ **1.** We (be) driving to San Jose in an old army ambulance. (present)

_____ **2.** We (be) driving to San Jose in an old army ambulance. (past)

_____ **3.** Sandy (be) rolling a keg down Hunnicutt Hill. (present)

_____ **4.** George Bailey (be) visited by an angel named Clarence. (past)

_____ **5.** The shepherds (be) discussing politics with Gus. (present)

_____ **6.** I (be) still not used to your crazy shenanigans. (present)

_____ **7.** You (be) talking in your sleep during the lecture on insomnia. (past)

_____ **8.** Dr. Legree (be) reciting a poem when the tornado struck. (past)

_____ **9.** The French painter Monet (be) color blind. (past)

_____ **10.** The Puritans (be) the first rum-distillers in America. (past)

_____ **11.** The game of hopscotch (be) invented by the Romans. (past)

_____ **12.** The elephant (be) the only animal with four knees in each leg. (present)

_____ **13.** King William IV's nickname (be) "Silly Billy." (past)

_____ **14.** There (be) 206 bones in the human body. (present)

_____ **15.** Attila the Hun (be) a dwarf. (past) ■

EXERCISE USING THE CORRECT PAST FORMS OF REGULAR AND IRREGULAR VERBS

Write the correct past or past-participle form of each verb in parentheses.

Hunger of Memory is the autobiography of Mexican-American Richard Rodriguez, who began his education in Sacramento, California, knowing just fifty words of English. In the following passage from his story, Rodriguez recalls his first experience with the pleasures of reading—an experience that eventually led him to obtain a Ph.D. in English.

The Achievement of Desire

OPEN THE DOORS OF YOUR MIND WITH BOOKS, read the red and white poster over the nun's desk in early September. It soon was apparent to me that reading (be) _____ the classroom's central activity. Each course (has) _____ its own book. And the information gathered from a book (be) _____ unquestioned. READ TO LEARN, the sign on the wall (advise) _____ in December. I privately (wonder) _____ : What was the connection between reading and learning? (Do) _____ one learn something only by reading it? (Be) _____ an idea only an idea if it could be written down? In June, CONSIDER BOOKS YOUR BEST FRIENDS. Friends? Reading was, at best, only a chore. I (need) _____ to look up whole paragraphs of words in a dictionary. Lines of type (be) _____ dizzying, the eye having to move slowly across the page, then down, and across. . . . The sentences of the first books I read (be) _____ coolly impersonal. Toned hard. What most bothered me, however, (be) _____ the isolation reading required. To console myself for the loneliness I'd feel when I read, I (try) _____ reading in a very soft voice. Until: "Who is doing all that talking to his neighbor?" Shortly after, remedial reading classes (be) _____ arranged for me with a very old nun.

At the end of each school day, for nearly six months, I would meet with her in the tiny room that (serve) _____ as the school's library but was actually only a storeroom for used textbooks and a vast collection of *National Geographics*. Everything about our sessions (please) _____ me: the smallness of the room; the noise of the janitor's broom hitting the edge of the long hallway outside the door; the green of the sun, lighting the wall; and the old woman's face blurred white with a beard. Most of the time we (take) _____ turns. I (begin) _____ with my elementary text. Sentences of astonishing simplicity (seem) _____ to me lifeless and drab: "The boys (run) _____ from the rain . . . She (want) _____ to sing . . . The kite (rise) _____ in the blue." Then the old nun would read from her favorite books, usually biographies of early American presidents. Playfully she (run) _____ through complex sentences, calling the words alive with her voice, making it seem that the author somehow was speaking directly to me. I (smile) _____ just to listen to her. I (sit) _____ there and (sense) _____ for the very first time some possibility of fellowship between a reader and a writer, a communication, never *intimate* like that I heard spoken words at home convey, but one nonetheless *personal*.

One day the nun (conclude) _____ a session by asking me why I was so reluctant to read by myself. I (try) _____ to explain; I (say) _____ something about the way written words (make) _____ me feel all alone— almost, I (want) _____ to add but didn't, as when I (speak) _____ to myself in a room just emptied of furniture. She (study) _____ my face as I spoke; she (seem) _____ to be watching more than listening. In an uneventful voice she (reply) _____ that I (have) _____ nothing to fear. Didn't I realize that reading would open up whole new worlds? A book could open doors for me. It could introduce me to people and show me places I never imagined existed. She (gesture) _____ toward the bookshelves. (Bare- breasted African women (dance) _____ , and the shiny hubcaps of auto- mobiles on the back covers of the *Geographic* (gleam) _____ in my mind.) I (listen) _____ with respect. But her words were not very influential. I was thinking then of another consequence of literacy, one I was too shy to admit but nonetheless (trust) _____ . Books were going to make me "educated." *That* confidence (enable) _____ me, several months later, to overcome my fear of the silence.

(Adapted from *Hunger of Memory: The Education of Richard Rodriguez,*
by Richard Rodriguez)

■

Writing Suggestion

Recalling specific experiences from your own childhood, write an essay in which you explain why your early education was generally pleasurable or not. When you are done, check to make sure that all of your verb forms are correct.

EXERCISE RECASTING PARAGRAPHS IN THE PAST TENSE

On your own paper, rewrite each paragraph below, putting the verbs into the past tense.

Example:
Original: There are vacant lots on either side of Billy Holsclaw's house.
Recast: There were vacant lots on either side of Billy Holsclaw's house.

Billy

There are vacant lots on either side of Billy Holsclaw's house. As the weather improves, they fill with hollyhocks. From spring through fall, Billy collects coal and wood and puts the lumps and pieces in piles near his door, for keeping warm is his one work. I see him most often on mild days sitting on his doorsill in the sun. I notice he is squinting a little, which is perhaps the reason he doesn't cackle as I pass. His house is the size of a single garage, and very old. It shed its paint with its youth, and its boards are a warped and weathered gray. So is Billy. He wears a short lumpy faded black coat when it is cold; otherwise he always goes about in the same loose, grease-spotted shirt and trousers.

(William H. Gass, "In the Heart of the Heart of the Country")

Example:
Original: The problems of the Indians are the weights and measures of Roger Stops.
Recast: The problems of the Indians were the weights and measures of Roger Stops.

The Weights and Measures of Roger Stops

The problems of the Indians are the weights and measures of Roger Stops. He fills saucers with cigarette butts while contemplating them. During the day, he stands behind the counter of his cafe, drinking coffee, playing with his granddaughter, talking to her in Crow; sometimes he cooks a hamburger or tells a kid that the juke box is broken because he is not yet ready to hear it; the whole of his day is pocked with the problems of washing machines: change is needed, the rinse cycle has failed, a machine has spun itself into collapse, and then there are the dryers and children who make too much noise. Through it all, he smokes and schemes and practices the art of exegesis and nostalgia on everything that touches his life.

(Earl Shorris, *How 114 Washing Machines Came to the Crow Reservation*)

Example:
Original: We drive through the country. . . .
Recast: We drove through the country. . . .

Appalachia

We drive through the country, out here where the people used to live, among forgotten general stores and deconsecrated churches. Hysterical hens tear across the path of the car, hogs root in the oak groves, an old horse rests his chin in the crotch of a butternut tree and watches life pass him by. We see hand-built WPA bridges arching polluted but pretty streams where great leprous-skinned sycamores lean above the water. We pass a farmhouse with a somewhat crumpled look, like a worn but comfortable shoe; a swing hangs by chains on the long front porch. We see an antique John Deere tractor, the kind with iron lug wheels, and a flatbed Ford with two flat tires. It is a poor but honest scene.

(Adapted from, *Appalachian Wilderness,* by Edward Abbey)

■

EXERCISE PROOFREADING FOR ERRORS IN VERB TENSE

In each paragraph below, some of the sentences contain errors in verb tense. Underline any verb that is used incorrectly, and write the correct form of the verb in the margin.

The following paragraph contains six errors in verb tense.

Hands Up!

Recently in Oklahoma City, Pat Roughen, a watchman, deposit thirty cents in a City Hall vending machine and reach in to get a candy bar. When the machine catch his hand, he pull out his pistol and shoot the machine twice. The second shot sever some wires and he got his hand out.

The following paragraph contains six errors in verb tense.

The Christmas Spirit

Mr. Theodore Dunnet of Oxford, England, run amok in his own house in December of 1972. He ripped the telephone from the wall, thrown a television set and tape-deck into the street, smash to bits a three-piece suite, kicked a dresser down the stairs, and torn the plumbing out of the bath. He offer this explanation for his behavior: "I was shock by the overcommercialization of Christmas."

The following paragraph contains six errors in verb tense.

Late Bloomers

Some very remarkable adults are known to have experience quite unremarkable childhoods. English author G. K. Chesterton, for instance, could not read until the age of eight, and he usually finish at the bottom of his class. "If we could opened your head," one of his teachers remark, "we would not find any brain but only a lump of fat." Chesterton eventually become a most successful novelist. Similarly, Thomas Edison was label a "dunce" by one of his teachers, and young James Watt was called "dull and inept."

The following paragraph contains ten errors in verb tense.

Mona Lisa

Leonardo da Vinci's *Mona Lisa* is the most famous portrait in the history of painting. Leonardo took four years to complete the painting: he begun work in 1503 and finish in 1507. Mona (or Madonna Lisa Gherardini) was from a noble family in Naples, and Leonardo may have paint her on commission from her husband. Leonardo is said to have entertain Mona Lisa with six musicians. He install a musical fountain where the water play on small glass spheres, and he give Mona a puppy and a white Persian cat to play with. Leonardo did what he could to keep Mona smiling during the long hours she sit for him. But it is not only Mona's mysterious smile that has impress anyone who has ever view the portrait: the background landscape is just as mysterious and beautiful. The portrait can be seen today in the Louvre in Paris.

The following paragraph contains ten errors in verb tense.

Hard Luck

A bank teller in Italy was jilted by his girlfriend and decide the only thing left to do was kill himself. He stolen a car with the idea of crashing it, but the car broken down. He steal another one, but it was too slow, and he barely dent a fender when he crashed the car into a tree. The police arrive and charge the man with auto theft. While being questioned, he stab himself in the chest with a dagger. Quick action by the police officers saved the man's life. On the way to his cell, he jumped out through a third-story window. A snowdrift broken his fall. A judge suspends the man's sentence, saying, "I'm sure fate still has something in store for you."

The following paragraph contains ten errors in verb tense.

The Worst Tourist

The least successful tourist on record is Mr. Nicholas Scotti of San Francisco. In 1977, he flew from California to his native Italy to visit relatives. En route the plane makes a one-hour fuel stop at Kennedy Airport. Thinking that he has arrived, Mr. Scotti got out and spend two days in New York believing he was in Rome. When his nephews are not there to meet him, Mr. Scotti assumes that they had been delayed in the heavy Roman traffic mention in their letters. While tracking down their address, the great traveler could not help noticing that modernization had brush aside most, if not all, of the ancient city's landmarks. He also notices that many people speak English with a distinct American accent. He just assumed, however, that Americans were everywhere. Even when told at last that he was in New York, Mr. Scotti refuses to believe it. He was return to the airport in a police car and sent back to California.

■

Postscript

In this chapter, you have practiced using the correct past forms of regular and irregular verbs. At the same time, you have gained further practice in combining sentences and in creating paragraphs and short essays of your own.

CHAPTER TWENTY

Pronouns

Preview

Pronouns are words that take the place of nouns. In this chapter, you will see how pronouns can be used effectively to make our writing concise and coherent. To be effective, they must refer clearly to the words they stand for. The exercises here will give you practice in using various types of pronouns clearly and correctly.

20.A Using the Different Forms of Pronouns

As seen in Chapter Fifteen, a pronoun takes the place of a noun, often serving as a subject or an object in a sentence. The common pronoun, short and unobtrusive, is an important device for making our writing both concise and coherent.

A pronoun is effective only if we use an appropriate form; otherwise, it may be distracting. There are three common pronoun forms: subject pronouns, object pronouns, and possessive pronouns. Be careful not to confuse them.

Subject pronouns are used as subjects of sentences or subordinate clauses. The subject pronouns are underlined in the sentences below:

I wasted a can of paint.
You remind me of a gray day in winter.
He (or She or It) looks peculiar.
We are the champions.
They rescued the pilot.

Object pronouns are used as objects of verbs or of prepositions. The object pronouns are underlined in the sentences below:

Mona sat between Melinda and me.
Professor Legree gave the cyanide tablets to you.
I saw him (or her or it) in St. Louis.
Our mother raised us to be cowboys.
The sailors rescued them.

Possessive pronouns show who or what owns something. The possessive pronouns are underlined in the sentences below:

My friends are in Toronto.   This glass is mine.
Your basement is flooded.   I liked yours best.

His (or Her or Its) dish is gone.   His (or Hers or Its) was cleaner.
Our days are numbered.   The problems are now ours.
Their children left.   The tickets are theirs.

Note that you do not use an apostrophe with a possessive pronoun.

EXERCISE USING CORRECT PRONOUN FORMS

On the line at the left of each sentence, substitute an appropriate pronoun for the underlined word or group of words.

_____ 1. I lent my car to Fred.

_____ 2. I lent my car to Fred and Mary.

_____ 3. I borrowed Kevin's notes.

_____ 4. Throw the Frisbee to Martha's dog.

_____ 5. The keys on this typewriter are sticking.

_____ 6. The Johnsons are moving to Little Rock.

_____ 7. We held a going-away party for the Johnsons.

_____ 8. The bike that belongs to you is underneath the wheel of my pick-up truck.

_____ 9. I sold more raffle tickets than Melanie did.

_____ 10. The petals on this plant are wilting.

_____ 11. This bagel is not the one that belongs to you.

_____ 12. Your chrysanthemums are tall and golden, but my chrysanthemums are shriveled and brown.

_____ 13. Your children are at camp this summer, while our children are in police custody.

_____ 14. Mrs. Klein and Mr. Verrioli attend different health spas.

_____ 15. Giving Leroy a spanking will hurt Leroy more than it will hurt me.

_____ 16. I ate more pickles than Katharine did.

_____ **17.** Mona sat between <u>John and me</u>.

_____ **18.** <u>Ms. Bowen and Mr. Arnold</u> attended different workshops. ■

EXERCISE RECASTING A PARAGRAPH WITH PRONOUNS

On your own paper, rewrite the following paragraph, substituting an appropriate pronoun for each underlined word or group of words.

Conversation

It is important to note that men and women regard conversation quite differently. For women <u>conversation</u> is a passion, a sport, an activity even more important to life than eating because <u>conversation</u> doesn't involve any weight gain. The first sign of closeness among women is when <u>women</u> find themselves engaging in endless, secretless rounds of conversation with one another. And as soon as a woman begins to relax and feel comfortable in a relationship with a man, <u>a woman</u> tries to have that type of conversation with <u>the man</u> as well. However, the first sign that a man is feeling close to a woman is when <u>a man</u> admits that <u>the man</u> would rather <u>the woman</u> please quiet down so <u>the man</u> can hear the TV. A man who feels truly intimate with a woman often reserves for <u>the woman and the woman</u> alone the precious gift of one-word answers. Everyone knows that the surest way to spot a successful long-term relationship is to look around a restaurant for the table where no one is talking. Ah . . . now *that's* real love.

(Adapted from *What the Dogs Have Taught Me*, by Merrill Markoe) ■

> ### Writing Suggestion
>
> **In a short essay developed with specific examples, compare and contrast the ways women and men generally carry on a conversation. When you are done, underline all of the pronouns that you have used in your report, and check to make sure that you have used the correct form of each one.**

20.B *Making Pronouns Agree with Their Antecedents*

A pronoun must agree in number with the word or words it stands for. That is, the pronoun must be singular if it stands for a singular word; it must be plural if it stands for a plural word. In each of the following sentences, the underlined pronoun agrees in number with its *antecedent*—the word that the pronoun stands for:

Melinda took <u>her</u> registration card to the front office.

Students should take <u>their</u> registration cards to the front office.

In the first sentence, the singular pronoun *her* refers to the singular noun *Melinda*. In the second sentence, the plural pronoun *their* refers to the plural noun *students*. The following *indefinite pronouns* (first seen in section 18.E) are singular:

one				
no one	anyone	everyone	someone	each
nobody	anybody	everybody	somebody	either
nothing	anything	everything	something	neither

A pronoun that refers to one of these indefinite pronouns should be singular:

One of these women lost her tennis racket.

Each of the voters placed his or her ballot in the box.

In the first sentence, the singular pronoun *her* refers to the indefinite pronoun *one*. In the second sentence, the singular pronoun phrase *his or her* refers to the indefinite pronoun *each*.

Unless we are sure that an indefinite pronoun refers exclusively to males or exclusively to females, we have to rely on a singular pronoun phrase: *he or she, his or her, his or hers*:

Everyone needs to renew his or her identification card.

However, when repeated too often in succession, such phrases can sound awkward and distract the reader:

Everyone needs to renew his or her identification card before he or she attends his or her first class.

One way to avoid such awkward phrasing is to eliminate any needless pronouns:

Everyone needs to renew his or her identification card before attending the first class.

Another way around the problem is to substitute a plural noun for the indefinite pronoun:

All students need to renew their identification cards before attending their first class.

Here the plural pronoun *their* refers to the plural subject *all students*.

EXERCISE COMPLETING SENTENCES WITH PRONOUNS

Complete each sentence with an appropriate pronoun.

1. When a student attends a local college, _____ can live quietly and inexpensively at home.

2. Students living in the dormitories must vacate _____ rooms during spring break.

3. An oak tree is just a nut that held _____ ground.

4. When a woman joins the Marines, _____ should not expect special treatment.

5. Nobody on the rugby team is working to ——————— ability.

6. In earlier days, the local drug store was different from the ones we have to-day: ——————— usually stood in the center of town and served as a meeting place for people from all walks of life.

7. Each of the women recited ——————— story.

8. Neither one of the men could make up ——————— mind.

9. Sarah is a person who sticks by ——————— principles.

10. Anyone who thinks wrestling is a legitimate sport must be out of ——————— mind.

11. Shakespeare left his second-best bed to ——————— wife.

12. The umbrella originated in Mesopotamia 3,400 years ago; ——————— offered protection not from the rain but from the sun.

13. Each woman at the workshop described ——————— project.

14. Most of the voters placed ——————— ballots in the wastebasket.

15. Neither one of the boys could remember ——————— address. ■

20.C Making Pronouns Refer Clearly to Their Antecedents

In formal writing, a pronoun should refer clearly to a specific word or phrase, not an implied one. See if you can locate the antecedent of *it* in this sentence:

> **X** Carving should be done no earlier than the day before Halloween so that it will re-main firm and not spoil.*

This sentence is faulty because the reader is left to deduce that the implied antecedent is *pumpkin* or *jack-o'-lantern*. One of those words should either precede the pronoun or take its place:

> Carving the pumpkin should be done no earlier than the day before Halloween so that it will remain firm and not spoil.
> Carving should be done no earlier than the day before Halloween so that the pumpkin will remain firm and not spoil.

Be particularly careful to provide specific antecedents for the pronouns *it, this, that, they, them, these*, and *those*. In everyday speech, we often use these pronouns casually to refer to implied ideas:

> **X** I applied for a student loan, but they turned me down.

In formal writing, however, these pronouns must refer to a specific word or group of words. We can correct our sample sentence either by replacing the pronoun with

---

*Throughout this text, examples of incorrect sentences are preceded by an **X** to remind you that they are faulty.

a noun or (if the antecedent is unknown) by rewriting the sentence in the passive voice:

> I applied for a student loan, but the loan officer turned me down.
> My application for a student loan was turned down.

In short, don't leave your readers guessing: provide specific antecedents for the pronouns you use.

Confusion may also arise if we provide more than one possible antecedent for a pronoun:

> **X** Beer in one hand and bowling ball in the other, Merdine raised it to her lips and swallowed it in one mighty gulp.

What did she raise and swallow? The beer, most likely, but possibly the bowling ball: *it* has two possible antecedents. To avoid such ambiguity, we need to change the beginning of the sentence and replace the first pronoun with a noun:

> With her bowling ball in one hand, Merdine raised the beer to her lips and swallowed it in one mighty gulp.

Again, don't leave your readers guessing: rewrite the sentence to remove the incorrect antecedent.

Finally, don't burden your sentences with needless pronouns. In particular, if a pronoun immediately follows its antecedent, consider whether the pronoun is necessary:

> **X** In the college catalog it says that students caught cheating will be suspended.

This same idea can be expressed more concisely and just as clearly without the pronoun:

> According to the college catalog, students caught cheating will be suspended.

Used effectively, pronouns can help make our writing clear, concise, and coherent. But if used carelessly, they can distract and even confuse our readers.

EXERCISE CORRECTING ERRORS IN PRONOUN REFERENCE

Each sentence below contains an error in pronoun reference. Rewrite each sentence, making sure that all pronouns refer clearly to their antecedents.

1. When the man gently picked up his puppy, his ears stood up and his tail started wagging.
2. My father is a mail carrier, but they wouldn't hire me.
3. Last year Dave played on the college boccie team, but this year he is too busy to do it.
4. On the menu it says that the chili is homemade.
5. She wore a black dress with a white front, and she wrinkled up her face in a

mischievous smile as her daughter pinned a rose on it so that she would look nice for the picture.

6. After Governor Baldridge watched the lion perform, he was taken to Main Street and fed twenty-five pounds of raw meat in front of the Fox Theater.

7. A few moments after the Countess had broken the traditional bottle of champagne on the bow of the noble ship, she slid slowly and gracefully down the slipway, entering the water with scarcely a splash.

8. After removing the meat from the broiling pan, allow it to soak in soapy water.

9. A broken board penetrated the driver's cabin and just missed his head; this had to be removed before the man could be released.

10. After drying your dog with a towel, drop it into the washing machine.

11. Because guilt and bitterness can be emotionally destructive to you and your children, you must get rid of them.

12. When a student is placed on probation, you may file an appeal with the dean. ■

EXERCISE **RECASTING AND COMBINING SENTENCES**

First, change the subject in the first sentence from *The industrial worker* to *Industrial workers*. Then, throughout the passage, replace the singular pronouns with plural pronouns that agree with their antecedents, and make any other changes that are necessary. Finally, on your own paper, combine the recast sentences into a paragraph of eleven or twelve sentences.

Example:

    Original: The industrial worker spends his best energy. He does this for seven or eight hours a day.

      Recast: Industrial workers spend their best energy. They do this for seven or eight hours a day.

Combined: For seven or eight hours a day, industrial workers spend their best energy producing "something" that is not theirs.

The Industrial Worker

1. The industrial worker spends his best energy.

2. He does this for seven or eight hours a day.

3. He does this in producing "something" that is not his.

4. He needs his work.

5. He must make a living.

6. His role is essentially a passive one.

7. He fulfills a function in a process of production.

8. The function is small.

9. The function is isolated.

10. The process is complicated.

11. The process is highly organized.

12. He is never confronted with "his" product as a whole.

13. He is not concerned with the whole product in its physical aspects.

14. He is not concerned with the whole product in its wider economic aspects.

15. He is not concerned with the whole product in its wider social aspects.

16. He is put in a certain place.

17. He has to carry out a special task.

18. He does not participate in the organization of his work.

19. He does not participate in the management of the work.

20. He is not interested.

21. He does not know why one produces this instead of another commodity.

22. He does not know what relation it has to the needs of society as a whole.

23. The shoes are produced by "the enterprise."

24. The cars are produced by "the enterprise."

25. The electric bulbs are produced by "the enterprise."

26. These are all produced using the machine.

27. He is part of the machine.

28. He is not its master as an active agent.

29. The machine has become his master.

30. The machine is not in his service to work for him.

31. This work once had to be performed by sheer physical energy.

32. The machine is not a substitute for human energy.

33. Instead, man has become a substitute for the machine.

34. His work is the performance of acts.

35. These acts cannot yet be performed by the machine.

36. This is how his work can be defined. ■

Writing Suggestion

In a paragraph or short essay, describe in detail some particular activity that you think is tedious, mechanical, or even dehumanizing. When you are done, check to make sure that all of your pronouns refer clearly and accurately to the words that they represent.

EXERCISE CREATING SENTENCES WITH PRONOUNS

On your own paper, add at least two or three sentences to each sentence below. Use your imagination to develop each idea, and use pronouns in your sentence to convey the ideas clearly and concisely.

1. The Pinto swerved across three lanes of traffic and headed directly for the front door of the Burger King. (*What happened next?*)

2. Some television programs reflect the violent times we live in. (*Give some examples.*)

3. With a tambourine in one hand, Merdine clambered onto the roof of her trailer during the thunderstorm. (*What did she do there?*)

4. A good parent provides both love and discipline. (*Explain why or give examples.*)

5. You must take some precautions to discourage burglars from entering your house. (*Suggest some precautions.*)

6. A student should participate in some of the extracurricular activities on campus. (*Explain why or give examples.*)

7. Computers appear to be taking over our lives. (*Show through examples how this may appear to be so.*)

8. As my friend and I crept down the darkened hallway of the old abandoned house, the floorboards creaked. (*What happened next?*)

9. A good professor can help you through the most difficult course. (*Explain how this is so or give an example.*)

10. I can remember how I felt my first day in a college classroom. (*Describe your feelings.*) ■

EXERCISE EDITING PARAGRAPHS FOR CORRECT AGREEMENT AND REFERENCE OF PRONOUNS

On your own paper, rewrite each of the following paragraphs, correcting all pronoun errors.

Registration

Registration at this college is an insult to mind and body. Everybody has to pre-register before they go to registration, but then you still have to spend hours waiting in a long line before they tell you that the courses you wanted to take are filled and that you will have to sign up for another one. Then we have to wait in another line. This drives me crazy. They treat you like animals here. A student goes to college to learn; they don't go to college to be bullied by Mafia-types on the registration lines. It should be stopped.

Writing on a Computer

Students should take advantage of the computers in the Writing Center. They can use them to type your papers so that your instructor doesn't have to strain their eyes trying to read it. They are easy to use, too. The student just slips in a disk, calls up the menu, and begins typing their paper. Then they save it and take it out and put it back in the box with the other disks. If mistakes appear in it, you can correct it before printing without having to retype it from start to finish. It can even check your spelling. Although a computer can't do the thinking for us, they can make your job a little easier.

Demand Your Rights!

If a person gets ripped off, they should not just lie back and sulk. You should demand your rights. For example, suppose you order a chicken sandwich at the cafeteria, and all they give you is a dried up little nugget inside a stale bun. Most people would just eat it. This is ridiculous. There is no reason why you should have to pay for something inedible. The counter person made a mistake, so they should do something about it. If she doesn't give you a fresh one, you should call the manager and demand an apology and a refund. This happens all the time, and we shouldn't have to put up with it. ■

Postscript

In this chapter, you have seen how pronouns can be used effectively to make writing concise and coherent. You have practiced editing sentences and paragraphs to make sure that pronouns refer clearly to the words that they stand for.

CHAPTER TWENTY-ONE

Punctuation and Mechanics

Preview

Punctuation marks are the small signals that guide the reader and help to bring out the meaning of our sentences. This chapter will show you how to use the common marks of punctuation. It will also explain how to follow certain other conventions of writing—the *mechanics* of underlining, capitalizing, abbreviating, and using numbers. The exercises here will give you practice in following these conventions correctly and consistently.

21.A Punctuation

In a paragraph that effectively illustrates some of the various uses of different punctuation marks, essayist Pico Iyer has also provided a clever explanation of the purpose served by these familiar marks:

> Punctuation, one is taught, has a point: to keep up law and order. Punctuation marks are the road signs placed along the highway of our communication—to control speeds, provide directions, and prevent head-on collisions. A period has the unblinking finality of a red light; the comma is a flashing yellow light that asks us only to slow down; and the semicolon is a stop sign that tells us to ease gradually to a halt, before gradually starting up again.
>
> (Pico Iyer, "In Praise of the Humble Comma")

In fact, you are probably already well acquainted with the "road signs" of punctuation. As you were introduced to various sentence structures in Chapters Fifteen and Sixteen, you were often given punctuation guidelines as well. The exercises that follow will give you an opportunity to review those guidelines.

21.A¹ End Punctuation

A sentence may end with a period (.), a question mark (?), or an exclamation point (!).

Use a *period* at the end of a sentence that makes a statement:

Television is chewing gum for the eyes.
Beware of the dog.

Felix asked if he could borrow my sleeping bag.
Robert Heinlein defined an elephant as "a mouse built to government specifications."

Notice that a period goes *inside* a closing quotation mark.
Use a *question mark* after direct questions:

What are we striving for?
Where do we go from here?

At the end of indirect questions, however, use a period, not a question mark:

Dorothy wondered if she was ever going to make it back home.

In rare instances, we may use an *exclamation point* after sentences expressing strong emotion:

She cried out, "I'm alive!"

Don't deaden the effect of the exclamation point by overworking it.

EXERCISE ADDING END MARKS OF PUNCTUATION

In the following paragraph, capitalize the first word of each new sentence, and insert the appropriate end marks of punctuation.

Down with Skool!

I am not against all schools I am very much in favor of schools that consist of groups of porpoises or similar aquatic animals that swim together I only wish that I had been to one no, I'm thinking more of school in the dictionary sense as an institution or building at which children and young people usually under nineteen receive education that dictionary definition tells the story what a school of porpoises does is to play skool is for work it is an institution why put children in an institution the real reason is that it gets the brats out from under the parents' feet the purported reason is that this is the best way to get useful information into the skulls of the little darlings how absurd children are more intelligent than adults and wiser instead of instilling into them the accepted knowledge and wisdom of the past, what we ought to be doing is learning from them that would be my idea of a good school: one run by children—or porpoises.

(Adapted from "Down with Skool!" by Richard Boston)
■

21.A² *Commas (,)*

There are four main guidelines for using commas effectively:

1. Use a comma before a coordinator (*and, but, yet, or, nor, for, so*) that links two main clauses:

The optimist thinks that this is the best of all possible worlds, and the pessimist knows it.
Character builds slowly, but it can be torn down again with incredible swiftness.

However, do *not* use a comma before a coordinator that links two words or phrases:

Jack and Diane sang and danced all night.

2. Use a comma between words, phrases, or clauses that appear in a series of three or more:

At the medical examination I was injected, inspected, and rejected.

Notice that a comma appears before but not after the coordinator.

3. Generally, use a comma after an introductory phrase or subordinate clause:

If one cannot invent a really convincing lie, it is often better to tell the truth.

If there is no chance of confusion, you may omit the comma after a short introductory phrase:

After lunch we drove to Thunder Bay.

4. Use a pair of commas to set off nonessential words, phrases, or clauses that interrupt a sentence:

Old George, the caretaker, escaped with the family's jewels.
Uncle Gus, his hands trembling, reached for the sawed-off shotgun.
Last week's pudding, which has turned green in the refrigerator, should be thrown away.

However, do *not* use commas to set off essential words, phrases, or clauses—words or groups of words that directly affect the meaning of the sentence:

Students who turn green should be sent to the infirmary.

For additional guidelines on using commas, turn back to section 15.D on coordination and to sections 16.A through 16.D on adjective clauses, appositives, adverb clauses, and participle phrases.

EXERCISE CREATING SENTENCES WITH COMMAS

Use each sentence below as the model for a new sentence of your own. Your new sentence should follow the rule in parentheses and use the same number of commas as in the original.

Example:
Model: Harold waited in the dining room, and Maude stayed in the car.
(*Rule:* Use a comma before a coordinator that links two main clauses.)

A. <u>Vera cooked the roast beef, and Phil baked the pumpkin pies.</u>

B. <u>Tom ordered steak, but the waiter brought Spam.</u>

Model 1: I rang the bell and pounded on the door, but no one answered.
(*Rule:* Use a comma before a coordinator that links two main clauses; do not use a comma before a coordinator that links two words or phrases.)

_____

_____

Model 2: I sent Elaine a basket full of apricots, mangoes, and dates.
(*Rule:* Use a comma between words, phrases, or clauses that appear in a series of three or more.)

_____

_____

Model 3: Because a politician never believes what he says, he is surprised when others believe him.
(*Rule:* Use a comma after an introductory phrase or subordinate clause.)

_____

_____

Model 4: Adrian Mole, who has not voted once in his life, is running for the post of County Commissioner.
(*Rule:* Use a pair of commas to set off nonessential words, phrases, or clauses that interrupt a sentence.)

_____

_____

■

EXERCISE USING COMMAS CORRECTLY

Insert commas wherever they are needed in the sentences below. Put an **X** through any unnecessary commas.

1. If you are the last person to leave the room please turn out the lights.
2. The last person to leave the room should shut off the copier machine turn out the lights and lock the door.
3. On Christmas Eve is going to marry Adam.
4. Pete Rose a professional baseball player for over twenty years broke Ty Cobb's record of 4,191 career hits.
5. People, who carry grenades and automatic rifles, should be prevented from boarding planes.

6. The new clerk the one with the phony eyeglasses and the red rubber nose is a real clown.

7. Edwina simplified her life by giving away her electric can opener automatic popcorn maker and ceramic bun warmer.

8. Clark County Landfill which was opened just last week has been declared an environmental hazard.

9. Cigarettes that contain low tar and nicotine, may be no safer than regular brands.

10. In autumn the leaves turn various shades of red orange and gold. ■

EXERCISE ADDING COMMAS TO A PARAGRAPH

Insert commas wherever they belong in the following passages.

Frederick Douglass

The son of a white man and a black slave Frederick Douglass spent his early years in slavery but escaped in 1838 and became a leading orator journalist and abolitionist. One stormy night Douglass was traveling from New York to Boston by boat. Because his African-American ancestry disqualified him from occupying a cabin or any of the public rooms he was obliged to curl up in a corner of the deck to sleep. An officer came across him there and took pity on him. Knowing that he could find Douglass a stateroom if he could pass him off as an American Indian the officer approached him with the words "You're an Indian aren't you?" Douglass immediately grasped the significance of the question. Looking the officer straight in the eyes he replied "No sir I'm a nigger" and curled up in his corner again.

The Least Successful Car

In 1957 Ford produced the car of the decade—the Edsel. Half of the models sold proved to be spectacularly defective. If lucky the proud owner of an Edsel could enjoy any or all of the following features: doors that wouldn't close hoods and trunks that wouldn't open batteries that went dead horns that stuck hubcaps that dropped off paint that peeled transmissions that seized up brakes that failed and push buttons that couldn't be pushed even with three people trying. In a stroke of marketing genius the Edsel one of the largest and most lavish cars ever built coincided with rising public interest in economy cars. As *Time* magazine reported "It was a classic case of the wrong car for the wrong market at the wrong time." Never popular to begin with the Edsel quickly became a national joke. One business writer at the time likened the car's sales graph to an extremely dangerous ski slope. He added that so far as he knew there was only one case of an Edsel ever being stolen.

Rap Music

For Lawrence C. Stringer and millions of other young blacks rap music is the voice of the voiceless. "Rap music has become the voice of the black community particularly the black male" said Stringer twenty an economics major at Valparaiso University in Indiana. "Rap music addresses the frustrations black men feel because we can't support our families and are constantly combating racism violence and capitalism." While not all rappers hint at violence as a solution to society's ills many of today's hottest rappers or "raptivists" as some are called combine powerful commentaries with hip-hop music. Rap music's most popular subjects include police brutality crime religion racism drug abuse AIDS and male/female relationships.

While many of these topics and lyrics may be unsettling the raps are about life says Sister Souljah. "Rap music includes curses because we are in a state of rage" says the New York City–based rapper who majored in history at Rutgers University in New Brunswick New Jersey.

But according to Robert Jagers a psychologist who teaches African-American studies and psychology at the University of Illinois-Chicago these self-appointed modern-day messengers should be mindful of the signals they send to their fans especially children who are listening to this music as they form their first impressions of the world. "Everyone has the right to an opinion and the Constitution gives rappers the right to say anything they want to say" Jagers said. "However given the present situation in the African-American community we need messages that facilitate social change." Such a change Jagers insisted can be brought about only through "a thorough understanding of our history and culture. Without this understanding some raps can be counterproductive." ■

Writing Suggestion

In a short essay, discuss what you perceive to be the significance of the lyrics of a song that you particularly like or dislike. When you are done, proofread to make sure that you have used commas correctly and effectively.

21.A³ *Semicolons (;), Colons (:), and Dashes (—)*

Semicolons, colons, and dashes are used less often than commas, but they are important marks of punctuation nonetheless. Be careful not to confuse them.

Use a *semicolon* to separate two main clauses not joined by a coordinator:

Those who write clearly have readers; those who write obscurely have commentators.

We also use a semicolon to separate main clauses joined by a conjunctive adverb:

The tail of the spider monkey is strong enough to hang by; <u>nevertheless,</u> it is also sensitive enough to probe for and pick up peanuts.

Semicolons and conjunctive adverbs are treated in section 17.B² on run-on sentences.

Use a *colon* to set off a summary or a series *after* a complete main clause:

There are three ingredients in the good life: learning, earning, and yearning.

Note that a main clause does not have to *follow* the colon; however, a complete main clause *must* precede it.

Use a *dash* to set off a short summary after a complete main clause:

At the bottom of Pandora's box lay the final gift—hope.

We may also use a pair of dashes instead of a pair of commas to set off nonessential words, phrases, or clauses that interrupt a sentence:

In the great empires of antiquity—Egypt, Babylon, Assyria, Persia—splendid though they were, freedom was unknown.

Dashes—more emphatic than commas in sentences such as this—are particularly useful for setting off a series of nonessential words within a sentence.

These three punctuation marks—semicolons, colons, and dashes—are most effective when used sparingly: don't overwork them.

EXERCISE CREATING SENTENCES WITH SEMICOLONS, COLONS, AND DASHES

Use each sentence below as the model for a new sentence. Your new sentence should follow the rule in parentheses and use the same punctuation contained in the model.

Model 1: The days were hot and dry; the nights were extremely cold.
(*Rule:* Use a semicolon to separate two main clauses not joined by a coordinator.)

_____

_____

Model 2: We have visited Australia several times; however, we have never seen a kangaroo.
(*Rule:* Use a semicolon to separate main clauses joined by a conjunctive adverb.)

_____

_____

Model 3: I divide all readers into two classes: those who read to remember and those who read to forget.
(*Rule:* Use a colon to set off a summary or a series after a complete main clause.)

_____

_____

Model 4: Chip could play the one musical instrument that no sane person can bear listening to—the bagpipes.

(*Rule:* Use a dash to set off a short summary after a complete main clause.)

Model 5: Today elaborate financial cushions—unemployment insurance, union benefits, welfare payments, food stamps, and so on—have made it less catastrophic to be out of a job for a while.

(*Rule:* For the sake of clarity or emphasis, use a pair of dashes to set off nonessential words, phrases, or clauses that interrupt a sentence.)

■

EXERCISE USING SEMICOLONS, COLONS, AND DASHES CORRECTLY

Insert semicolons, colons, or dashes wherever they are needed in the sentences below.

1. The three primary colors red, yellow, and blue appear in every one of Randolph's paintings.

2. A great many people may think they are really thinking however, most are merely rearranging their prejudices.

3. An American's devotion to McDonald's rests in part on uniformities associated with all McDonald's restaurants setting, architecture, food, ambience, acts, and utterances.

4. When in doubt mumble when in trouble delegate.

5. Staged in outdoor arenas, the modern rodeo comprises five classes bareback bronc-riding, saddle bronc-riding, bull riding, calf roping, and steer wrestling.

6. Today many of us are eating vegetables, fruits, and spices that our parents scarcely even heard of garbanzos, chili peppers, avocados, bean sprouts, adzuki beans, tofu, nori, daikon.

7. Myths are public dreams dreams are private myths.

8. Our three children Larry, Curly, and Moe have decided to enter show business.

9. There is one bird that can fly all day without even flapping its wings the albatross.

10. Baseball is a pastoral game, timeless and highly ritualized its appeal is to nostalgia. ■

EXERCISE ADDING PUNCTUATION TO A PARAGRAPH

Insert commas, dashes, colons, and semicolons wherever they are needed in the following passages.

Bad Trip

In 1985 the British Association of Travel Agents held a memorable conference in Sorrento Italy because of fog and delayed flights most people arrived a day late two fell down a marble staircase many contracted food poisoning one marketing director developed septicaemia following a snake bite the annual golf tournament had to be cancelled because there was no golf course.

(Adapted from *Cannibals in the Cafeteria and Other Fabulous Failures* by Stephen Pile)

Pasta

Pasta a large family of shaped dried wheat pastes is a basic staple in many countries. Its origins are obscure. Rice pastes were known very early in China pastes made of wheat were used in India and Arabia long before they were introduced into Europe in the twelfth century. According to legend Marco Polo in 1295 brought back from China a pasta recipe. Pasta quickly became a major element in the Italian diet and its use spread throughout Europe.

Pasta is made from durum wheat flour which makes a strong elastic dough. Hard durum wheat has the highest protein value. The flour is mixed with water kneaded to form a thick paste and then forced through perforated plates or dies that shape it into one of more than one hundred different forms. The macaroni die is a hollow tube with a steel pin in its center the spaghetti die lacks the steel pin and produces a solid cylinder of paste. Ribbon pasta is made by forcing the paste through thin slits in a die shells and other curved shapes are produced with more intricate dies. The shaped dough is dried carefully to reduce the moisture content to about twelve percent and properly dried pasta should remain edible almost indefinitely. Pastas can be colored with spinach or beet juice. The addition of egg produces a richer, yellower pasta that is usually made in noodle form and is often sold undried. ■

Writing Suggestion

In a short essay, discuss what you perceive to be the significance of the lyrics of a song that you particularly like or dislike. When you are done, proofread to make sure that you have used commas correctly and effectively.

21.A⁴ Apostrophes (')

There are two main guidelines for using apostrophes effectively.

1. Use an apostrophe to show the omission of letters in a contraction:

I'm (I am)	isn't (is not)
you're (you are)	aren't (are not)
he's (he is)	can't (cannot)
she's (she is)	don't (do not)
it's (it is)	who's (who is)
we're (we are)	won't (will not)
they're (they are)	

Be careful to place the apostrophe where the letter or letters have been omitted, *not* where the two words have been joined.

2. Use apostrophes with nouns to show possession:

Victoria's Secret	Larkin's poetry
my daughter's husband	a student's report
the woman's scarf	the students' reports
today's newspaper	my daughters' husbands

As you can see, some of these possessive forms end in *'s*, others in *s'*. If the noun does not end in *-s*, add *'s* to show possession:

the man's magazine	the men's magazine
the girl's swingset	the children's playthings

As a general rule, if the noun already ends in *-s*, simply add the apostrophe to show possession:

the girls' swingset (the swingset belonging to the girls)
the students' projects (the projects belonging to the students)

Do *not* use an apostrophe with the possessive pronouns:

yours	its
his	ours
hers	theirs

Don't confuse the contraction *it's* (*it is*) with the possessive pronoun *its*, or the contraction *you're* (*you are*) with the possessive pronoun *your*.

EXERCISE COMBINING SENTENCES WITH CONTRACTIONS

On your own paper, combine the sentences and convert the underlined words into contractions. Be sure to insert an apostrophe to show where letters have been omitted.

Example:
Original: You are tired. You should not try to study.
Combined: You shouldn't try to study when you're tired.

1. It is too cold to go swimming this morning. I will stay home and read a book.
2. I left a message for Sam this morning. He has not returned my call.
3. We are lost. Here we are on a road that does not go anywhere.
4. We will be joining you in St. Louis. We hope you do not mind.
5. There is the podiatrist. He is the man who is engaged to my sister.
6. She is quitting her job. She did not say why.
7. It is not fair. You are going to Hawaii. I am stuck at home.
8. I would like to help you. You are a close friend. I am too busy right now. ■

EXERCISE COMBINING SENTENCES WITH POSSESSIVE NOUNS

On your own paper, combine the sentences and change the word order so that each underlined noun shows possession. Supply an apostrophe or an apostrophe-plus-*s* wherever necessary.

Example:
Original: John sings. His singing drives me crazy.
Combined: John's singing drives me crazy.

1. Our neighbors have a dog. It chews gum. It drinks rum.
2. My grandfather lives in the playhouse. The playhouse is in the back yard. The playhouse belongs to our children.
3. Sarah has a younger sister. Her younger sister lives in the Yukon. Her younger sister is a lumberjack.
4. Do you remember the World Series? The World Series was last year. Do you remember which team won?
5. Harry owns a Volkswagen bus. The bus is old. It was stolen last night. It was abandoned in a junk yard.
6. I read the newspaper. The newspaper came out this morning. The newspaper said that the concert has been canceled. The concert was supposed to be tonight.
7. The pick-up truck crushed the motorcycle. The pick-up truck belongs to Sally. The motorcycle belongs to Oliver.
8. The Johnsons have a garden. It is a vegetable garden. Raccoons visit the garden frequently. The raccoons enjoy a midnight snack there. ■

EXERCISE USING APOSTROPHES CORRECTLY

In the following passage, insert apostrophes where needed to indicate possession or contractions.

The Art of Remembering Names

No ones ability to remember names is perfect. Yet this important skill gives you the advantage in business and personal relations. "A persons own name is the sweetest and most important sound," Dale Carnegie wrote in *How to Win Friends and Influence People*. Its often the ticket to a friendship, a closed deal, or a new partnership, and it generates good will in a way no other courtesy can. Forgetting someones name, on the other hand, can cause hurt feelings and make you feel socially inept and uncomfortable. Even worse, it can create a powerfully negative impression that works against you long afterward.

When you find yourself wrestling with a forgotten name ten seconds after an introduction, its because you were inattentive. This happens primarily because we often are preoccupied with ourselves. When youre meeting someone new, clear your thoughts of outside concerns. If your mind wanders during an introduction, ask that the name be repeated. At large gatherings, decide in advance to whom youre going to pay attention. (Youll never remember more than a few names from any group.) If you say to yourself, "Im going to be very conscious of my bosss wifes name," youll retain it.

The best way to retain new names is by "association-exaggeration," or forging connections between unlike things. Heres how: after youve been told a persons name, focus on his *face*. Is there something particularly interesting or attractive about it? Is the hair bright red? Are the eyebrows heavy? Are the eyes striking? Select just one feature and commit it to memory by exaggerating or animating it. If the person has red hair, set it on fire in your minds eye. If the eyebrows are bushy, see them wriggling like worms.

Once youve memorized a particular feature, transform the persons name into an unforgettable image through some rudimentary and even amusing connections. Say youve just met Fred Smith. If you envision Fred Astaire in a blacksmiths outfit, youd have to work hard to get Fred Smith out of your mind. After youve found a dramatic image for a name, place it over the distinct feature of the persons face. For example, upon meeting Dennis, you might associate his name with "tennis." You can then substitute a racquet for his long face. Dont be put off by bizarre concepts that come to mind; strange and ridiculous images are memorable ones.

Training yourself to remember names may take a lot of practice. But once youve mastered the art, you can be sure that people will remember *you*.

(Adapted from *How to Remember Names*, by Thomas Crook and Christine Allison)

■

> **Writing Suggestion**
>
> In a paragraph or short essay, describe your favorite food—its appearance, taste, texture, and varieties. When you are done, proofread to make sure that you have used punctuation marks correctly and effectively.

21.A⁵ *Quotation Marks (" ")*

There are four main guidelines for using quotation marks effectively.

1. Use double quotation marks (" ") to enclose a direct quotation:

     The president calls the new weapon a "peacekeeper."
     "No good deed," wrote Clare Booth Luce, "will go unpunished."

   However, do *not* use quotation marks around indirect quotations:
   Direct: Felix said, "I am tired."
   Indirect: Felix said that he was tired.

2. Use double quotation marks to enclose the titles of songs, stories, essays, poems, and articles in newspapers and magazines:

     Dr. Legree recited a poem titled "I am a Bug on the Windshield of Life."
     Who sang "Every Time I Itch I Wind Up Scratching You"?

   Do *not* put quotation marks around the titles of books, newspapers, and magazines; underline them instead.

3. Use single quotation marks (' ') to enclose a quotation or title within another quotation:

     Dean Buck once said, "I have never read much Shakespeare, but I love his sonnet 'Be-bop-a-lula.'"

   Notice that two separate quotation marks appear at the end of the sentence: a single mark to close the title and a double mark to close the direct quotation.

4. When you use a comma or a period at the end of a quotation, put it *inside* the quotation marks:

     "Gluttony is an emotional disease," Peter DeVries once wrote, "a sign that something is eating us."

   When you use a semicolon or a colon at the end of a quotation, put it *outside* the quotation marks:

     John Wayne never said, "A man's gotta do what a man's gotta do"; however, he did say, "A man ought to do what's right."

   When you use a question mark or an exclamation point at the end of a quotation, put it *inside* the quotation marks if it belongs to the quotation:

     Bobo sang "What Kind of Fool Am I?"

However, if the question mark or exclamation point does not belong to the quotation, put it *outside* the quotation marks:

> Did Bobo sing "I'm a Fool for You"?

Never place a period directly after a question mark or exclamation point.

EXERCISE USING QUOTATION MARKS CORRECTLY

Insert quotation marks (double and single) wherever they are needed in the sentences below. Cross out any unnecessary quotation marks.

1. Last week we read The Lottery, a short story by Shirley Jackson.
2. Last week we read The Lottery; this week we are reading A & P, a short story by John Updike.
3. The only thing we have to fear, Franklin Roosevelt said, is fear itself.
4. Natasha asked if "we were going to the concert without her."
5. Natasha asked, Are you going to the concert without me?
6. Uncle Gus said, I once heard your aunt singing The Star Spangled Banner out behind the barn at three o'clock in the morning.
7. It doesn't much signify whom one marries, Samuel Rogers wrote, for one is sure to find next morning that it was someone else.
8. Did Nelda ask you "to play Chopsticks for her on the piano?" ■

REVIEW EXERCISE PUNCTUATING SENTENCES CORRECTLY

Add appropriate punctuation marks to the sentences below.

1. The bear rears back his jaws agape and slowly spins on his feet as if in a gentle dance.
2. Music has always had a visual element of a sort the images that the listener sees in his mind's eye when a favorite song or symphony comes on.
3. More than 1,800 miles of ocean dams and inland dikes protect the Netherlands without them nearly two-thirds of the country would be inundated twice daily by the tides.
4. One of the many talents lost in this increasingly technological age is that of putting pen to paper in order to communicate with family friends and lovers.
5. In the old days about fifteen years ago I could sit down in front of my television on a Sunday afternoon in the fall and spend a few relaxing hours watching a professional football game but those days are gone.
6. I was flying cross-country recently when a woman occupying the seat next to me asked Do you mind if I smoke

7. Harbor Springs is now a summer resort for the very affluent but a hundred years ago it was the Indian village of my Ottawa ancestors.

8. Women who work outside the home whether by choice or by need do not deserve to feel the anxiety guilt and exhaustion that they do.

9. When a friend dies part of yourself dies too.

10. We took photographs of a statue of the patron saint of nail-biters the Venus de Milo. ■

REVIEW EXERCISE PUNCTUATING PARAGRAPHS

Add appropriate punctuation marks to the sentences in the paragraphs below.

Lost in the Witchcrafted Woods

I'll never forget summer camp two weeks of cramps and campfires and slugs in my underwear. One night I got lost in the woods the witchcrafted spine tingling woods. I don't know how I managed to get lost one moment I was marching along with my fellow scouts and the next I was marching alone. When I realized what had happened I responded like a true Boy Scout of America I sat down on a toadstool and sobbed. Oh I knew I was going to die out there. I waited for the gnats that sew your lips shut the owls that peck out your eyes the spiders that drop eggs on your tongue and the wolves that drag you to their dens. I knew that by the time they found me there would be nothing left of me but my neckerchief slide. I imagined them taping it to a postcard and mailing it home to my dad. When I ran out of tears I started singing Oh they built the ship Titanic to sail the ocean blue. And just then a flashlight found me. My patrol leader asked me what I was doing out here in the woods and I said Don't worry about me, I can take care of myself. That night I dreamed of dragons in the pines and I woke up screaming.

As American as . . . Corn

Corn is absolutely indigenously American. It runs with the land. It was here thousands of years before pale-skin rovers swooped in from Europe for nearly three centuries thereafter its cultivation harvest and conversion to foodstuffs occupied more time in the lives of most Americans than any other farm pursuit bar none. It was corn as well as the soils needed to grow it that pulled the Republic west to the sundown sea. It was corn that made it possible for many of the earliest settlers to survive. And as it runs with the land so does the husky heritage of corn course through our language. Our slang is starched with it our songs are too. I'm as corny as Kansas in August wrote Oscar Hammerstein II with scant concern for the fact that Kansas is much better known for its wheat.

Corn unlike wheat is practically ubiquitous. It is grown in every one of the coterminous United States. It covers in season a full quarter of the nation's cropland. In total volume of production it ranks Number One. Of all the grains it is the most efficient converter of solar energy one acre of corn can yield the equivalent in bushels of three acres of wheat. Even in an off-year such as 1983 when devastating drought and a new federal payments program cut production nearly in half corn growers here harvested more than four billion bushels almost enough to supply one bushel to every single human on earth.

(Adapted from "Where Corn Is King," by John G. Mitchell)

21.B Mechanics

This section recommends certain conventions you should follow when underlining, capitalizing, abbreviating, and using numbers.

21.B¹ Underlining

Underline the titles of specific books, plays, magazines, newspapers, movies, and television programs:

<u>Native Son</u> (book)	<u>New York Times</u> (newspaper)
<u>Death of a Salesman</u> (play)	<u>E. T.</u> (movie)
<u>Newsweek</u> (magazine)	<u>Roseanne</u> (television program)

However, do *not* underline the titles of stories, essays, poems, or articles in magazines and newspapers; instead, enclose these titles in quotation marks.

Underline words referred to *as* words:

Many people frequently misspell the words <u>separate</u>, <u>receive</u>, and <u>their</u>.

Occasionally, we underline words to emphasize them:

It is not love that we all want so much as <u>respect</u>.

But be careful: excessive underlining will only distract your reader, not emphasize your ideas.

EXERCISE UNDERLINING WORDS AND PHRASES

In the following sentences, underline words and phrases as needed. Some sentences require no underlining and are correct as they stand.

1. I have never seen Gone with the Wind, but I have read the novel.
2. I subscribe to Time, Ebony, and National Geographic.
3. I am not sure how to pronounce the word bathos.
4. Last night we saw The Glass Menagerie performed at the Roxy Playhouse.
5. My favorite quiz show is Jeopardy.
6. I rarely watch the news on television; I prefer to read the newspaper.
7. Professor Legree assigned three chapters in our textbook, The History of Western Culture and Civilization.
8. Have you ever read the Frost poem "Mending Wall"?

9. Although the reruns are over twenty-five years old, Fred's favorite television program is still the original Star Trek.

10. The words okay, all right, and nice have been overworked to death. ■

21.B² *Capitals*

Capitalize the first word of every sentence:

Sometimes a walk is as good as a hit.
Go home.
She has forgotten the words; however, she can still hum the tune.
I have three main worries: yesterday, today, and tomorrow.

Notice that the first word after a semicolon or a colon is usually *not* capitalized.
Capitalize proper names:

Alice Walker	(a specific person)
Laramie, Wyoming	(a specific place)
Sunday	(a specific day)
September	(a specific month)
Christmas	(a specific holiday)
Spanish	(a specific language and nationality)
Odd Fellows Club	(a specific organization)
Methodists	(a specific religion and its followers)
Mazda	(a specific trade name)

Do *not* capitalize the names of seasons, compass directions, plants, or sports.
Capitalize certain words in titles:

Return of the Native
"On the Photograph of a Corps Commander"
"The Whole of the Moon"

Always capitalize the first and last words in a title. Also, capitalize the words in between *unless* they are coordinators (*and, but,* and so on), short prepositions (*to, of,* and so on), or the articles *a, an,* and *the.*

EXERCISE USING CAPITALS

In the following sentences, add capital letters where they are needed; cross them out where they are not.

1. Mona lost ruth's copy of michael jackson's CD.

2. George sold his toyota and bought a new Convertible.

3. On the first saturday in april, we always visit the blue ridge mountains to celebrate the start of another Spring.

4. We walked four miles and then turned East and followed the Arnold River to its bitter end.

5. I enjoy my english course, but I am having trouble with Statistics.

6. Felix is a member of the rotary club and a fund-raiser for the united way.

7. Kathryn read "Ode On The Death Of A Favorite Cat," a poem by Thomas Gray.

8. Bobo was born in a log cabin; Now he lives in a lean-to.

9. E. B. White wrote three Children's Books: <u>stuart little</u>, <u>charlotte's web</u>, and <u>the trumpet of the swan</u>.

10. Reginald plans to drop his Badminton course and take either French or Botany instead. ◼

21.B³ *Abbreviations and Numbers*

As a general rule, avoid using abbreviations in formal writing. However, you should use the standard abbreviations before proper names:

Mr. Rogers	Dr. Ruth Westheimer
Mrs. Miller	St. Peter
Ms. Harriet Lahrman	

Abbreviate the names of well-known organizations:

ITT	CIA
ABC	FBI
IBM	YMCA

You may also abbreviate the name of a less well-known unit or organization if you intend to mention it several times in your paper. Just be sure that you write the name out in full the first time you use it, and indicate its abbreviation in parentheses. Thereafter, use the abbreviation.

Another general rule concerns the use of numbers in formal writing: spell out numbers that are under one hundred or that take no more than two words to write:

<u>seven</u> patients
<u>twenty-three</u> cases of plagiarism
<u>ninety-nine</u> bottles of beer on the wall
<u>a thousand</u> pages

Use figures for numbers that require more than two words:

We ordered <u>743</u> cartons of erasers.
The population of Kiev is <u>2,192,000</u>.

Also, use figures for dates, times, phone numbers, and exact amounts of money:

Katie was born on September <u>20, 1973</u> (or <u>20</u> September <u>1973</u>).
The bus leaves at <u>2:20</u>.
The number of the Consumer Response Center is <u>1-800-431-1004</u>.
Ms. Didriksen offered to pay him <u>$1.08</u> a day for writing the book.

However, always spell out numbers that begin sentences.

EXERCISE USING ABBREVIATIONS AND NUMBERS

In the sentences below, correct any errors in the use of abbreviations and numbers. If there are no errors in a sentence, write *correct* on the line at the left.

_____ **1.** 4 people died in the zeppelin collision.

_____ **2.** We visited the YWCA to hear Mister Marcus play twenty-eight different versions of "Stardust" on his harmonica.

_____ **3.** Dr. Noble is leaving to teach at Brunswick Junior College (BJC).

_____ **4.** The population of Paramaribo is approximately one-hundred-and-two thousand, three-hundred-and-four.

_____ **5.** I am still stuck on the 1st page of this textbook.

_____ **6.** My cousin used to be an undercover agent with the FBI.

_____ **7.** Forty people showed up for the first meeting of the SPC (the Shy People's Club), but only 1 person said anything.

_____ **8.** At 2:38 on Wed. morn., Professor Legree flung open his 2nd story window and sang "Bye, Bye Blackbird" at the top of his lungs.

_____ **9.** Approx. 7 out of every 10 students never speak to their univ. prof. outside of the classroom.

_____ **10.** If you have reached the end of this chapter and still have questions about punctuation and numbers, please call 912-927-5210 for additional information. ■

Postscript

In this chapter, you have practiced applying the guidelines for effectively using the common marks of punctuation: periods, question marks, exclamation points, commas, dashes, colons, and semicolons. In addition, you have reviewed the mechanics of underlining, capitalizing, abbreviating, and using numbers.

CHAPTER TWENTY-TWO

Words

Preview

Throughout this book we have been concerned with words—their arrangement in sentences, their different forms, their various shades of meaning. This final chapter provides additional advice on using words correctly and effectively. First, you will learn how to use the dictionary as a reference tool. Next, you will be given some pointers on how to spell correctly and how to distinguish between commonly confused words. And finally, you will see the value of not wasting words in a final draft.

22.A Using the Dictionary

There are several good dictionaries available—*The American Heritage Dictionary, Webster's New Collegiate Dictionary,* and *Webster's New World Dictionary,* among others. You will find any one of these to be a valuable reference tool. In fact, you may want to invest in two dictionaries—an inexpensive paperback that you can carry to class and a larger hard-cover edition to work with at home. But owning a dictionary isn't enough; you must know how to use what's in it.

A dictionary contains information about various things. Depending on the size and edition, it may include brief biographies, a list of place names, a list of American colleges, a short history of the English language, and a guide to grammar and punctuation. But the most important information in any dictionary is that found in its entries on words.

The arrangement of a word entry differs from one dictionary to the next, but the type of information is similar in all. Here we will examine a typical entry from *The American Heritage Dictionary of the English Language.* After reading the entry and our discussion of it, turn to the guide at the front of your own dictionary for additional information.

22.A¹ Spelling

The spelling of a word with its division into syllables is given in bold print. How, then, do we look up a word if we are unsure of its spelling? Usually one or two informed guesses should take us right to the spot. For instance, unsure of the spelling of *pacify,* we might start our search by glancing at words that begin with *pass-.* Finding nothing suitable there, we next consider what letters other than *s* can represent an *s* sound. The most likely answer is *c,* and so we turn to those words begin-

(3) Part of Speech (4) Other Forms

(2) Pronunciation ↘

↓ ↓

(1) Spelling ⟶ pac·i·fy (păs'ə-fī') *tr.v.* -**fied**, -**fy·ing**, -**fies**. **1.** To ease the anger or agitation of. **2.** To end war, fighting, or violence in; establish peace in. ◄— (5) Meanings
[Middle English *pacifien*, from Old French *pacifier*, from Latin *pācificāre*: *pāx, pāc-*, peace; see **pag-** in Appendix + *-ficāre*, -fy.] ◄— (6) History
—**pac'i·fi'a·ble** *adj.*

Synonyms: *pacify, mollify, conciliate, appease, placate.* These verbs all refer to allaying another's anger, belligerence, discontent, or agitation. To *pacify* is to restore calm to or establish peace in: *"The explanation . . . was merely an invention framed to pacify his guests"* (Charlotte ◄— (7) Synonyms Brontë). *An army was required in order to pacify the islands. Mollify* stresses the soothing of hostile feelings: *"In that case go ahead with the project," she said, mollified by his agreeable manner. Conciliate* usually implies winning over, often by reasoning and with mutual concessions: *"A wise government knows how to enforce with temper or to conciliate with dignity"* (George Grenville). *Appease* and *placate* suggest the satisfaction of claims or demands or the tempering of antagonism, often through the granting of concessions: *The child is adept at appeasing her parents' anger with a joke or compliment. Even a written apology failed to placate the indignant hostess.*

From *The American Heritage Dictionary of the English Language,* 1992.

ning with *pac-*. Glancing down the column, we spot a likely spelling: *p-a-c-i-f-y*. Then we check the pronunciation and meaning to make sure that this is indeed the word we have been looking for. The syllable divisions (*pac·i·fy*) show us where we can divide the word with a hyphen at the end of a line.

EXERCISE USING THE DICTIONARY TO CHECK SPELLING

Use your dictionary to check the spelling of each word below. If the word is misspelled, correct it on the line at the right.

1. arguement _____

2. achieve _____

3. benefit _____

4. catagory _____

5. cemetery _____

6. imatation _____

7. irrelavent _____

8. neccessary _____

9. occassion _____

10. occurred _____

11. peculiar _____

12. quanity _____

13. recieve _____

14. separate _____

15. truly _____

■

22.A² *Pronunciation*

The version of the word in parentheses tells us how to pronounce it. We can translate the pronunciation symbols with the help of the key at the bottom of each page (or of every other page) in our dictionary:

p as in **pop**	ə as in edible
ă as in pat	**f** as in **fife**
s as in **sauce**	**i** as in pie

The inverted *e* (ə), called a *schwa*, represents a very common vowel sound, one that may be represented by an *a* (about), *e* (item), *i* (edible), *o* (gallop), or *u* (circus). Many misspellings result from matching this vowel sound with the wrong letter.

EXERCISE USING THE DICTIONARY TO CHECK PRONUNCIATION

Use your dictionary to answer the following questions.

1. Does the final syllable of epitome rhyme with home or be? _____

2. Is the second a in assuage pronounced like the a in pay or the a in father? _____

3. Do we pronounce the t in often? _____

4. Does the final syllable in <u>malaise</u> rhyme with <u>be</u>, <u>wise</u>, or <u>haze</u>? _____

5. Does <u>wreak</u> rhyme with <u>neck</u> or <u>seek</u>? _____ ■

22.A³ *Parts of Speech*

This item tells us whether the word is a *noun, verb, pronoun, adjective, adverb, preposition,* or *conjunction.* Here we learn that *pacify* is a verb, one that may be either active or passive (*transitive*).

Note that some words may serve as more than one part of speech. *Round,* for example, may be used as a noun, verb, adjective, adverb, or preposition. When you look up the meaning of a word, be sure to check its function as well.

EXERCISE **DETERMINING PARTS OF SPEECH**

Identify the part(s) of speech given in your dictionary for each word below.

1. antidote _____

2. malinger _____

3. down _____

4. score _____

5. volatile _____ ■

22.A⁴ *Other Forms of the Word*

Dictionaries do not give separate entries for all forms of every word, but often different forms are listed after the base form of the word. In the *pacify* entry, for example, three endings are listed: the ending of the past form (*-fied*), the present-participle form (*-fying*), and the singular present form (*-fies*). So, if you have trouble finding a word in the dictionary, see if it is listed under another form.

EXERCISE **FINDING OTHER FORMS OF WORDS**

Use your dictionary to answer the following questions.

1. What is the plural of banjo? _____

2. What is the present-participle form (<u>-ing</u>) of <u>study</u>? _____

3. What is the past-participle form of <u>swim</u>? _____

4. What is the plural form of <u>swine</u>? _____

5. What is the past form of the verb <u>crow</u>? _____

■

22.A⁵ *Meanings*

A word may carry several meanings, so be sure to read them all. Some dictionaries begin with the oldest meaning of a word and then proceed to more recent ones. However, most dictionaries (like *The American Heritage*) begin with the most common meaning. Check the guide at the front of your dictionary to see which arrangement it follows.

When you want to find the definition of a word that you have run across in your reading, be sure to consider the *context* (the sentence or paragraph) in which the word appears as well as the meanings given in the dictionary. Imagine, for instance, that we first encountered *pacify* in this sentence:

Irma relied on a rubber frog to <u>pacify</u> her baby.

When we check the meanings given in the dictionary entry, we see that only the first definition fits the way the word has been used in the sentence:

1. To ease the anger or agitation of; restore calm to; appease. . . .

Simply memorizing dictionary definitions is not an effective way of building a precise vocabulary. Instead, we need to match those definitions with sentences that illustrate how the words are used.

EXERCISE DEFINING WORDS IN CONTEXT

Study how each underlined word below is used in its sentence, and then look up the word in your dictionary. Copy the definition that best fits the way the word is used in the sentence.

1. Carl's <u>pungent</u> wit hurt many people's feelings.
2. He was more concerned with <u>corporal</u> pleasures than with spiritual pursuits.
3. The water that comes from the reservoir is <u>hard</u>.
4. One needs a great deal of <u>capital</u> to start a new business these days.
5. Unable to face the truth, George continued to <u>rationalize</u> his behavior.

■

22.A⁶ *History of the Word*

Larger dictionaries will often explain the history of a word—how it has changed in form and meaning over the years. For instance, we see that *pacify* comes originally from two Latin words: *pax* (meaning "peace") and *facere* ("to make").

Although the form of the word has changed, its basic meaning has not. Checking the history of the word can help us to remember it and relate it to words that we already know.

EXERCISE TRACING THE ORIGINAL MEANINGS OF WORDS

The words listed below have experienced some interesting changes in meaning over the centuries. Look up each word in a large dictionary, and then copy the following information: (a) the original meaning of the word (often as it appeared in a different form in another language); (b) the most common meaning of the word today.

1. sophomore _____

2. dandelion _____

3. assassin _____

4. gorilla _____

5. nice _____

6. manure _____

7. manufacture _____

8. saxophone _____

9. mentor _____

10. company _____

11. hippopotamus _____

12. ruminate _____

■

22.A⁷ Synonyms

Synonyms are words that have similar meanings. Notice that we are given several synonyms for *pacify*, but that none of these words means exactly the same thing as any other. We can become more precise in our writing by recognizing the differences as well as the similarities between words.

EXERCISE FINDING SYNONYMS

Use your dictionary to find at least two synonyms for each word below.

1. chief (adj) _____

2. follow _____

3. last _____

4. prone _____

5. relevant _____

■

22.B Correct Spelling

Even some of the most experienced writers have difficulties with spelling. Do we use *ie* or *ei*? Double the *l* or keep it single? These are questions we often find ourselves asking when we come to revise, edit, and proofread our writing. We know that correct spelling is important, not because a misspelled word would utterly befuddle our readers, but bekuz it would distract from our message—as that peculiar spelling of *because* just did.

You have seen how to use a dictionary to check spelling. In fact, you're probably already in the habit of looking up words that you know are tricky—*chlorophyll*, for example, or *rheumatism*. But what about those everyday words that we have gotten into the habit of misspelling? How do we track them down and correct them? Here are some suggestions.

22.B¹ Using a Spell-Checker

If you have any experience at all in writing with the help of a computer, you are probably familiar with a useful word-processing tool: the spell-checker. Most word-processing programs have a built-in spell-checker that allows you to identify any word that is not contained in its dictionary. For instance, a spell-checker would quite likely highlight the misspelled version of *oppose* in this sentence:

I opose the planned route of the new expressway.

In addition, the spell-checker may suggest one or more correctly spelled words that resemble the highlighted word:

oppose

With the tap of a key, you can substitute the recommended word for the highlighted word.

But we have to be careful not to put too much trust in the spell-checker. For one thing, because even the best spell-checker is incomplete, not all highlighted words are necessarily incorrect. More importantly, the spell-checker has no way of determining that you have inadvertently typed in the correct spelling of the wrong word. In the following sentence, for instance, a spell-checker would not highlight the word *weigh*:

I had forgotten the weigh home.

However, good old-fashioned proofreading should help you to recognize that the word should be *way*.

Therefore, when using a spell-checker, keep these three tips in mind:

1. *In addition to* using a spell-checker, be sure to proofread your work carefully with the aid of a standard dictionary.

2. When your spell-checker highlights a word, check a standard dictionary to make certain that you really have made an error.

3. When your spell-checker suggests an alternative spelling, make sure that it *is* the word you want to use.

Though the spell-checker can be useful, it's not a substitute for careful proofreading.

22.B² *Keeping a Spelling List*

If you have found yourself checking the spelling of the same words time and time again, it's *now* time to start a spelling list. Or if your papers have been marked off frequently for the same misspelled words, you should start a spelling list. It's not difficult.

Set aside a few pages in your notebook—or buy a special notebook—just for spelling. Whenever you look up a word in the dictionary or find a misspelling in your writing, enter the word in your notebook. An excerpt from one student's spelling list appears below:

receive	I received a raise.
separate	Separate the men from the boys.
cemetery	Take it easy in the cemetery. (3 e's)
their	Their house is on fire. (possession)

As you can see, the student has listed the words (spelled correctly) in the left-hand column and followed each word with a simple sentence that uses the word. In some instances she has jotted down clues that will help her remember the correct spelling.

For your list to be effective, you must *use* it. When you first enter a word, copy it letter by letter from the dictionary, making sure that you are copying it accurately. Then slowly spell the word *out loud* several times until you can do so without looking at the page. Each time you enter a new word, review the words already in the list by again spelling them out loud. If you follow this method carefully, you won't become a perfect speller overnight, but your spelling will show steady improvement.

22.B³ *Learning the Basic Spelling Rules*

Spelling rules are imperfect: they *all* have exceptions. But some writers find that certain rules help them remember how to spell particular types of words, especially those formed by adding *suffixes* (endings). Of all the spelling rules, the four that follow should be the most helpful to you:

Rule 1: Use i before e, except after c, except when sounded as a, as in neighbor and weigh.

believe	deceive
chief	receive
piece	weigh
thief	freight

(Some common exceptions: efficient, weird, neither, ancient, foreign)

Rule 2: Drop the final e before a suffix beginning with a vowel but not before a suffix beginning with a consonant.

please + ure = pleasure	entire + ly = entirely
ride + ing = riding	like + ness = likeness
guide + ance = guidance	arrange + ment = arrangement

(Some exceptions: noticeable, truly)

Rule 3: Usually change a final y to i before a suffix, unless the suffix begins with i.

defy + ance = defiance	occupy + ing = occupying
try + es = tries	try + ing = trying
pity + ful = pitiful	copy + ing = copying

Rule 4: Double a final single consonant before a suffix beginning with a vowel when *both* these conditions exist: (a) a single vowel precedes the consonant; (b) the consonant ends an accented syllable or a one-syllable word.

stop + ing = stopping	stoop + ing = stooping
admit + ed = admitted	benefit + ed = benefited
occur + ence = occurrence	delight + ful = delightful

22.B⁴ *Studying the Most Commonly Misspelled Words*

The following list contains two hundred of the most commonly misspelled words. On your own paper, spell out the words as a friend reads them to you (or as you listen to a recording of your own reading). Then check your work, correcting any misspellings and adding those words to your own spelling list.

absence	address	argument
accommodate	advertise	athlete
achieve	advice	awful
acquire	among	balance
across	apparent	basically

becoming
before
beginning
believe
benefit

breathe
brilliant
business
calendar
careful

category
ceiling
cemetery
certain
chief

citizen
coming
competition
convenience
criticize

decide
definite
deposit
describe
desperate

develop
difference
dilemma
disappear
disappoint

discipline
does
during
easily
eight

either
embarrass
environment
equipped
exaggerate

excellent
except
exercise
existence
expect

experience
experiment
explanation
familiar
fascinating

finally
foreign
forty
forward
friend

fundamental
generally
government
grammar
guarantee

guidance
happiness
heroes
humorous
identity

imaginary
imitation
immediately
incidentally
independent

intelligent
interesting
interfere
interpretation
interruption

invitation
irrelevant
irritable
island
jealous

judgment
knowledge
laboratory
length
lesson

library
license
loneliness
losing
lying

marriage
mathematics
medicine
miniature
minute

mysterious
naturally
necessary
neighbor
neither

noticeable
occasion
occurred
official
often

omission
operate
optimism
original
ought

paid
parallel
particularly
peculiar
perceive

perform
permanent
persevere
personally
persuade

picture
piece
planning
pleasant
political

possess
possible
practical
prefer
prejudice

presence
privilege
probably
professional
promise

proof	sacrifice	temperature
psychology	safety	temporary
quantity	scissors	through
quarter	secretary	toward
quiet	separate	tries
quit	shining	truly
quite	similar	twelfth
realize	sincerely	until
receive	soldier	unusual
recognize	speech	using
recommend	stopping	usually
reference	strength	village
religious	studying	weird
repetition	succeed	welcome
restaurant	successful	whether
rhythm	surely	writing
ridiculous	surprise	

EXERCISE SPELLING CORRECTLY

Add any letter(s) to complete the correct spelling of each word in parentheses. In some cases, no letters are needed. Write the *complete word* on the line at the left of each sentence.

GROUP A: Some of these words require an e; others are correct as they stand.

_____ 1. Dave is (tru-ly) sorry for keeping you awake last night.

_____ 2. We were beaten (sever-ly) by hooligans.

_____ 3. The trailer was (complet-ly) demolished.

_____ 4. Marvin was (sincer-ly) grateful for the reprieve.

_____ 5. The Flintstones are (argu-ing) again.

_____ 6. They (argu-d) last night for hours.

_____ 7. When is Alfalfa (com-ing) home?

_____ 8. Pearl is (writ-ing) her autobiography.

_____ **9.** Mr. Faulk is (judg-ing) the beauty contest.

_____ **10.** Be (car-ful) when you light the stove.

GROUP B: Some of these words require ie; others require ei.

_____ **1.** Paint the (c--ling) before you paint the walls.

_____ **2.** Gus has been (rec--ving) crank phone calls.

_____ **3.** That (w--rd) noise came from the house on the hill.

_____ **4.** I paid over two dollars for that (p--ce) of pie.

_____ **5.** I don't (bel--ve) a word of what she says.

_____ **6.** All the guests brought (th--r) kids to the wedding.

_____ **7.** (N--ther) of us can help you today.

_____ **8.** The (n--ghbors) complained about our puma.

_____ **9.** Linda (w--ghs) less than ninety pounds.

_____ **10.** We waited at the crossing for the (fr--ght) train to pass.

GROUP C: Some of these words require i; others require y.

_____ **1.** Have you (tr-ed) this fine dessert yet?

_____ **2.** The baby (cr-ed) throughout the night.

_____ **3.** We compared two (theor-es) of evolution.

_____ **4.** Reggie felt (betra-ed) by his manager.

_____ **5.** I will be (stud-ing) for tomorrow's exam.

_____ **6.** (Lonel-ness) was never a problem for Thoreau.

_____ **7.** He (fl-es) on broken wings.

_____ **8.** Felix has never (rel-ed) on an editor.

_____ **9.** Give Mr. Flannery my (apolog-es).

_____ **10.** It was a (pit-ful) sight.

GROUP D: Complete each word with the letter <u>a</u>, <u>e</u>, or <u>i</u>.

_____ **1.** Gus stole these flowers from the (cemet-ry).

_____ **2.** The parrot eats large (quant-ties) of bird seed.

_____ **3.** The tax cuts will (ben-fit) the wealthy.

_____ **4.** It is a (priv-lege) to meet you.

_____ **5.** Jane has an (unpleas-nt) disposition in the morning.

_____ **6.** We placed the children in (sep-rate) bunks.

_____ **7.** Herb is an (independ-nt) thinker.

_____ **8.** I found an (excell-nt) excuse to leave the party.

_____ **9.** We selected items from different (cat-gories).

_____ **10.** Professor Legree made another (irrelev-nt) remark.

GROUP E: Some of these words require the doubling of a consonant; others are correct as they stand.

_____ **1.** The sun was (shin-ing) down like honey.

_____ **2.** The experiment was (control-ed) by a madman.

_____ **3.** This campus is (begin-ing) to resemble a wasteland.

_____ **4.** Doug (pour-ed) raisins over Yoddy's oatmeal.

_____ **5.** I keep (forget-ing) my own name.

_____ **6.** Fred (admit-ed) his error.

_____ **7.** We were (sweat-ing) in the classroom.

_____ **8.** The thought of apologizing never (occur-ed) to me.

_____ **9.** The little bunny went (hop-ing) down to the abattoir.

_____ **10.** My doctor (refer-ed) me to a dimple specialist.

GROUP F: Some of these words require the addition of one or more letters; others are correct as they stand.

_____ **1.** Marriage comes without a (g-arantee).

_____ **2.** Mr. Caley (su-prised) me.

_____ **3.** We are (prob--ly) going to be late.

_____ **4.** Do you (reali-e) that your socks don't match?

_____ **5.** (D-scribe) the truck that ran into you.

_____ **6.** We waited (until-) the trashmen arrived.

_____ **7.** Bob (recom-ended) a psychiatrist.

_____ **8.** Take two (asp-rin) and go to bed.

_____ **9.** She supports a strong (ath-letic) program.

_____ **10.** The (temp-rature) reached 109 in Yuma.

GROUP G: Some of these words require the addition of one or more letters; others are correct as they stand.

_____ **1.** We (a-quired) a good tan and a bad debt.

_____ **2.** Frodo is (basic--ly) lazy.

_____ **3.** What can we do to improve the (envir--ment)?

_____ **4.** I wish Hansel would simply (dis--pear).

_____ **5.** Mr. Winters should attend to his (bus-ness).

_____ **6.** George Orwell wrote an essay (sim-lar) to yours.

_____ **7.** The Cubs have (fin-lly) won a ball game.

_____ **8.** I was (dis-appointed) by the guanabanas in dill sauce.

_____ **9.** The mad scientist was working in his (lab-ratory).

_____ **10.** Baron Leibnitz works for the (gover-ment). ■

22.C Choosing the Correct Word

It is easy to confuse words that are similar in sound, spelling, or meaning. But it is also easy to clear up such confusions. The most common of these troublemaking words appear below. Study the definitions and examples in each set, and then fill in each blank with the appropriate word.

1. *a, an, and*

Use *a* and *an* before nouns: *a* before a noun that begins with a consonant sound (*a doctor, a horse, a university*); *an* before a noun that begins with a vowel sound (*an envelope, an hour, an umbrella*). *And* is a coordinator: use it to join words, phrases, or clauses.

> *Example:* A bank is a place where they lend you an umbrella in fair weather and ask for it back when it begins to rain.

(a) Writing is just having _____ sheet of paper, _____ pen, _____ not a shadow of _____ idea of what you are going to say.

(b) _____ good coach is _____ understanding tyrant _____ a hard-headed friend.

2. *accept, except, expect*

Accept is a verb that means "to take in." *Except* is a preposition that means "other than." *Expect* is a verb that means "to depend on" or "to await."

> *Example:* Everyone except the safety squad accepted the latest wage offer. We expect to go back to work on Thursday.

(a) No one _____ a fool would _____ your story that a platypus ate your check for the rent.

(b) I _____ you to pay me by tomorrow; I will _____ no more excuses.

3. *advice, advise*

Advice is a noun meaning "guidance." *Advise* is a verb meaning "to recommend" or "to counsel."

> *Example:* Donna's father advised her not to marry John. She should have followed his advice.

(a) The _____ you gave me resulted in my arrest.

(b) I _____ you to mind your own business from now on.

4. *affect, effect*

Affect is usually a verb meaning "to influence." *Effect* is usually a noun meaning "result." When used as a verb, *effect* means "to cause."

> *Example:* The increase in tuition has <u>affected</u> many students. One <u>effect</u> is declining enrollments.

(a) Scientists are still studying the _____ of NutraSweet on humans.

(b) The controversy over artificial sweeteners has not seriously _____ the sales of diet soft drinks.

5. *all ready, already*

The phrase *all ready* means "completely prepared." *Already* is an adverb meaning "previously" or "by this time."

> *Example:* We have <u>already</u> packed our clothes. We are <u>all ready</u> to go.

(a) Both teams have _____ taken batting practice.

(b) The players are _____ to start the game.

6. *a lot (much, many)*

A lot is spelled as two words, not one. In formal writing, avoid the phrase *a lot of* and instead use *much* or *many*.

> *Example:* <u>A lot of</u> people left early. *(informal)*
> <u>Many</u> people left early. *(formal)*

(a) Professor Legree received _____ complaints. *(informal)*

(b) Professor Legree received _____ complaints. *(formal)*

7. *amount, number*

Use *amount* to refer to a quantity. Use *number* to refer to people or objects that can be counted.

> *Example:* A large <u>number</u> of students devoured a great <u>amount</u> of food.

(a) An enormous _____ of energy was exerted by a small _____ of people.

(b) The police discovered a(n) _____ of counterfeit bills in Ashmore's wallet.

8. *beside, besides*

Beside is a preposition meaning "next to." *Besides* is a preposition meaning "in addition to." As a conjunctive adverb, *besides* means "also."

Example: Ella was too proud to sit beside her husband. Besides, she preferred sitting in the front of the church.

(a) _____ being a top scholar, Sidney is a talented soccer player.

(b) His diploma stands _____ the soccer trophy on his bookcase.

9. *breath, breathe*

Breath is a noun; *breathe* is a verb.

Example: Finding it hard to breathe inside the auditorium, I stepped out for a breath of fresh air.

(a) I held my _____ as I watched Jenny shinny up the flag pole.

(b) I was too frightened to _____ .

10. *choose, chose, chosen*

Choose is an irregular verb, with *chose* as the past form and *chosen* as the past-participle form. (See Chapter Nineteen on *Verb Tenses*.)

Example: I chose my courses for next term, but I haven't yet chosen a major. I find it hard to choose between podiatry and penology.

(a) We must _____ partners for the relay race.

(b) I would have _____ Genghis, but he _____ not to come.

11. *clothes, cloths*

Clothes means "clothing." *Cloths* is the plural of *cloth* ("fabric").

Example: Put your filthy clothes in the hamper, and then wipe your face with a damp cloth.

(a) Crazy Jane's _____ appeared to have been made out of old _____ sewn together.

(b) Gus left his wedding _____ on the line during the storm.

12. *complement, compliment*

Complement means "something that completes or brings to perfection." *Compliment* is "an expression of praise." Both words have a noun and a verb form.

Example: Art's singing complemented Paul's guitar playing. The two men earned high compliments for their perfect performance.

(a) I _____ Jocko on the exquisite meal he had prepared. (Use the past form of the verb.)

(b) The fine meal was _____ by the fine service. (Use the past-participle form of the verb.)

13. conscience, conscious

Conscience is a noun meaning "the sense of what is right and wrong." *Conscious* is an adjective meaning "being aware" or "deliberate."

> *Example:* Sally was troubled by a guilty <u>conscience</u>. She was <u>conscious</u> that she had done wrong.

(a) Sally made a _____ effort to change her ways.

(b) Her troubled _____ would not let her rest.

14. device, devise

A *device* is "a gadget" (noun); *to devise* is "to plan" (verb).

> *Example:* This simple <u>device</u> turns a pencil into a divining rod. It was <u>devised</u> by a Latvian shepherd.

(a) We must _____ a way to rescue Merdine from the well.

(b) Perhaps a _____ involving pulleys and moonshine will work.

15. few (fewer), little (less)

Few and *fewer* refer to people or objects that can be counted. *Little* and *less* refer to a small quantity.

> *Example:* A <u>little</u> juice was spilled on the rug. There are still a <u>few</u> bottles left in the ice box. Because <u>fewer</u> people showed up this time, we had <u>less</u> trouble than last time.

(a) I have _____ money than I thought.

(b) A _____ bills are missing from my wallet.

(c) I have _____ time to argue.

(d) I have _____ friends now that I am poor.

16. formally, formerly

Formally means "in a formal manner." *Formerly* means "at an earlier time."

> *Example:* This ice cream parlor was <u>formerly</u> a swank restaurant. Guests were <u>formally</u> greeted by the owner.

(a) The hostess asked her guests to dress _____ .

(b) She had _____ been a waitress at the Rainbow Restaurant.

17. *have, of*

Use *have*, not *of*, as a helping verb with *could*, *must*, *should*, *would*, *may*, and *might*. *Of* is a preposition.

> *Example:* One of the first things you should have done was call me.

(a) One _____ us made a mistake.

(b) It must _____ been Ernestine.

18. *hear, here*

Hear (verb) means "to listen"; *here* (adverb) means "in this place."

> *Example:* Everyone can hear if you place the speaker here.

(a) Did you _____ the announcement?

(b) The bus is _____ .

19. *hoping, hopping*

Hoping is the present-participle form of *hope* ("to wish for"). *Hopping* is the present-participle form of *hop* ("to skip").

> *Example:* Hoping that he would not fall, Alice watched her son hopping along the edge of the cliff.

(a) Frank is _____ along on one foot.

(b) We are _____ he'll be all right.

20. *imply, infer*

A speaker *implies* ("suggests") something; a listener *infers* ("deduces").

> *Example:* The bank manager implied that I was ineligible for a loan. I inferred from her letter that she considers me a poor risk.

(a) This newspaper report _____ that one of the employees started the fire.

(b) I _____ from this report that the police have a suspect.

21. *in, into*

A person is *in* a place but may move *into* another one. *Into* suggests movement.

> *Example:* After waiting in the hallway for twenty minutes, I finally walked into the room.

(a) Douglas stepped _____ the time capsule, and _____ a minute he was gone.

(b) The chief value of money lies _____ the fact that one lives _____ a world _____ which it is overestimated.

22. *its, it's*

Its is a possessive pronoun. *It's* is a contraction of *it is* or *it has*. An apostrophe never follows *its*.

> *Example:* Because it's such a hot day, the dog is sleeping in its hiding place under the porch.

(a) Although _____ not yet autumn, this tree is losing _____ leaves.

(b) Either _____ dying, or _____ signaling that cold days are coming soon.

23. *lay, lie*

Lay is a verb meaning "to put" and requires a direct object. *Lie* is a verb meaning "to rest" and does not take a direct object. Don't confuse the past and past-participle forms of these verbs:

Present:	lay	lie
Past:	laid	lay
Past Participle:	laid	lain

> *Example:* The pumpkin I had laid on the bench lay there for two weeks.

(a) The cat always _____ curled up in a ball under the table.

(b) Don't shout when you _____ your cards on the table.

(c) Ginger _____ down for a nap after yoga last night.

24. *lead, led*

Led is the past and past-participle form of *lead*.

> *Example:* We led the game until the bottom of the fifth inning. Now the Pirates lead.

(a) Your suggestions will _____ me into trouble.

(b) Your advice has _____ me into trouble many times before.

25. *loose, lose*

Loose means "not tight"; *lose* means "not to win" or "not to keep."

> *Example:* You will probably lose your pants because your belt is so loose.

(a) The knob on this radio is _____.

(b) If we _____ that knob, we won't be able to replace it.

26. *many, much*

Many refers to people or objects that can be counted. *Much* refers to a large quantity.

Example: Because so <u>much</u> food had spoiled, <u>many</u> of the picnickers went home hungry.

(a) _____ critics praised Mildew's first play.

(b) Mildew's first play earned _____ praise from the critics.

27. *maybe, may be*

Maybe is an adverb meaning "perhaps." *May be* is a verb showing possibility.

Example: The instructor <u>may be</u> absent today. <u>Maybe</u> class will be cancelled.

(a) Omar _____ hiding in his room.

(b) _____ Omar is hiding in his room.

28. *passed, past*

Passed is both the past and past-participle form of *pass*. *Past* is a noun (meaning "a previous time"), an adjective (meaning "ago"), and a preposition (meaning "beyond").

Example: The <u>past</u> two weeks have been difficult for Leonard. He has not <u>passed</u> any of his exams. When he walked <u>past</u> me, I told him to forget the <u>past</u> and look toward the future.

(a) We drove _____ the exit five minutes ago.

(b) We _____ the exit five minutes ago.

(c) In the _____ , students were required to study a foreign language.

(d) In _____ years, students were required to study a foreign language.

29. *precede, proceed*

Precede means "to come before." *Proceed* means "to go forward."

Example: Bush <u>preceded</u> Clinton in the White House. Clinton <u>proceeded</u> with his plans to decrease military spending.

(a) After detaining us for several minutes, the guard let us _____ .

(b) The storms of April _____ the gentle rains of May.

30. *principal, principle*

As a noun, *principal* means "administrator" or "sum of money." As an adjective, *principal* means "most important." *Principle* is a noun meaning "basic truth" or "rule."

> *Example:* The Peter Principle is the notion that an employee will rise to his or her level of incompetence.
> Ms. Cottrell said that boredom was her principal reason for leaving the job.

(a) Mr. Flotsam recently retired as school _____.

(b) His _____ ambition now is to tend to his garden.

(c) The _____ of gardening is the same as the _____ of teaching: to provide nourishment.

31. *quiet, quit, quite*

Quiet means "silence." *Quit* means "to leave." *Quite* means "very" or "actually."

> *Example:* I was quite tired, and all I wanted was a quiet place to rest. I asked the children to quit playing the radio.

(a) He needed peace and _____ .

(b) Henry _____ his job and moved to a cabin in the woods.

(c) Now he is _____ content.

32. *than, then*

Use *than* when making a comparison. Use *then* when referring to time.

> *Example:* The test was harder than I had expected. I answered two questions and then got stuck.

(a) I completed an application form and _____ waited in the lobby.

(b) I had to wait much longer _____ you did.

33. *their, there, they're*

Their is the possessive form of *they*. *There* is an adverb (meaning "at that place") and a pronoun used to introduce a sentence. *They're* is a contraction of *they are*.

> *Example:* There are four children in our family. They're all boys. Two of them are sitting over there. Their brothers are in school.

(a) _____ are geese in the garden.

(b) _____ nibbling the roses.

(c) _____ honking can be heard for miles.

34. *to, too*

To is a preposition referring to place, direction, or position. *To* is also used before the verb in an infinitive. *Too* is an adverb meaning "also" or "excessively."

> *Example:* Celeste was too tired to walk home. I was tired too. We walked to a phone booth and called a cab.

(a) I have wanted _____ visit River Junction for a long time.

(b) I was always _____ busy _____ go.

(c) Next weekend I am going _____ River Junction, and you may come _____ .

35. *were, we're, where*

Were is a past form of the verb *to be*. *We're* is a contraction of *we are*. *Where* refers to a place.

> *Example:* We were lost in the middle of the city. No one knew where we were. We're going to bring a map with us next time.

(a) _____ driving to New Orleans for the Mardi Gras.

(b) We don't know _____ we'll be staying.

(c) Last year we _____ forced to sleep in the car.

36. *which, who*

The pronoun *who* refers to people; *which* refers to things.

> *Example:* The man who wants to buy the Pinto now owns a Pacer, which was once called "the car of the future."

(a) Brad's book, _____ was first published in 1975, is now a bestseller.

(b) An essayist is a lucky person _____ has found a way to speak without being interrupted.

37. *whose, who's*

Whose is the possessive form of *who*. *Who's* is the contraction of *who is* or *who has*.

> *Example:* Whose turn is it to wash the dishes? Who's going to wash them?

(a) Gloria pummeled the man _____ car ran into hers.

(b) He is the same man _____ been directing the campaign for safer driving.

38. *your, you're*

Your is the possessive form of *you*. *You're* is the contraction of *you are*.

Example: <u>You're</u> responsible for the conduct of <u>your</u> pet ocelot.

(a) _____ car is blocking mine.

(b) _____ going to have to move _____ car.

EXERCISE CHOOSING THE CORRECT WORD

Underline the word in the parentheses that completes the sentence correctly.

1. I (maybe, may be) late for the skeet shoot.
2. He worked harder (than, then) he had ever worked before.
3. If I had known your number, I would (of, have) called.
4. (Whose, Who's) shorts are hanging from the flagpole?
5. The game has (all ready, already) started.
6. Foster has (alot, a lot) of problems.
7. The curriculum changes will not (affect, effect) you.
8. If you (lose, loose) your temper you will probably (lose, loose) the game.
9. What is your (principal, principle) reason for going to college?
10. She (implied, inferred) that she had a good alibi, but I (implied, inferred) otherwise from her nervous manner.
11. Last year Bowser (lead, led) the league in home runs.
12. Although my (clothes, cloths) were ragged and dirty, Vera (complimented, complemented) me on my tidy appearance.
13. I was (conscience, conscious) after the collision, but (to, too) frightened (to, too) move.
14. Although (much, many) people attended the conference, only a small (amount, number) stayed for the evening lecture.
15. (You're, Your) not the first person (who's, whose) had such problems.
16. (Quiet, Quite, Quit) was restored, and the judge (preceded, proceeded) with the case.
17. I was (choose, chose, chosen) to (led, lead) the expedition.
18. Gus opened (a, an, and) umbrella (an, and) (preceded, proceeded) to dance across the lawn.
19. (There, Their, They're) (maybe, may be) visitors this weekend.
20. The handle was (lose, loose) and could (of, have) fallen off at any minute. ■

EXERCISE COMBINING SENTENCES WITH THE CORRECT WORD

First, underline the word in parentheses that completes the sentence correctly. Then combine the sentences in each set.

Example:

The bank has a policy. The policy is new. The policy concerns loans. The policy (<u>affects</u>, effects) all students.

Combined: The bank's new loan policy affects all students.

1. George read the report. The report concerned the bad (affects, effects) of smoking. George puffed on his cigarette. He puffed nervously.
2. The jogger stopped. He helped me. A tire was flat. We changed the tire. The jogger would not (accept, except) any money.
3. Bobo gets up early every morning. He brews coffee for his wife. His wife leaves for work. (Than, Then) Bobo (lays, lies) down for a nap.
4. The woman is running for mayor. She is a political animal. Yet this is also a woman (who, which) has strong moral (principals, principles).
5. The Pirates have (lead, led) the league. They have (lead, led) for the (passed, past) three years. They have (lead, led) in strikeouts.
6. Reggie (laid, lay) the strange (device, devise) on the table. (Than, Then) he (preceded, proceeded) to explain how it worked.
7. I would (have, of) called sooner. I was (hoping, hopping) that you would call first.
8. There are (fewer, less) students majoring in social work now. There are (fewer, less) students (than, then) in (passed, past) years.
9. The ambulance (passed, past) us on the right. It was traveling at eighty miles an hour. (Its, It's) lights (were, we're, where) flashing. (Its, It's) siren was blasting.
10. (Alot, A lot) of my friends buy (there, their, they're) (clothes, cloths) second-hand at Benny's Bargain Store. (There, Their, They're) unable to afford new (clothes, cloths). ■

22.D *Directness*

Our final guideline is simple: *don't waste words.* When revising your papers, cut out unnecessary words. Try reducing clauses to phrases:

Wordy: The clown <u>who was in the center ring</u> was riding a mule.
Revised: The clown <u>in the center ring</u> was riding a mule.

And try reducing phrases to single words:

Wordy: The driver of the cab demanded a larger tip.
Revised: The cab driver demanded a larger tip.

Eliminate redundant expressions:

Wordy	*Revised*
blue in color	blue
oval in shape	oval
basic fundamentals	basics
the reason is because	because
at this point in time	now
by means of	by (*or* with)
descend down	descend
a convertible-type car	a convertible
new innovation	innovation
in the event that	if
very unique	unique
join together	join

And don't overwork *There is, There are*, or *There were* as sentence openers:

Wordy: There is a possibility that the team may lose.
Revised: The team may lose.
Wordy: There are two exits that are blocked.
Revised: Two exits are blocked.

Unnecessary words are those that add nothing to the meaning or the rhythm of our writing. They bore the reader and distract from our ideas. Cut them out.

EXERCISE REVISING FOR DIRECTNESS

The sentences below contain unnecessary words. Without eliminating any essential information, revise each sentence to make it more concise.

1. This morning at 7:30 A.M., I woke up out of sleep to hear my alarm go off, but I turned off the alarm and returned back to a sleeping state.

2. In the cellar there are four wooden-type crates with nothing in them that we might perhaps use for storing paint cans inside of.

3. Duke and I, we returned back to the hometown where we both grew up to attend a reunion of the people that we went to high school with ten years ago.

4. The reason that Flicka was not able to be at the hockey game was because she had jury duty.

5. The man that collects tickets from people at the movie theater asked us for some sort of identification that would show how old we are.

6. At that point in time when Merdine was a teenager she first learned the basic fundamentals of how to dance.

7. In view of the fact that it was raining, orders were given that the game be canceled.

8. It is possible that one of the causes of so many teenagers running away from home is the fact that many of them have indifferent parents who don't care about them.

9. She used her money to purchase a large-type desk made of mahogany wood that is dark brown in color and handsome to look at.

10. Melba has designed a very unique kind of shirt that is made out of a polyester type of material that never creases into wrinkles when it rains and the shirt gets wet. ■

EXERCISE PROOFREADING

In each paragraph below, six words are either misspelled or misused. Underline each error, and write the correct word or the correct form of the word in the margin.

Traveling with a Notebook

The keeping of a regular diary is dificult and apt in most lives to be dull as it plods through good and bad at one even pace. But the art of the notebook is selective. One's own sensations and emotions should be left out, while the *causes* that produced them are carfully identified. These are usually small concrete facts not particlarly spectacular in themselves, and a single word may recall them. . . . Colors, odors (good and bad), even aparently irrevelant details like the time of day, are far more evocative then a record of feelings, which represent the writer and not the scene and are, usually, a mere embarrassment in later reading.

(Adapted from *The Zodiac Arch*, by Freya Stark)

Christmas in Michigan

Christmas, without any question, was the greatest day of the year. It was not just that it was a time for recieving gifts, although Heaven knows that was enough in itself. . . . This was a religous holiday and we never lost sight of the fact. The most sacred of all legends revealed itself then as the incredable truth, and all but literally we went about on tiptoe. On starry evenings durring Christmas week groups of young people would go about town, stoping before various houses to sing Christmas carols, and as there harmonies floated off across the night we could see the town of Bethlehem not far away, and our snowy Michigan hills became one with the tawny slopes of Palestine.

(Adapted from *Waiting for the Morning Train*, by Bruce Catton)

How to Build a Fire in a Fireplace

Though "experts" differ as to the best technique to follow when building a fire, one genrally excepted method consists of first laying a generous amount of crumpled newspaper on the hearth between the andirons. Kindling wood is then spread generously over this layer of newspaper an one of the thickest logs is placed a cross the back of the andirons. This should be as close to the back of the fireplace as possable, but not quiet touching it. A second log is then placed an inch or so in front of this, and a few additional sticks of kindling are laid across these two. A third log is then placed on top to form a sort of pyramid with air space between all logs so that flames can lick freely up between them.

(Adapted from *The New York Times Complete Manual of Home Repair*, by Bernard Gladstone)

Night Sky

One of our evening entertainments was to watch the night sky. My dog, a dingo bred to herd sheep, also came on the trip. He is so use to the silence and empty skies that when an airplane flys over he always looks up and eyes the distant intruder quizzically. The sky, lately, seems to be much more crowded then it used to be. Satellites make there silent passes in the dark with great regularity. We counted eighteen in one hour's viewing. How odd to think that while they circumnavigated the planet, Martin an I had moved only six miles into our local wilderness and had seen no other human for the two weeks we stayed their.

(Adapted from *The Solace of Open Spaces*, by Gretel Ehrlich)

Cows

To my mind, the only possible pet is a cow. Cows love you. They are harmless, they look nice, they keep the grass down, and they are so trusting and stupid that you can't help but loose your heart to them. Where I live in Yorkshire, theirs a herd of cows down the lane. You can stand by the wall at any hour of the day or night, and after a minute the cows will all waddle over and stand with you, much to stupid to know what to do next, but happy just to be with you. They will stand there all day, as far as I can tell, possibly till the end of time. They will listen to you're problems and never ask a thing in return. They will be your freinds forever. And when you get tired of them, you can kill them and eat them. Perfect.

(Adapted from *Neither Here Nor There: Travels in Europe*, by Bill Bryson)

Reverence for Life

Life means strength, will, arising from the abyss, dissolving into the abyss again. Life is feeling, experiance, suffering. If you study life deeply, looking with perceptive eyes into the vast animated chaos of this creation, it's profundity will seize you suddenly with dizziness. In everything you reconize yourself. The tiny beetle that lays dead in your path—it was a living creature, struggling for existance like yourself, rejoicing in the sun like you, knowing fear and pain like you. And now it is no more than decaying matter—which is what you will be sooner or later, too.

(Adapted from *Reverence for Life*, by Albert Schweitzer, translated by Reginald H. Fuller)

■

Postscript

In this chapter, you have concentrated on using words correctly and efficiently. After considering some ways to use the dictionary as a reference tool and the spell-checker as a proofreading aid, you worked on eliminating common spelling errors and wordiness from your writing.

Testing Word and Sentence Skills

(DIAGNOSTIC TESTS)

Preview

The three tests in this section will help you to measure your ability to use words and sentences correctly and effectively. You may want to take the first test at the start of your composition course to determine the sort of writing problems you need to work on. You may then take the second test later in the course to evaluate your progress. Tests Three and Four allow you to evaluate your sentence skills in the context of paragraphs and short essays.

Test One: Word and Sentence Skills

Part of each word group below is underlined. If the underlined part appears to be correct, write **C** on the line at the left. If the underlined part appears to be faulty, write **F**.

Fragments (Chapter 17)

_____ 1. When you are worried, talk things over with someone who cares. Don't keep your troubles bottled up inside.

_____ 2. Using a bobby pin to pick the lock. Heloise broke into the storeroom.

_____ 3. Wild animals do not make good household pets. A wombat, for instance, may claw up your carpet looking for roots.

_____ 4. After several delays throughout the afternoon. The game was finally canceled because of rain.

_____ 5. Some sports are much more popular outside America. Soccer and rugby, for example.

_____ 6. While walking home, I noticed a stranger following me in the shadows. He was wearing a hockey mask and carrying an ax.

_____ 7. Jason stood in the doorway. His eyes blinking nervously, his fingers tapping on the sill.

_____ 8. Two weeks at summer camp and a week at Maggie's farm. I was ready to go back to school.

Run-ons (Chapter 17)

_____ 9. We stayed at the Stratford Inn, which had recently been renovated.

_____ 10. I drove a thousand miles to visit Jane, she wasn't home.

_____ 11. Some students insist on taking all their courses in the morning others prefer to attend night classes.

_____ 12. If we want things to stay as they are, things will have to change.

_____ 13. All afternoon he lay on the bed, eating crackers, sipping water, and watching rock videos on a miniature TV.

_____ 14. He searched the sky for a target, the gray sky looked as if it had been rubbed with a soiled eraser.

_____ 15. Most of my best friends have left town, Gina, for instance, has moved to Watertown.

_____ 16. George has a problem he has lost his license.

Subject-Verb Agreement (Chapter 18)

_____ 17. Gus bake brownies every Halloween.

_____ 18. Agnes never takes the bus to work.

_____ 19. Melanie and Vicki is arguing again.

_____ 20. Both of my daughters are professional dancers.

_____ 21. One of these mechanics have a set of jumper cables.

_____ 22. The people who own that house carry no insurance.

_____ 23. Music soothes me.

_____ 24. Every one of the workers receive the same benefits.

Verb Tenses (Chapter 19)

_____ 25. Last night Lazlo pick a fight with Bottleneck Jones.

_____ 26. Professor Legree has promised to resign at the end of the year.

_____ 27. Long ago she give me the golden apples of the sun.

_____ 28. When the wolfman arrived, the children begun to laugh.

_____ 29. Wendy has tore her cape.

_____ 30. The workers have laid the foundation for the new church.

_____ 31. I have wrote to the president several times.

_____ 32. I would help you if I could.

Pronouns: Agreement and Reference (Chapter 20)

_____ 33. A student should register their vehicle with the security staff.

_____ 34. Each performer sang his or her favorite song.

_____ 35. Neither of the candidates expressed their views on the plight of the American farmer.

_____ 36. The parakeet flew back into its cage.

_____ 37. A doctor must take their job very seriously.

_____ 38. I enjoy watching NBA games on television, but I am too short to play it myself.

_____ 39. The Raymonds asked me to repair their sump pump, but they did not explain how.

_____ 40. When I tossed the plate at the window, it broke.

Punctuation (Chapter 21)

_____ 41. Wounds heal and become scars, but scars grow with us.

_____ 42. Jeff ran downstairs, and answered the door.

_____ 43. If the grass is greener in the other fellow's yard let him worry about cutting it.

_____ 44. Celeste handed out apples, peaches, and pears, to the children.

_____ 45. We know what happens to people who stay in the middle of the road: they get run over.

_____ 46. A pessimist is a man who looks both ways; when he is crossing a one-way street.

_____ 47. At last night's concert, did Springsteen sing "Born to Run?"

_____ 48. The cockatoo has escaped from it's cage.

Word Use and Spelling (Chapter 22)

_____ 49. I recieved a nickel tip from the duchess.

_____ 50. Frank and Queenie left their swimming trunks in the trailer.

_____ 51. Teddy has an excellant driving record.

_____ 52. Last year Hugh lead the campaign to save the whales.

_____ 53. I interviewed the woman <u>which</u> won the swimming competition.

_____ 54. In <u>past</u> years, we had trouble finding volunteers.

_____ 55. I should <u>of</u> tried harder.

Test Two: Word and Sentence Skills

Part of each word group below is underlined. If the underlined part appears to be
correct, write **C** on the line at the left. If the underlined part appears to be faulty,
write **F**.

Fragments (Chapter 17)

_____ 1. Holly works at the pizzeria. <u>Every weekend and on Tuesday and
Thursday nights.</u>

_____ 2. <u>Before we entered the house, Corina peeked through all the
windows.</u> No one appeared to be home.

_____ 3. Many foods contain large amounts of sugar. <u>Such as cereals,
ketchup, and hamburger buns.</u>

_____ 4. <u>Raising the window so that I could clean the outside panes.</u> I
strained my back.

_____ 5. <u>Hearing the old song, I started to cry.</u> It reminded me of you.

_____ 6. Simon danced across the rain-soaked lawn. <u>His shirt-tail flapping in the breeze.</u>

_____ 7. <u>Whenever you get the urge to sing.</u> Stifle that urge.

_____ 8. Amphibians are the most primitive of terrestrial vertebrates. <u>For
example, toads, salamanders, and newts.</u>

Run-ons (Chapter 17)

_____ 9. I looked for the can opener, <u>it was gone.</u>

_____ 10. The man who can smile when something has gone wrong has
thought of someone <u>he can blame it on.</u>

_____ 11. Ginger has a dollar, <u>she won't lend it to me.</u>

_____ 12. <u>Of all the gin joints in all the towns in all the world,</u> she walks
into mine.

_____ 13. Under the trees he collected an armload of branches <u>near the
dunes he located some heavy boxwood.</u>

_____ 14. The train yanked its long tail out of the thundering tunnel, <u>he
felt a surge of freedom at the view of the moon-hazed Western
hills.</u>

_____ 15. She swept up the cards and began to shuffle with the abandoned virtuosity of an old riverboat gambler, standing them on end, fanning them out, whirling them through her fingers, dancing them halfway up her arms.

_____ 16. Seattle is the largest city in the Pacific Northwest, it is the region's cultural, financial, and commercial hub.

Subject-Verb Agreement (Chapter 18)

_____ 17. Cindy always ride alone.

_____ 18. Doug and his brother is mending the wings of butterflies.

_____ 19. The man who owns those cars lives in Key Largo.

_____ 20. One of my uncles dance at the Rainbow Cafe.

_____ 21. Both of my essays is brilliant.

_____ 22. Every one of the professors drives a used car.

_____ 23. Phil and Jeremy has gone to the concert.

_____ 24. The pulses emitted by a neutron star recur at precise intervals.

Verb Tenses (Chapter 19)

_____ 25. Yesterday Melinda carry a bazooka to work.

_____ 26. Dr. Demento has never played our song.

_____ 27. Gippy has wore the same shirt for a week.

_____ 28. When the desserts arrived, we choose the pecan pie.

_____ 29. After chasing away the mountain lion, Dolly return to her cabin.

_____ 30. Brutus laid his hand on my shoulder.

_____ 31. He had ran ten miles every morning for four months.

_____ 32. Kelly's record has never been broke.

Pronouns: Agreement and Reference (Chapter 20)

_____ 33. My daughter has invented her own mathematical system.

_____ 34. The dog forgot where it had buried its bone.

_____ 35. Professors should follow his or her own rules.

_____ 36. Neither of these products lives up to their reputation.

_____ 37. The policeman ordered me to move the car, but they would not help me move it.

_____ 38. Each child must be accompanied by their parent.

_____ 39. Last year I performed in three plays and held a part-time job, but now I don't have time to do it.

_____ 40. After Larry talked with Arthur, he got angry.

Punctuation (Chapter 21)

_____ 41. If Adam comes home for Christmas, Eve will have to sleep in the den.

_____ 42. Homer told a story about a little gray hen_and Faye pretended to pay attention.

_____ 43. There is only one kind of game worthy of human time, thought, and esteem; the game of chance.

_____ 44. We laughed and sang old songs together, but soon the morning arrived and made us strangers again.

_____ 45. One gift remained at the bottom of Pandora's box—hope.

_____ 46. Katie reached for the silver apples of the moon, and the golden apples of the sun.

_____ 47. Is Stephen Crane the author of "The Open Boat"?

_____ 48. Professor Legree posted a sign over his door; "Abandon all hope, ye who enter here."

Word Use and Spelling (Chapter 22)

_____ 49. Victor decieved me into believing him.

_____ 50. Do you believe in the existance of poltergeists?

_____ 51. Mr. Benny asked for separate checks.

_____ 52. Alot of people disagreed with the referee's decision.

_____ 53. Was the first test simpler then the second one?

_____ 54. I get along with people which don't take themselves too seriously.

_____ 55. I could of danced all night.

Answers to TEST ONE

1. C	9. C	17. F	25. F	33. F	41. C	49. F
2. F	10. F	18. C	26. C	34. C	42. F	50. C
3. C	11. F	19. F	27. F	35. F	43. F	51. F
4. F	12. C	20. C	28. F	36. C	44. F	52. F
5. F	13. C	21. F	29. F	37. F	45. C	53. F
6. C	14. F	22. C	30. C	38. F	46. F	54. C
7. F	15. F	23. C	31. F	39. C	47. F	55. F
8. F	16. F	24. F	32. C	40. F	48. F	

Answers to Test Two may be provided by your instructor.

Test Three: Sentence Skills in Context
40 Questions—40 Minutes

In the following passages, certain words and phrases are underlined and numbered. In the right-hand column you will find alternatives for each underlined part. Choose the one that best expresses the idea, makes the statement appropriate for standard written English, or is worded most consistently with the style and tone of the passage as a whole. If you think that the original version is best, choose "No change."

Read each passage through once before you begin to answer the questions that accompany it. You cannot determine most answers without reading several sentences before and after the phrase in question.

Passage 1: Circus Rider

After the lions had returned to their cages,
₁

creeping angry through the chutes, a little bunch of us
₂

drifted away and into an open doorway nearby, where we

standing for awhile in semidarkness, watching a big
₃

brown circus horse go harumphing around the practice

ring. His trainer was a woman of about forty, the two
₄

of them seemed caught up in one of those desultory

treadmills from which there is no apparent escape. She
₅

had on: a short-skirted costume and a conical straw hat.
₆

Her legs were bare, and she was wearing on both of her feet
₇

high heels, which probed deep into the loose

tanbark and kept her ankles in a state of constant

turmoil.

1. A. No change
   B. into they're
   C. to its
   D. back into their

2. A. No change
   B. angrily through
   C. angrily; through
   D. angrily, through

3. A. No change
   B. stand
   C. are standing
   D. stood

4. A. No change
   B. forty and
   C. forty, and
   D. forty,

5. A. No change
   B. which there is
   C. from which there are
   D. from that, there is

6. A. No change
   B. had on
   C. has on
   D. had—

7. A. No change
   B. and, on
      both of her
      feet, she
      was
      wearing
   C. and she
      wore
   D. on both
      feet she
      was
      wearing

Passage 2: The Fountain Pen

There is young people growing up today who have
        8   9
never had the experience of using a fountain
   9
pen. All they know is a ballpoint. I haven't used

a fountain pen for many years myself, moreover, I
                              10
remember what it was like.

A fountain pen, for those who have never seen

one had liquid ink inside, sloshing around. Such
   11
a pen was filled by holding the point in a bottle of

ink, working a lever so that it would press down on a

rubber sack, and then you released the lever,
                      12
permitting the rubber sack to expand and suck in the

ink. If the lever was worked when the pen wasn't

empty a stream of ink would squirt out, inundating
   13
anyone or anything in their path. That is why it is
                        14
called a fountain pen.

Unlike the ballpoint pen, which requires a cartridge
                              15

8. A. No change
   B. They're
   C. There are
   D. Their

9. A. No change
   B. today, who
      never had
   C. today,
      which have
      never had
   D. today that
      has never
      had

10. A. No change
    B. myself, but
       I
    C. myself, I
    D. myself; as a
       result of
       the fact
       that I

11. A. No change
    B. them, had
    C. a fountain
       pen had
    D. one, had

12. A. No change
    B. then release
       the lever,
    C. then
       releasing
       the lever,
    D. then the
       lever was
       released,

13. A. No change
    B. empty.
       Then a
    C. empty, a
    D. empty;
       subse-
       quently a

refill, a fountain pen could be filled anywhere there

was a supply of <u>ink. On the other hand, I</u> filled my own
16

pen at the post <u>office, the ink</u> there was thin and
17

linty. Another source of ink was a bank. At banks,

however, the inkwells were made so shallow that they

prevented a capacity filling.

14. A. No change
    B. in its
    C. on their
    D. in the general vicinity of its

15. A. No change
    B. pen, its required
    C. pen, which require
    D. pen that require

16. A. No change
    B. ink, however, I
    C. ink, for example, I
    D. ink. I

17. A. No change
    B. office, even though the ink
    C. office: because the ink
    D. office— being that the ink

18. Consider the order of the three paragraphs in the passage that you have just read. What changes, if any, should be made in this arrangement?
    A. No changes
    B. The first paragraph ("There is . . .") should be inserted between the second and third paragraphs to make a clearer transition from the past to the present.
    C. The second paragraph ("A fountain pen . . .") and the third ("Unlike the ballpoint . . .") should be combined into one: both discuss exactly the same thing.
    D. The third paragraph ("Unlike the ballpoint . . .") should appear ahead of the first paragraph ("There is . . ."): the third paragraph clearly introduces the subject and provides a thesis for the whole paper.

Passage 3: Inanimate Objects

Inanimate objects are classified scientifically

into three major <u>categories; those</u> that don't work,
19

those that break down, and those that get lost.

The goal of all inanimate objects <u>are to</u>
20

resist man and ultimately to defeat him, and

19. A. No change
    B. categories. Those
    C. categories
    D. categories: those

20. A. No change
    B. have been to
    C. is to
    D. to

the three major classifications are based on the
$\underline{\hspace{3cm}}$
                                        21

method each object uses to achieve its purpose.

As a general rule, any object capable of breaking
$\underline{\hspace{3cm}}$
        22

down at the moment when it is most needed

will break down just at the moment when it is most
$\underline{\hspace{5cm}}$
                              23

needed. The automobile is typical of the category.
$\underline{\hspace{1cm}}$
  23

     With the cunning typical of its breed, the

automobile never breaks down before entering a filling
                       $\underline{\hspace{2cm}}$
                              24

station with a large staff of idle mechanics. It

waits until it reaches a downtown intersection in the
$\underline{\hspace{3cm}}$
              25

middle of the rush hour, or until it is fully loaded

with family and luggage on the Ohio turnpike.

21. A. No change
    B. based on
       the
    C. having
       been based
       on a
    D. were based
       on this

22. A. No change
    B. However,
    C. Here's
       what I'm
       going to
       talk about
       in my essay:
    D. Even so,

23. A. No change
    B. will do it
    C. will do so
    D. will

24. A. No change
    B. down, when
    C. down, until
    D. down while

25. A. No change
    B. waits until
       reaching,
    C. waits until
       they reach
    D. reaches

Passage 4: Horror Movies

     The popularity of horror movies are no doubt partly
                                  $\underline{\hspace{1cm}}$
                                        26

explained by its ability to engage the spectator's
           $\underline{\hspace{1cm}}$
              27

feelings without making any serious demand on the

mind. In addition, however, horror movies covertly
                   $\underline{\hspace{2cm}}$
                        28

embody certain assumptions about science that reflects
                                         $\underline{\hspace{3cm}}$
                                              29

popular opinion.

     Horror movies can be divided into three major

categories: Mad Doctor, Atomic Beast, and
            $\underline{\hspace{1cm}}$
               30

26. A. No change
    B. (omit)
    C. is
    D. was

27. A. No change
    B. it's
    C. a
    D. their

28. A. No change
    B. , besides,
    C. however
    D. , therefore,

29. A. No change
    B. in which is
       reflected
    C. that reflect
    D. in reflecting
       on

Interplanetary Monster. <u>One of my favorite movies is</u>
31
<u>a musical comedy starring Steve Martin.</u> They do not
31
exhaust all the types, but <u>each contain</u> two essential
32
characters, the Scientist and the Monster.

The Mad Doctor series is by far the most long

lived of the <u>three, it</u> suffered a temporary decline in
33
the forties. Films about Dracula, the Werewolf, and

even Frankenstein find their roots in European folk

myths. Dracula <u>inspired by</u> an ancient Balkan
34
superstition about vampires, and the Werewolf is a myth

recorded in the Breton *lais* of Marie de France.

Frankenstein, though created by Mary Shelley in the

Gothic tradition, has a medieval prototype in the

Golem, <u>it is a monster</u> the Jews fashioned from clay
35
and earth to free them from oppression.

30. A. No change
    B. categories.
       Mad
    C. categories;
       Mad
    D. categories
       Mad

31. A. No change
    B. (Shift this
       sentence to
       the top of
       the first
       paragraph.)
    C. (omit)
    D. (Add to
       this
       sentence
       the specific
       title of the
       movie.)

32. A. No change
    B. each of the
       types
       contain
    C. each
       containing
    D. each
       contains

33. A. No change
    B. three, and
       it
    C. three, as it
    D. three,
       although it

34. A. No change
    B. was
       originally
       inspired
       in the
       beginning
       by
    C. having
       been
       inspired by
    D. was
       inspired by

35. A. No change
    B. . The
       Golem
       being a
       monster
    C. , a monster
       that
    D. The
       monster
       in which

Passage 5: New York

New York is a city of things unnoticed. It is a city with cats sleeping under parked cars, two stone armadillos <u>crawl</u> up St. Patrick's Cathedral, and
 36
thousands of ants on top of the Empire State Building.

The ants <u>were probably carried up there to the top of</u>
 37
<u>the Empire State Building in New York</u> by winds or
 37
birds, but nobody is sure; <u>nobody in New York knows</u> any
 38
more about the ants than they do about the

<u>panhandler who</u> takes taxis to the Bowery or the
 39
dapper man who picks trash out of Sixth Avenue trash

cans.

New York is a city for eccentrics and a center for odd bits of information. <u>When they clean the sea</u>
 40
<u>lions' pool at the Bronx Zoo,</u> coins, paper clips,
 40
ball-point pens, and little girls' pocketbooks are

found by workmen.

36. A. No change
    B. crawled
    C. crawling
    D. which crawled

37. A. No change
    B. probably carried there
    C. were certainly being carried there
    D. probably were carried there

38. A. No change
    B. , nobody in New York knows
    C. , but nobody in New York knows
    D. ; nobody in New York know

39. A. No change
    B. panhandler, who
    C. panhandler, which
    D. panhandler: who

40. A. No change
    B. (Move this clause to the end of the sentence.)
    C. Cleaning the sea lion's pool at the Bronx Zoo,
    D. Having cleaned the sea lion's pool at the Bronx Zoo,

Test Four: Sentence Skills in Context
40 Questions — 40 Minutes

In the following passages, certain words and phrases are underlined and numbered. In the right-hand column you will find alternatives for each underlined part. Choose the one that best expresses the idea, makes the statement appropriate for standard written English, or is worded most consistently with the style and tone of the passage as a whole. If you think that the original passage is best, choose "No change."

Read each passage through once before you attempt to answer the questions that accompany it. You cannot determine some answers without reading the sentences before and after the phrase in question.

Passage 1: Saving Egypt's Sphinx

For more than three thousand years, people been
<u>1</u>

<u>trying</u> to save the Sphinx. From the pharaohs, Greeks,
<u>1</u>

and Romans to Napoleon and present-day scientists, the

preservation process has puzzled, intrigued, <u>and</u>
<u>2</u>

<u>humiliated</u> restorers.
<u>2</u>

In fact, after so much restoration work, <u>a miracle</u>
<u>3</u>

<u>that</u> the world-renowned half-man, half-lion still sits
<u>3</u>

majestically on the Gaza plateau. It is thinner.

The neck, of lighter stone, <u>looking</u> bandaged and
<u>4</u>

distorted. The stones of the figure's <u>hindquarters,</u>
<u>5</u>

<u>which are</u> patched or falling, and a weather vane sits
<u>5</u>

on <u>its</u> rump.
<u>6</u>

The problems facing the Sphinx are innumerable.

The monument was hewn from fifty-million-year-old

1. A. No change
   B. are trying
   C. try
   D. have been trying

2. A. No change
   B. it has humiliated
   C. humiliating
   D. humiliated,

3. A. No change
   B. a miracle being that
   C. it is a miracle that
   D. a miracle is

4. A. No change
   B. (omit)
   C. look
   D. looks

5. A. No change
   B. hindquarters are
   C. hindquarters that are
   D. hindquarters,

6. A. No change
   B. it's
   C. it is
   D. its'

limestone <u>rock, some of it strong</u> and some weak.
$$7$$
While the head is made of relatively durable <u>rock.</u>
$$8$$
<u>The body</u> and shoulders are not, raising concerns that
$$8$$
the head could <u>fall down off of the body of</u> the
$$9$$
sixty-five-foot-high creature.

  Pollution, temperature changes, and wind erosion

<u>increase</u> decay. <u>However,</u> underground sewage water
$$10 \qquad 11$$
and vibrations from nearby quarries, cars, and

buses also contribute to the monument's decline.

Yet despite a deterioration <u>rate that is greater</u> in
$$12$$
the last fifty years than in the previous centuries

combined, the Sphinx continues to survive.

7. A. No change
   B. rock; some of it strong
   C. rock, some of it was strong
   D. rock some of it strong

8. A. No change
   B. rock, the body
   C. rock, while the body
   D. rock, and the body

9. A. No change
   B. fall down of the body of
   C. fall from
   D. be falling down off of

10. A. No change
    B. increases
    C. is increasing
    D. increasing

11. A. No change
    B. Consequently,
    C. Otherwise,
    D. In addition,

12. A. No change
    B. rate has been greater
    C. rate that has been greater
    D. rate greatest

Passage 2: Digital Satellite Radio

  While television offers national broadcasts through

networks and <u>superstations, radio</u> remains primarily
$$13$$
local. At best, the most powerful amplitude modulation

13. A. No change
    B. superstations. Radio
    C. superstations and radio

(AM) stations <u>may be picked up</u> halfway across the
14
United States on a good night. <u>As a result,</u> digital
15
radio broadcasts by satellite would change all that.

A single satellite in orbit could beam messages in
CD-quality sound to an entire country or even a
<u>continent, a dozen</u> such satellites linked up could
16
broadcast to the world. Because a satellite beam can be
split up into many separate <u>beams, broadcasters</u> would
17
be able to target audiences geographically.

The idea of direct satellite broadcasts <u>having been</u>
18
<u>around</u> for years. Ships have long carried big antennas
18
to communicate by satellite. <u>Not surprisingly, many</u>
19
<u>existing radio stations in the United States are</u>
19
<u>resisting the technology.</u> The challenge of
19
commercializing the technology has been to build a
cheap, portable receiver--a satellite dish that fits in
the pocket. Engineers predict that within the next few
years they will be able to build a receiver the size of
a Sony Walkman <u>in the beginning at an initial cost of</u>
20
<u>about $300 in price.</u> If the technology catches on,
20
mass-production could push the cost down to about $50.

D. superstations, however radio

14. A. No change
    B. maybe picked up
    C. (omit)
    D. may pick up

15. A. No change
    B. Consequently,
    C. Plus
    D. However,

16. A. No change
    B. continent; a dozen
    C. continent. While a dozen
    D. continent a dozen

17. A. No change
    B. beams. Broadcasters
    C. beams and broadcasters
    D. beams, therefore broadcasters

18. A. No change
    B. have been around
    C. has been around
    D. been

19. A. No change
    B. (Shift this sentence to the beginning of the paragraph.)
    C. (omit)
    D. (Shift this sentence to the end of the paragraph.)

20. A. No change
    B. at an initial cost of about $300 in price in the beginning.
    C. at an initial cost of: about $300.
    D. at an initial cost of about $300.

Passage 3: Scream Machines

For the first time since the 1920s, the number of big roller coasters in the United States are on the $\underline{}$
21
rise, from 147 in 1978 to 203 today. Some look as if the doodlings of a student have materialized in tubular steel across the skyline.

The amusement parks spend millions to build these
          22
monsters know what they are up to. And most parks have
                            23
daily equipment maintenance and an annual inspection
                 23
that includes X-ray testing of structural parts. Exit
          23
polls show that what brings customers back is the thrill ride, and no thrill ride is more marketable than
       24
a coaster with new technology--such as the corkscrew, the vertical loop, and the stand-up coaster. A top amusement park has to have the latest advances if they
                           25
want to convince visitors that they are getting some-
25

21. A. No change
    B. were
    C. was
    D. is

22. A. No change
    B. parks, which
    C. parks that
    D. parks who

23. A. No change
    B. (Shift this sentence to the beginning of the paragraph.)
    C. (Shift this sentence to the end of the paragraph.)
    D. (Shift this sentence to the end of the next paragraph.)

24. A. No change
    B. ride, although
    C. ride, because
    D. ride, but

25. A. No change
    B. they
    C. it wants to
    D. they will

thing special for the typical $15 to $22 admission

charge.

How can killer coasters be multiplying at a time

when risk-averse insurers look sideways even at

seesaws? The reason that insurance companies have

tagged along is because of the dark secret of the
                26

roller-coaster world: statistically, coasters are safer
                          27

than merry-go-rounds. A passenger-restraint system
27

effectively keeps people from stepping off in midride,
                                28

preventing them from getting out of the cars. Many
                28

coasters use computerized braking systems and rely

on wheels inside, as well as above and below, the

rails. To keep cars from flying off into space. Insurers
        29

require that operators be trained in how to load and

unload cars.

26. A. No change
    B. is
    C. because of
    D. is because

27. A. No change
    B. world,
       statistically,
       coasters are
       safer than
    C. world.
       Statistically,
       coasters are
       safer then
    D. world
       statistically;
       coasters are
       safer then

28. A. No change
    B. keeps
       people
       from
       stepping
       off in
       midride, it
       prevents
       them from
       getting out
       of the cars.
    C. preventing
       people
       from
       getting off
       in midride.
    D. prevents
       people
       from
       getting off
       in midride.

29. A. No change
    B. rails, this
       keeps
    C. rails to
       keep
    D. rails. Thus,
       keeping

Passage 4: Jeans

A few utilitarian garments--leather jackets,

sneakers, T-shirts, and, most significantly, blue

jeans--has long made up the key elements of the American
      30

30. A. No change
    B. have
    C. are
    D. did

casual-wear uniform. In the beginning, the uniform's

components, which symbolize youthful rebellion and,
          31

for the most part, toughness and masculinity. Over
                                    32

time, all have become standard middle-class wear for
    32

both genders, their popularity also spans all age
             33

groups and social classes.

    By adapting to the needs of the baby-boom market,

blue jeans become the most enduring fashion statement
           34

of the past few decades. Yet it began strictly as work
                    35

clothes.

    In the 1850s, a merchant from California, who was
                      36

young and named Levi Strauss turned tent canvas into
    36

durable garments for prospectors and miners. Later,

Strauss switched to material called "serge de Nimes,"
                      37

customers Americanized it to "denim." For a century,
        37

denims remained primarily work clothes for cowboys,

ranchers, and farmers. Then, in the 1950s, James Dean

and Marlon Brando donned them portraying non-

conformists in *Rebel Without a Cause* and *The Wild Ones*.

A decade later, blue jeans became the uniform of the

youth movement, usually ripped, painted, patched,

embroidered, tie-dying or they were studded to reflect
                    38

the wearer's personality. Bell bottoms were favored--the

31. A. No change
    B. compo-
       nents will
       symbolize
    C. compo-
       nents
       symbolized
    D. compo-
       nents that
       symbolized

32. A. No change
    B. On the
       other hand,
       all
    C. Conse-
       quently, all
    D. As a result,
       all

33. A. No change
    B. genders,
       even
       though
       their
       popularity
    C. genders,
       from which
       their
       popularity
    D. genders.
       Their
       popularity

34. A. No change
    B. have
       become
    C. has become
    D. (omit)

35. A. No change
    B. they begin
    C. they began
    D. it begins

36. A. No change
    B. a merchant
       who was
       young from
       California
       named
    C. a young
       California
       merchant
       named
    D. a young
       merchant
       from
       California,
       who was
       named

bigger, the better. Designer jeans made their debut in

the late 1970s. Straight-legged and sleek people, often
<u>39</u>

had to lie down to wriggle into them, sometimes needing

pliers to pull up the zippers. This type jean usually
<u>40</u>

also featured the designer's name on a back pocket. More

recently, comfort has returned with baggy jeans, looser

cuts, and elastic waistbands.

37. A. No change
    B. Nimes," which customers Americanized it to "denim."
    C. Nimes," which customers Americanized to "denim."
    D. Nimes," for which customers Americanized to "denim."

38. A. No change
    B. tie-dyed or studded to reflect
    C. tie-dyed, studded, reflected
    D. tie-dyed or studded, they reflected.

39. A. No change
    B. Straight-legged and sleek they were cut so tight people
    C. Straight-legged and sleek, they were cut so tight that people
    D. Straight-legged and sleek, they were cut tight, people

40. A. No change
    B. This
    C. These type jeans
    D. These jeans

APPENDIX B

Essay Examinations

Preview

English is not the only college course that calls on you to exercise your writing skills. Essay examinations are commonly given in subjects as diverse as history, art, business, engineering, biology, and psychology. But while the subjects vary, the requirements of a good essay do not. Your work throughout this textbook should help you to develop and organize an effective exam essay on any topic you have studied. In this section you will find some additional advice on planning, writing, and revising such an essay.

Planning an Exam Essay

Imagine that you have just been handed an examination that opens with these instructions:

> Write a well-organized, soundly supported essay on one of the topics below. You have an hour.

You then read over your choice of topics and select the one you feel most comfortable with—the one you have studied for and taken notes on. And then, not wanting to waste any time, you immediately begin to write. Or do you? In fact, the best way to use your time is to spend the first few minutes studying the topic and planning your approach before you start to write.

Studying the topic will give you an opportunity to relax and collect your thoughts. Just as importantly, it will help you to understand just what your instructor is asking for. Read the topic several times, word by word, looking for clues as to how you should develop and organize your essay. Here, for example, are a few essay-exam topics and some tips on how to respond to them:

1. *Discuss the relationships between sociology and one other natural science or social science.*

   Although the topic is broad, your essay will need to provide brief specific examples of the general relationships you identify. Many of the assignments in Part One (beginning with Chapter Four, *Virtues and Vices*) offer advice on using examples in your writing.

2. *Trace the impact of Freud upon psychology at large.*

   Here is another broad topic, one that needs to be explored with references to specific leaders and movements in psychology. Notice that the topic asks you to consider *effects*—a type of writing discussed in Chapter Ten (*Modern Times*).

3. *How is information retrieved from memory?*
   This question calls for a step-by-step explanation of a process—similar to the kind of writing discussed in Chapter Eight (*Skills*). But be careful: there may be different theories concerning a single process, and you may be expected to comment on each one.

4. *Do the best men become President?*
   A question such as this may look deceptively easy. True, the instructor is asking for your opinion, but you will be evaluated on your ability to support your views with facts. Remember the advice given throughout Part One: *support general ideas with specific information.*

In some cases, a single word in the topic may suggest the approach you should take in your essay:

When you are asked to *state* something, present the main points in a logical order.
When you are asked to *list* or *enumerate* something, be brief and to the point, as if you are making an outline. Nonetheless, use complete sentences.
When you are asked to *summarize* or *review* something, give a shortened version of the main points.
When you are asked to *criticize*, *discuss*, *evaluate*, or *justify*, use specific examples and facts to back up your judgments.

As you can see, the assignments in Part One of this book have prepared you for the types of questions that are often asked in essay exams.

Once you have selected a topic and studied it carefully, calculate the time you have in which to write the essay. While working under a one-hour time limit, for instance, you might designate the first five or ten minutes for discovering ideas, the next forty minutes or so for writing, and the last ten or fifteen minutes for revising and editing. Or you might allot a shorter period to the initial drafting and devote more time to revising the essay. Plan a realistic schedule—one based on your own writing habits—and then stick to it.

Writing the Essay

Trying to write the essay before you have discovered what you want to say can be a very frustrating and time-wasting experience. Therefore, plan to spend a few minutes putting your thoughts down in any fashion that works for you: freewriting, listing, probing—any of the discovery techniques discussed in the early chapters of Part One. Then, after filling a page or so with notes, you might want to make a simple list outline (Chapter Eleven, *Reasons*) as a guide to developing and organizing the essay.

Decide from the start whether you are writing a draft that you will later revise or a final version that you will have time only to polish and proofread. If you are drafting, write quickly and waste no time checking your spelling or struggling over sentence structures. The important thing is to get your ideas down on paper before you lose them. You can straighten out the writing and correct any errors later when you revise.

Sometimes, however, because of restrictions imposed by the instructor, a full revision will not be possible. In such cases, you will need to spend more time planning the essay and put more care into composing it. Write legibly, but don't waste time fussing with an eraser or correction fluid; if you make an error, simply strike it out with a single line. It is also a good idea to skip a space between lines so that you will have room to make additions and corrections when you are done. And finally, don't get stuck: if you find yourself tangled in a sentence or at a loss for the right word, jump down a line or two and carry on with your next thought. You can return to the trouble spot later to repair the damage or fill in a word.

A good exam essay is clear, concise, and complete. You need no long introductions or interesting sidelights: just the answers to the questions stated or implied in the topic. And make sure that your answers are backed up with specific information that you have gained from your studies.

Revising and Proofreading the Essay

Whether or not you have the opportunity to rewrite your essay, you will need time to review it carefully when you are done. If you find yourself running short on time, don't worry about crafting a brilliant conclusion; instead, clearly *list* the points you still want to make so your instructor will see that lack of time, not lack of knowledge, was your problem. Then spend several minutes revising and proofreading the essay.

When you reread your paper, you may discover that you left out an important piece of information or that you need to move a sentence or even an entire paragraph. Don't panic. Use the margin (or the space between lines) to insert new information. Draw an arrow (perhaps accompanied by a note in the margin) to show where a sentence or paragraph should be shifted. If you need to correct a misspelling or change a word, don't attempt to write *over* the original word; instead, cross out the original and write the corrected version just above it.

The skills involved in writing an exam essay are similar to those you have been practicing throughout this book. You may have to write more quickly than you would like, but you should not be intimidated by time limits. Schedule what time you do have so that you will still be able to plan, write, revise, and proofread your essay. You may be surprised: strict deadlines have a remarkable way of motivating us to work hard and work well without wasting time.

APPENDIX C

The Résumé and Letter of Application

Preview

Whether you are applying for a part-time job after classes or a full-time position that might be the start of a career, you will usually need to provide your prospective employer with two important pieces of writing—a résumé and a letter of application. In this section you will find suggestions on how to prepare both.

Preparing a Résumé

A résumé is a concise record of your skills, interests, educational background, and work experience. It should allow a prospective employer to recognize your qualifications at a glance. To ensure that it is current and accurate, you will need to update your résumé regularly, perhaps every six months to a year. But you do not have to prepare a new résumé for every job you apply for. Instead, you should send each prospective employer a clear photocopy of the original. Make sure, therefore, that the original is concise, complete, and attractive.

There is no single format that you must follow in preparing a résumé, but it should contain the following information: *identification, educational background, work experience, personal information,* and *references.* Following the guidelines below, you should be able to provide all of this information on one typed page.

1. *Identification.* At the top of the résumé, type your name, full address, and telephone number. If you have two addresses (home and college), include them both.

2. *Educational background.* Name the college you are currently attending, your year in college, and your major. After that, identify any other colleges you may have attended and the high school from which you graduated.

3. *Work experience.* First, identify your current job (starting date of employment, employer's name and address, title of your position), and then list any other jobs you have held that you think are worth mentioning. You may include volunteer work in this section.

4. *Personal information.* Identify those interests (hobbies, extracurricular activities, and the like) that might make a good impression on a prospective em-

ployer. You are not required to state your age and marital status, though you may wish to do so.

5. *References.* You may either give the names of three or four references or direct your reader to the placement folder that contains letters from these individuals. The counselors in the Placement (or Careers) Office at your college will show you how to create a placement folder and make it available to prospective employers.

Here we have outlined the basic information contained in a standard résumé, but keep in mind that the résumé should fit *you*—not a single prescribed format. Compare the two sample résumés on the following pages. Sample A was prepared by a nineteen-year-old freshman who had never held a full-time job. Sample B was prepared by a recent graduate whose work experience had been interrupted by the job of raising two children. These two individuals have prepared their résumés differently because their backgrounds and experiences are quite different. Both résumés are effective, however, because they share certain qualities:

They are clearly organized.
They emphasize the strengths of the individual.
They provide specific information.
They are concise.
They are free of errors.
They are easy to read, with wide margins and spaces between major divisions.

Therefore, be guided by these samples, but imitate neither. Your résumé should clearly reflect your individual interests, achievements, and experiences.

Writing Suggestion

Based on the guidelines in this chapter, develop a one-page résumé that accurately records your skills, interests, educational background, and work experience.

Preparing a Letter of Application

When applying for a job, you need to mail a letter of application along with your résumé. This letter should be brief—no longer than a page—and tailored to fit the particular job you are applying for. The letter should not simply rehash material that's in your résumé but rather emphasize particular qualities and experiences that relate to the job you are seeking.

Organize your letter according to the standard format discussed in Chapter Seven (*Complaints*).

```
Your Name
Your Address
Date

Name and Title of Prospective Employer
Employer's Address
```

ANTHONY FORREST CLARKE

College Address: Home Address:
1095 Macon Highway 21   121 Wilshire Road
Athens, Georgia 30605   Savannah, Georgia 31410
(706) 555-6439   (912) 555-9733

Objective   An entry-level position with ample
                   opportunity for advancement in
                   marketing or purchasing.

Education   University of Georgia, Athens, Georgia
                   Degree Expected: B.F.C.S. in Consumer
                   Economics, August 1998.

Areas of   Economics   Personal finance
Study   Demography   Consumerism
                   Marketing

Work   Saint Mary's Hospital, Athens, Georgia
Experience   1994 to present
                   Volunteered in Public Relations Department

                   Lofton Professional Insurance Services,
                   Inc., Savannah, Georgia
                   Christmas 1994
                   Involved in analyzing demographics to deter-
                   mine advertising strategies

                   Alps Elementary School, Athens, Georgia
                   1994 Fall Quarter
                   Tutored first-grader in math and reading

                   J. Parker Limited, Savannah, Georgia
                   Christmas 1993
                   Sales Associate, wrapped gifts

Special   Lotus 1-2-3, Harvard graph packet,
Skills   Macintosh's Kricket graph packet,
                   IBM's 20-20 program, WordPerfect.

Member   Council on Consumer Interest (CCI)

Personal   Hobbies: music, photography.
                   Responsible for recruiting four
                   students into the School of Consumer
                   Economics at the University of Georgia.

References   Available upon request

Sample Résumé A

Jane Nineham
345 Brooklawn Drive
Rochester, New York 14618
(716) 555-0101

WORK EXPERIENCE

1985–present EVERGREEN EQUIPMENT COMPANY, Pittsford, New York General clerical work as well as some telephone sales and counter sales of industrial equipment—primarily engineered products and components (pumps, valves, compressors, fittings).

1983–1985 BAKER SUPPLY COMPANY, Madison, Wisconsin Clerical work and sales.

1982–1983 MARX UTILITIES LEASING CORP., Miami, Florida General clerical and credit work.

1977–1980 EPSOM ADVERTISING, Miami, Florida Advertising copywriter and designer (layouts, research, proofing).

In addition, I have worked part-time for a political organization doing public relations, for WBBF radio and WXIX-TV as a copywriter, and for various Rochester businesses doing freelance public relations work. I am skilled in word processing and database management.

EDUCATION

1989–present Bachelor's degree in Communications, June 1995 from the State University of New York at Brockport. Course work includes technical writing, business computing, journalism, media productions, and speech.

1992 Associate's degree in General Studies from SUNY at Brockport. GPA: 3.45.

PERSONAL

1980–present Raised two children and managed a household. Interests include reading; writing; raising and training dogs.

Sample Résumé B

```
Dear Mr. (or Mrs. or Ms.) _____ :

Brief Introduction

Body (one or two paragraphs)

Conclusion

Sincerely,


Your Signature and Name
```

Although the exact content and arrangement of the letter will vary according to your qualifications and the job you are applying for, certain basic information should appear in the introduction, body, and conclusion of any letter of application.

Your introduction may be as short as one or two sentences. In it, be sure to identify the particular position you are interested in; you may also want to state where or how you learned of this job opening. Also, give a brief indication of why you think you are qualified for the job. In each of the sample letters that follow, notice how this information is provided.

In your body paragraph(s), you may refer to your enclosed résumé, but don't retell everything that is in it. Instead, emphasize those aspects of your education and work experience that show you are qualified for the job. Stress not only what you have already done but also what you are capable of doing for your prospective employer. In the first sample letter of application, the writer deals with his work experience and his educational background together in a single body paragraph. The writer of the second letter, in contrast, focuses exclusively on her work experience, which is quite varied and extensive.

Your conclusion should, again, be brief and direct. State that you look forward to an interview, and explain how and when you can be reached.

The tone and appearance of your letter are as important as its content. The tone should be confident, enthusiastic, and polite—never arrogant or apologetic. And you should type the letter neatly (or have someone type it for you), making sure that the information is accurate and the writing is clear and correct.

The career counselors at your college can give you additional advice on applying for a job and preparing an effective résumé and letter of application. In addition, you may want to consult any one of several books designed to help you in your search for a job. One of the most popular is *What Color Is Your Parachute? A Practical Manual for Job-Hunters and Career Changers*, by Richard N. Bolles (Berkeley: Ten-Speed).

Writing Suggestion

Based on the advice in the chapter, write a concise letter of application for a particular job, real or imagined.

Anthony Clarke
1095 Macon Highway 21
Athens, Georgia 30605
20 May 1995

Ms. LaVonya Burke, Personnel Director
Gallery Marts
1770 Peachtree Boulevard
Atlanta, Georgia 30313

Dear Ms. Burke:

My work experience and educational quali cations appear well
suited to the part-time position of Purchasing Assistant at
Gallery Marts. As a consumer economics major at the
University of Georgia, I look forward to this
opportunity to apply my energy and skills in this
challenging job.

I am con dent that the public relations experience I have
gained at St. Mary s Hospital--writing, editing, and, most importantly, communicating with the public--will serve me well
as a Purchasing Assistant. I have had many
opportunities to apply the information that I have gained in
management and marketing courses. Likewise, my
temporary and part-time work experience at Lofton Professional
Insurance Services and J. Parker Limited have allowed me to
apply demographic principles in a practical setting and gain
 rsthand knowledge of consumer interests and needs. In short,
I will come to Gallery Marts with solid experience and an
earnest wish to
succeed.

I would welcome the opportunity to begin working with you
part-time immediately. I will call your of ce next week
to set up an appointment for an employment interview.

Sincerely,

Anthony Forrest Clarke

Anthony Forrest Clarke

Sample Letter of Application A

Jane Nineham
345 Brooklawn Drive
Rochester, New York 14618
10 June 1995

Ms. Brenda Lain, Station Manager
WAXC Radio
1490 East Avenue
Rochester, New York 14610

Dear Ms. Lain:

Edward Baxter, the sales director at WXIX-TV, recently informed me that your station is now conducting interviews for the position of sales manager. If you are looking for someone with diverse experience in advertising and the media, I hope you will consider inviting me for an interview.

To be effective in a marketing region the size of Rochester, a sales manager needs to maintain personal contact with her clients as well as keep up to date with the latest advances in media marketing. You will nd that I meet both requirements. In my sales position with Evergreen Equipment Company over the past ten years, I have worked closely with managers at most of the major businesses and industries in this area. At the same time, my part-time work as a copywriter with WXIX and WBBF has enabled me to learn rsthand how to apply advertising strategies based on market research. I look forward to applying those skills at WAXC.

Now that I have completed my degree at Brockport, I am ready to combine my skills, interests, and experience in a challenging full-time position. My r sum demonstrates my quali cations, but I would welcome an opportunity to demonstrate my energy and enthusiasm in person. You can reach me at 927-5348 during the day and at 555-0101 in the evening.

Sincerely,

Jane Nineham

Jane Nineham

Sample Letter of Application B

Composing on a Computer

Preview

The computer can be a useful tool to the writer. With a little guidance and practice, you should not have much difficulty learning how to perform basic word-processing functions. This chapter suggests some ways that you can apply your knowledge of word processing to the various stages of the writing process.

For many writers, the computer has become an important, if not essential, writing tool. Far more than just a costly typewriter, a computer equipped with a good word-processing program can assist you through all stages of the writing process, from discovering ideas through editing final drafts. Popular word-processing programs include WordPerfect©, Microsoft Word©, and MacWrite©—all of which have several features in common. In addition, there are several brands of less expensive, stand-alone word-processing machines. Despite some individual differences, all of these word-processing programs and machines perform the same basic functions: inserting, deleting, and rearranging words on a screen as well as saving and printing full-length texts.

If you don't own a computer or stand-alone word processor, you shouldn't be at a disadvantage: the computing labs and writing centers of most colleges and universities contain all of the equipment that you will need, as well as staff members willing to teach you how to use it. After a short tutorial and a little practice, you should feel right at home composing on a computer.

Discovering and Drafting

Though some writers prefer to begin a project with pen and paper before turning to the computer, others have found that the computer provides some excellent ways of overcoming writer's block. You should at least try your hand at exploring ideas and composing drafts with the help of a word processor. If you are not satisfied with the results, you can always pick up your pen again.

With a little bit of typing experience, freewriting on the computer can be an especially productive exercise. For five or ten minutes, simply type in words and phrases as they come to mind, without stopping to criticize or edit. To avoid the temptation to begin editing your work prematurely, you might try freewriting with your computer monitor darkened or turned off. Not being able to see the words that you have typed may encourage you to play with ideas as they come to you. After five or ten minutes of this so-called "invisible" writing, turn the monitor back on to work with the notes you have generated in the freewriting session.

Similarly, the discovery strategies of listing and brainstorming can be carried out as easily on a computer as with pen and paper. Not only can you type in key words and phrases as they come to mind, but you can easily insert new ideas, delete irrelevant ones, and rearrange those that remain.

Moving from discovering ideas while sitting at a computer to composing a rough draft should not be a difficult transition. Drafting on a word processor has several advantages—in particular, legibility and flexibility. Though the writing we do in a rough draft usually reflects a good deal of confusion as we work out our ideas, a word-processed version will not be as hard to read as handwritten drafts often are. And the ease with which we can move around in a word-processed text tends to encourage experimentation. If we get stuck working on one paragraph, we can simply jump ahead to another or switch to a blank screen to test out new ideas as they come to us.

As you become more experienced in using the computer, you can also take advantage of it as a research tool: accessing the computerized card catalog from your college library (or from libraries throughout the world); calling up programs and information sources by means of CompuServe©, Prodigy©, and America-on-Line©; and recalling information from reference works contained on CD-ROMs.

Whether you are a newcomer to computers or an old hand, one piece of advice holds true for everyone: *save your work often.* An unexpected power failure or a slip of your finger on the keyboard can cruelly erase hours of effort. Every fifteen minutes or so, use the *save* command on your word processor to make sure that your work will not be lost. Likewise, at the end of each work session print out a hard copy of your paper, and create a backup file on a separate disk. The few seconds it takes to follow these steps could one day save you from the arduous chore of trying to re-create a draft from memory.

Revising

All word-processing programs allow you to perform the basic revision functions: inserting, deleting, and moving words, sentences, and paragraphs. In fact, the ease with which you can perform these functions on a computer may encourage you to be more creative when it comes to revising. Experiment with various arrangements, making sure that you save each version in a separate file: on occasion, an earlier revision effort may turn out to be superior to the versions produced later.

At some point in the revision process, you should find it helpful to print out a copy of your draft and review it carefully. You may see problems or opportunities on the printed page that you missed when looking at your text on the monitor. It is a simple matter to transfer changes made by hand to the word-processed version. As you revise, practice moving back and forth between a hard copy and the computer screen until you become familiar with the relative advantages of each method.

Editing and Proofreading

Although word processors are particularly helpful during editing, many writers prefer to begin the editing process in the old-fashioned way—with a pen and a printed copy of the paper. Word-processing tools such as spell-checkers, grammar- and style-checkers are still no substitute for careful reading of our own work.

As discussed in Chapter Twenty-two, most word-processing programs have a built-in spell-checker that allows you to identify any word that is not contained in its dictionary. But we have to be careful not to put too much trust into the spell-checker: because even the best dictionary is incomplete, not all highlighted words are necessarily incorrect. Therefore, when using a spell-checker, keep these three tips in mind:

1. *In addition to* using a spell-checker, be sure to proofread your work carefully with the aid of a standard dictionary.

2. When your spell-checker highlights a word, check a standard dictionary to make certain that you really have made an error.

3. When your spell-checker suggests an alternative spelling, make sure that it *is* the word you want to use.

Though the spell-checker can be useful, it is not a substitute for careful proofreading.

In addition, keep in mind that editing involves much more than simply a search for spelling errors. Read your work aloud, testing each word to determine if it is appropriate and accurate, testing each sentence to determine if it is clear and concise. Though the computer makes editing less arduous, *you* must still do the thinking.

Postscript

This chapter has offered some suggestions on ways to use word-processing software effectively through all stages of the writing process. With a little practice, you will discover those strategies that work best for you.

APPENDIX E

Original Passages

Preview

This section contains the paragraphs and essays that served as models for the paragraph-building exercises in Chapters Fifteen and Sixteen. As you compare your combinations with the works of the original writers, keep in mind that *various* effective combinations are possible. Indeed, your work may at times be superior to the original.

Paragraph Building with Adjectives and Adverbs (Chapter 15, page 225)

Martha's Departure

Martha waited patiently on her front porch. She wore a plain white bonnet and a long calico dress. She watched the sun sink beyond the empty fields. Then she watched the thin, white light in the distant sky. Carefully she listened for the soft, familiar sound. Suddenly through the warm evening air a long silver ship descended. Martha calmly picked up her small black purse. The shiny spaceship landed smoothly in the empty field. Slowly and gracefully, Martha walked toward the ship. Minutes later, the field was again dark, silent, and empty.

Paragraph Building with Prepositional Phrases (Chapter 15, page 230)

The Chase

[The man] ran after us, and we ran away from him, up the snowy Reynolds sidewalk. . . . He chased Mikey and me around the yellow house and up a backyard path we knew by heart: under a low tree, up a bank, through a hedge, down some snowy steps, and across the grocery store's delivery driveway. We smashed through a gap in another hedge, entered a scruffy backyard and ran around its back porch and tight between houses to Edgerton Avenue; we ran across Edgerton to an alley and up our own sliding woodpile to the Halls' front yard. . . . We ran up Lloyd Street and wound through many mazy backyards toward the steep hilltop at Willard and Lang.

He chased us silently, block after block. He chased us silently over picket fences, through thorny hedges, between houses, around garbage cans, and across streets. . . . He chased us through the backyard labyrinths of ten blocks before he caught us by our jackets.

(from *An American Childhood,* by Annie Dillard)

Paragraph Building with Coordination (Chapter 15, page 234)

The Coming of Rain

Over the high coast mountains and over the valleys the gray clouds marched in from the ocean. The wind blew fiercely and silently, high in the air, and it swished in the brush, and it roared in the forests. The clouds came in brokenly, in puffs, in folds, in gray crags; and they piled in together and settled low over the west. And then the wind stopped and left the clouds deep and solid. The rain began with gusty showers, pauses and downpours, and then gradually it settled to a single tempo, small drops and a steady beat. . . . For two days the earth drank the rain, until the earth was full.

(from *The Grapes of Wrath,* by John Steinbeck)

Paragraph Building with Adjective Clauses (Chapter 16, page 241)

Yamacraw

Yamacraw is an island off the South Carolina mainland not far from Savannah, Georgia. . . . The twentieth century has basically ignored the presence of Yamacraw. The island is populated with black people who depend on the sea and their small farms for a living. . . . Thus far, no bridge connects Yamacraw with the mainland, and anyone who sets foot on the island comes by water. The roads of the island are unpaved and rutted by the passage of ox carts, still a major form of transportation. The hand pump serves up questionable water to the black residents who live in their small familiar houses. Sears, Roebuck catalogues perform their classic function in the crudely built privies, which sit, half-hidden, in the tall grasses behind the shacks. Electricity came to the island several years ago . . . , [b]ut there are no telephones. To call the island you must go to the Beaufort Sheriff's Office and talk to the man who works the radio. Otherwise, Yamacraw remains aloof and apart from the world beyond the river.

(from *The Water Is Wide,* by Pat Conroy)

Paragraph Building with Appositives (Chapter 16, page 245)

Mrs. Bessie Taylor Gwynn

Born in 1895, in poverty, Bessie grew up in Athens, Alabama, where there was no public school for blacks. She attended Trinity School, a private institution for blacks run by the American Missionary Association, and in 1911 graduated from the Normal School (a "super" high school) at Fisk University in Nashville. In later years, Mrs. Bessie Taylor Gwynn, the essence of pride and privacy, never talked about her years in Athens; only in the months before her death did she reveal that she had never attended Fisk University itself because she could not afford the four-year course. At Normal School she learned a lot about Shakespeare, but most of all about the profound importance of education—especially for a people trying to move up from slavery. . . . Mrs. Gwynn taught hundreds of economically deprived youngsters, including my mother, my brother, my sister, and me, during her remarkable forty-four year career. Miss Bessie, a blessing to children and an asset to the nation, was an example of an informed, dedicated teacher.

(from "Unforgettable Miss Bessie," by Carl T. Rowan)

Paragraph Building with Adverb Clauses (Chapter 16, page 249)

Learning to Hate Reading

From the very beginning of school we make books and reading a constant source of possible failure and public humiliation. When children are little we make them read aloud, before the teacher and other children, so that we can be sure that they "know" all the words they are reading. This means that when they don't know a word, they are going to make a mistake, right in front of everyone. Instantly they are made to realize that they have done something wrong. . . . Perhaps the teacher will say, "Are you sure?" or ask someone else what he thinks. Or perhaps, if the teacher is kindly, she will just smile a sweet, sad smile—often one of the most painful punishments a child can suffer in school. In any case, the child who has made the mistake knows he has made it, and feels foolish, stupid, and ashamed, just as any of us would in his shoes.

Before long many children associate books and reading with mistakes, real or feared, and penalties and humiliation. . . . [I]f books cause them humiliation and pain, they are likely to decide that the safest thing to do is to leave all books alone.

(from "How Teachers Make Children Hate Reading," by John Holt)

Paragraph Building with Participle Phrases (Chapter 16, page 256)

A Slippery Thief

In September 1979, Carlo Colodi parked his car outside a bank in Milan, Italy, and then dashed in with a scarf hiding his face and a revolver in his hand. Hitting his foot on the corner of the mat, he slid across the marble floor. His scarf dropped off, revealing his face, and, as he fell, he accidentally fired his revolver. Scrambling hastily to his feet, he ran to the cashier's desk, skidded wildly, and grabbed at a counter to keep his balance. In the process, he dropped his gun, and the entire bank rocked with laughter. Offended by this lack of appreciation, the man turned, ran, slipped again, and finally crawled out of the bank. Outside he found a police officer writing out a ticket for his car, which was parked in a no-waiting zone.

Paragraph Building with Absolutes
(Chapter 16, page 258)

Running

Zipped up in his leather jacket, each fist squeezing a small rubber ball, he ran along the dirt road past burst mattresses, water heaters, fenders, sodden cartons, worn-out tires, and rusty cans strewn down by the deep bank. By the time Ernie was opposite the warehouses he was hot and sweaty. His breathing fixed to the plopping of his long black tennis shoes, he pounded past the port. As larks rose with flashes of yellow from the dead weeds and wild grass, he came unflaggingly on, feeling he would never tire. The oaks of Dad's Point stood ahead in the distance, their trunks painted white. Mouth gaping, his damp hair in his eyes, his body like a fired-up furnace, Ernie held his stride opposite Rough and Ready Island, where rows of moth-balled warships, their gun mountings sealed in protective pods, were moored three abreast for the future. Gagging on a dry throat, he chose some object as his finish line and, plodding up to it on weighted legs, plodded right on past. He did not quit there either. He fought on with himself to the edge of the park and, stumbling over the lawn past picnic tables and barbecue pits, careened with flailing arms farther and farther under the trees, until at last he stood gasping on the muddy bank of the point with nowhere else to run.

(from *Fat City*, by Leonard Gardner)

Further Practice in Building Paragraphs
(Chapter 16, page 260)

The first three paragraphs of the following essay by George Orwell served as the model for the paragraph building exercise on pages 260–261 of Chapter Sixteen.

A Hanging

It was in Burma, a sodden morning of the rains. A sickly light, like yellow tinfoil, was slanting over the high walls into the jail yard. We were waiting outside the condemned cells, a row of sheds fronted with double bars, like small animal cages. Each cell measured about ten feet by ten and was quite bare within except for a plank bed and a pot for drinking water. In some of them brown, silent men were squatting at the inner bars, with their blankets draped round them. These were the condemned men, due to be hanged within the next week or two.

One prisoner had been brought out of his cell. He was a Hindu, a puny wisp of a man, with a shaven head and vague liquid eyes. He had a thick, sprouting mustache, absurdly too big for his body, rather like the mustache of a comic man on the films. Six tall Indian warders were guarding him and getting him ready for the gallows. Two of them stood by with rifles and fixed bayonets, while the others handcuffed him, passed a chain through his handcuffs and fixed it to their belts, and lashed his arms tight to his sides. They crowded very close about him, with their hands always on him in a careful, caressing grip, as though all the while feeling him to make sure he was there. It was like men handling a fish which is still alive and may jump back into the water. But he stood quite unresisting, yielding his arms limply to the ropes, as though he hardly noticed what was happening.

Eight o'clock struck and a bugle call, desolately thin in the wet air, floated from the distant barracks. The superintendent of the jail, who was standing apart from the rest of us, moodily prodding the gravel with his stick, raised his head at the sound. He was an army doctor, with a grey toothbrush mustache and a gruff voice. "For God's sake, hurry up, Francis," he said irritably. "The man ought to have been dead by this time. Aren't you ready yet?"

Francis, the head jailer, a fat Dravidian in a white drill suit and gold spectacles, waved his black hand. "Yes sir, yes sir," he bubbled. "All iss satisfactorily prepared. The hangman iss waiting. We shall proceed."

"Well, quick march, then. The prisoners can't get their breakfast till this job's over."

We set out for the gallows. Two warders marched on either side of the prisoner, with their rifles at the slope; two others marched close against him, gripping him by arm and shoulder, as though at once pushing and supporting him. The rest of us, magistrates and the like, followed behind. Suddenly, when we had gone ten yards, the procession stopped short without any order or warning. A dreadful thing had happened—a dog, come goodness knows whence, had appeared in the yard. It came bounding among us with a loud volley of barks and leapt round us wagging its whole body, wild with glee at finding so many human beings together. It was a large woolly dog, half Airedale, half pariah. For a moment it pranced around us, and then, before anyone could stop it, it had made a dash for the prisoner, and jumping up tried to lick his face. Everybody stood aghast, too taken aback even to grab the dog.

"Who let that bloody brute in here?" said the superintendent angrily. "Catch it, someone!"

A warder detached from the escort, charged clumsily after the dog, but it danced and gambolled just out of his reach, taking everything as part of the game. A young Eurasian jailer picked up a handful of gravel and tried to stone the dog away, but it dodged the stones and came after us again. Its yaps echoed from the jail walls. The prisoner, in the grasp of the two warders, looked on incuriously, as though this was another formality of the hanging. It was several minutes before someone managed to catch the dog. Then we put my handkerchief through its collar and moved off once more, with the dog still straining and whimpering.

It was about forty yards to the gallows. I watched the bare brown back of the prisoner marching in front of me. He walked clumsily with his bound arms, but quite steadily, with that bobbing gait of the Indian who never straightens his knees. At each step his muscles slid neatly into place, the lock of hair on his scalp danced up and down, his feet printed themselves on the wet gravel. And once, in spite of the men who gripped him by each shoulder, he stepped lightly aside to avoid a puddle on the path.

It is curious; but till that moment I had never realized what it means to destroy a healthy, conscious man. When I saw the prisoner step aside to avoid the puddle, I saw the mystery, the unspeakable wrongness, of cutting a life short when it is in full tide. This man was not dying, he was alive just as we are alive. All the organs of his body were working—bowels digesting food, skin renewing itself, nails growing, tissues forming—all toiling away in solemn foolery. His nails would still be growing when he stood on the drop, when he was falling through the air with a tenth-of-a-second to live. His eyes saw the yellow gravel and the grey walls, and his brain still remembered, foresaw, reasoned—even about puddles. He and we were a party of men walking together, seeing, hearing, feeling, understanding the same world; and in two minutes, with a sudden snap, one of us would be gone—one mind less, one world less.

The gallows stood in a small yard, separate from the main grounds of the prison, and overgrown with tall prickly weeds. It was a brick erection like three sides of a shed, with planking on top, and above that two beams and a crossbar with the rope dangling. The hangman, a greyhaired convict in the white uniform of the prison, was waiting beside his machine. He greeted us with a servile crouch as we entered. At a word from Francis the two warders, gripping the prisoner more closely than ever, half led, half pushed him to the gallows and helped him clumsily up the ladder. Then the hangman climbed up and fixed the rope round the prisoner's neck.

We stood waiting, five yards away. The warders had formed in a rough circle round the gallows. And then, when the noose was fixed, the prisoner began crying out to his god. It was a high, reiterated cry of "Ram! Ram! Ram! Ram!" not urgent and fearful like a prayer or cry for help, but steady, rhythmical, almost like the tolling of a bell. The dog answered the sound with a whine. The hangman, still standing on the gallows, produced a small cotton bag like a flour bag and drew it down over the prisoner's face. But the sound, muffled by the cloth, still persisted, over and over again: "Ram! Ram! Ram! Ram! Ram!"

The hangman climbed down and stood ready, holding the lever. Minutes seemed to pass. The steady, muffled crying from the prisoner went on and on, "Ram! Ram! Ram!" never faltering for an instant. The superintendent, his head on his chest, was slowly poking the ground with his stick; perhaps he was counting the cries, allowing the prisoner a fixed number—fifty, perhaps, or a hundred. Everyone had changed colour. The Indians had gone grey like bad coffee, and one or two of the bayonets were wavering. We looked at the lashed, hooded man on the drop, and listened to his cries—each cry another second of life; the same thought was in all our minds; oh, kill him quickly, get it over, stop that abominable noise!

Suddenly the superintendent made up his mind. Throwing up his head he made a swift motion with his stick. "Chalo!" he shouted almost fiercely.

There was a clanking noise, and then dead silence. The prisoner had vanished, and the rope was twisting on itself. I let go of the dog, and it galloped immediately to the back of the gallows; but when it got there it stopped short, barked, and then retreated into a corner of the yard, where it stood among the weeds, looking timorously out at us. We went round the gallows to inspect the prisoner's body. He was dangling with his toes pointed straight downwards, very slowly revolving, as dead as a stone.

The superintendent reached out with his stick and poked the bare brown body; it oscillated slightly. "*He's* all right," said the superintendent. He backed out from under the gallows, and blew out a deep breath. The moody look had gone out of his face quite suddenly. He glanced at his wristwatch. "Eight minutes past eight. Well, that's all for this morning, thank God."

The warders unfixed bayonets and marched away. The dog, sobered and conscious of having misbehaved itself, slipped after them. We walked out of the gallows yard, past the condemned cells with their waiting prisoners, into the big central yard of the prison. The convicts, under the command of warders armed with lathis, were already receiving their breakfast. They squatted in long rows, each man holding a tin pannikin, while two warders with buckets marched around ladling out rice; it seemed quite a homely, jolly scene, after the hanging. An enormous relief had come upon us now that the job was done. One felt an impulse to sing, to break into a run, to snigger. All at once everyone began chattering gaily.

The Eurasian boy walking beside me nodded towards the way we had come, with a knowing smile: "Do you know, sir, our friend (he meant the dead man) when he heard his appeal had been dismissed, he pissed on the floor of his cell. From fright. Kindly take one of my cigarettes, sir. Do you not admire my new silver case, sir? From the boxwallah, two rupees eight annas. Classy European style."

Several people laughed—at what, nobody seemed certain.

Francis was walking by the superintendent, talking garrulously: "Well, sir, all has passed off with the utmost satisfactoriness. It was all finished—flick! Like that. It iss not always so—oah, no! I have known cases where the doctor was obliged to go beneath the gallows and pull the prisoner's legs to ensure decease. Most disagreeable!"

"Wriggling about, eh? That's bad," said the superintendent.

"Ach, sir, it iss worse when they become refractory! One man, I recall, clung to the bars of hiss cage when we went to take him out. You will scarcely credit, sir, that it took six warders to dislodge him, three pulling at each leg. We reasoned with him, 'My dear fellow,' we said, "think of all the pain and trouble you are causing to us!' But no, he would not listen! Ach, he wass very troublesome!"

I found that I was laughing quite loudly. Everyone was laughing. Even the superintendent grinned in a tolerant way. "You'd better all come out and have a drink," he said quite genially. "I've got a bottle of whiskey in the car. We could do with it."

We went through the big double gates of the prison into the road. "Pulling at his legs!" exclaimed a Burmese magistrate suddenly, and burst into a loud chuckling. We all began laughing again. At that moment Francis' anecdote seemed extraordinarily funny. We all had a drink together, native and European alike, quite amicably. The dead man was a hundred yards away.

(from *Shooting an Elephant and Other Essays*, by George Orwell)

This passage served as the model for the exercise on page 262.

Clipper Ships

The clipper was the fastest, the most beautiful, and the most short-lived of the great sailing ships. Developed in the United States in the 1820s, the clipper reached the height of its fame in the 1850s and 1860s, and it was obsolete by the end of the century. Since it was built primarily for speed, the clipper was slim and light, with a limited cargo space, and carried an enormous area of canvas. The clipper served many needs, including the Californian gold rush, the China tea trade, and the Australian wool trade. There was competition between shipping companies in the race to make fast passages and high profits, and this produced crews of the highest quality. Several factors, among them steamships, transcontinental railroads, and the opening of the Suez Canal, made the clippers obsolete. The clippers were replaced by windjammers and, later, steamships. Although the days of the great sailing ships are gone, the clipper remains as a symbol of craftsmanship, efficiency, and beauty.

This passage served as the model for the exercise on page 263.

The Gramercy Gym

The Gramercy Gym is two flights up some littered, lightless stairs that look like a muggers' paradise, though undoubtedly they are the safest stairs in New York. Inside, two dozen bodies are chopping up and down, self-clocked, each fellow cottoned in his dreams. Some are skipping rope, turbaned in towels, wrapped in robes in order to sweat. These are white-looking figures, whereas the men who are about to spar have on dark headguards that close grimly around the face like an executioner's hood. There are floor-length mirrors and mattresses for exercising and rubdowns, and two speedbags banging like drums, and three heavy bags swinging even between the rounds with the momentum of more than a decade of punches. The bell is loud; the fighters jerk like eating and walking birds, hissing through their teeth as they punch, their feet sneakering the floor with shuffly sounds. They wear red shoelaces in white shoes, and peanut-colored gloves. . . . They are learning to move their feet to the left and right, to move in and out, punching over, then under an opponent's guard, and other repetitive skills without which a man in the ring becomes a bag of straw. The speed bags teach head-punching, the heavy bags teach body work, and one bag pinned to the wall has both a head and torso diagrammed, complete with numbers, so that the trainer can shout out what punches his fighter should throw. "Bounce, bounce!" the trainers yell.

(from *Walking the Dead Diamond River*, by Edward Hoagland)

Acknowledgments *(continued)*

Jill Young Miller. "Making the Grades: How to Cram" from *Campus Voice*, Fall, 1987. Copyright © 1987 by Jill Young Miller.

Enid Nemy. "You Are How You Eat" from *The New York Times*, September 20, 1987. Copyright © 1987 by The New York Times Company. Reprinted by permission.

Irene Oppenheim. "On Waitressing" by Irene Oppenheim. Copyright © 1986 by Irene Oppenheim. First published in *The Threepenny Review*.

Jane O'Reilly. "In Las Vegas: Working Hard for the Money" from *Time*, August 27, 1984. Copyright © 1984 by Time, Incorporated. Reprinted by permission.

George Orwell. "A Hanging" from *Shooting an Elephant and Other Essays* by George Orwell. Copyright © 1950 by Sonia Brownell Orwell and renewed 1978 by Sonia Pitt-Rivers. Reprinted by permission of Harcourt Brace & Company and the estate of the late Sonia Brownell Orwell and Martin Secker & Warburg.

Ishmael Reed. "My Oakland, There is a There There" from *Writin' Is Fightin': Thrity-Seven Years of Boxing on Paper* by Ishmael Reed. Copyright © 1988 by Ishmael Reed. Reprinted by permission of Simon & Schuster.

Carl T. Rowan. Excerpt from "Unforgettable Miss Bessie" from *Reader's Digest*, March, 1985. Copyright © 1985 by The Reader's Digest Assn., Inc.

Collette H. Russell. "A Day in the Homeless Life" from the *Utne Reader*, Sept./Oct. 1990; excerpted from *Street Magazine*, April, 1989. Copyright by Jonathan Fountain. Reprinted by permission of Jonathan Fountain.

William Safire. "On Keeping A Diary" from *The New York Times,* September 9, 1974. Copyright © 1974 by The New York Times Company. Reprinted by permission.

Frederick Turner. "Blushing Monday: A Day Set Aside to Revel in Shame" in *Harper's Magazine*, August, 1991. Copyright © 1991 by *Harper's Magazine*. All rights reserved. Reprinted from the August issue by special permission.

Andrew Ward. "They Also Wait Who Stand and Serve Themselves" from the *Atlantic Monthly*, May, 1979. Copyright © 1979 by Andrew Ward. Reprinted by permission of the author.

Eudora Welty. "The Little Store" from *The Eye of the Story* by Eudora Welty. Copyright © 1975 by Eudora Welty. Reprinted by permission of Random House, Inc.

E. B. White. "Open Letter to the A.S.P.C.A." from "Two Letters, Both Open" from *Poems and Sketches of E. B. White* by E. B. White. Copyright © 1951 by E. B. White. Copyright renewed. Reprinted by permission of HarperCollins Publishers Inc.

James Wolcott. "An Airhead Exercise in Aimless Activity" (original title, "Everyone's a Critic") from *The New Yorker*, February 28, 1994. Copyright © 1994 by The New Yorker.

Index